Planning Paris before Haussmann

Nicholas Papayanis

PLANNING PARIS
BEFORE HAUSSMANN

THE JOHNS HOPKINS UNIVERSITY PRESS · BALTIMORE & LONDON

© 2004 The Johns Hopkins University Press
All rights reserved. Published 2004
Printed in the United States of America
on acid-free paper

2 4 6 8 9 7 5 3 1

The Johns Hopkins University Press
2715 North Charles Street
Baltimore, Maryland 21218-4363
www.press.jhu.edu

Library of Congress Cataloging-in-Publication Data
Papayanis, Nicholas.
Planning Paris before Haussmann / Nicholas Papayanis.
    p. cm.
Includes bibliographical references and index.
ISBN 0-8018-7930-2 (hardcover : alk. paper)
    1. Paris (France)—History. 2. Urban renewal—France—Paris—History.
3. City planning—France—Paris—History. 4. Cities and towns—Plan-
ning—France—Paris. 5. Haussmann, Georges-Eugène, baron, 1809–1891.
I. Title.
DC723.P28 2004
711'.4'094436109033—dc22   2004002763

A catalog record for this book is available
from the British Library.

For Marilyn, once more, with all my love

Contents

Illustrations

Acknowledgments

ONE OF the great pleasures of completing this book is the opportunity it affords me to thank the several friends, colleagues, and institutions that facilitated my research and writing.

Most of the research for this book was completed over several summers in Paris, principally at the Bibliothèque historique de la Ville de Paris (BHVP), the Bibliothèque administrative de Paris (BA), and, to a lesser extent, at the Bibliothèque nationale de France (BNF) the New York Public Library, and the Bobst Library of New York University. For their invaluable assistance, I am grateful to Luc Passion, Odile Sampson, and Geneviève Morland of the BHVP. Frédéric Lions, a *conservateur* at the BHVP and a dear friend, played an especially important role in the research stage of this project. Pierre Casselle, the *conservateur général* of the BA, facilitated my use of the many important documents in his facility. He was particularly generous in granting me complete access to the Siméon papers and archives before his publication of a considerable part of this collection. I thank, too, Henri Zuber of the Régie Autonome des Transports Parisiens and François Gasnault of the Archives de Paris for their generous cooperation. Michèle Bonnard of the BNF and also a dear friend has always made my research days at the French National Library agreeable. Patrick Fridenson, an old friend and colleague, continues to be an important source of good fellowship and advice.

I have also benefitted from important institutional support. Grants from the Research Foundation of the City University of New York in 1997, 1998, 2000, and 2001 helped fund summer research in Paris. A fellowship from the National Endowment for the Humanities, grant number FB-35609-99, for the academic year 1999–2000, in conjunction with a fellowship leave of absence from Brooklyn College, enabled me to complete most of the research necessary for this book. I am most grateful to the staff of the National Endowment for the Humanities for their kind cooperation and patience in answering my questions about the preparation of my grant proposal. During the academic year 2000–2001, immediately following my NEH/sabatical year, I was awarded a fellowship by the Ethyle R. Wolfe Institute for the Humanities of Brooklyn College. This provided an academic year free of all teaching responsibilities, during which time I completed the first draft of the book. For her generosity in establishing this foundation, which provides release time from a heavy undergraduate teaching schedule for select faculty research projects, I am grateful to the former provost of Brooklyn College, Ethyle R. Wolfe, and I thank too the director of the institute, Robert Viscusi, for his support, as well as those colleagues who voted to fund my proposal. I also thank the former chair of my department, Professor Philip Gallagher, for his strong support of my application for the Wolfe Fellowship.

Three friends and colleagues, Christopher Johnson, Barrie Ratcliffe, and Anthony Sutcliffe, took time out from their own very busy work schedules to read the entire manuscript. They made detailed and important comments throughout, saved me at times from various errors of fact, or caused me to sharpen certain assertions. They have not always agreed with my conclusions or approach, but they have always been supportive. They are not, of course, responsible for any errors that might remain or my thesis.

I would also like to thank Mr. Henry Tom, executive editor of the Johns Hopkins University Press, for his strong interest in this project. Ms. Claire McCabe facilitated my contact with the press during the last stages of the book's gestation as did Ms. Andre Barnett. Ms. Barbara B. Lamb has been a superb copyeditor. Rachel Fuchs read the manuscript for the Press, and I am grateful for her very helpful comments.

Some information in chapters 2 and 3 formed the basis for a chapter I wrote, "L'Émergence de l'urbanisme moderne avant Haussmann," which appeared in *La Modernité avant Haussmann: Formes de l'espace urbain à Paris, 1801–1853,* edited by Karen Bowie (Paris: Éditions de la Recherche, 2001). A version of chapter 5 first appeared as an article, "Urbanisme de Paris souterrain: Premiers projets de chemin de fer urbain et naissance de l'urbanisme des cités modernes," in *Histoire, Économie, et Société,* No. 4 (Oct.–Dec. 1998). I also presented material related to this book to two annual meetings of the Society for French Historical Studies, to the New York City Area French Historians Seminar, to the Columbia University Seminar on the City, and to an international conference in Paris on modernity before Haussmann. I appreciate the positive reception of my findings and the many useful comments they elicited. And a very special acknowledgment to Drs. Robert L. Fine and Steven Schreibman for their care and humanity.

Acknowledgments

My greatest debt belongs to my wife, Marilyn Adler Papayanis, who has been associated with this project from its inception, accompanying me to Paris on each of my research trips. She made Paris very much her own, a city where she was able to pursue her own professional projects and where, over the years, we developed together many dear friendships. At home she took time out from her own research and writing to read carefully and with sensitivity all drafts of the manuscript as they unfolded. She performed valued copyediting work, productively discussed my ideas, made important suggestions with respect to theory, and found this project worthwhile and significant even when I had my own reservations about my approach. Always a loving companion, her encouragement and confidence in my work, as in all aspects of my life, have sustained me throughout our life together.

Planning Paris before Haussmann

INTRODUCTION

WALTER BENJAMIN, in a celebrated text, referred to Paris as "the capital of the nineteenth century."[1] By this he meant that, in the development of urban forms of life, nineteenth-century Paris exemplified certain distinct features of modernity. While no single element can be made to stand for the totality of modernity, a few features may be taken as central and emblematic. Among these are speed, circulation, and a compression of space and time; architects as diverse as Hector Horeau and Le Corbusier and writers like Louis-Sébastien Mercier and Maxime du Camp remind us that these features are central to modern urban life. So too is official concern with hygiene, dramatic population growth, intensified industrial and commercial activities, and the potentially destabilizing effects of uneven standards of living. Also basic to the modern vision of the city is that it be regarded as a single entity, an organic whole, all of whose parts function together efficiently, and that its planning be comprehensive rather than piecemeal. From the late eighteenth century onward, engineers, architects, intellectuals, and urban planners, as well as poets and novelists, tried to understand the modern city and, in the case of the nonliterary writers, generated plans or proposals or simply articulated ideas designed to bring order and reason, health, rapid and smooth circulation, and control to the expanding and eventually seemingly fragmented metropolis. Their aim or dream was to create a rational, well-policed, intelligible, and "networked" city in which social harmony and order prevailed.

There are important studies on Paris urbanism during the eighteenth century, on the rebuilding of the French capital under the Second Empire, and on city planning in the post-Haussmann period, and there are literary perceptions of nineteenth-century Paris.[2] There is, however, very little work covering the emergence and history of modern urban planning ideas with respect to Paris from the late eighteenth century through the first half of the nineteenth century.[3] This study is intended to fill that void. Primarily an investigation of elite attitudes toward space, this book explores new ideas about the

ideal physical layout of the city in the age of industrial capitalism as they in-
tersect with, on the one hand, the state's need to control its population and
shape the environment and, on the other, capitalism's general need for the efficient circulation of commerce, industrial goods, and wealth.

Most histories of the transformation of Paris into a modern capitalist city
begin with the regime of Napoleon III and his prefect of the Seine Department, Baron Georges-Eugène Haussmann, ascribing to them, and to Haussmann in particular, a new vision of the city which, when combined with the
public works of the Second Empire, resulted in the creation of a modern metropolis, one whose physical layout was suited to the industrial-capitalist age.
It is as if there is a sharp dividing line, both in terms of the space of Paris and
ideas about its ideal forms, between all that came before Haussmann and all
that followed. And always the key figure in the emergence of modernity in
Paris is Haussmann. The writings of Françoise Choay are typical of the standard estimation of Haussmann's importance. Choay, for many years a professor
of the history of ideas and the history of urbanism at the French Institute for
Urbanism in Paris, published, among other studies, two important essays
dealing with the concept of urbanism, including Haussmann's place in modern urban planning.[4] Primarily interested in the intellectual roots of urban
modernity, Choay also wrote the chapter on ideas about the modern city in
the important collective history of French urban life during the industrial period, a work that appeared in 1983, and restated her interpretation of Haussmann's significance most recently in her introduction to the new edition of
Haussmann's memoirs.[5]

It is Choay's view—one that has become commonplace—that without
knowing it, Haussmann was one of the founders of modern urban planning.
In Choay's thinking Haussmann emerges as a towering figure, both in terms
of the projects planned during his administration and with respect to a new
vision of the modern city, because he understood something not grasped before. According to Choay, "it had apparently never occurred to the successive
authors of earlier plans that Paris as a whole, or simply the right and left
banks, could one day become a single organism quickened with a unique
life." Such a revelation had broad implications, as the "the now thoroughly familiar idea of the *big* city as a unified entity was still foreign to the mentality
of Haussmann's period."[6] Haussmann's originality, according to Choay, lay in
his "holistic treatment" of urban space. This constituted the "epistemological
foundation" upon which his reforms of Paris rested, reforms that made Paris
"the first paradigm of the industrial metropolis and of the discipline (urban
planning) which assigns itself the task of transforming urban space into an
object of applied science." We should be clear, moreover, that this compre-

hensive approach to planning, in both theory and practice, and the understanding that the modern city was an "isotropic space," should be attributed neither to Napoleon III nor to any of his collaborators. The honor, according to Choay, belongs solely to Haussmann.[7]

Other writers have made similar arguments, and the view of Haussmann as the seminal figure in the modern conception of the city, whether one is favorable to or critical of Haussmann's form of planning, is widespread. Typical, for example, is Richard Sennett's view that Haussmann "was the first to look at these problems [housing, transport, political control] as essentially related," or David Donald's estimation that "Haussmann represents, in part at least, a new conception of the city." Sennett explained further that "as industrial cities grew in population and economic importance, they came to be uncontrolled, and the rules of social welfare lost their historic power. We know now the evils of this transformation—the intense poverty, the uncertainty of health and vocation, the unending boredom of the physical appearance of these cities; so did the more enlightened men of the nineteenth century. It is to one such man, Baron Haussmann, that we owe the impetus to urban reform that has come to dominate our era." David Harvey, himself one of the most original and perceptive writers on the Second Empire, economically summed up the standard judgment with respect to Haussmann: "Part of what was special about it all was the conception of space employed." Instead of partial plans or piecemeal reforms, Haussmann wished to employ a general, all-embracing plan to guide the comprehensive reform of Paris. "Urban space," Harvey observed, "was seen and treated as a totality in which different quarters of the city and different functions had to be brought into relation to each other to form a working whole."[8]

Haussmann also figures significantly in the trajectory of modern urban planning. According to Choay three forms of planning emerged during the nineteenth century, forms of planning that she identified as "regularization, pre-urbanism, and urbanism." All were an outcome of a new order created in the western city as a result of industrialization and dramatic population growth. As a consequence of these twin forces and the structural transformations they engendered, such as the insertion of railways into the city, the specialization of urban districts, the opening of new streets, the visible crowding of people and shops, and increasing suburbanization, the city dweller was initially unable to conceptually assimilate the break between the industrial and the preindustrial city. One outcome was that the industrial city was confronted as a new object for investigation, and nineteenth-century forms of urban planning evolved as an attempt to impose order over it. Choay labeled the form of planning practiced by Haussmann the "regularization" model. It aimed to reform Paris so that it could function effectively as a space of production and consumption in the industrial era. Haussmann achieved such a space by privileging the "designing of a circulatory system and opening a system of ventilation. Problems of traffic flow were given priority."[9] With respect to the system of new boulevards, streets, and open spaces that Haussmann would create, Choay estimated that "the real basis as well as the originality of [Haussmann's] planning lies in the dual concept of a circulatory and respiratory system. The schema of regularization emerges during the last third of the nineteenth century as the fundamental verity of the capitalist-industrial order."[10]

"*Urbanisme,*" now also rendered in English as *urbanism,* originated in the late nineteenth century and was first closely associated with the writings of the Spanish planner Ildefonso Cerdá. Its important characteristics are that it is the preserve of specialists rather than generalists, that it is depoliticized, that it is eventually concerned with practical tasks, and that it adopts a metascientific language in its planning proposals. It is Choay's identification of a third form of planning, the "preurbanism" model, that is of greatest interest here, as it is the form of planning that preceded Haussmann's regulatory model and came to maturity during the first half of the nineteenth century. How one understands this period will bear directly on the issue of Haussmann's originality. Choay divided preurbanism into two models, each taking as its problem the new industrial city, which they found wanting, and each characterized by utopian elements. Choay labeled one model, or subgenre, of preurbanism "culturalist," and its proponents include all those—like John Ruskin and William Morris in England—who looked backward to an idealized past as an alternative to the modern city. There are no French representatives of this form of planning during the first half of the nineteenth century.

Choay referred to the second form of preurbanism as the "progressist" model. It is embraced by all those thinkers who—like Charles Fourier, Robert Owen, and Étienne Cabet—while rejecting the industrial city as then organized under a system of private property and laissez faire, looked forward to its complete transformation under a regime of rational planning so that its benefits would be shared equitably by all its inhabitants. The hallmarks of this system of planning were faith in the power of reason, science, and technology; an optimistic vision of the future; a division of urban functions according to some preconceived logic; and the importance of standardized housing. This form of planning also embodied a repressive element, as progressive utopian planners were convinced that their model represented the ideal form of the city and that all existing or newly planned cities, no matter how their subjects might articulate their subjective needs, should conform to some preconceived rational form.[11] The rationally planned city, in turn, would have a beneficial effect on all its residents.

While Choay's schematization and approach to the history of ideas with respect to the city is a useful starting point, I take issue with some of her interpretations and conclusions. First, I question the broad treatment of the first half of the nineteenth century as one uniform period; as we shall see in this study, insofar as Paris is concerned, there are distinct phases in the emergence of new ideas about the city. A second problem, one not unique to Choay, is the view that any history of modern planning ideas with respect to the industrial city begins with the nineteenth century.[12] An important point here, however, is the existence in numerous eighteenth-century writings on Paris of many elements of modern planning. These include ideas about regulating, ordering, and making the city safe for its inhabitants, as well as the relationship of the city's physical layout to effective political authority, to industry, and to commerce. An analysis of the formation of modern ideas about the city that takes Paris as its object must not, in other words, assume some sharp break between the eighteenth and nineteenth centuries. Although there are significant differences in the manner in which the city is understood during these two time periods, it is more accurate to note an element of continuity in thinking about the city over this time period.

This observation leads directly to a third objection to Choay's conceptualization of planning during the nineteenth century as it relates to Paris: her division of planning models into preurbanism, Haussmann's regulatory model, and urbanism. Choay used as a standard for this periodization only the writings of major thinkers representing each model, but she ignored the many urban commentaries belonging to either of these models or to the followers of the first-line thinkers. An examination of the period of preurbanism, however, brings us to the major point of this study. What is revealed by an investigation of the writings before Haussmann, before both the regulatory and modern planning models, on the morphology of Paris is the existence of an extensive archive of theoretical and practical speculations on the nature of the modern city which is extremely significant in its own right, a universe of thinking about Paris that must not be regarded, as the term *preurbanism* implies, as merely a prelude to modern planning or to Haussmann. This archive of ideas about the forms and functions of Paris, moreover, while it contains some utopian elements, is too complex and more often than not too rooted in perceptions of real urban problems to be labeled "utopian."

Lastly, one may identify three forms of planning before Haussmann, which, though relatively distinct from one another, share many elements and form a powerful intellectual foundation not only for Haussmannization but for modern planning as well. In turn, these forms, which reached their maturity during the first half of the nineteenth century, rest firmly on eighteenth-century foundations.

I refer to these three forms of planning as the *functionalist,* the *Saint-Simonian,* and the *Fourierist.* Collectively they may be referred to as the *progressive urban planning model,* as each accepts the new industrial city as a starting point for any program of urban transformation. Building upon eighteenth-century insights into the changing requirements of Paris, each contributed to the shaping of a modern vision of Paris and, indeed, of the modern city. Eighteenth-century thinkers had already begun to speculate on the necessity of a general plan for reforming Paris, that is, on comprehensive planning to tie all parts of the city together, on the importance of infrastructural reforms, on the relationship of the city's form to its health and its state of order and security, and on commerce. What distinguished eighteenth- and nineteenth-century planning, however, was that in the latter there was a decided and widespread sense of urgency about the need for urban reforms, reforms that privileged the infrastructure and the overall physical structure of Paris. This was the result of the twin forces of dramatic population growth and industrialization, which began to intrude into the mental universe of Paris intellectuals and which brought to the surface a plethora of urban problems that demanded resolution. Moreover, several nineteenth-century urban-planning proposals offered more meticulous details than eighteenth-century plans on projected urban reforms, including extensive data on the cost of reform of the urban physical structure and environment. Some nineteenth-century speculations on the ideal city, in fact, evinced a scientific rigor that was lacking in eighteenth-century plans.

The working out of comprehensive planning proposals for the new industrial, densely populated city would be the great intellectual accomplishment of nineteenth-century planners and was a major element in the thinking of all planning models during the first half of the nineteenth century. Within this intellectual universe, the functionalist model encompassed planning proposals of many intellectuals, architects, and especially engineers that did not for the most part contain the slightest hint of utopian formulations. Like Haussmann's regulatory model of planning, these speculations accepted the industrial city as a reality; with one notable exception included in chapter 2, and another in the Saint-Simonian model, discussed in chapter 3, there is no nostalgic look backward, no look forward to a totally transformed city of the future. The aim of this model was to create an industrial-commercial city that simply worked efficiently. Moreover, plans for such a city adopted, however loosely, a "scientific" approach to planning. The scientific dimension was also shared by the Saint-Simonian and Fourierist planning proposals.

The Saint-Simonian model placed an enormous emphasis, indeed faith, in the capacity of public works to solve all manner of urban problems, especially in the area of health. While the prescription for public works found in Saint-Simonian planning texts might intuitively appear to be the most "realistic" part of this planning tradition, it may be characterized, ironically, as the most "utopian." Although no one in the early nineteenth century knew what caused cholera, Saint-Simonians believed, for example, that urban public works projects would eradicate the disease. And it was a Saint-Simonian, Charles Duveyrier, who proposed a sweeping transformation and organization of space and labor in Paris. Even if Saint-Simonians included utopian elements in their public works projects or openly utopian plans, however, they understood correctly that the planned reform of the physical environment could result in great social benefits. In contrast to this part of their planning proposals, the Saint-Simonians also theorized about cities, all cities, as critical nodal points in a global network of communication routes that would pull the entire earth together in peaceful commercial and trading enterprises. Given the centrality of Paris in so much of their writing, one may assume that it would be at the center of this global network. The entire conception was an ideological justification for, and in some respects an anticipation of, the contemporary globalization phenomenon.

There also emerged out of Saint-Simonian circles a highly abstract theory, in which Paris served as the explicit model, for understanding the hierarchy of village and city placement in any given territory, and this too anticipated an important twentieth-century theory of the same topic. More than most planners studied here, moreover, the Saint-Simonians argued for the constant circulation of capital as a requirement of modern industrial society. Finally, note should be taken of the centrality, in Saint-Simonian thinking, of efficient communication routes to modern urban national and international life, a vision Saint-Simonians shared, to one degree or another, with all the schools of planning that emerged during the first half of the nineteenth century.

The third form of planning, the Fourierist, has traditionally been regarded as the most utopian of the socialist schools. Here we will see, in the writings on Paris of select followers of Fourier, the degree to which its focus was on real, albeit radical, reforms for the capital, in which the center and the internal road system of the city became the key to the city's effective functioning as a site of production and consumption. In addition, this school, dismissed as being wedded to ideal cities in nonurban settings, centered its planning proposals on Paris, while the Saint-Simonians, reputedly the most "realistic" owing to their emphasis on public works, were the most abstract and theoretical of the planners discussed here.

Having delineated the important features of these planning models, two important caveats are in order. First, my use of the words *models* or *forms* of planning should not necessarily be taken to indicate the existence of acknowledged or coherent "schools" of planning. I have used these terms partly to bring some order to an extensive archive of ideas about Paris. They are not purely arbitrary categories, however, as the intellectuals who make up each group do imagine Paris in a manner determined partly by attitudes related to whether they were essentially pragmatic, like the functionalists, largely theoretical, like the Saint-Simonians, or whether they envisaged a sweeping reform of Paris based upon Fourier's architectonics. The boundaries between the three planning models were always quite porous, and a lively cross-fertilization of ideas existed among them. Second, I extend the discussion of some planning proposals beyond the first half of the century, as in chapter 5, in order to show their ultimate realization or import.

What emerged from the proposals and plans that came out of these planning models during the first half of the nineteenth century was a modern vision of the city and an almost fully modern model of urban planning. I alluded to a definition of the modern Western industrial city, which needs to be made explicit at this point. Taking nineteenth-century Paris as a standard, the modern city may be defined as one whose infrastructure above and below ground and whose general physical layout are designed to facilitate simultaneously the rapid and efficient communication and circulation of people, commerce, air, sunlight, police power, waste matter, and even knowledge and information within its boundaries and beyond to national and international territories. It is also a city with a stable and clearly recognizable center or centers, with public institutions easily accessible from all its extremities. In a capitalist society, it is, in short, a city made safe for commerce and production and for the tranquility and safety of its inhabitants. Prized above all else in the classic Western city in the age of industrial capitalism are order, safety, health, and circulation—all closely related elements.

As for city planning of the kind advocated during the eighteenth and the first half of the nineteenth centuries, it was the domain of intellectuals, architects, and engineers; the profession of urban planner, that is, a self-conscious practitioner in a discipline with its own scientific language, associations, rules, and regulations, did not exist at this time. Nevertheless, I refer to those who thought about space at this time as "planners" because they recognized the importance of urban form and structure to the effective functioning of modern life and expended a considerable amount of intellectual energy devising projects and plans intended to order and control the modern city. While they lacked a self-consciously styled metascientific language to serve as their exclusive and distinct badge, they understood that their enterprise was scientific in nature and that their approach to planning, the application of reason to the physical environment, was universally applicable. And, to repeat, the planners of the first half of the nineteenth century, following ideas already expressed by the mid-eighteenth century, articulated the requirement that city planning had to be comprehensive. It is for these reasons that the corpus of thinking that constitutes the planning tradition in Paris before Haussmann is best described, at a minimum, as "early modern urban planning," with the understanding that it was a very short step away from the formation of a fully modern urban planning profession in the late nineteenth and early twentieth centuries.

We are now in a better position to distinguish between the significance of the eighteenth and the first half of the nineteenth century and what follows with respect to new conceptions of city life. The first thing to note is that the importance of Haussmann as a figure of modern planning is not in question. What is being claimed here is simply that one must separate Haussmann's accomplishments, his public works projects, from the so-called originality of his form of city planning. Haussmann accomplished what planners before him had already articulated as the correct form for modern Paris, what they had already laid out in countless planning proposals. By the first half of the nineteenth century, these proposals had been debated in the leading architectural journals of the day and were the subject of numerous texts. The new ideas were part of lively public discussions on matters like urban health and the cholera epidemic, the siting of a new wholesale food market for Paris, the siting and construction of railway termini in the capital, the crowding of its central districts, the fear of revolution and public disturbances, and a remarked-upon population movement during the 1840s of many of the well-to-do in the direction of the western end of capital. Government officials at the highest levels of the administration were aware of these debates and also participated in them.

Thus, Haussmann had available to him, when he assumed office in 1853, in addition to strong support from a powerful court, something lacking in previous administrations, namely, a vast archive of planning projects, proposals, and ideas that drew a picture of a well-functioning Paris not unlike the program that Haussmann and Napoleon III had in mind for Paris. According to François Loyer, the author of an important architectural history of Paris in the nineteenth century, "what is especially remarkable is that Haussmann's approach was worked out in the field and was never given any theoretical underpinnings. Yet his approach reflected a global vision of the city and city life that was deeply embedded in France and European culture."[13] What I show in this book, however, is the existence of a powerful intellectual and theoretical foundation both for Haussmannization and for modern planning in the corpus of reflections on Paris which preceded Haussmann, but which he did not acknowledge.

What I aim to demonstrate is that this period is significant in its own right as the birthplace of modern concepts of city life and functioning. One might say that the modern city was born in the thinking of many intellectuals at that time. This process was set in motion by eighteenth-century intellectuals who had begun to speculate on the links between the urban physical environment and form and crime, safety, health, commerce, and convenience. A limited but important building program in Paris also suggested urban planning on a citywide scale. It was during the first half of the nineteenth century, however, that relatively modern ideas about the city's forms and functions became widespread and common among a large group of urban intellectuals and government officials. A study of the emergence of urban modernity during the first half of the nineteenth century in Paris, this book is largely about ideas, about the discovery in contemporary thinking of the ideal form and function of the modern industrial city. An ideal Paris was imagined, planned, and hoped for by the numerous intellectuals who are the subjects of this study. Their plans were a product of the Enlightenment belief that reason, combined with science and technology, is the essential determinant of material progress. Early modern urban planners, all children of the Enlightenment, held that the rational transformation of city space would fulfill the Enlightenment project of social betterment for the city's inhabitants. Their projects, however, were also rooted in a real urban context, in a real city, and were designed to make it an orderly and safe site for those who lived there. We are not dealing here, for the most part, with some study of ideal forms imagined for their own sake, and the dreams of the urban planners did find expression in the reform of Paris during the nineteenth century and beyond. Furthermore, underlying the plans and proposals that form the subject of this study were powerful interests, which complicated the meaning of any potential reform or transformation of the urban environment.

While I did not set out to chart the emergence of hegemonic political and social order in Paris, it became evident, as my writing progressed, that early modern progressive urban planning, whether socialist or functionalist, lent itself powerfully, as a function of its vision of order and safety in the city, to the creation of a hegemonic order that suited the needs of the state, of capitalism, and of the average middle-class city dweller. Moreover, whether planners alternatively privileged social progress and equality, order and strategic considerations, health, or commerce, the authentic voices and subjective interests of the common people, and especially the workers, are missing from these proposals.[14] When plans for a new city did address workers' issues they did so from upper-class needs and perspectives. All plans and projects considered here are, in a broad sense, the product of middle-class male elites and experts, no matter what their political or ideological underpinnings. Note, too, that missing from these proposals is any extensive discussion of the effect of urban spatial reform on gender relations, on how the reforms would impact the structure of daily life for women, for example. This might appear surprising given the strongly held middle-class view by 1848, as Victoria Thompson showed, that lower-class working women, so prominent as merchants in public markets in Paris, were associated with disorder and fear of revolution and, as a consequence, were subject by the police to surveillance and control. The renovation and regulation of the marketplace to facilitate authority over lower-class women in the public sphere was especially important.[15] The failure to deal explicitly with gender issues might be the result of the particular texts under consideration, texts more focused on the physical landscape of Paris. When they do deal with class, a category that would include female workers, they do so in broad terms, and fear of "unruly" and "dangerous" women is most likely subsumed under that classification. Planning on a citywide scale, therefore, during both the nineteenth and the eighteenth centuries, addressed all possible (real or imagined) impediments, and not merely one portion of the lower classes, to the comprehensive reform of the urban environment.

This leads to a final introductory consideration. As issues of power, urban safety and order, health, and commerce coalesced with openly expressed or implicit Enlightenment ideals, I found the work of certain theorists especially useful in suggesting interpretive insights and strategies in my reading of urban planning texts. The most important of these for me have been Zygmunt Baumann, Gilles Deleuze and Félix Guattari, Mary Douglas, Henri Lefebvre, Karl Marx, Richard Sennett, and Paul Virilio. Standing somewhat apart in importance is the work of Michel Foucault. I have appropriated these writers' insights, where useful, on issues like the relationship of space to state power, control, and knowledge, middle-class fears of urban masses and strangers, middle-class dreams of an orderly and healthy public space, the government's need for urban surveillance and control, and the capitalists' requirement for a well-policed and well-designed city. In this spirit I have tried to unpack and decipher the meaning of urban planning texts set within the context of a real city. What I hope will be evident at the end of this investigation and analysis is the extent to which the idea of modern Paris in the plans, projects, and imaginings of urban intellectuals' plans—plans that would eventually make Paris the "capital of the nineteenth century"—was bound up with issues of power, order, control, and the economy, elements that provided the ground for, and shaped the external beauty of, a great world capital.

CHAPTER ONE

Eighteenth-Century Roots of Modern Planning

AN EXAMINATION of a wide range of eighteenth-century writings on Paris—well-known treatises as well as obscure or anonymous pamphlets and brochures—reveals the existence of a rich fund of texts on the form and function of the city with decidedly modern features.[1] These texts are not, for the most part, a response to the kind of serious dislocation brought about by the dramatic population growth and urban industrialization that occurred during the first half of the nineteenth century. These twin forces, and the planning they engendered—planning that was frequently considered urgent and always absolutely necessary for the city's health and effective functioning—constitute a major dividing line between the planning schemes of the eighteenth and nineteenth centuries. Nevertheless, a significant degree of industrial and commercial development and a rise in population did occur in eighteenth-century Paris and were remarked upon by eighteenth-century writers. David Garrioch concluded that Paris in the eighteenth century experienced "urbanization on a scale unknown elsewhere in Europe, except in London." By the end of the century Paris had a population of 547,736. The next largest French city at this time was Marseille, with 111,130 people, followed by Lyon, with 109,500, and Bordeaux, with 90,992.[2] The large number of individuals in eighteenth-century Paris was especially striking as so much of daily living then was carried on outdoors, in the streets. Selling, buying, looking for work, ceremonies, playing—all these activities were part of the usual street life of Paris.[3]

James Leith noted that eighteenth-century intellectuals writing about Paris believed it was possible to improve the welfare of its inhabitants through extensive urban reforms. He writes, for example, that during the time of the Revolution many of the projects designed to celebrate its accomplishments were also aimed "at improving the city of man."[4] The Enlightenment faith in the capacity of reason to improve the human condition was extended to the ability of urban intellectuals to create an ideal city, one that would serve as the material basis for an improved life for all its inhabitants. As David Harvey commented, Enlightenment writers believed "that the world could be controlled and rationally ordered if we could only picture and represent it rightly." Imagining city space was part of this tradition, a tradition that assumed "one possible answer to any question," a manner of thinking about urban space that extended from Voltaire well into the nineteenth century.[5] In his study of French Enlightenment architecture, Richard Etlin stated that "one of the most striking aspects about French culture at this time [the eighteenth century] was the extent to which intellectuals—not only architects but also clergym[e]n, doctors, lawyers, scientists, and writers as different as Mercier and Voltaire—took an active interest in the physical aspects of the city [Paris]."[6]

While new building and other public constructions in Paris during the eighteenth century did not match similar activity during the Second Empire, or even during the July Monarchy, what did take place was not without consequences for ideas about planning the entire city. The same holds true for building codes and regulations. Royal ordinances for the regulation of building heights and the alignment of houses with the street date back to the seventeenth century; in 1600 and 1607 Henri IV issued such codes with respect to building lines. Not always enforced, their effect was limited. During the eighteenth century, however, significant new codes were promulgated and enforced, the most important being the royal ordinance of 1783, amended in 1784. The 1783/84 code fixed the maximum height of Paris buildings in relation to the size of the street. This legislation was a major turning point in the history of domestic Paris architecture and an important foundation for the architectural look of the city during the nineteenth century, as it required architects to produce their best efforts within common height regulations.[7] Also in 1783, Edme Verniquet, a royal surveyor, was commissioned to produce a survey map of Paris showing the building lines throughout the city, a project he completed in 1791. This effort reinforced the sense that the entire city should conform to common building regulations. What is also important about Verniquet's map and the building codes is that they represent important instances during the eighteenth century of people seeing the city whole rather than focusing on one part of it.

The construction of important building and infrastructural amenities was also characteristic of the eighteenth century, and these, too, were citywide. As the population of Paris grew from about 500,000 in 1700 to about 620,000 in 1789, royal officials became increasingly occupied with providing the city with material amenities that would improve its safety and health. In the seventeenth century Henri IV had already installed a pump at Samartaine to obtain water from the Seine River for the city. In the eighteenth, the brothers Périer used steam to operate a pump they constructed at Chaillot (1778–81) for the same purpose, and authorities designed plans for canals to access the waters of the rivers Ourcq, Yvette, and Bièvre for Paris. Public officials also equipped Paris streets with oil-reflector lamps, began limited sidewalk construction, and, under the administration of the lieutenant of police, Grégoire de Sartine (1759–74), created a fire brigade. Parisians had available to them, in addition, several gardens open to the public, those of the Tuileries and Luxembourg Palaces and the Palais-Royal, as well as the Jardin des plantes. The large avenues and grand boulevards, which date from the seventeenth century, also served as pleasurable walks for the population.[8]

It was the construction of public and domestic buildings and squares, however, that related most closely to urban planning. Huge piazzas, for example, had already been constructed or planned during the early seventeenth century, the most important being the place Dauphine, the Place Royale (currently the Place des Vosges), and the Place de France, which was begun in 1609 but never built, owing to Henri IV's death in 1610. Its plan was significant, however, because the major street intended to extend from this *place* to the Place Royale, the rue de Turenne, was constructed. The latter and seven other streets were planned, but not executed, for the *place* would have transformed the entire east end of Paris.[9] By the end of the century Paris also had important royal piazzas in the Place des Victoires (1685) and the Place Vendôme (1697).

It was during the eighteenth century, however, that "the new classical architecture was applied on a scale large enough to transform Paris."[10] An important number of public buildings, constructed to face the streets—unlike private mansions, which guarded their entrances from the public roadway—went up during the eighteenth century. These included the École militaire (1752–57), the Hôtel des Monnaies (1768–75), the École de Droit (1770–83), the École de Médecine (1779–86); and the Théâtre Français at the Odéon (1779–82). In addition, the Catholic Church planned huge development projects associated with the construction of the churches of Saint-Geneviève (the current Panthéon) (1755–90) and of Saint Sulpice (1733–77), and, from the mid-eighteenth century onward, private entrepreneurs began constructing apartment houses in less-developed districts of the city to relieve housing densities in its center. In 1748, moreover, as a result of the impending end of France's participation in the War of the Austrian Succession (1742–48), the city of Paris announced a competition for the design of a public piazza in which to place a new statue of Louis XV, who was currently quite popular with the French people. The competition, which is discussed below, and the intellectual ferment associated with the new piazza revived interest in urban planning, which had waned since the great building programs of Colbert during Louis XIV's reign. Another major project of this century was the freeing up of space around the Louvre, which had gradually been encroached upon by houses, a process that began in 1758. All this public construction necessitated thinking about the relationship between new, large buildings and the street on a citywide scale.

Reflections by intellectuals on an ideal Paris revolved around the theme of *embellissement,* a French word that refers both to adornment and infrastrutural amenities.[11] In the classical ideal, the goal of *embellissement* was beauty and magnificence in building styles within a city conceived as a closed, walled entity. In the language of the *Encyclopédie,* a city is "a collection of houses arranged by streets and bounded by a common enclosure, usually of walls and moats. But to define a city more precisely, it is a space enclosed by ramparts which includes several quarters, streets, public squares, and other buildings."[12] As for magnificence, J.-G. Legrand and C.-P. Landon wrote in 1809, in a description of Paris at the time, that "one cannot deny that it was appropriate to construct edifices of a grand character for the embellishment of a city such as Paris and for the honor of the arts that the government causes to flourish there."[13] What begins to emerge in eighteenth-century Paris, however, is a shift in mental attitudes: the city is increasingly seen as the site of convenience, utility, and safety, rather than as a site of majesty and splendor. The new ideal city is also seen as open, without walls, a feature that would enhance the circulation of people and commerce. A modern city was emerging in the consciousness of urban thinkers in which the key elements were concern with urban functions and the economic sphere.[14]

Eighteenth-century "urban planning literature," moreover, contained many elements that became important components of nineteenth-century urbanism. As Emmanuel Le Roy Ladurie wrote, the eighteenth century "abolishes the aestheticised and fictive image of the city [and] invents a real urbanism." That is to say, many urban intellectuals addressed issues such as social suffering and the sheer number of people in the capital,[15] concerns that became more prominent by the end of the century. These new attitudes are significant in that they established a program, important parts of which resonated in the creation of modern Paris under Georges-Eugène Haussmann, as well as in the emergence of modern city planning. Increasingly, the management of space rather than the design of buildings became the main preoccupation of urban writers. A form of knowledge about space, in other words, became an essential ingredient both in the destruction of the classical ideal of urban planning and in the creation of modern planning proposals that preceded the actual creation of the modern city.[16] It is also evident from an examination of eighteenth- and nineteenth-century speculations on Paris that, while there are important differences between eighteenth- and mid-nineteenth-century attitudes toward the capital, many of the urban-planning issues taken up during the latter century have their origin in the former. Although the treatment of space in Paris during the nineteenth century and plans for its reform were more thorough, more rigorous, and more quantitative than in the eighteenth century, there was not so sharp a break between the two periods in terms of their larger aims with respect to the capital.

An entree into this important literature is suggested by Richard Etlin, who, for analytical purposes, divided the rich and multilayered ideal of *embellissement* into four categories. In Etlin's construction eighteenth-century Parisians wished to establish Paris as a "space of magnificence, of hygiene, of clarity, and of emulation." Etlin, whose primary subject is architecture, was thinking here both of the layout of the city as well as of public buildings.[17] A reading of and greater focus upon those elements that relate to the design of the city and to its infrastructure, rather than to its individual buildings, yields a slightly different set of analytical categories. For the eighteenth century, I would group texts on *embellissement* around five categories, which constitute a program for the ideal city. Increasingly and to varying degrees, urban planning literature on Paris addressed (1) comprehensive planning, (2) infrastructural amenities, (3) public health, (4) order and security, and (5) commerce. As we shall see, however, these divisions can be quite slippery and often overlap so closely that it is difficult to separate them, even for analytical purposes.

GLOBAL VISION AND
COMPREHENSIVE PLANNING

The idea that urban reform must be based upon a global, organic vision of the city came into its own by the mid-nineteenth century. A central component of planning texts in the first half of the century was the argument that Paris was an organic entity that must be treated and understood, both as a physical entity and as an intellectual construct, as a whole. An organicist vision of the city held that a reform in one part of the city would have consequences in another, necessitating, therefore, that all major transformations conform to an overarching plan. This contrasted with ideas about Paris current in the early seventeenth century, when, as Hillary Ballon wrote, "Henri IV's architects did not perceive Paris as an organic whole; intervention in one part was generally not considered in relation to the functioning of the entire city."[18] An early intimation of global planning for Paris, however, may be found later in the century in the work of François Blondel, a royal architect who, in 1672, was appointed by Louis XIV to head the Académie royale d'architecture, founded by Colbert the previous year. In that same year Blondel had designed the Porte Saint-Denis. Three years later, with the cooperation of his student, the architect Pierre Bullet, who in 1674 had designed the Porte-Saint-Martin, Blondel created a map of Paris for the purpose of managing and guiding urbanism and embellishment there. While it was the first such comprehensive plan, it remained locked in an older vision of Paris in the sense that Blondel and Bullet were mostly concerned with the state of Paris as it was rather than with its future possibilities or growth. It was the same with Blondel's *Cours d'architecture,* a three-volume work published in 1675. In it he wrote about facilitating circulation within Paris but focused mostly on architectural matters like the decorations on Paris *portes.*[19]

There were more extensive writings on comprehensive planning in the eighteenth century, and it is on these that the nineteenth-century planners would rest their own understanding of the same subject. The eighteenth-century conceptions of comprehensive planning, however, were not as fully articulated as those of the following century or completely free of older elements of planning, for example, planning for aesthetic effect rather than for convenience. This is not to say that nineteenth-century proposals did not address aesthetic issues—many did—but only that their focus on such issues as the city's infrastructure, health, and commerce were more sophisticated and comprehensive. By the end of the eighteenth century Paris, moreover, still lacked any official comprehensive plan for urbanism. At this time Paris fell under the administrative authority of the king, the municipal government, and the Parlement de Paris, the chief law court of France. The king's authority was represented by the lieutenant-general of police at the Châtelet, police at this time signifying broad civil and criminal administrative matters; the municipal government was headed by an official known as the prévôt des marchands et les échevins, who met in the bureau de Ville and oversaw such matters as the Paris infrastructure; the Parlement de Paris registered royal edicts associated with the city and also oversaw public administration.[20]

While the population of the city was increasing steadily, from about 220,000 in 1600 to 510,00 in 1700 to 620,00 by 1789, a total that represents the exceptional influx of people into the city during the Revolution, neither the royal nor the municipal governments adopted any guiding principles for new building-lot developments or street openings beyond the building code of 1783/84. Most new streets were opened by private individuals—aristocrats interested in having access to their private residences or entrepreneurs planning some real estate speculation. New streets rarely had any relationship to each other. By the end of the century, moreover, there was already a significant expansion of the city toward the north and west, a drift of the population that became especially troublesome to public officials and Paris intellectuals in the early 1840s. In the eighteenth century the unchecked growth of Paris also worried municipal authorities concerned with public order who feared a shortage of construction materials for public and private buildings, neglect of the important buildings and monuments in the center of the city, and the inability of authorities to provide public services over a wider territory.

Among those intellectuals in the eighteenth century who began to understand that urban reforms should be based upon a comprehensive, global view of the city, perhaps the most famous to address the issue of *embellissement* in Paris was Voltaire,[21] who lived in a Paris whose architectural magnificence had been determined by Louis XIV's wishes for a classically ordered capital city. *Hôtels,* churches, impressive boulevards, piazzas, gardens, and burgers' houses were constructed on an extensive scale throughout the city, and an important extension of the Louvre had been decided upon in the 1670s.[22] Unlike his contemporary Jean-Jâcques Rousseau, who approached Paris from a decidedly antiurban perspective and who preferred the "authentic" life of the countryside,[23] Voltaire expressed great pride in the French capital, whose monuments, he believed, "surpass the beauties of ancient Rome."[24]

He was not uncritical, however, and in 1749, following a trip to London, he published an essay on ways in which to improve the material condition of Paris.[25] Here he addressed comprehensive planning in the sense that he expressed an ideal for the entire city, beginning with the observation that a fundamental contradiction characterized the French capital. On the one hand, Paris consisted of great monuments and, on the other, of squalor and an inadequate infrastructure. He complained: "The center of the city, obscure, dense, hideous, is an example of the most shameful barbarism."[26] In Voltaire's program for urban reform three points stand out as a legacy for modern city planning. First, he called upon public authorities and leading citizens, "those who are at the head of the most opulent capital of Europe, to make it more agreeable and more magnificent." It is telling that Voltaire placed "agreeable" (*commode*) before "magnificent," because it suggests infrastrutural amenities. What Paris required, he wrote, were new public markets, larger streets, fountains to deliver water, and crossroads to facilitate the flow of traffic. With respect to *embellissement,* therefore, Voltaire emphasized issues of daily living over monuments. This would become a common consideration and emphasis in the early nineteenth century.

Second, Voltaire proposed a thoroughly modern program, centered on the circulation of capital, to finance the reform of Paris. Starting with the assumption that the king's treasury had been depleted, and that, in any case, no national monies should support purely Parisian reforms, he suggested a moderate municipal tax, either on personal wealth, on houses, or on produce, to finance the *embellissement* of Paris. Tax money, he believed, would create jobs for workers, circulate capital, stimulate construction-related industries, and make Paris more attractive to tourists and denizens, so that it would yield considerable benefits to all Parisians. A third important element in Voltaire's thinking was his wish that there appear on the scene "an individual with enough zeal to embrace all these projects, with a rather strong heart in order to follow them through, with a sufficiently enlightened spirit to draw them up, and [with] enough standing to make them succeed."[27] This did, of course, happen with the advent to administrative power over Paris of Georges-Eugène Haussmann about a hundred years later.

Voltaire's significance as an urban commentator thus lies in his clear recognition that Paris required infrastructural reforms, that these reforms would be economically productive and thus justified a tax levy, and that strong leadership was needed to undertake their execution. For those Enlightenment thinkers who, like Voltaire and Louis-Sébastien Mercier after him, thought about space, no matter how briefly, the application of reason to the creation of an orderly city landscape represented an integral aspect of the emergence of a progressive society. Voltaire's essay is not, however, an actual plan for Paris, nor does it offer a real vision of the city, as it lacks any details on what reforms to undertake. Neither did he work out a theoretical defense for *embellissement*, which, in its broad eighteenth-century sense, was an assumed part of French royal culture, and the need for urbanism was simply taken for granted. Many nineteenth-century urban planners, unlike Voltaire, theorized about and rigorously justified the more extensive comprehensive projects they projected. But Voltaire's essay was a statement of principle, an agenda whose specifics could be filled in later by some enlightened official or city planners.

Marc-Antoine Laugier's 1753 publication, *Essai sur l'architecture*,[28] represents a slight advance over Voltaire's thinking in that it at least announced three principles upon which to base a reform of Paris and was explicit about the need for comprehensive planning. Laugier, an ordained priest, had had a lively interest in architecture as a young man. His book, clearly written and highly opinionated, became one of the most widely discussed treatises on the subject within six months of its publication, coming as it did at a time of great interest on the part of a wide public in art criticism and on the emerging style of neoclassicism.[29] Following a discussion of architectural principles and style, which occupies the greatest portion of the work, Laugier turned his attention to the embellishment of towns, in particular, Paris. He began with an observation that would be repeated in the nineteenth century by, among others, a utopian socialist critic of Paris, Victor Considerant. "Our towns," Laugier wrote, "are still what they were, a mass of houses crowded together haphazardly without system, planning or design. Nowhere is this disorder more noticeable and more shocking than in Paris." In another critique, which also forms part of a tradition among Paris commentators, he described the center of the French capital as consisting of "the same number of little, narrow and torturous streets smelling of dirt and filth where the encounter of carriages causes constant obstruction."[30] The overarching problem was that among French cities Paris exemplified the total absence of "system, planning or design." The city, he wrote, lacks those "things that make a town convenient, agreeable and magnificent. Its avenues are miserable, the streets are badly laid out and too narrow, the houses plain and banal, the squares few in number and insignificant and nearly all the palaces badly placed." To rectify the disorder, Laugier suggested that *embellissement* be applied not merely to the construction and adornment of private homes and public buildings but also to entire towns. In order to advance the reform of Paris and the construction of a genuinely beautiful capital, therefore, he proposed principles of planning for "its entries, its streets and its buildings." Three rules would govern *embellissement:* "The entries into towns must be (1) free and unobstructed; (2) numerous, proportionate to the wall; [and](3) sufficiently ornate."[31]

Paris streets and avenues were central to Laugier's project. He compared the planning of streets to the design of roads through a forest or in a park. The major aim was that city streets be wide and properly aligned with one another. He analogized streets to park roads in order to establish the rule that streets should be simultaneously orderly and symmetrical, yet varied. As in the example of parks and forest or garden roads, not only streets but the entire city should be designed in a way to "avoid excessive regularity and excessive symmetry" or "boring repetition of the same objects." Streets and the city should achieve this effect while at the same time expressing order and rationality. Laugier's image of the garden as a model for the city and its streets may have derived from a purely aesthetic sense; as he notes, the gardens of Versailles, although "accepted by us as one of the wonders of the world," struck him as boring because of their formal and strict regularity.[32]

It is also possible that Laugier did not wish to create a sharp distinction between city and countryside in his suggestions for new streets in Paris. As John Merriman noted, city and countryside were not as sharply divided up to the first half of the nineteenth century as they would become in more modern

times, and this applied to Paris as well as to other French cities, as so many agricultural pursuits were practiced at the edge of the city and many rural types
inhabited its immediate suburbs and actively interacted with the city, whose
boundaries were so often not clearly delineated from those of its immediate
suburbs.[33] Laugier was perhaps simply reflecting this fact in his design principles. We will encounter this image of the street as functional but also organic
and curving, as in a park or forest, in the Saint-Simonian Charles Duveyrier's
1832 proposal for an ideal Paris; it also resonates in Adolphe Alphand's plans
for Paris parks under Georges Haussmann.

Laugier also affirmed that a capital city like Paris needed "a great avenue,
very wide and straight, lined with two or four rows of trees; it ends in a triumphal arch . . . ; from there one enters a large piazza formed by a half-sec-
tion of a circle, of an oval or of a polygon; several streets extend fanlike from
it of which some lead to the center, others to outlying districts of the town
and all with a vista of a beautiful work." Since the seventeenth century, Paris
already had in the Champs-Élysées what one historian described as "the most
grandiose and potentially symbolic urban perspective in Europe."[34] Laugier's
wish for a triumphal arch, of course, would be realized in the early nineteenth
century, with the further development of the avenue and, at the end point of
its vista, the Arc de Triomphe (1806–36). As for town entry points, which
were built later in the eighteenth century, Laugier advised that they be designed in a manner to facilitate movement as well as to suggest grandeur and
magnificence. Within the city, the facades of buildings and houses should be
decided by a public authority following a plan for an entire street, which
would also determine their height in relation to the width of the street. The
entire city, finally, had to be mapped out according to an overarching plan,
the most difficult part of the work of *embellissement,* according to Laugier.[35]

Like Voltaire, however, Laugier did not lay out a plan of his own or provide any details beyond his general principles. There is no sense in his universe of how much time a rebuilding of the city would take or of how such a
project would be financed. Voltaire, in addition to dealing with financing, at
least estimated that a reform of Paris would take approximately ten years.[36]
Moreover, while Laugier's treatise contains many modern elements—an argument for wide boulevards and streets and the construction of traffic circles—
it was primarily concerned with the beauty of a town, its overall visual impression, rather than with matters like utility and health.

Three years later, in 1756, Guillaume Poncet de la Grave, a historian and
lawyer working for the admiralty, published his *Projets des embellissemens de la
ville et des faubourgs de Paris.*[37] Unlike Voltaire and Laugier, Poncet identified
projects, often interesting in themselves, that covered wide areas of Paris.

Thus, he had important suggestions on improving streets, on safety and order in the city, and on health. His understanding that large parts of Paris had to be reformed was intuitive rather than theoretical, however, and, although his ideas are detailed and specific, he targeted individual projects rather than the city as a whole. Ansquer de Londres represents another type of limited thinking. Appealing to Laugier's authority for legitimation, he bemoaned the lack of planning and order in Paris, especially in the city's center. His proposals to rectify the disorder lack specificity and his vision of Paris remains static, still rooted in a baroque ideal.[38] In 1778, J.-B.-M. Jaillot went further and treated the entire city, section by section, with an even higher degree of specificity.[39] Michel Fleury and François Monnier regard Jaillot's plan as the first ever to present a complete proposal for Paris which avoided the "unpleasant theoretical and rhetorical spirit" characteristic of so many eighteenth-century city planning proposals.[40] It is true that Jaillot seems to have canvassed the entire city, and he seems simply to have taken it for granted that the aim of urban reform must be to facilitate circulation through the city.[41] As we shall see, however, it was precisely the ability to combine sophisticated theory with data that by the mid-nineteenth century constituted an important advance in ideas about space management.

More inclined toward theory than detailed suggestions was Pierre Patte (1723–1814). As a theoretician, however, he was far more sophisticated than most urban commentators in eighteenth-century Paris. Although trained as an architect, his fame rests largely on two remarkable publications, the *Monuments érigés à la gloire de Louis XV* (1765) and *Mémoires sur les objets les plus importans de l'architecture* (1769).[42] In the first he presents an ideal rational urbanism for Paris; in the second he writes about cities generally, positing a model of their ideal form. The intellectual starting point for Patte's analysis of planning in Paris was his application of reason to spatial problems; or, as Sophie Descat writes, Patte presented "the principles of a reasonable urbanism," which became increasingly characteristic of the second half of the eighteenth century. Another writer, going further, saw in Patte's attention to urban problems "the most complete expression of the desire for rationalization in the whole of the Age of the Enlightenment."[43] Moreover, it is only with the publication of Patte's *Monuments érigés* that the town became a central preoccupation of architectural theorists.[44] Writers before Patte had also placed urban problems at the center of their concerns, among them Nicolas Delamare in the early part of the century and Poncet de la Grave slightly before Patte, but none had Patte's comprehensive theoretical vision.

The immediate occasion for Patte's speculations on Paris urbanism was the June 27, 1748, decision of Paris municipal authorities to construct an equestrian statute of Louis XV in some prominent public square in the French capital; the city turned to Edme Bouchardon to design the statue, a model of which he completed in 1749. Paris officials invited France's leading artists and architects to design a new piazza for this statue anywhere in Paris they deemed appropriate, guided only by their aesthetic sense in the choice of location. The competition for a new royal square attracted all members of the Royal Academy of Architecture, as well as independent architects, including some who had only recently completed their studies, and even some members of the public. In addition to the formal proposals submitted, which totaled about fifty, numerous letters in *Mercure de France* dealt with the problem of the location of the king's statue. Eventually the king rejected all plans submitted, believing that a new royal piazza in any of the already developed parts of Paris would seriously disrupt the material life of the neighborhood upon which it was imposed, and he designated land belonging to the crown between the Tuileries and the Champs-Élysées as the only appropriate site.

The realization of this project was long: the statue was installed on the site and officially dedicated in 1763 and the buildings forming the square, the current place de la Concorde, were completed only during the Revolution. What is also important about the competition is that it attracted, in addition to plans that only considered the eventual site's effects on a local neighborhood, projects that gave thought to its location in relation to the entire city.[45] Taken as a whole the submissions for this competition had, Patte believed, "given birth to ideas about embellishment for this capital." From the approximately fifty plans originally submitted Patte choose those he found most interesting and instructive as a point of departure for an analysis of the means "to embellish this city in its totality, and thus to render it as agreeable as it is pleasing."[46] His analysis of these plans was a manner of expressing an ideal physical layout for Paris.

Patte was boldly announcing a new program, one that would combine infrastructural amenities and beauty for the entire city. Like many others in the eighteenth and nineteenth centuries, Patte was intellectually offended that Paris consisted of "a mass of houses crowded together pell-mell, where it seems that chance alone has presided. There are entire quarters that had virtually no communication with others."[47] He identified the underlying problem as the absence of a general plan for the entire city. Focusing on streets as the means to tie the city together, to make it into an organic entity, he complained that streets were poorly distributed throughout the city and that public authorities had failed to use public space to connect streets. Patte proposed a dramatic alternative, an ideal of planning whose imagery was also a central motif of certain mid-nineteenth-century planning proposals. He suggested an almost total reconstruction of Paris, save for the great monuments and elegant private houses. The process would begin only after a detailed map of the city had been drawn. The project for the rebuilding of the capital should then be submitted to all the great artists of France as part of a competition. A group of "connoisseurs" would make the final choice and the plan would be printed and displayed in the Hôtel de Ville, while the central government would buy up properties necessary to complete the project.

As no political will existed during this century for such a daring undertaking, one can characterize Patte's vision as utopian. His discussion of Paris, moreover, was, for all its modernity, still rooted in a baroque dream of a beautiful city.[48] Nevertheless, Patte's vision of an improved Paris must rank as an important forerunner of the Commission of Artists formed in 1793 to study the integration of expropriated Church lands into the public space of Paris. Beyond this there is in Patte's analysis a clearly articulated understanding that a city is a unified entity and that urban reform requires comprehensive planning directed by experts. This would be a powerful legacy for those who followed in the nineteenth century.

In 1769, four years after *Monuments érigés,* Patte published *Mémoires sur les objets les plus importans de l'architecture,* a work in which he extended his discussion of the infrastructure of a city. While this work was not about Paris, or any real city for that matter, it being his conception of an ideal city, Patte nevertheless drew on many examples from Paris or wished to apply his conclusions to it. Although in his previous work Patte had used the placement of a monument as a springboard for a discussion of infrastructure, in *Mémoires* he privileged the materiality of the city. In his mental construction of an ideal city Patte emphasized, among other topics, the necessity of a sewage system, the distribution of water, building regulations to prevent housing fires, and security. He devoted a great deal of analysis, however, to the morphology of the ideal street, which he regarded as the key to the successful functioning of a city. Such a street, he believed, would be paved, wide, and divided into three parts separated by gutters. He reserved the middle section for coaches and animals and the two remaining sections for pedestrians. He also wanted quays and bridges free of all obstructions in order to permit a free flow of traffic, the circulation of air currents, and an aesthetically pleasing vista up and down a river.[49]

Patte also anticipated an insight held by an urban planner of the July Monarchy, the pseudonymous Perreymond (see chapter 4), namely, that a central characteristic of the ideal city was the ability of people and coaches to move easily from its center to its periphery. As one often entered cities, especially capital cities like Paris, on a road passing through a triumphal arch or gate,

Patte maintained that it was essential "that all these access [points] be easy, that there be sufficient opening from one *quartier* to another for the transportation of merchandise and the free circulation of coaches, and finally that the farthest locations be capable of effortless linkage from the center to the city's perimeter without confusion."[50] While Patte was acutely aware of the necessity of well-designed streets and boulevards to the effective functioning of the city, in this work, however, he also remained wedded to a baroque ideal. Wide streets and boulevards were not only necessary for efficient circulation; they would, he opined, better show off "buildings, temples, and palaces, which are the city's ornaments."[51] Still, as the recognition of the relationship of periphery to center in the ideal city and in Paris was a key element of nineteenth-century modern thought about urban planning, Patte's understanding of this relationship must rank as a portentous insight.

Patte was not alone in calling for comprehensive planning. The idea of submitting any new general plan for Paris to experts is also found in Maille Dussausoy's very original *Le Citoyen désintéressé, ou diverses idées patriotiques concernant quelques établissemens et embellissemens utiles à la ville de Paris,* which appeared in two volumes in 1767 and 1768.[52] Unlike Patte, who only expressed the ideal of planning experts to evaluate projects, Dussausoy outlined an institutional framework for a committee of such experts. In this sense, he too is an important forerunner of the Commission of Artists and nineteenth-century planners.[53] Starting with the recognition that Paris was growing in population and size, Dussausoy expressed surprise that no plan existed to govern urbanism in the city.[54] Such a plan, he advised, was especially needed to designate "the opening, the aligning and the straightening out of streets that would suit the decoration of this city and the convenience of its inhabitants."[55] Once completed, a copy of the plan should be distributed in each quarter, an idea that was expressed later by the Commission of Artists. On the plan should be engraved the different buildings in Paris to be constructed or those that only needed to be decorated. What he had in mind, as he assured his readers, was not "useless destruction" but a focus on "the principal streets" with the aim of creating a coherent and rational use of public space in the capital.[56] This would address the lack of planning that had resulted in the confusion of narrow streets with no easy communication

Facing page

A plan proposed by Maille Dussausoy, as part of his larger urban renewal projects, to create a new cultural, academic, and administrative center for Paris in and around the old royal palace. Avery Architectural and Fine Arts Library, Columbia University

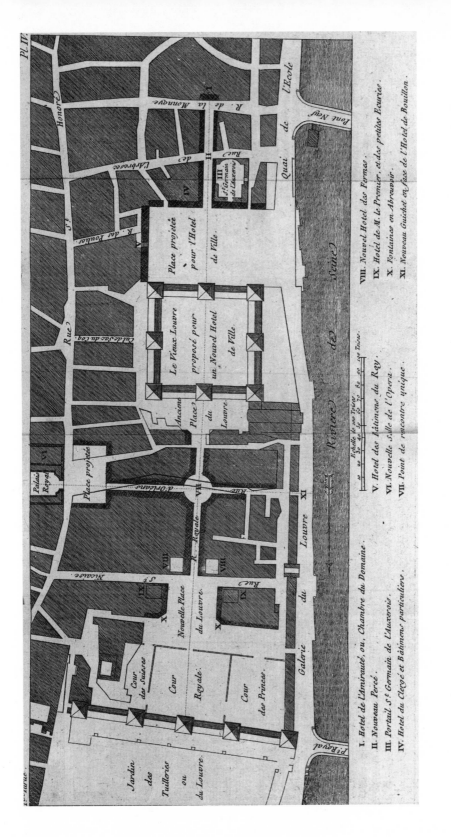

Pl. IV.

I. Hôtel de l'Amirauté, ou, Chambre du Domaine.
II. Nouveau Percé.
III. Portail St Germain de l'Auxerrois.
IV. Hôtel du Clergé et Bâtimens particuliers.
V. Hôtel des bâtimens du Roy.
VI. Nouvelle salle de l'Opera.
VII. Point de rencontre unique.
VIII. Nouvel Hôtel des Fermes.
IX. Hôtel de M. le Premier, et des petites Ecuries.
X. Fontaines en Abreuvoir.
XI. Nouveau Guichet en face de l'Hôtel de Bouillon.

Echelle de 100 Toises.

throughout the city and the replication of this pattern into the suburbs that characterized Paris urbanism in the eighteenth century. As Dussausoy noted, there already were laws that governed the opening of new streets and the erecting of buildings, but "we see every day the construction of houses in the most interesting parts of the city, without any alignment of the public roadway."[57] If private builders conformed to a coherent plan, Dussausoy predicted that Paris could be reformed in about thirty years.

Who would draw up such a plan? Dussausoy's answer is the key to his originality. He proposed a "commission" to address issues of Paris *embellissement,* a planning commission, to use modern terminology. Like all other writers under review here, Dussausoy understood *embellissement* to mean the functional and the beautiful, with a great emphasis on the infrastructure. A planning commission to guide all public building projects in Paris, especially the construction and widening of streets would be established under the direction of each of the authorities that had some control over Paris, the secretary of state for the Seine Department, the controller general of finances, the first president of the Parliament of Paris, the director general of buildings, the prévôt des marchands, the first president of the Bureau of Finances, and the lieutenant general of the police. It would consist of twelve members, "people of taste and enlightened amateurs," six appointed and six honorary. Dussausoy did not indicate who would appoint the members, although one may assume it would be the royal government, given the agencies to which the commission was responsible. The commissioners would designate from among the appointed members a treasurer and a secretary general of plans and treatises. The commission's principal functions would be to review plans and proposals for Paris *embellissement* submitted to it by any interested party, to choose the most interesting of these for discussion or submit them to a competition, and, finally, to pick the best project for execution, following a formal report to the Bureau of the Commission, a clear reference to its appointed members.[58]

Dussausoy's planning commission had one additional important role to fulfill. It would direct all urban projects it authorized. In this sense it would function as a kind of modern ministry of public works, planning and supervising Paris urbanism. This aspect of its responsibilities may be linked with another of Dussausoy's proposals. Dussausoy pointed out that in Roman times the army had been used not only to fight but also to build public roads, aqueducts, the urban infrastructure, and monuments. He suggested for his own times that "the use of troops and of the people for the construction of public buildings makes them less expensive and their building quicker and easier."[59] He did not develop this idea further but, given his other proposals, such a work force would obviously operate under the control of the planning commission. It is also interesting to note that we have in Dussausoy's recommendation an important forerunner of a planning idea found among the Saint-Simonians during the nineteenth century, namely, the establishment of a "workers' army" to execute the important public works projects needed by the public authorities. Proposals almost identical to Dussausoy's for a planning commission and a workers' army are also found in Stanislas Mittié's 1804 tract on the *embellissement* of Paris, and for the use of the army for public works projects in an 1830 work on a comparison of city planning in Paris and London, suggesting the birth of a recurring idea in planning.[60] Mittié, who had been a royal tax collector, went further and also proposed that the French state take the lead in developing its fallow lands into productive agricultural units, using soldiers to do the initial reclamation work during peace time and investing the income from those lands both in the embellishment of Paris and for relief of the poor.[61] Dussausoy concluded his section on the planning commission by advocating the creation of a permanent fund, made up of money from a lottery and a tax on playing cards, to finance its work and projects, a proposal that speaks to its author's farsightedness and realistic vision.

Louis-Sébastien Mercier wrote some twenty years after Voltaire's text on Paris and a decade later than Patte and Dussausoy. Like Voltaire and several other eighteenth-century urban writers, he had an overarching vision of what an orderly and rational Paris should look like, without, however, a detailed blueprint for its design. Mercier is best known as the author of the multivolume *Tableau de Paris,* published between 1782 and 1788, and the earlier *L'An 2440,* published in 1770.[62] The *Tableau* is a minute description of daily life in Paris in the late eighteenth century. According to one historian, Mercier invented a new manner of portraying a great and complex city like Paris by focusing on the social interaction of Parisians at street level rather than on its monuments or political institutions.[63] Another noted that, given Mercier's intense interest in the world around him, "there is no better writer to consult if one wants to get some idea of how Paris looked, smelled, and felt on the eve of the Revolution."[64] What emerges from Mercier's portrait of the French capital is a somewhat critical stance, although he loved the city. What disturbed Mercier about Paris, about the daily activities on its streets and in its public places, was its total chaos and irrationality. It was a city of traffic jams, accidents, and drunken driving. It lacked sidewalks, public latrines, and adequate sewers. It was so fixed in its physical structure, the product of a long history of unplanned growth, and so tightly controlled by a self-interested elite that, he believed, any reform or rational planning that would override individual interests would be difficult.

In *L'An 2440,* however, Mercier had permitted his imagination to roam in order to visualize a totally reformed Paris set in the distant future, in the year 2440 of the title. Despite this literary device, the book was not a classic utopian text, that is, one set in a purely imaginary space. It was set in a real city, although projected to a future time. In this fashion Mercier could propose reforms based upon real problems and imagine, in his "thought experiment," what Paris would look like if they were adopted.[65] There is also a sense in this work that time is not fixed and perfection achieved, as in classic utopian texts, but that history unfolds toward a better future. What emerges, therefore, is a new Paris, an outcome of Mercier's belief in progress.[66] Infrastructural reforms do not occupy much of the text, but when they appear they are designed to produce a more rational and orderly city, often mixed with a democratic vision of the new Paris. And all is colored by an Enlightenment faith in the goodness and rationality of the individual.

Thus Mercier envisioned a Paris where the streets were "perfectly lit. The lanterns were attached to all walls and their combined light eliminated all shadows." This feature of the new Paris, combined with the presence of an internal security guard, provided the necessary surveillance to assure security and tranquility in the city. The soldiers of the city guard, moreover, were the only ones necessary, as wars had been given up by sovereigns as irrational.[67] Writing about nineteenth-century utopian literati, among them Fourierists and Saint-Simonians, Christopher Prendergast observed that "light, both literal and figurative, will . . . play a part in the utopian imagining of the alternative city as the site of progress and justice," which was exactly Mercier's dream.[68] Fancifully, he also imagined a rebuilt Hôtel de Ville opposite the Louvre and the use of an immense space between the Louvre and the Tuileries Palace for public festivals "staged for the people." In another instance of linking material transformation and a democratic ideal, he projected the destruction of the Bastille fortress/prison and its replacement with a Temple of Clemency, as well as the free use of the Tuileries gardens by the public. In addition, he visualized height restrictions on all Paris houses, a reform that had already been decided upon by the ordinance of 1793/94, the construction of gardens on all roof tops, the placing of fountains on each street corner, the provision of water to each Paris house, and the removal of the Hôtel-Dieu, the major Paris hospital, from the center of the capital, and its replacement by twenty individual buildings, each located in some extremity of the city.

All these measures insured cleanliness and a healthier air quality for Paris. Like other reformers of this and the next century, Mercier also stressed the free and safe movement of the population through the streets of Paris. His aim was that "the greatest people [the Parisians] establish a free, convenient, and completely orderly circulation." One such reform, he wrote, came to him in a sudden flash. It was that all vehicular traffic drive on the right side of the road. One commentator concluded that Mercier's "Paris of the future . . . merges with the great preoccupations of the proposals for city planning [in the eighteenth century]: circulation and hygiene."[69]

Many other writers also recognized the need for a global plan for Paris urbanism. A.-C. Quatremère de Quincy, a prominent intellectual whose writings on art and politics extended from the last years of the Old Regime to the Restoration, proposed in 1809 major Paris street constructions that one urban historian characterizes as essentially "a Haussmannian program" before Haussmann.[70] Earlier, in 1769, Pierre-Louis Moreau, the official architect of the city of Paris, had put forth a proposal, in the form of etchings, for the reform of the capital. Entitled *Le Plan général du cours de la rivière de Seine et de ses abords dans Paris avec les différents projects d'embellissements dont cette ville est susceptible,* this work remained in manuscript form at the time and thus had less influence on contemporaries than if it had been published. It is important, however, in that it was part of contemporary discussions on urbanism in the capital and it expressed a principle that others, too, were elaborating. Moreau's key insight was that the various public and private works projects being planned for Paris should somehow be connected, that they should "form a general project of embellishment so that the different quarters of the city would obtain the greatest advantages."[71] In 1787, the royal architect, the count Charles de Wailly, proposed a plan for urban improvement in Paris. It focused on the less-developed Left Bank of the city and called for the construction of wide major streets. His plan also proposed a new east-west street on the Right Bank running from the rue Saint-Antoine to the Louvre, the route of the future rue de Rivoli, which Napoleon I would begin to construct.[72]

In an institutional sense the Commission of Artists is of primary importance. The Commission was formed by the Directory in 1793, as indicated earlier, to determine the integration of land expropriated from the Church into the fabric of Paris. It drew many of its ideas on streets and squares from Patte and Wailly.[73] Its most important tool was a detailed map, produced several years earlier by the architect and land surveyor, Edme Verniquet. This map, intended as the basis for a program of urban reform that embraced the entire city, focused principally on the road system of Paris, which would be the means to bind the city's new properties to public space. The commission also wished to plan new streets throughout Paris to facilitate the movement of air and sanitation, as well as eliminate those streets that were "narrow and winding, where air scarcely circulated, streets that were sources of corruption and unwholesomeness." While the Plan of the Artists embraced the entire city, and may therefore be characterized as comprehensive, it did not explicitly articulate the principle of general reforms. This represents a slight lack when compared to Pierre Patte's acknowledgment of this requirement. Still, the Plan of the Artists represents an important practical step in the direction of global and organic urbanism. Nothing came of this plan in the hectic days of the Revolution, and the commission disbanded in 1797. One central feature of its proposal, however, the opening of a west-to-east street in Paris, the future rue de Rivoli, received the support of Napoleon I, who completed the western section of this street.[74]

P. J. Le Moine stands apart from most eighteenth-century urbanists in that he proposed in 1793 a total reconstruction of the center of Paris, replacing part of it with a monumental public building that reminds one of Charles Fourier's Phalanstère.[75] Even this clearly utopian project, however, was concerned with the proper alignment of streets, the height of houses, the ease of communication throughout Paris, and the creation of a master plan. Another extensive project for public works throughout the city was designed by François Cointeraux, a professor of architecture. Responding to a competition for the development of the Champs-Élysées announced by the minister of the interior, Cointeraux submitted an extensive proposal in 1798 which embraced the entire city. He called for, among other reforms, the construction of new housing and hospitals, the multiplication of public squares, the enlargement of streets, the expansion of the Jardin des plantes, and, most importantly, the development of the area between the Louvre and the Tuileries, with the aim of making the latter a magnificent government center. Despite offering a plethora of details on individual projects, however, Cointeraux clearly articulated at the outset of his essay the need for one comprehensive plan to guide all urban reforms in Paris. An introduction to one of his works stated that if his proposal was examined "with the greatest impartiality, one would be convinced of the absolute necessity of halting temporarily all partial embellishment projects in Paris, and to proceed beforehand and immediately to the construction of a general plan" to pull together all urban reforms. Such a plan, a "universal program," should, moreover, be approved by the municipal authorities and published.[76]

B. A. Houard's 1807 plan for Paris is a fitting conclusion for this section as it typifies some of the strengths and limitations of eighteenth-century approaches to planning Paris.[77] In this work Houard outlined thirty disparate projects that seemed to him central to the well-being of the city, including the construction of several new bridges over the Seine, the expansion of the place des Innocents, the building of a new market in the place Maubert, the construction or expansion of several central streets, the establishment of new ports, the improved delivery of water to the city, and the construction of a large boulevard around Paris. While so many of these projects exhibit an understanding of the centrality of circulation flow in the city and of infrastrutural reform, Houard's plan, in its details, is a program for piecemeal reform. Nevertheless, Houard, who appealed to the authority of both Laugier and Verniquet, also recognized the importance of having a general plan of the capital serve as a guide to individual reforms. In language that sums up an understanding that had emerged in the thinking of some advanced urban intellectuals by the end of the eighteenth century, he observed that "it is perhaps very essential that the government order the office of Paris Streets and Boulevards (*le bureau de la grande voirie*) of this vast city to consult as quickly as possible the general plan of Paris, among others, that constructed by Verniquet, architect, in order to examine all the new streets that it would be feasible to open, continue or extend in a straight line or to enlarge in the interior of this city, in order to facilitate and multiply the means of communication." Such a map would be also useful as a guide to the city's purchase of property so that it could better align streets, as Verniquet intended. Houard hoped, too, that his plan and his proposals would engender new, "more vast projects, better thought out, more useful, more advantageous and easier to execute than those that we have detailed."[78] A map of Paris accompanied his suggested reforms.

Contrary to Françoise Choay's assertion that the conception of the modern city as an organic whole originates with Haussmann,[79] these writings suggest that the idea of comprehensive planning and the perception of Paris as a unified entity was becoming a common element in the planning literature by the end of the eighteenth century, even though a plan comprising both extensive details and hard data with respect to individual projects and a true general vision had yet to be devised. This would be the important accomplishment of several nineteenth-century planners. The eighteenth century, however, was already pointing in this direction. Infrastructural reform was also becoming part of the planning agenda by the eighteenth century.

THE PARIS INFRASTRUCTURE

Discussion of infrastrutural reform in Paris, especially the planning and alignment of new and old streets, was for many theorists the principal avenue for intellectually grasping Paris as a whole and demonstrating the need for comprehensive planning. It was also, however, a reform sought in its own right, not always linked to arguments for general planning, and for this reason may

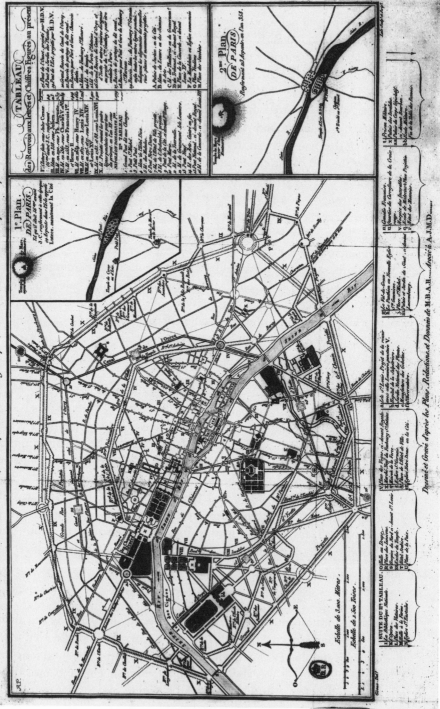

PLAN DE PARIS,

Où sont indiquée 4 Nouveaux Ponts 4 Monuments Publics Commerciaux et plusieurs Bassins pour Porte et Garce 2 Canaux de Navigation qui se partagent chacun en deux parties;
Plusieurs rues, Places et autres Objets utiles et nécessaire au Commerce et à la Salubrité de cette grande Ville. Le tout tel qu'il est plus amplement expliqué et détaillé aux
Articles mentionnée aux VII VIII et Xme Cahiers Ime Volume imprimé du Recueil Polytechnique de l'an XI Ime année du Consulat de Napoléon Bonaparte. Premier de l'Empire Français.

be treated as a separate category for analysis. It might seem obvious today that the street system of a modern city must be extensive, rationally laid out in connecting the entire city, and a purely public space. Matters were not so simple in the eighteenth century, before the 1783/84 royal edict establishing a minimum width for new streets, when private individuals as well as the government could take primary responsibility for opening new streets and no plan existed for linking them. As in the case of comprehensive planning, public officials and urban thinkers recognized the centrality of the street to the life of Paris and began to produce an important literature on the correct design, use, and importance of this facility.

One of the earliest such officials was Nicolas Delamare (1639–1723), a councillor to the king in the Châtelet de Paris, the police headquarters of the city. Delamare's major work was the *Traité de police,* a glossary on police power published in the early years of the eighteenth century.[80] In Delamare's time, police power in Paris included civil as well as criminal matters. Thus, one of the central responsibilities of the police was to oversee the *voirie de Paris,* the public roadway, a power that included standards for the construction of buildings as well as the streets. The aim of the police, already evident in this early stage of its development, was to "monitor people's movements" and to "ensure more effective control of a larger, more mobile population. . . . Theorizing about police work was directed toward the same end as philosophizing about space," according to Daniel Roche. Its program fitted within the Enlightenment ideal of stability.[81] Delamare's treatise provided the intellectual rationale for the broad powers assigned to the police at that time. The fourth and last volume of this work, on which Delamare worked over the last two years of his life, focused on the police and the road system of the capital. While not a classic treatise on urbanism per se, Delamare's study lays out all the principal ideas concerning the importance of the street found in and developed more fully not only by later eighteenth-century writers but also by Georges Haussmann in the nineteenth century, thus forming the ground, as it were, for modern notions of the form and function of streets.

According to Delamare, in order for the police to exercise its power to administer the city and maintain public order and for the city's commerce to function, police agents as well as citizens of Paris had to have easy access to all parts of the city, and this meant police control over, and public access to,

Facing page

A map of central Paris in 1807, showing the very dense network of roads there at the time. Avery Architectural and Fine Arts Library, Columbia University streets. In a statement of great economy, considering the themes it encompassed, Delamare defined police power, all aspects of which revolved around the street, as follows:

> It [the police] has as its appropriate and immediate business housing and the regularity of buildings; the expansion, the alignment, the freedom and convenience of streets, of public places, and of large roads; and as a more long-range but more considerable aim the ease of commerce and the correspondence of citizens among themselves and their neighbors as well as foreigners; . . . health, the abundance of provisions necessary to maintain it . . . ; the ease and the speed of mail delivery, of public vehicles, and of the advance of armies.[82]

Well-constructed streets, he knew, assured the circulation of merchandise and people necessary for successful commerce, the circulation of air and sunlight for health, and the circulation of police and armies for order and security. The principal charge of police commissioners concerning streets, Delamare wrote, was therefore to secure their "cleanliness, their convenience, and their safety."[83]

Delamare also identified an aesthetic component of street construction, an appreciation that runs through the writing of virtually all eighteenth- and many nineteenth-century urban commentators. The "paved street," he asserted, "is the principal ornament of a city." As he explained, paved streets provide access to the important "Temples, Palaces and Public Places" of the city. This was one reason why the police should maintain streets in a clean and uncluttered state, a condition that ensured not only the city's health and commerce but its beauty as well.[84] Additionally, Delamare coupled the aesthetic properties of streets with building construction. He maintained that the police, in order to assure both the beauty and functionality of Paris, must reserve to itself the right to regulate the form of buildings, "to proscribe the alignment, the construction and the height of houses; to maintain the width and freedom of the public way." He meant by this that there is an ideal relationship between the height of buildings and the width of the street, and this should be respected for its aesthetic impact on the city. For the sake of public safety and order, he believed also that the police should determine the soundness of building construction. The prefecture of police, he concluded, was interested in anything that concerned "either the decoration of the city or the convenience of its inhabitants."[85]

Having established the logic of urban street construction and the general principles of their design—they should be wide, paved, and uncluttered—Delamare employed a simple classificatory scheme for streets that was adopted in almost the same form by Patte later in the same century and by Chabrol de Volvic, prefect of the Seine Department, in the early nineteenth century. Although no law at this time fixed the width of Paris streets, Delamare estimated that they clustered into three groups. In his classification large streets ranged from fourteen to twenty meters across ("seven or ten *toises*," a *toise* being equal to about two meters), medium-sized streets—Delamare referred to them as "communication and distribution streets"—were six to ten meters wide, and small streets, whose primary function was to provide shortcuts to large streets, measured six to eighteen feet from side to side (a foot being 0.3 meters). Ideally, any street should be wide enough for two coaches to pass each other from different directions. Following this discussion Delamare drew a conclusion that would have fundamental implications for modern urban planning. "The width of streets being determined," he wrote, "anything found to interfere with their alignment must be demolished without distinction to persons, to whatever state and office they belong, because, following the general maximum of the kingdom, all particular interests must yield to the public welfare, save nevertheless for compensation, which is regulated by the opinion of commissioners named by the king."[86] Effective laws governing the expropriation of private property for public projects did not come into existence until the nineteenth century. Delamare, however, in his capacity as councillor to the king, was a champion and agent of centralized state power, and he articulated an important theoretical principle, the right of eminent domain, for modern state planning.

In one small portion of his treatise Delamare, using the street as starting point, gave flight to his imagination and expressed a thought that also became an important ideal among a segment of modern planners. Turning to a reading of history, Delamare observed critically that ancient Roman cities, before the time of Nero, lacked laws governing their arrangement and land use. At that time there was "so little order," a quality that disturbed Delamare as it did many nineteenth- and twentieth-century planners. Lack of order, he wrote, "rendered this city [Rome] considerably distorted; there were at that time only two sorts of streets, some rather straight, but the majority of the others oblique, tortuous, full of turns and bends." Then Nero burnt the city, he wrote approvingly, and the new streets were rationally planned and magnificent.[87] Georges Haussmann, according to a recent biographer, also disliked disorder, and this was one impulse behind his transformation of Paris in the mid-nineteenth century.[88] In a broader sense the articulations of both men represent, more than a hundred years apart, what Paul Rabinow referred to in a discussion of planning as "the emergence of certain practices of reason in France."[89] Both men, in other words, made contributions to the discipline of city planning which may be seen as part of the project of regulating the modern world. Delamare and Haussmann dreamt of the perfectly ordered society, not surprising given their respective positions of political power. These same impulses were shared by many outside the government, as we shall see throughout this study.

Writers after Delamare also regarded the street as the key element in the infrastructure of Paris and suggested additional reforms. Poncet de la Grave called for the alignment of all entry points into Paris as well as of all streets in the capital, which was not only a necessity but would also "produce a charming effect." He recommended the construction of a major boulevard ringing the city, the removal of chains closing certain streets to public vehicles, and the elimination of any object, like a fountain, that impeded traffic flow.[90] Patte, as we have seen, saw the street as the key to tying the city together into one organic entity. Jaillot believed that circulation throughout the city "must always guide our projects."[91] François Cointeraux had an especially dynamic view of the efficacy of street construction. He believed that the judicious opening of new streets, along with other amenities like sidewalks, gardens, new housing, and new hospitals, could determine the equitable spatial distribution of the Paris population and somehow—he never explained exactly how—insure that Paris would be neither too small nor too large.[92] Many planners from the seventeenth century to the time of the Revolution had called for the development of the area between the Louvre and the Tuileries Palace and of the Champs-Élysées. Cointeraux's plan also aimed at improving this section of the capital. Referring to the major east-west artery that Napoleon I decided to complete, the rue de Rivoli, Cointeraux opined that "this famous street is the beginning of all the work necessary for the general embellishment" of Paris. Without this street, he continued, one could create neither "the space nor the form of the most beautiful public square in the world. This unique square, the most majestic square of which I wish to speak is that which already exists between the Louvre and the Tuileries but whose beauty is obstructed by a multitude of streets and crossroads, of houses and shops."[93]

With respect to streets and the police, police power became increasing rationalized throughout the eighteenth century, a power that was increasingly visible over the streets, which the police wished to keep free for vehicular and pedestrian traffic. The impulse to keep streets clear of rubbish, street merchants, stalls of any kind, and the gathering of people related to games and other social activities was linked to the growth of the centralized state, the needs of commerce, and even aesthetic sensibilities. As a result, by the end of the century the police had defined the street in mostly functional terms, as a site for traffic flow rather than neighborhood socializing, and considerable progress had been made in this domain, although not as much as in modern times.[94] Along these lines, Arlette Farge summed up the police attitudes with respect to streets and security by noting the police "obsession" with alleys, those narrow street corridors where so much could be hidden from the watchful eyes of authorities. Control over the streets, and especially their dark corners and narrow passageways, fell under "this [police] passion for control."[95]

Closely related to streets in modern times is the sidewalk, although the first-rank theorists dealt with here did not always link the two, being content to expound only on the former. For Patte it was far more important to pave streets than to have sidewalks, although sidewalks should be an element of an ideal street.[96] Poncet de la Grave and Jaillot limited their discussion to new streets and their alignment. Cointeraux mentioned sidewalks but only as a remote possibility.[97] The issue of sidewalks became increasingly important as the eighteenth century wore on, however. While the first sidewalk within Paris was constructed in 1601 on the Pont Neuf, the first sidewalk construction for a street took place in 1781, on the rue de l'Odéon. Before, and even after, that time Parisians risked grave accidents simply trying to negotiate Paris on foot. Mercier, the eighteenth-century chronicler of daily life in the capital, complained that "from the moment one is on the streets of Paris one clearly sees that people do not obey the laws. No convenience for pedestrians; no sidewalks. The common people seem a body separate from the other orders of the state; the rich and the great men who have coaches have the barbarous right to crush or mutilate the common folk in the streets." He concluded that "the lack of sidewalks renders nearly all streets dangerous."[98]

Mercier joined two critiques here. One sprang from his democratic sentiments. The second was a statement about the material conditions of the Paris roadway. With respect to the physical state of Paris streets, two conceptually related texts, one written in the late eighteenth century, at the time Mercier penned his complaint, and the other at the beginning of the nineteenth century, presented wide-ranging arguments for sidewalk reform which encapsulated thinking on this subject at this time.[99] They were also early stages in similar reflections that were taken up later in the nineteenth century. That they were not written by a major writer—the first was an anonymous pamphlet and the second by one Arthur Dillon—also points to the increasing concern with infrastructural reforms by a wide range of urban thinkers and is a sign of more specialized and technical writing on the urban environment. It is significant, too, that both writers saw the construction of sidewalks as inextricably connected to other issues, including health, safety, tourism, and commerce, so much so that any attempt to separate these elements for analysis would distort their arguments. With that caveat, therefore, let us first examine the 1784 text.

So many Parisian writers thinking about the urban infrastructure, including the author of the 1784 brochure, compared their city to London and found it wanting. Comparisons between the two capital cities were apt. By 1750 London's population was about 675,000, whereas that of Paris by 1789 was about 620,000. By the mid-eighteenth century, however, London already had elegant and wide streets. New streets on the West End estates were about sixty feet wide, constructed with broad sidewalks, and were about double the width of Paris streets. Especially critical in London urbanism was the passage of the first Westminster Paving Act of 1762, soon followed by others for the City and other places. The act mandated paving commissioners with paid staffs; gutters and pavements were constructed on either side of roads and the pavements were used as pedestrian walkways. Donald Olsen, in a comparative history of Paris, London, and Vienna, concluded that, "with respect to paving, lighting, and sanitation, and to the material conditions of life, Georgian London (1714–1830) far surpassed Paris."[100] We have already noted that Voltaire was inspired to write his essay on Paris following a trip to the English capital. The author of *Projet sur l'établissement de trottoirs,* with the apt subtitle *For the Safety of the streets, and the embellishment of Paris,* was also partly inspired by London, which, he wrote, had set the model for sidewalk construction "so that people can walk safely on the streets." He added, clearly as a rhetorical flourish, that "since the establishment of sidewalks, there are no longer any accidents in London."[101] His main objective, however, was to offer a convincing argument for the construction of sidewalks in Paris. This was especially important, in his mind, considering that a new vehicle, the cabriolet, was currently popular. It was lighter and faster than the traditional coach but as a result more dangerous to anyone walking on Paris streets.

The author of *Projet* advanced two principal reasons for Paris sidewalk construction, one philosophical and the other pragmatic. He based the first argument upon a democratic interpretation of the space needs of Paris. "Every sumptuary law, every police regulation must have as its end this mass of men that one calls the people. Most assuredly, it well merits this: it is the people which validates the land, which provides the greatest number of subjects to the State, which causes the arts, commerce, and industry to flourish, which pay the greatest amount of taxes and duties; in a word it is the people which composes the Republic."[102] "Republic" in the above context was only meant to signal the tradition of urban corporate freedoms. The author, following his goal of social utility for the widest number of people, concluded that since ninety-eight out of one hundred people in Paris walked on the capital's streets rather than took coaches, as the small wealthy minority did, the law would not be unjust in abolishing coaches. He did not argue this position, however, but merely used it to demonstrate that the government was obliged, given the needs of the largest part of the population, to provide infrastrutural reforms to protect the majority. In the matter of Paris streets this meant the construction of sidewalks.

Toward the latter part of the eighteenth century intellectuals increasingly began to judge projects in terms of their social utility; the idea that public building projects should demonstrate a concern for the welfare of the people became dominant during the time of the Revolution.[103] This attitude is reflected by the author of *Projet,* who, having laid out the governing principle of infrastructural reform, then offered a practical argument for sidewalks which centered on the issue of public health. Lack of sidewalks on Paris streets, he wrote, was especially dangerous to four special categories of the population, comprising people who could not walk Paris streets without running a great risk of being "knocked down" by vehicles: the deaf, the blind, the old, and children. To highlight the danger to these groups he once more painted an idyllic portrait of young children on London streets: "It is there, with others of the same age, that they run, play and frolic together as if they were in a room." The children of Paris, even those of the rich, suffered from the lack of sidewalks. Rich children, who rarely walked in the city because of the danger coaches posed on the street, rode in their own carriages. Consequently they could not prevent illnesses—unnamed—associated with lack of exercise. Children of moderately well-to-do families also "are locked in their rooms, or one takes them by the hand on the streets; something which, in depriving them of necessary exercise, exposes them to a great number of infirmities: from this comes without doubt that the Bretons in general are vigorous and stronger than the French. There is more: this difference in exercise maintains the preservation of some and the destruction of others."[104]

The author concluded this argument linking health and exercise to the ability to negotiate public space with another equally forward-looking precept. He observed that "in an immense capital, full of useful and agreeable manufacturing, trades, and professions, it is imperative that the transactions of the civil society have a regular movement"—by which he meant that circulation had become an essential aspect of the emerging modern city. Not only would sidewalks facilitate movement, they would stimulate health, cleanliness, tourism, and, finally, adornment, thus combining the infrastructural reform program of London with the magnificence of Paris buildings, and Paris would therefore surpass London.[105]

In addition to laying out reasons for sidewalk construction, the author of the *Projet,* like Delamare and Patte, also classified Paris streets but, in his case, according to their capacity to support sidewalks. His criterion with respect to street width, including sidewalk construction, was the ability of coaches to move freely over streets. The author claimed to have measured every street in Paris—"and that has not been a small task for me"[106]—and that a street thirty feet wide could accommodate three vehicles passing each other and ten feet of sidewalk, five along each of its sides; streets only twenty feet wide could have sidewalks on one side only; streets too small to permit sidewalks and coaches should be closed, he believed, by means of a chain across the street, reserving the latter for pedestrian use only.[107]

In 1803, Arthur Dillon, an abbot who wrote on ecclesiastical and political matters, also compared Paris to London and used the ability to walk over Paris streets as a form of exercise to argue the virtues of sidewalk construction.[108] He went much further, however, and tied sidewalks to issues of morality, commerce, and surveillance. Sidewalks, Dillon thought, produced urban cleanliness, and it was this element that had a positive moral influence on the population. Anthropologist Mary Douglas's insights on dirt are relevant here. Douglas observed that "dirt offends against order. Eliminating is not a negative movement, but a positive effort to organize the environment." Stripped of its association with Western knowledge about hygiene, according to Douglas, dirt becomes symbolic of things out of order, of matter being disorganized. By demanding cleanliness, culture or society demands that everyone conform to order and control, she argues.[109]

This is what Dillon seems to have been aiming for when he wrote that "cleanliness elevates man, inspires him with confidence; it disposes him to decency; it induces him to respect others so that one respects him; finally, one can say that it gives a new force to all social relations by taming manners. All travelers have remarked that cleanliness and civilization always march with the same step among the savages." One can easily read for "savages" here the working and lower classes. "Man is," he explained further, "degraded by uncleanliness; the mud which covers his clothing humiliates him; it penetrates his heart; and if this kind of humiliation does not render him more servile and low, surely he will become insolent through cynicism." It is interesting that *la fange,* the French word for *mud,* can also mean *degradation* or *vileness.* For Dillon the cycle of uncleanliness was perpetuated because dirt picked up on the streets by individuals was also brought inside homes.[110] Here is another example of reason and planning at the service of social control over space and the individual.

Closely aligned with control over the environment to produce middle-class order and values—Dillon's voice is surely that of the respectable bourgeoisie—was a form of space management linked to police power. Dillon observed that "the police of Paris are particularly interested in the construction of sidewalks" because in a country like France, where political convulsions had been great, "the police cannot be too vigilant and its agents too encouraged to maintain safety." Arguing as Delamare had done at the beginning of the eighteenth century, Dillon observed that sidewalks would permit police agents to patrol a city day and night and were therefore essential. Moreover, "the construction of sidewalks in the capital, and in all the large cities which imitate its example, shall have a direct influence on public safety throughout the kingdom." This was the case not only because all major French cities would be equipped with sidewalks but also because their construction would provide significant public employment, or, in his words, "useful work," especially following wars, to eliminate "vagrancy and idleness."[111]

Perhaps the most modern element in Dillon's argument for sidewalk construction had to do with commerce. In the eighteenth century, *commerce* had two meanings: "it was the driving force in the development of manufacturing . . . ; and, in a more general sense, it was a force that promoted reciprocal social relations, a key factor in sociability."[112] Dillon, without neglecting the second meaning, focused on the first and captured perfectly a modern sensibility with respect to shopping and merchandising.

It is worth recalling first, however, Walter Benjamin's insight that in early-nineteenth-century Paris methods had been devised for the "phantasmagoric" display of commodities, among them posters, internal shop lighting, and mirror displays, and especially the arcades—"a recent invention of industrial luxury," in the language of the 1852 *Illustrated Guide to Paris,* "those glass-roofed, marble-paneled corridors extending through whole blocks of buildings, whose owners have joined together for such enterprises"—walkways where goods were publically displayed to stimulate the customer's desire for purchases. These were, according to Benjamin, "the forerunners of the department stores." The art of display was paramount in the success of the arcades, an attraction both for Parisians and tourists.[113] On a more practical level, the arcades helped the Parisian middle classes avoid the dirty, dangerous streets in shopping, and no arcades were built after about 1840, as the streets improved. If the arcades led to the department stores, eighteenth-century shop windows preceded the arcades. By the late eighteenth century, as the trade in luxury goods extended broadly beyond the aristocracy, bourgeois merchants took to opening their stores to shopping traffic on the streets. Windows, formerly merely observation portals into the shop and a key source of light, were increasingly used as a stage setting to display goods found within the shop.[114]

Two eighteenth-century infrastructural developments advanced the use of shop windows: street lighting and sidewalks. Street lighting not only complemented the store's internal illumination, it also extended the shopping day and provided safety, bringing light into night, a great appeal to evening strollers. The candle lamp was the first form of street lighting. The number of these lamps grew steadily in Paris: in 1697 the French capital had 2,736 street lanterns; in 1740 the number was 6,400, and in 1766 it had grown to about 7,000 or 8,000. Lighting street lamps was a police responsibility, and after 1769 lamps remained lit until dawn; before this time they had operated until 2 a.m. The first gas lamps were employed in Paris in 1817 to light up, appropriately, an arcade, the passage des Panoramas. By 1830, some 6,000 lamp posts were lighting the boulevards and main streets with gas lamps. Given the surveillance function of street lamps, we should note, too, that their installation often provoked a reaction from below, and lantern smashing became both a symbolic and a real act of defying authority in the seventeenth and eighteenth centuries and during the revolutions of the nineteenth century.[115]

Shop windows were not so effective, however, if the shopper could not easily get to them and linger before their displays. This is where Dillon's insight on sidewalks was so prescient.[116] Dillon linked the form of urban space and the correct siting of an establishment to commercial success. Any kind of boutique had to be visible to all who passed by in order to flourish. Another element of its prosperity would be a location in the busiest and most heavily trafficked urban districts. Some boutiques already had achieved these requirements, he wrote, like those in central Paris, where existing sidewalks encouraged walking. A program of sidewalk constructions "would convert all the streets of Paris into agreeable promenades, would increase the number of strollers, and would thus make possible, more often than not, the display of objects under the eyes of the public that could excite its desires." He explained that he did not mean to imply by this that sidewalks would "increase the needs of the populace." It was only that "merchants speculate as much about the fantasies of buyers as about their real needs; and certainly nothing is more suitable to stimulate the desire to buy than the sight of the objects for sale."[117] Sidewalks conferred additional benefits: merchants could more easily make deliveries to all parts of the city; labor could be employed in their construction; general sociability would result as people could stroll the city's streets; and, lastly, sidewalks were "objects of pure decoration or agreement, like public squares, promenades, and theaters."[118]

Dillon's vision of a Paris equipped with sidewalks extended to a consideration of urban and national circulation and its economic importance. Sidewalks should be constructed in Paris, he suggested, following a master plan, modeled on that used for the national highway system. During the eighteenth century "the hierarchy of roads—royal roads, highways, royal ways, and crossroads—was defined and widths specified for each type of road." Improved and safer highways facilitated and represented the power of the national state, improved commercial intercourse, and linked cities, especially Paris, to a burgeoning national economic system.[119] Following the national territorial model, Dillon proposed that Paris sidewalk construction begin on the major communication routes of the city and extend to others based on their size and importance. These sidewalks should be linked with each other in such a manner as to divide the whole city into seven or eight grids. The entire system, he proposed, should connect with the national highways, which would result in the efficient circulation of goods and services in Paris and beyond. Considering the national and local economic benefits of sidewalks, their construction, he suggested, should be financed by the government for the major Paris routes; on secondary streets, builders of new houses would be required to construct sidewalks fronting them following a government-determined plan.[120] Dillon's proposal, while not developed further, is a forerunner of the Saint-Simonians' theorization about a national and international communications system built around the railroad and waterways (see chapter 3) and also of Chabrol de Volvic's similar suggestion that Paris could be spatially unified by a system of sidewalks (see chapter 2).

HEALTH AND THE CITY

In addition to wanting a beautiful and magnificent city, eighteenth-century Parisians were greatly preoccupied with creating a healthy city, according to Richard Etlin. The free and effective circulation of air was considered essential for such a city, and three spatial improvements would facilitate its flow: the construction of low buildings, wide streets, and urban gardens.[121] Additionally, reformers were also concerned with the circulation of water in the city, the construction of sewers, what to do with urban cemeteries, slaughterhouses, and hospitals, which people believed all spread disease, and public toilet facilities. The need for effective refuse disposal was of special concern to eighteenth-century Parisians. As Donald Reid made clear, worries over refuse were related to new fears in the eighteenth century—similar anxieties arose following the plague of 1530—over the supposed harmful effects of miasmas emanating from rotting refuse in the city. As a result public officials passed ordinances intended to improve sanitation in the capital. In 1758, a royal ordinance required that new dumps be located outside the city; in 1761, municipal authorities designated Montfaucon, in northeast Paris, as the capital's principal dump; and, in 1781, as authorities had closed all other Parisian garbage heaps, Montfaucon, a site of refuse as well as public executions, became the city's only dump. The latter was a mixed success, however, as the stench emanating from this refuse heap made Montfaucon "the epicenter of stench in Paris," and, in the imagination of many scientists, ironically itself a source of the unhealthy state of Paris.[122]

The city's sewer system was also decidedly inadequate during the eighteenth century; writers of the time believed that ancient Rome had a sewer system far superior to their own, a reflection, they believed, of the superior public spirit and services of the ancient capital. Paris had 26 kilometers of sewers at the time of the Revolution. Often many of these were nothing more than a channel running down the center of a street. Moreover, the crown was not especially interested in the construction of sewers, and Paris city authorities did not regularly maintain those that existed; private contractors were frequently hired to clean sewers. Although municipal authorities began to cover sewers at this time, covered sewers became difficult to clean, air did not circulate effectively in them, and authorities often forgot the site of buried sewers until they overflowed into some Paris neighborhood. Such incidents only added to Parisians' fears of air-borne diseases.[123]

It was in this context that the well-known writers of this period, like Delamare, Patte, and Jaillot, acknowledged the ideal of a healthy city. This goal was also expressed by intellectuals, and not merely medical doctors, who focused exclusively on health issues, producing thereby a prototechnical literature on this subject. As early as 1726 one Alphonse L.—as he had his name printed on a brochure—decried the "dirtiness" of the public roadway, the mud and puddles of the streets, and the trash thrown onto public spaces. Sewers, he complained, emptied out into the Seine, with the result that there was formed along its banks "a bed of mud which putrefies the water that serves the majority of the population for washing, bathing, and drinking." Continuing a litany of charges that become part of a standard dialogue of urban discourse, Alphonse remarked that people who lived on small impassable streets, where air did not circulate and filth accumulated, "generally have a pale and ghastly color, a sign of bad health and misery." He completed his prologue to suggestions for reform by noting that men far from their lodgings often took part in "the most disgusting and the most insupportable" abuse of relieving themselves publically, which not only contributed to uncleanliness but also "offended" the sensibility of women.[124] To remedy these conditions, Alphonse proposed an eighteen-point reform program. Its most important articles called for the establishment of a professional sanitation department for Paris and the appointment of an "inspector-general of public health," who, with "assistant inspectors," would circulate throughout Paris on horse to insure the city's cleanliness. A private firm would provide each district of Paris with regular trash pickup at fixed hours, and the passing cart would be announced by a bell on one of the horses pulling it. He concluded by calling for the paving of all Paris streets and squares and the installation of new open sewers.

In 1782, Jacques Hippolyte Ronesse identified an important context for the steady interest in sanitation in Paris: he attributed the public health problems of Paris to "a surprising growth" of the French capital over the decade of the 1770s. Significant population growth, Ronesse observed, determined the need for street reforms that would assure cleaner air, a water supply, and the ability of sunlight to penetrate the city.[125] Writers later in the century proposed methods to clean Paris that required technical sophistication. Henri de Goyon de la Plombanie believed that the city's air should be purified by having streets washed each day and trash removed. Each house too should be equipped with water through a system of pipes running below ground. Fountains, with water running continuously, would also help purify the air.[126] Writing about ten years later, in 1789, Antoine Tournon drew an elaborate model of a canal system beneath Paris streets which would evacuate water from houses and streets, an underground sewer system network intended for the constant circulation of water through Paris. Tournon also submitted a new classification system for Paris streets, this one based not upon their width but upon their cleanliness. With tongue in check perhaps, but making a point about public health, he observed that Paris streets were either clean, less clean, or unclean. His major point was that air should circulate more freely in Paris, a condition to be achieved by building wider streets and opening up more gardens.[127]

Another proposal for the delivery of water to Paris was L. Bruyère's 1804 plan to divert water from the Ourcq River to Paris through a system of canals connecting to the capital. At the time Bruyère was the engineer-in-chief of the Ponts et Chaussées, and, while he was not the first to propose tapping the Ourcq River as a supply of water for Paris, he is representative of a strong interest at the time in such a project. Jean-Antoine Chaptal, minister of the Interior between 1800 and 1804, wrote in his memoirs that he had suggested to Napoleon I a policy to assure the abundant delivery of water to Paris, and the idea of utilizing the waters of the Ourcq River for this purpose date back to Colbert. Napoleon I did set into motion the construction of the Ourcq canal, a project that was completed under the Restoration.[128] Bruyère wrote that abundant water was essential for use by people, for the cleaning of streets, for use in sewers, for drinking-troughs for animals, for public laundry facilities, and for embellishment. Such water, moreover, had to be clean "but also agreeable."[129]

Water had become an important preoccupation of engineers and intellectuals writing on Paris at this time. Charles Lambert wrote a book in 1808, partly in response to a call that year from the Académie française for an essay on embellishments for Paris, in which he imagined a city of magnificent monuments but which also had a significant section on the construction of a new canal in Paris that would prevent future flooding in the city.[130] Opening wider streets and constructing buildings that would not overwhelm the street was not a great technical feat; it merely required political will, something that was lacking until the great street reforms of Haussmann. The delivery of water to a city was another matter, however, bringing engineers into the realm of urban planning, since they were the only ones with the technical knowledge to accomplish this goal. At this point in the history of urban planning, however, engineers and architects were not so sharply divided; the rift between them occurred during the nineteenth century.[131]

The above discussions of infrastructural amenities with respect to health in Paris are an indication of how far the eighteenth century had moved away from the baroque objective of the city as a work of art. Ronesse concluded that "*great projects are needed for a great city, for the capital of a great kingdom.*"[132] By this he meant infrastrutural reforms, not great monuments. Tournon expressed the same idea more forcefully. Writing that Paris needed public fountains, gutters, bridges, and sewers, he opined that "it is by these objects of utility that a wise government distinguishes itself; these are the real riches of the nation." Monuments and temples "only offer an incoherent melange of pride and misery, much more suited to inspire the pity rather than the admiration of the foreigner."[133] Even an 1802 work by C. A. Guillaumot, an administrator of the Gobelins tapestry works, whose primary intent was as a brief for the building of new monuments in Paris of a "majestic character," recognized the importance of the construction of sewers, the delivery of water for the health of the population, and the establishment of sidewalks. All projects related to monuments and the infrastructure were necessary, he wrote, for "the embellishment, for the convenience, and for the health of Paris."[134] Enlightenment writers also believed that public gardens would contribute to the health of Paris. In 1778, Jaillot deemed "that what is needed, without contradiction, are gardens in the cities; but they must be dedicated to public utility. What cities require are walks for the infirm, for those convalescing, for professionals, even for idlers." In Paris such public gardens could be carved out from a small portion of the property of religious establishments, but only after fair financial compensation, he advised. Roads could be cut through part of these estates, providing access to the gardens, while raising the value of the remaining property.[135] In 1804 a legislator, Sedillez, addressed the national legislative body on the importance of public gardens for the health and beauty of Paris. Provincials, he observed, were regularly in touch with nature in their daily rounds and thus used their gardens only for produce. On the other hand, Parisians, who were far removed from the countryside, needed to bring the benefits of the rural landscape into Paris by creating public gardens. "Numerous motives combine so many people in the same place! One person comes to get away from business; the other comes to recharge himself; one comes looking for company; another finds solitude; the greatest number is only drawn there by the need to breathe free air, to finally be able to see the sky and the play of light." A public garden, he concluded, should have "the character of an institutional space as necessary to the happiness of a great people as the insights of a wise government."[136] Gardens would thus bring nature into the city, and their construction became a major aim of planners during the first half of the nineteenth century, although the opening of important public gardens would have to await the regime of Napoleon III.[137]

If gardens were supposed to bring clean air into Paris, urban planners wished to remove sources of foul and unhealthy air from the city as well. Chief among these were slaughterhouses, cemeteries, and hospitals. Patte wanted cemeteries removed from the center of Paris, where they infected the air, and Poncet de la Grave proposed that Paris cemeteries be removed to the four extremities of the capital. Maille Dussausoy, attributing the foul air of Paris, the most serious cause of diseases in the thinking of the time, primarily to the cemeteries inside the city, wanted the government to address this subject, especially the presence of the cimetière des Saints-Innocents within the shadow of the main food market of the city.[138] The Saints-Innocents cemetery was one of the largest in Paris; it also served as a widely used public social space. Fear of odors emanating from rotting corpses in cemeteries became acute by the later eighteenth century, so Paris authorities decided to deconsecrate Saints-Innocents and remove it from Paris, a process they began in 1785; new cemeteries would also be constructed outside Paris.[139]

Patte complained, as Mercier would do later, that the Hôtel-Dieu, the very large public hospital in the center of Paris, housed people with infectious diseases, polluted part of the Seine River, generally infected the air, and should therefore be removed from its location in the center of Paris. As for slaughterhouses, Poncet de la Grave complained that as a consequence of their presence throughout Paris one continuously saw "a surge of blood flowing in the gutters, infecting the quarters and constituting a horrible spectacle." He suggested the construction, under government supervision, of a central slaughterhouse in each quarter or on the outskirts of Paris.[140] As for the construction of sewers, a major aim of the Enlightenment program for a healthier Paris, Ronesse advanced the boldest reform by calling for the construction of sewers under every street of the city. Equipped with an underground sewer system Paris would take on a "new face" of "cleanliness and sanitation."[141] This reform would be accomplished only during the Second Empire.

ORDER AND SECURITY

Infrastructural improvements and a healthier Paris are closely related to another aim of eighteenth-century urban intellectuals: the safety and order of the city. Michel Foucault's insights are germane here. Foucault interpreted the classical age as an important stage in the rise of the disciplines, professions like medicine, that devised methods of control over the body. While for Foucault disciplinary power operated over discrete spaces that blanketed the entire society—hospitals, prisons, army barracks, schools, circular buildings with courtyards—one may also argue that different elites, political and intellectual, also dreamt of subjecting urban space to a form of rational planning that would ensure order throughout the city. Foucault recognized this aspiration when he observed, in a suggestive insight, that eighteenth-century intellectuals began to develop a "political literature" that addressed issues of order and "collective infrastructure" in the city, in which the city was increasingly seen as a political model for governing the larger territory. This concern with social order—it did not originate in the eighteenth century—reached a new stage during the classical period because of a double conjuncture: a large demographic push resulting in the perception on the part of more-settled Parisians of a kind of nomadism, as people moved from the countryside to the city, and of increased production associated with capitalist industrialization and urbanization, even if in its early stages. In police reports and treatises of that time, according to Foucault, "one finds that architecture and urbanism occupy a place of considerable importance."[142] Delamare is a classic example of this linkage.

The desire for order and security, however, was also taken up by urban intellectuals, for whom these elements became a vital amenity of city life. Not only did urban planners almost universally call for wider and better aligned streets in Paris, essential to the ability of the police and troops to penetrate the city; they also focused on individual projects or reforms that would be inserted into the urban fabric to assure order, like city guards, troops, barracks, public lighting, a fire brigade, even inexpensive housing for workers. The organization of state power in Paris ranked highest among these elements. Poncet de la Grave devoted two chapters on the police and public safety in his work on Paris *embellissements*.[143] Because of an increase in the size of the Paris population, he recommended the doubling of the city guard (*Troupe du Guêt*), the stationing of a regiment of the guard in each Paris quarter at regular distances from each other, and the installation of a large bell, secured by a chain, on each corner of the city to raise an alarm for the guard, day or night. In addition, he proposed that commissioners, who managed the administration of the police service under the lieutenant-general of police, have permanent residences in each district of the capital. His point was that they have maximum visibility throughout the city. To this end he proposed that the state identify a site in each quarter for the construction of an Hôtel des Commissaires, which would be the permanent lodging place of each commissioner, and pay for the building from the caisse des Embellissements he had proposed. Commissioners would then pay a very low rent for this housing, clearly an important benefit of the post. Alongside the Hôtel des Commissaires would be housing facilities for the day- and night-time watches, along with stables for the latter.

Dussausoy also addressed the issue of city guards. Like Poncet de la Grave, he identified the expansion of Paris as the factor that necessitated better urban policing. Dussausoy, however, made a brief for the permanent stationing of the king's troops throughout Paris and for state construction of barracks to house them. More concerned apparently about order in the city than municipal rights, Dussausoy noted that royal troops would "prevent the disorders that they were accused earlier of committing."[144] By this he meant that troops were currently more disciplined than they had been in earlier times, and that this would translate into urban discipline. Dussausoy also proposed a regular fire brigade for Paris as a critical element of urban safety.[145]

We have already seen that artificial lighting was an important aspect of the urban shopping experience. Street lighting was also considered important for public security. Night was an opportune time for criminals, as darkness provided cover for their activities. The eighteenth-century Paris police perceived the greatest threat of crime as coming not from the working poor but from mendicant vagabonds, of whom there were about ten thousand in Paris, from servants, and from prostitutes.[146] Nightfall magnified the danger of crime and street lighting could provide a measure of real and psychological security. Truly modern street lighting, electrical lighting capable of flooding the entire street, did not come into existence until the 1870s. Before that time lanterns with candles and, from 1769, oil lamps with reflectors "had generally cast a kind of private light." Gas lighting, introduced in the early nineteenth century, expanded the reach of lanterns, but not to the extent of electric lighting.

Gaston Bachelard offered a psychological interpretation of public lighting, no matter how dim, namely, that it was intended to fix in the mind of the urban walker an expression of the state's power to observe its citizens. Average law-abiding citizens submitted to public lighting, which is coincident with the rise of the absolute state, "because it promised to guarantee stability and security."[147]

Poncet de la Grave's prescription for a visible city guard included illuminating the Hôtels des Commissaires with lanterns at all times so that individuals could locate them easily if they needed assistance. An inscription identifying the Guard's buildings would be displayed prominently above their doors, also illuminated by the lanterns.[148] In addition, Poncet de la Grave called upon the state to double the number of lanterns throughout Paris and to light them each night, even if the moon was bright. He faulted the police for not being more attentive to lanterns, asking if it "had not therefore reflected on the notable harm that results from darkness, often quite fatal on the streets of Paris." He was especially concerned that lanterns be operative during times of pleasant weather, giving as a reason the case of a merchant who, following a long day of work, might wish to take a brief walk on the ramparts or on a public walk during part of the evening. In this comment Poncet de la Grave was alluding to the increase in theft, which accounted for the majority of crime in Paris, generally went up during the month of August, when many wealthy Parisians left the city, and a large number of strangers, tourists, businessmen, and others, entered it. At that time of year, too, many unemployed servants, whom the police, as indicated above, suspected of criminal activity, also wandered about town.[149] Poncet de la Grave undoubtedly expressed the fear of the average law-abiding or middle-class Parisian, who would be quite willing to submit to the watchful eye of public authorities, in the form of a question: "Doesn't darkness which reigns in all the quarters therefore favor thieves and assassins, despite the regular vigilance of the *troupes du guêt?*" Because the answer was meant to be obvious, Poncet de la Grave dreamt of bathing all Paris in light.[150]

The working poor of eighteenth-century Paris also figured in planning literature in the context of security issues. Jaillot has a short and portentous insight on the population structure of Parisian quarters relating to order and security in the capital. He observed that it was politically dangerous to have districts in Paris composed only of poor people; the ideal manner of preventing riots, he advised, was to divide the common people. Ideal quarters, therefore, were those that combined a population of well-to-do persons with the working poor. In these mixed neighborhoods the rich could provide poor relief to the indigent and sick. He noted, too, that workers could always find lodgings they could afford in decent surroundings, and he criticized those who built inferior houses in less well-to-do quarters, as these only "announce misery and dishonor the capital" and, as he implied, also spatially concentrate the lower classes.[151] It is too early in the history of Paris to talk about the discovery of the "social question," that is, the systematic sociological investigation by government officials and intellectuals of poverty, workers, and social unrest, and the programs designed to deal with these matters. That "discovery" took place in the nineteenth century.[152] It is interesting to note, however, that when the poor did enter into the consciousness of one eighteenth-century writer, Jaillot, the solution he offered to potential unrest emerging from below was a particular spatial geography for Paris. Thinking along spatial lines as a solution to the "social question," though not in Jaillot's terms, became far more pronounced during the nineteenth century.

COMMERCE

A last major concern that may be detected in the planning literature of the eighteenth century was the effect of an orderly and safe city on commerce and production. As indicated at the beginning of this chapter, many of the principal themes that run through the planning literature of the eighteenth century overlap. Thus, we have already examined Arthur Dillon's insights on street improvements and their potential effect on commerce. Early in the eighteenth century, Delamare summed up an obvious maxim concerning the life of cities. All cities, he wrote, need commerce, and in medium-sized cities people can walk throughout the city in order to complete their business affairs. A large city, such as Paris, needed vehicles to accomplish the same end, and this meant that its streets had to form an effective communications network covering the city.[153] Voltaire made the connection between the embellishment of Paris and the hiring of new labor, including foreign workers, two processes that would circulate wealth in the kingdom as gainfully employed workers spent money on food and commodities.[154] The anonymous author of *Anti-Radoteur* characterized the ideal state as one in which wealth circulated easily from its capital—his example was Paris—throughout the state, something to be accomplished only with the reform of the capital's infrastructure. He also observed that Paris was becoming too large, that entrepreneurs were putting up too many buildings, with the result that air and sunlight were being blocked in the city. Unlike other writers, however, he also linked the building glut to negative economic consequences. In the spirit of Adam Smith and applying the metaphor of the body to the state, not uncommon at this time, he observed that "money must be regarded as the blood of the state; the political body begins to languish, its constitution alters, when wealth passes from the provinces to the capital; all is lost when it passes from the capital to the court: it results in the ebb and concentration of the blood in the head; apoplexy is inevitable." What was needed for economic health, therefore, was efficient circulation of wealth throughout the kingdom and not its concentration in building enterprises in Paris.[155]

The link between urban improvement and commerce is perhaps best captured by another anonymous author, writing in 1784. Advocating street construction, he noted that new streets "shall increase the wealth of the city of Paris by multiplying the number of people there. It is one of the first maxims of state policy to attract people to its capital by all the means it can adopt. Three things are needed for this outcome: *low prices for foodstuffs, public security, the suitability of streets.*"[156]

TOWARD A NEW MENTAL
FRAMEWORK OF THE CITY

It was evident by the beginning of the early nineteenth century that the mental universe of some urban intellectuals had shifted decidedly from imagining the city as a work of art to perceiving it as a space of utility benefiting the largest number of people. Two planning documents, each published in 1808, may stand for this shift in outlook, one by the architect Nicolas Goulet on Paris embellishments and monuments and the other an almanac by an anonymous author on the same themes.[157] In one important sense both authors still belonged to the traditional world of eighteenth-century-planning intellectuals in that their projects were not technical and did not offer an exact ground plan for the reform of Paris, each being content to outline the principles for a program of urban transformation. They embody the alteration in the structure of thinking about the city, however, in their respective definitions of the aim of architecture and planning.

That both texts were published in 1808 was not a coincidence. In that year the Académie française announced a poetry prize on the subject "Les Embellissemens de Paris." This topic, the academy suggested, would appeal to artists and philosophers alike as it invited speculation on varied objects of the urban environment, from canals to the completion of the Louvre. The aim of the embellishments was to assure "the health of the capital," to promote "new delights for its inhabitants," and to add "to the grandeur of the empire and the glory of the sovereign."[158] This echoed Napoleon I's goal of creating an imperial capital of distinction. As the minister of the interior reported to the Corps législatif in August 1807, "the Emperor wishes that his capital become the first capital of the universe, to achieve such a glorious end through its appearance."[159] In this broad context, Goulet thought about embellishments that "if the French Academy has determined that this subject is worthy of a poetry prize, it is no less a subject in the field of architecture," and he would submit his proposals for a reform of Paris.[160]

Goulet had been an architect in the Department of National Domains and had earlier submitted plans for a Temple of Laws, to be built near the Tuileries and the Louvre, a building intended to disseminate the laws of the Revolution among the people.[161] His essay, *Observations sur les embellissemens de Paris,* offered, beyond the individual building, a definition of the architect and architecture that brings us close to the discipline of modern urban planning. Goulet began this definition with an autobiographical note: "For more than twenty years," he wrote, "I have been concerned with projects for the amelioration and embellishment of the city of Paris, and always steering them toward the goal of public utility and for the greatest benefit of its inhabitants." Goulet's beginning point for a new architecture was the principle that "it is not a single monument, nor even several that can make a city beautiful" if the infrastructure and health of the city were lacking, that is, if streets were narrow, dirty and unpaved, houses poorly constructed, pedestrians in danger from coaches, the air foul, and the like. An architect, he believed, had to change his focus from the individual monument or building to consider the entire city's needs, especially infrastructural, to plan buildings only "within the universal conjuncture of the embellishments of Paris." The first consideration of planning had to be utility within an overall and precise plan of embellishment.[162] As he explained further, "the opening and enlargement of streets, the construction of bridges, walls for the quays, fountains, matters of current concern, are without doubt the most important ameliorations" in the program of embellishments in the capital.[163]

Having announced a modern program for architecture, Goulet devoted the rest of his essay either to individual monuments or to material improvements in the capital. Concerning the latter his suggested projects represented typical concerns of eighteenth-century planning, like proposals for more effective water fountains, new quays, better cesspools, and fire prevention. With respect to streets, an important preoccupation of Goulet's, he, like others of his time, welcomed work on the principle east-west street of Paris, the rue de Rivoli. There was another street project, however, that "would be yet more beautiful and useful," and that was the alignment of the rue Saint-Jacques on the Left Bank with the rue Saint-Martin on the Right Bank. These two streets ran north-south and Goulet proposed that they be widened and extended from one end of Paris to the other, crossing the rue de Rivoli at a right angle. Haussmann achieved the conjuncture of two streets bisecting Paris north-south and east-west through the construction and alignment of the Boulevards de Strasbourg and Sébastopol on the Right Bank with the boulevard Saint-Michel on the Left Bank, but the north-south route that Goulet proposed to traverse Paris north-south was just slightly to the east of Haussmann's route.[164]

Goulet proposed an additional reform that represented the Enlightenment planners' desire for urban order and rationality. Following his agenda for the transformation of the physical structure of Paris, he proposed completing the process of urban rationality with a new administrative order for the city.[165] In his time Paris was divided into twelve arrondissements and forty-eight quarters. Nine arrondissements were on the Right Bank and three, the Tenth, the Eleventh, and the Twelfth, on the Left Bank. The sizes of the arrondissements were unequal: the smallest was the Fourth, at 523,300 square meters, and the largest the Eighth, at 6,126,031 square meters. Quarters within each arrondissement also varied in size.[166] Goulet wished to divide Paris into nine arrondissements, one in the center, four at an angle and four laterally to the center. The center one he designated the Arrondissement of the Center, and it comprised the île Notre-Dame and the île Saint-Louis, and the others, the Arrondissement of the North, of the South, of the North-East, of the South-East, and so forth. He then divided each arrondissement into five quarters for a total of forty-five. Each division of Paris would have, to the extent possible, an equal population.

Goulet would also change most Paris street names, dropping those that were associated with some historical event or person to prevent their having to be renamed if the event or person being celebrated fell out of historical favor. Streets should thus be designated with common nomenclature, like proper names. Also, names of principal streets, the long connecting urban roads between the arrondissements, should not change along any portion of the street, as this would only cause confusion. He welcomed, too, the system of house numbering, which had been regularized under Napoleon's regime. And, as in the case of conquered cities, administrative reform would conclude with the production of a map of the new Paris, which the government would post on public buildings, on letter boxes, on the barriers, and at public coach stations; it would also sell copies to individuals. Goulet's main reasons for suggesting the administrative change, as he noted, were to inform strangers and locals in Paris about ideal routes to follow and to facilitate the government's management of the city.

The second document under consideration, the 1808 *Almanach des embellissemens de Paris,* is a seminal text in that it represents a summation of the new sensibility toward Paris. It also announced an agenda for urban reform that is taken up, with different degrees of specificity, by nineteenth-century reformers, ultimately culminating in Haussmann's program. The author's starting point was a rejection of baroque principles of urban planning, finding uniformity of style and symmetry boring. He also faulted baroque architects—his example was Paris under Louis XIV—for their focus on individual buildings and lack of planning for the city as a whole. He contrasted these times with his own, praising Napoleon I, who wished to reform the entire city and to combine the beautiful with the useful, the construction of majestic buildings, and the creation of large, aligned streets that were both paved and clean. Such streets were sites for public edifices, important factors in the city's health, and also critical elements in urban circulation and commerce. To facilitate the latter he proposed traffic circles in strategic parts of Paris, crossroads, and additional squares throughout the city. While he did not offer a diagram of these traffic circles and squares or other technical details, as Eugène Hénard did in the early twentieth century, he did at least indicate where he believed they would be useful.[167] And he certainly had a sense that circulation was central to the life of modern Paris.

It was not merely the recognition of circulation and communication as an element of urban life that rendered the author of the *Almanach* modern but also his planning of specific streets or avenues as a means of restructuring entire sections of Paris. He proposed, for example, the same north-south and east-west street system as Goulet, and he planned a huge traffic circle around the place du Châtelet, to provide street access between both sides of the Seine River at that point. The place du Châtelet was a vital geographic center in Paris; the old fortress of the Châtelet was taken down in 1802 and in its place Napoleon had constructed a victory fountain (1806). It was for this reason, according to the *Almanach,* that "one of the most important communication routes between the two parts of the city" must be unblocked by "a vast traffic circle" there and a corresponding one at the end of the Saint-Michel bridge, occupied then by a market that should be moved.[168] The *Almanach* also observed, in a narrative that became increasingly common in the nineteenth century, especially among public health officers, that the Cité, "the oldest part of Paris, is still today a mass of obscure haunts, poorly ventilated, unhealthy, and infected. There are streets which, ever since their existence, have never been lit with the beneficial rays of the sun. There one breathes a thick and noxious air." The solution offered was "to open three or four large streets there to clean the quarter." The author, as part of his program, favored the destruction of the Hôtel-Dieu, the central Paris hospital in the Cité district. This would create a space where, he hoped, "a magnificent street would be opened in the direction of the Hôtel de Ville, and communication would be established by a bridge that would become extremely beneficial for commerce and pedestrians."[169] This proposal was realized with the construction of a modest pedestrian bridge, the pont de Grève, in 1828 and the rue Arcole in 1834.

There are many other examples of specific street reforms in the *Almanach,* but what is interesting about its author is the wide range of other improvements he suggests, all having to do with aspects of the infrastructure. Covered in his work are urban markets, sidewalks, water delivery, fountains, bridges, sewers, entries into Paris, avenues, water pumps for the fire brigade, slaughterhouses, and street lighting. All his comments on these topics are related to improving commerce, safety, health, and circulation in Paris. He even proposed the creation of a public outdoor gymnasium in the garden of the Arsenal, with government inspectors in charge of the facility, which would include a swimming school and exercise equipment. More than other contemporary writers he also favored the use of the quays and the Seine River as components of a circulatory system in the capital.

The *Almanach*'s interest in commerce, circulation, and safety is expressed in a short proposal concerning the early Paris arcades.[170] At the time of its publication in 1808 Paris already had several arcades; the author mentions, as examples, the passage du Caire, the passage des Panoramas, and the passage de Feydeau. The greatest number of arcades, however, were constructed between 1815 and 1830. One historian estimated that "the creation of the covered merchant galleries remains perhaps the most original trait of Paris urbanism during the time of the Restoration."[171] Their potential was grasped earlier, however, as Dillon's text and the *Almanach* demonstrate. The author of the *Almanach* characterized the few that existed in Paris at the time as being "very convenient for pedestrians; they provide an agreeable route, shelter from the rain, and comfort for an instant from the painful vigilance that one must constantly exercise to protect oneself from all the hindrances of the often-frequented streets." He believed that these should be multiplied in Paris, and gave as a reason that many boutiques currently obstructing public monuments, streets, and quays should be transferred to the arcades. This motive for more arcades coupled the needs of Paris circulation and commerce, to which he added a safety consideration. This is evident in his warning to arcade merchants that they not spread their wares too far out on the public space before their shops, as this impeded the flow of pedestrians and also acted as a cover for pickpockets when theaters let out and people frequented the arcades.[172]

While the *Almanach* does not develop an economic theory, its recognition of the importance of urban forms, new streets, boulevards, traffic circles, and the like, to a well-functioning urban economy runs throughout the work. Beyond infrastrutural reforms, moreover, its author also favored a symbolic expression of the centrality of commerce to the life of Paris. He was, he wrote, "truly surprised" that Paris had no school, no square, no monument dedicated to commerce. Richard Etlin explains the importance of the symbolic aspects of eighteenth-century Paris urban planning. Eighteenth-century architects aimed to design buildings that projected a monumental or magnificent impression and whose function and purpose, at the same time, could clearly be grasped "through . . . expressive and possible metaphorical character."[173] The author of the *Almanach* imagined just such a building to represent commerce. "All slightly important cities have a stock exchange, and in some capitals of Europe this stock exchange is a building which by its importance or by the beauty of its architecture deserves to rivet the attention of the traveler." He concluded, therefore, that "Parisian commerce requires the establishment of a stock exchange, and the general interest calls for it to be situated in the center of the city: one has proposed the quai de Dessaix [today the quai de la Cité]."[174] A Palais de la Bourse (the stock exchange palace) was begun in 1808 under Napoleon's regime, but in its present location in the Second Arrondissement, off the rue Vivienne, and completed in 1825.

Two additional proposals found in the *Almanach* merit attention, especially as they constitute the book's conclusion.[175] First, the author proposed a fund designated for urban improvement (*une caisse des embellissemens*). He wished the government to subsidize a caisse des embellissemens "by a tax on the opulent class and on luxury items" and recommended as a standard to define this class those who had several domestics and horses and government employees whose net annual income was more than 8,000 francs. He noted, too, that the tax, to be levied on horses, coaches, and any luxury imported items, had to be "progressive." The fund could also obtain revenues from lotteries, gaming houses, and other places and items of public pleasure.

Second, noting that the proposals outlined in the *Almanach* would require a large work force, the author proposed that an immense encampment be established where such a concentration of workers could be housed, fed, and clothed. This workers' corps, composed of people from "different classes," would also wear a distinctive badge, identifying them as members of the corps.[176] These workers would be salaried and have deducted from their pay—there were no details on wage scales—one sou per day to provide an insurance fund to support them in a retirement home when they were too old or sick to continue working and to contribute benefits to their wives or children if they died while on the job. To head the entire program of urban reform the *Almanach* recommended a "director-general of embellishments," who "must be a former engineer of the national administration of roads and bridges, known for his talents and integrity." The *Almanach* set the compensation for this post at 15,000 francs per annum and free lodgings.[177] This proposal was not exactly the same as those recommending use of the army for public works, but it did plan for workers to be organized in the form of an army corps. In its outline the plan appears more akin to the French National Workshops of 1848 or to those public works corps in the United States at the time of the depression during the 1930s.

Paris as the rational city of the urban planners did not materialize during the eighteenth century. With the exception of the construction of three important theaters between 1779 and 1783, the Comédie-Française, the Comédie Italienne, and the Théâtre des Italiens, not much building or general urban transformation went on during the Revolution, as intense political activity and military events preoccupied the public leaders. The Commission des Artistes settled upon the practical work of integrating lands expropriated from the Church and others into the public space of Paris. Despite Napoleon I's wish to create a great imperial capital, his regime was blocked in terms of urbanism, both by the resistance of Parisians to the expropriations necessary for such a transformation and by the government's need to expend large sums of money and energy on foreign wars. Two great monuments were begun during his administration, the Arc de Triomphe and the Madeleine Church, the first completed in 1836 and the second in 1845. Napoleon's most important urban accomplishment was to improve the great axes of circulation that centered on the place de la Concorde, especially the beginning of the rue de Rivoli. He also launched the construction of two new towns, Napoléonville, in Pontivy, Brittany (see chapter 2), and La Roche-sur-Yon, in the Vendée. In Paris, his regime also added three kilometers to the system of quays, and, as indicated above, tore down the Châtelet, freeing that part of Paris for improved circulation. On the whole, however, Napoleon's regime had abandoned large-scale projects in Paris for partial reforms.[178]

Something important, outside the realm of the purely material, however, becomes apparent in the history of Paris urbanism during the eighteenth century. By the end of the century a decided shift was evident in perceptions of the ideal city, at least by those who were actively engaged in thinking and writing about the city. By the end of the eighteenth century infrastructural reforms, especially those related to the street and intended to facilitate commerce, health, movement, and safety, had become an important preoccupation of many eighteenth-century urban intellectuals. Most importantly, Paris intellectuals of all kinds—architects, the clergy, social commentators, philosophers—began to state the belief that a comprehensive plan or map should guide all partial or individual public works projects. This notion became a central tenet of nineteenth-century urban reformers. While planning for aesthetic effect remained a goal, both during the eighteenth and nineteenth centuries, citywide planning for largely practical reasons—planning to make Paris function efficiently from the point of view of its health, order, commerce, and circulation—became increasingly important. The dream of an orderly and rationally planned capital city became even more clear and urgent during the following century as a result of a significant increase in the capital's population and the quickening of its commercial and industrial life.

CHAPTER TWO

"Functionalist Planners" before Haussmann

T HE FIRST DECADES of the nineteenth century, the period that corresponds roughly with the opening of the Restoration, witness the appearance of a new kind of planning literature, one that aimed at making sense
of and imposing order on a city that was becoming significantly more populated and whose economy was expanding and that ended with Paris as the
center of a railway system. With respect to population alone, in 1801 Paris had
547,736 people compared to 1,053,262 in 1851. This doubling of the population over fifty years represents what one historian characterized as "an explosion without precedent."[1] Older histories of planning, especially those that
see the Second Empire as the critical period in the history of Paris, treat the
first half of the nineteenth century as a relatively uniform period, when, in
fact, one can identify at this time at least two stages in the formation of new
attitudes concerning the appropriateness of government intervention into
public space.[2]

The first new attitude is apparent during the Restoration as the architectural treatise gave way to the technical or purely urban planning text, whose
focus, sometimes almost exclusively, was on comprehensive spatial design and
infrastructure rather than architecture and individual buildings. In the fore-
front of this transition were engineers, concerned with matters like the delivery of water to the city, and even some architects whose writings on the city
increasingly focused purely on spatial planning issues. At this time, too, and
extending into the early years of the July Monarchy, we see a deep concern in
the planning literature with the "social question," with the relationship of
space to the economy, and with health and sanitation. While some of these
subjects appeared in the late eighteenth century, by the first half of the nineteenth century concerns with social issues, with the economy, and with health
had assumed a privileged position in many texts on planning. Writings on

these subjects are treated with greater sophistication, detail, and, at times, anxiety.

By the 1840s a decidedly new stage in planning was apparent, one in which much writing on the shape of Paris was reduced to the circulatory needs of the capital. While the centrality of urban circulation and communication was developing over the entire first half of the century, it became an especially pressing issue as a result of an awareness by public authorities and intellectuals in the 1840s of a serious population dislocation in Paris characterized by a steady movement of the well-to-do classes toward the northern and western borders of the city and beyond. There was, in addition, considerable crowding in the central districts of Paris, owing largely to an abundance of employment and administrative services there. New arrivals in Paris tended to congregate in the old Fourth, Seventh, and Ninth Arrondissements, "where crowding became particularly intense."[3] The growing influx of people to the center and the fact that the working classes began to outnumber the middle and upper classes became menacing. This new population and its poverty could not be ignored or hidden. Moralists and reformers, as Rachel Fuchs noted, were concerned with this population increase, which the upper classes "perceived as debauched if not actually dangerous."[4] Urban intellectuals, property owners, and businessmen also focused on the shift of the population, fearing that the center and Left Bank districts would gradually be abandoned by the well-to-do, resulting in a serious inequality of services between the two parts of the city. An important planning literature, generated by this population displacement "crisis" and by the crowding in the central districts of the capital, represented a critical step in the emergence of modern urban planning.

In this chapter I deal with the "functionalist" model of planning as it emerged up to about the 1850s; the socialist modes of planning are discussed in chapters 3 and 4. Unlike the Saint-Simonian and Fourierist models of urban planning, which emerged from identifiable ideological traditions and schools, the functionalist model, which was not made up of an ideological school of reformers, consisted of a disparate archive of texts that collectively constituted its approach to planning modern Paris. The main aim of the functionalists was to design reforms for Paris that would permit the infrastructure of the capital to operate efficiently. Their plans and projects did not spring from an implicit or explicit political perspective. These were practical reformers addressing specific problems within the context of comprehensive planning. They were primarily interested in the smooth functioning, especially in terms of circulation and efficient movement, as well as in the order, health, and security, of the modern city.

THE RESTORATION

Restoration Paris has not fared well in the historical literature on urbanism in the capital when compared to the July Monarchy or especially the Second Empire.[5] Guillaume Bertier de Sauvigny observed that Paris streets at the time of the Restoration remained "pitifully" inadequate to accommodate the steady increase in vehicular traffic that became a characteristic of this regime and that "only a politics of massive expropriation" to open up new streets and quarters could address the problem—which is precisely what the Restoration never accomplished.[6] As contemporary statistics show, in 1819 more than 18,000 coaches and carts of all types regularly circulated through the narrow, winding streets of Paris. In 1828 the first omnibuses began to ply the streets and by the end of the following year, some 221 of these coaches provided regular service through the center of the capital, adding to the density of Paris traffic.[7] The best officials could do to alleviate this situation was to open 65 new streets between 1816 and 1828, whereas under the July Monarchy 112 new streets were opened, including the very substantial rue Rambuteau, which served Les Halles in the center of Paris.[8] Public works under the Restoration did not involve much more than the development by private capitalists of some new quarters, minor work on sewers and cemeteries, and the construction of eight new churches,[9] none of which followed any master plan. André Morizet, the author of a standard older work on Paris from the Restoration to the Second Empire, said of Restoration Paris that "history has known few periods as flat."[10] These are especially negative views of Paris urbanism under the Restoration.

There were important urban developments, however, not the least of which were the shopping arcades. In addition, we have under the administration of the count G. J. G. Chabrol de Volvic, the Restoration's prefect of the Seine Department and the chief administrator of Paris urbanism, the completion of three important canals serving Paris—the canals Saint-Denis, de l'Ourcq, and Saint-Martin—new fountains, some sewer construction, and the introduction of public gas lighting. And there was considerable housing construction throughout the city in cooperation with private developers.[11] Paris was also at this time, although not to the extent of English cities, a center of industry, especially in luxury goods, textiles, metal production, and wallpaper, tobacco, chemicals, and furniture establishments. The capital was, moreover, the principal seat of French banking and finance, a hub of international trade, and a huge consumption market for French provincial products.[12]

If we expand our horizon just beyond Paris to its immediate suburbs we notice "an explosion of industry" at this time. Typical was Belleville to the northeast, which, at the time of the Restoration, was already known for its quarries and also had five factories and many workers among its population of five thousand.[13] On the other hand, nothing much was done in the realm of public health in Paris, and it was not until the July Monarchy that authorities turned seriously to urban reform, which one recent historian of Paris characterized as "a veritable program of modernization of the capital."[14] The virtual reconstruction of most of Paris under the Second Empire is well known.

The Restoration government failed to undertake significant public works in Paris as compared to successive regimes partly because of its preoccupation with paying off a huge military debt incurred by the Napoleonic wars, the outcome of the laissez-faire mentality of Chabrol de Volvic, and partly because no major urban crisis, like the cholera epidemic of 1832, impinged upon the consciousness of urban administrators. This is not to say, however, that contemporaries did not worry about the suitability of the Paris infrastructure, its extent and design, to support the rapid growth of the city's population. The contemporary literature frequently indicated that the adequacy of the infrastructure and the population expansion were the fundamental double problem for Paris administrators during the early nineteenth century. For example, few houses had been built during the French Revolution and the First Empire. That situation was reversed under the Restoration, and between 1824 and 1827 some three thousand housing units went up in Paris. These were, however, often speculative constructions designed for the well-to-do in the well-off quarters of northwestern Paris. The housing entrepreneurs, many of whom went bankrupt trying to raise capital to finance their projects, largely ignored the old central quarters of the city, with the result that the center of Paris, the present-day Third, Fourth, and Ninth Arrondissements, because of inadequate housing construction, became increasingly more densely populated: whereas about thirty people had occupied each building in central Paris in 1817, that number increased to about thirty-five in 1826.[15] As for population growth, according to official statistics the total population of Paris in 1817 was 713,966, a figure that climbed to 785,862 by 1831.[16]

In both absolute and proportional terms, the most dramatic incidence in the growth of the Paris population came under the July Monarchy, when 267,400 people were added to the Paris rolls. A considerable percentage of the increase in the Paris population was due to the inmigration of non-native Parisians rather than to a natural increase in the birth rates of natives. Barrie Ratcliffe and Christine Piette pointed out, moreover, that those newly arrived in the capital were part of a long tradition of migration to Paris, that they assimilated relatively easily, and that they were dispersed fairly evenly spatially and occupationally.[17]

The doubling of the Paris population at this time, however, and the sheer volume of people crowding the center of the city registered in the minds of elites. While this increased population affected all parts of the city, its consequences were most visible in the center, as we have already seen. The congregation of poor people in the old Second, Third, and Fifth Arrondissements circling the Cité was troublesome to the authorities, as so many poor people occupied central Paris, a population that was increasingly entering into the vision and consciousness of the authorities and intellectuals. Jeanne Gaillard concluded that by the 1850s there had developed "in the heart of Paris all kinds of opaque cores thwarting urban circulation and public security, menacing with decrepitude and paralysis the entire center."[18] For government officials, social and business elites, and urban intellectuals, the most serious problem in Paris at this time was the perception of a significant and noticeable increase in parts of the city's population; at least, that was a fact the officials employed to argue for urban reform. These elites often framed urban issues in terms of population, whether there was a real danger or not, as a means of exercising social control over the general population, especially the lower classes.

Writing in 1824, Guillot, the associate inspector-general of sanitation and lighting in Paris, observed that over the previous ten years Paris had experienced, without any significant physical growth in its boundaries, a "kind of extraordinary development" internally. He explained: "New streets have been opened on several points; numerous new constructions arise everywhere; entire new quarters have, as it were, loomed up, risen from the earth as if by magic; building developers are currently busy, and will be for a long time, in several new quarters." These entrepreneurs, in turn, were flooding neighborhoods with carts of all kinds filled with building materials.[19] Primarily concerned with increasingly unsanitary conditions in Paris and how to alleviate them, Guillot identified other causes of the capital's generally squalid state. He cited, in addition to street and building construction, "the prodigious increase of the population" and the "no less prodigious development of industry and commerce, a development which gives birth to a multitude of factories and other large establishments all of which today combine to increase the mass of household garbage." Not wishing to exclude the upper classes from their role in the unsanitary condition of the capital, Guillot also pointed to the habit of the well-to-do of keeping in Paris horses whose droppings had to be removed from the streets each morning by sanitation workers.[20]

What matters in Guillot's testimony is not whether population figures and construction starts during the Restoration were not as important as they were during the July Monarchy, but that a public official in charge of streets perceived them as dramatic and impressive events necessitating some form of government action, in Guillot's case, the proposal of a new organization of the city's sanitation department. This sense that the population of Paris was growing at a troublesome rate was also evident at the highest levels of the national administration, especially in the official publication of the Seine Department, the *Recherches statistiques de la ville de Paris et le département de la Seine,* whose first four volumes appeared between 1821 and 1829,[21] a remarkable statistical study of the material life of Paris and its inhabitants, directed by Chabrol de Volvic, with the important assistance of Frédéric Villot, the director of the Bureau spécial des archives et de la statistique, the statistical office within Chabrol's administration, and J. B. J. Fourier, the famous mathematician who was Chabrol's teacher at the École polytechnique, the elite French military engineering school created in 1794.

As prefect of the Seine Department during the Restoration, Count G. J. G. Chabrol de Volvic was the chief administrator of Paris.[22] Pierre Lavedan said of Chabrol de Volvic that "he does not appear to have been an urbanist with a large vision."[23] It is true that he did not build much in Paris when compared with his successors Claude-Philibert Barthelot de Rambuteau and Georges-Eugène Haussmann. However, Chabrol de Volvic was personally responsible for the production of the *Recherches statistiques de la ville de Paris.* This text must rank as one of the landmark accomplishments in the field of urbanism, broadly defined to include ideas as well as material constructions. The single most important subject of this publication was the statistical representation of the Paris population. Under Chabrol de Volvic's authority, Villot, the editor of the *Recherches statistiques,*[24] wrote in the introduction to the first volume that its main object was "the complete census of the population of the capital" in order to have an "exact knowledge of the territory, of the condition of its people, and of the sources of public revenue." Such knowledge was an essential foundation for wise government policy. The introduction noted, too, as if for emphasis, that among the many topics contained in the *Recherches statistiques,* meteorological tables, data on agriculture, public welfare, vehicles, and the like, the subject of population was "the most important of all."[25] With respect to the gathering of statistics, eminently exemplified by the *Recherches statistiques,* Bernard Lepetit has shown that the statistical representation of various material aspects of French life became increasingly important and then dominant between 1770 and 1830.[26] Paris population statistics, in this context, were a particular source of interest because, according to Louis Chevalier, "the basic problem [in Paris during the first half of the nineteenth century], and the one seen to be basic, was in fact the population problem."[27]

The first census of the Paris population under the Restoration was conducted by Chabrol de Volvic's office in 1817 and published in the first volume of the *Recherches statistiques* in 1821.[28] In 1824 Chabrol de Volvic noted the population increase as a common fact of the rapid material transformation of Parisian life. That year he reported to the general council of the Seine Department that since 1818 several "striking changes have been apparent," notably, that "the population of the capital has increased greatly," that housing constructions had multiplied throughout the city and more were planned, that commerce was expanding both within and outside the fortifications, that vehicular traffic was increasing as a result, and that the regions immediately surrounding Paris were experiencing significant development. All these changes, resulting in a "great growth in public prosperity," were having an effect "on the thinking of the administration," which planned more efficient roads for the Seine Department.[29]

In 1829, J.-L.-M. Daubanton, one of two chief Paris road inspectors in Chabrol de Volvic's administration, published a report in volume 4 of the *Recherches statistiques* on the availability of housing in relation to the Paris population.[30] He concluded that during the years 1821–26 "there had been a progressive and constant augmentation in the population [of Paris], and that the number of residences has also increased, but not in the same proportion."[31] This gap was especially serious in the central quarters, where the lower classes clustered. The Third and Fourth Arrondissements were classic examples of the situation. The population of the Third Arrondissement had increased over these years by 9,235 persons, but the 114 new houses constructed there could only accommodate 4,560 persons. A similar lack of housing in relation to the growth of the population existed in the neighboring Fourth Arrondissement, where, in addition, "there are no public squares, no public walks. There are many streets but these are almost all narrow, winding, and dirty."[32]

The lack of housing in relation to the overall population had also evoked a response outside the administration. In 1824 an anonymous brochure, *Coup d'oeil sur Paris* (a bird's-eye view of Paris) criticized the great amount of luxury housing in Paris while the needs of a rising general population were not being addressed.[33] In 1829, two writers, Mirbel and A. Bareau, representing a group of property owners, architects, and builders, addressed the minister of the interior with proposals to revive the building trades industry, recently suffering from a depression. In their report, citing Chabrol de Volvic's population census of 1817, they noted that the Paris population was growing at a rate of 25 per 100 while the housing stock was only increasing at a rate of 10 per 100. The downturn of building starts had resulted in a "state of crisis" affecting the entire financial community. In addition to the report's general analysis of

Paris urbanism, this was one of the earliest Paris publications to employ the word *crisis* to describe an urban condition. In the same report the authors also remarked that the administration had to enlarge and clean up the center of Paris, where mortality rates were especially high.[34]

Official focus on the Paris population in relation to housing during the time of the Restoration brought with it problems that escaped the domain of the architect. Increasingly, infrastructural improvements became an object of discussion within and outside government circles. As noted earlier, these were matters, especially the delivery of water to the city, that fell within the expertise of the engineer. As a result engineers began to emerge from under the shadow of architects and propose their own ideas in the realm of city planning, planning that focused on the infrastructure rather than on individual buildings.[35]

The shift from architecture to engineering as the critical element in town planning was in the making throughout the last decades of the eighteenth century. But the story begins even earlier, as engineers were seen as an increasingly important element of state policy in mastering the national territory. This was the result of the French state's increasing preoccupation, dating from the time of Colbert in the seventeenth century, with uniting the national territory into an effective unit of circulation and production. To do so, roads, canals, river ways, and bridges would have to be developed as effective means of communication and circulation flows. The management of space and circulation flows was precisely what the engineer, as opposed to the architect, mastered. It was not a large step from managing the national territory to planning cities. Cities and towns were not at the center of architectural theory during the seventeenth and eighteenth centuries until we come to Pierre Patte. In the engineers' world, however, cities and towns, hitherto thought of as closed systems, began to be considered as open spaces linked to the national territory, critical points in the circulation of people, goods, and even ideas. It should not be surprising, therefore, that engineers had a strong presence in cities, especially Paris, during the eighteenth and nineteenth centuries. They focused on cleaning the city by insuring the delivery of water, on embellishment, and on linking the city to the national space.[36]

Central to the emergence of the engineer as city planner was the national school of civil engineering, the École des Ponts et Chaussées.[37] Founded in 1747, it was part of a complex of engineering networks, military engineers, mining engineers, and private engineers. The Ponts et Chaussées, however, became the French state's most prestigious school of engineering, coordinating all important national and city projects on the ground. As architects' "projects were limited in space and time," engineers coming out of the Ponts et

Chaussées developed the tools and policies needed to conquer physical space and also to advance social progress, which likewise became part of the aim of the school and its engineering corps. The importance of engineers as city planners can be seen not only in specific projects, like the building of roads or the delivery of water, but also in the emergence of the city planning text.

THE CITY PLANNING TEXT

Alexandre de Laborde, who was in charge of the Ponts et Chaussées of the Seine Department from 1810 to 1816, was responsible for Paris streets and boulevards, bridges, quays, canals, and the supply of water. Of these he considered the distribution of water the city's most important and the least developed infrastructural service. He observed that English and American cities distributed abundant water to homes by pipes, whereas Paris still depended upon "an army of water carriers," whom he characterized as "the shame of civilization."[38] Water carriers were quite enterprising and hard working, much like Paris coachmen, another group that was frequently maligned by the well-to-do,[39] and Laborde's characterization was meant to appeal to a popular middle-class stereotype in order to advance his argument. Since war had prevented the Napoleonic administration from completing important material reforms in Paris, Laborde wished to present his agenda for such improvements as a record for posterity and as an attempt to influence public opinion and the administration of Chabrol de Volvic.

The title of his treatise was, significantly, *D'embellissemens de Paris,* but its focus and content were largely technical. Laborde proposed five major objectives for Paris urbanism: (1) the distribution of water by pipes to homes, (2) the construction of a public washhouse, (3) the creation of a major water reservoir on the heights of Chaillot Hill, (4) the placing of several "monumental fountains" throughout the city, and (5) the laying out of sidewalks everywhere in the capital. In a coda to his book, he proposed the construction of a public

Facing page

In 1816, Alexandre de Laborde drew up a detailed plan for the construction of a public wash house, hoping thereby to regulate the work of laundresses, at the time considered dangerous to public health because of the kinds of chemicals used. This plan also exemplifies Laborde's privileging of infrastructural reforms, as opposed to monuments, as the basis for Paris's greatness. Avery Architectural and Fine Arts Library, Columbia University

Elevation du Lavoir public

à Construire près la Pompe à feu du Gros Caillou.

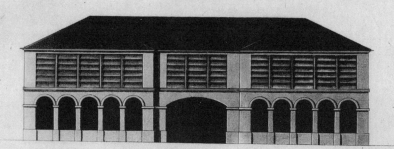

Plan du Lavoir.

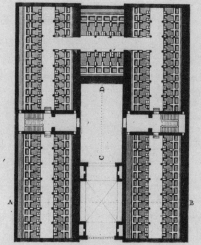

Coupe sur la
Ligne A.B.

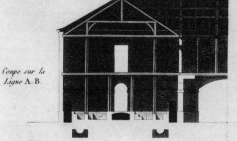

Coupe sur la
Ligne C.D.

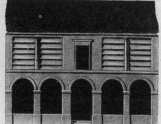

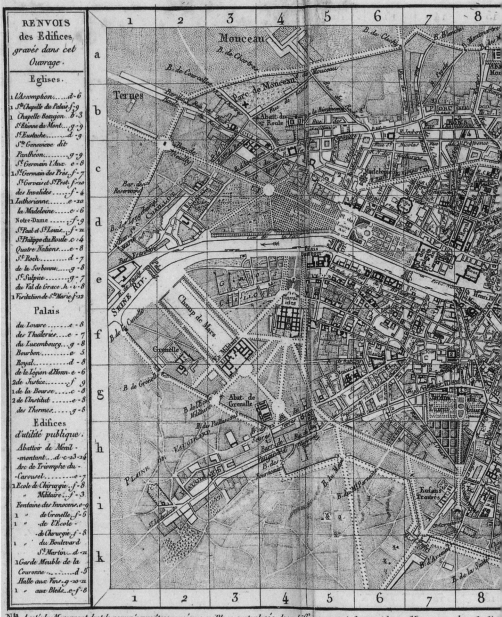

RENVOIS des Edifices gravés dans cet Ouvrage.

Eglises.

1 L'Asomption......d-6
1 Ste Chapelle du Palais.f-9
1 Chapelle Beaujon...b-3
St Etienne du Mont....g-9
St Eustache.....d-9
Ste Geneviève dit Panthéon....g-9
St Germain l'Aux..e-8
1 St Germain des Prés..f-7
St Gervais et St Prot. f-10
des Invalides.....f-4
1 Luthérienne.....e-10
la Madeleine.....c-6
Notre-Dame.....f-9
St Paul et St Louis. f-11
St Philippe du Roule.c-4
Quatre Nations....e-8
St Roch.....d-7
de la Sorbonne....g-8
St Sulpice.....g-7
du Val de Grace.h-i-8
1 Visitation de Ste Marie.f-12

Palais

du Louvre......e-8
des Thuileries.....e-7
du Luxembourg....g-8
Bourbon.......e-5
Royal.......d-8
de la Légion d'Honn..e-6
2 de Justice......f-9
1 de la Bourse....c-8
2 de l'Institut.....e-8
des Thermes....g-8

Edifices d'utilité publique.

Abattoir de Ménil-montant...d-c-13-14
Arc de Triomphe du Carousel.....e-7
1 Ecole de Chirurgie..f-8
" Militaire..f-3
Fontaine des Innocens.e-9
1 " de Grenelle.f-5
1 " de l'Ecole de Chirurgie.f-8
1 " du Boulevard St Martin..d-11
1 Garde Meuble de la Couronne....d-5
1 Halle aux Vins.g-10-11
1 " aux Bleds..e-f-8

Nta. A coté du Monument dont le nom n'a pu être gravé sur ce Plan, sont placés des chiffre en avant du nom de ces Monuments dans la liste

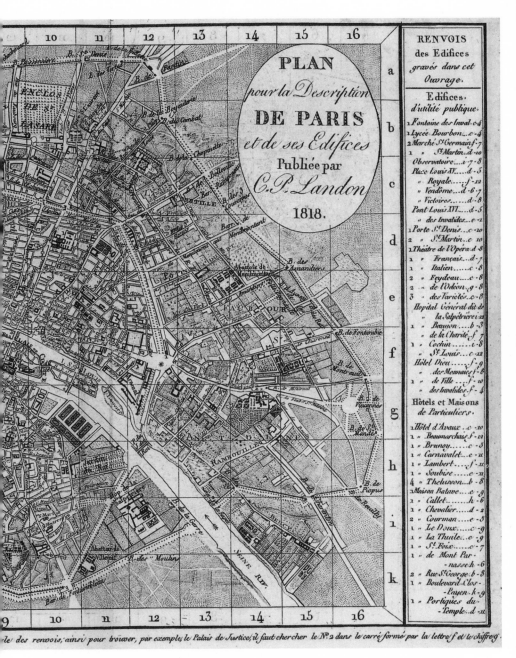

A map of central Paris in 1818, showing the continued density of streets and lack of major connecting arteries there and throughout Paris. General Research Division, New York Public Library, The Astor, Lenox, and Tilden Foundations

promenade for pedestrians and horseback riders on part of the Champs-Élysées, a subject more suitable to the older definition of embellishment. The entire text, in marked contrast to the architectural treatise of Pierre Patte, was rooted in scientific and engineering details: maps, statistics, measurements, financial calculations, drawings (for a public laundry facility and for fountains), and the kind of stone to use for sidewalks. Laborde's text represented the creation, on paper, of a new city in which infrastructural amenities, rather than great public buildings, would become the hallmark.

Others, and not only engineers, approached Paris in a similar fashion, although the monumental did not completely disappear from planning proposals. The architect B. A. H. Devert wrote in 1825 that "the great truth" in Paris at the time was the need for public authorities to focus on "commerce" and "public sanitation." Devert's own contribution to plans for Paris was the design of a model street crossroad to facilitate the movement of vehicular traffic.[40] J. G. Legrand and G. P. Landon, in their *Description de Paris et de ses édifices* (1818), defined Paris as a city that combined the beautiful and the useful, and this, they wrote, made it unique in the modern world.[41] The architects, building entrepreneurs, and property owners who spoke through Mirbel and A. Bareau linked the design of space in Paris to matters of health, the lower classes, and the economy.[42] Leblanc de Ferrière's book on Paris and its suburbs, a work largely about individual monuments, also argued for a program of public works in Paris and its metropolitan area.[43] Two architects, P. Levicomte and F. Rolland, encapsulated an important aspect of the new focus with regard to Paris. In 1833 they designed a model for a new building type in Paris, a *Maison commune*—the modern equivalent of a *mairie,* or town hall—for each arrondissement, whose function was to house all offices specializing in urban services. The first point to notice is that the Levicomte and Rolland proposal did not aspire to some noble architecture, a theater or church, perhaps. Commenting on architecture, they observed that "in our time it is no longer a question that something must be beautiful and grand; it must also be useful and inexpensive." The purpose of their building, they believed, should be reflected in its simple and economical architecture; its spare design symbolized the urban services it provided, and their concept and building design attracted favorable comments in contemporary journals devoted to Paris urbanism.[44]

The most remarkable example of this shift from architectural treatise to planning document, however, was a collective work, one not normally thought of as an urban planning text, the *Recherches statistiques* mentioned above.[45] Historians are in agreement that the *Recherches statistiques* was a pioneering compendium of raw statistical data intended to serve as the basis for an enlightened administration of the welfare of the Paris population.[46] It was, however, more. The *Recherches statistiques* represented a new manner of looking at the city, a description of the city expressed through statistics. What mattered most in this publication were the material features that determined the underlying structure of Paris: its climate, infrastructure, topography, population profile, for example, rather than monuments or architecture, which did not figure in its pages. Such knowledge, when complete, would then make possible an overarching plan for the capital's reform.

On the surface the *Recherches statistiques* offers no grand narrative vision of a new Paris. In fact, there is only limited narrative text of any kind, the form of the work being largely statistical. It would also appear that it expresses no authorial point of view, that what we are dealing with, moreover, is not one "work" but a collection of volumes, under one title, whose aim was to publish population statistics and data on all aspects of Paris life that could be counted and rendered statistically.[47] In my reading, the *Recherches statistiques,* or at least its first four volumes, does constitute a new discursive vision of Paris, a new knowledge about the city. And while no single author was responsible for its publication, Chabrol de Volvic was its principle animator, working closely with the mathematician J. B. J. Fourier and the statistician Frédéric Villot to realize its form. Its vision of the new city was not invented by either of these individuals, however, but fit into the newly emerging science of statistics and the reduction of knowledge, where possible, to statistical representation. This will be apparent in an exploration of the structure and content of the work as well as of other materials.

Chabrol de Volvic's direction of the *Recherches statistiques* project was not the first instance of his supervising the collection and publication of comprehensive data on an administrative unit of France or its empire. Between 1806 and 1810 Chabrol de Volvic had been the prefect of the Department of Montenotte, formally an Austrian possession, on the gulf of Genoa, where he was responsible for a policy of tying an outlying region of France to Paris, its administrative center. To that end he improved land communications between the French capital, Montenotte, and Piedmont. He also launched public works projects that upgraded the delivery of water to the department, the condition of roads and sewers, and port facilities, which facilitated trade with France. All this, however, was based upon a thorough knowledge of the resources and characteristics of the department. In 1810, in a response to a call from Napoleon's government to prefects regularly to submit data on the populations under their jurisdictions, Chabrol de Volvic began gathering information on Montenotte. In 1824, he published a two-volume work summarizing the results of his investigations.

The *Statistiques des provinces . . . de Montenotte* resembled in structure and content the *Recherches statistiques,* so much so that one may be thought of as a model for the other. The former provided both descriptive and statistical information, in tabular form, on the material and institutional life of the Department of Montenotte. Included in its two volumes was, in the following order, information on topography and geology; a description of cantons and communes in the department; a statistical, "physical and moral" portrait of the population; and an account of the domestic economy. This was followed in volume 2, again in order, with chapters on the history of the department, public instruction, the administration, agriculture, industry, and commerce. All this knowledge was meant to serve as the enlightened basis for the administration, control, and reform of the department. Of this publication and his use of statistics, Chabrol de Volvic wrote that "the data that statistics generate are of interest to governments and people. The administration in gathering the information that it studies, that it classifies systematically, comes to know more precisely its resources, its means, its revenues." He also observed, quite accurately, that "over the last several years statistics has become an unusual science in Europe: the enlightened sovereigns extend and favor this science."[48] He would apply the same approach and philosophy to Paris, starting with the collection of population data.

In 1816 Chabrol de Volvic issued a call for a population census of Paris. It was completed the following year, and he decided to publish it as part of a larger record of the material life of the capital. In order to assist him with this project, he turned to his former mathematics instructor at the École polytechnique, Fourier, to guarantee the theoretical soundness of the work, and to the head of the office of statistics within the prefecture, Villot, to edit its volumes. The first four volumes appeared during the Restoration (1821, 1824, 1826, and 1829). The fifth volume, which had been under preparation between 1827 and 1836, appeared only in 1844, delayed because of Villot's death. The sixth volume appeared in 1860. Aside from not having the guiding hand of Villot or Chabrol de Volvic, volumes 5 and 6, moreover, have a quite narrow focus when compared to the previous tomes. Volume 5 deals with topography and population and the last volume essentially with population alone. Each of the first four, on the other hand, range in their focus from population to public institutions, agriculture, public transit, public assistance, commerce, and industry. Both in terms of subject matter and editing, therefore, volumes 1-4 constitute a recognizable unity, and E. Lavasseur characterized them as "extremely remarkable" in their presentation "of the most varied information on the city of Paris."[49]

The unsigned introduction to the first volume of the *Recherches statistiques* makes it clear that Paris administrators wished to gather a statistical profile of the capital as a tool of public policy. In the words of the introduction, public policy had to be based upon an "exact knowledge of the territory, of the condition of its people, and of the sources of public revenue." In the third volume the editor wrote that "in publishing the statistical reports of the city of Paris the administration aims to call general attention to the great number of authentic facts which it believes need to be known."[50] The use of the expressions "exact knowledge" and "authentic facts" reflected the belief that statistical knowledge was somehow "true" and not open to challenge. To reinforce this impression the editors of the *Recherches statistiques* decided that whenever it was possible the information they had gathered would be "reduced to tables so that these almost countless details can be understood and compared more easily." In his memoirs, Chabrol de Volvic, who had trained as an engineer at the École polytechnique and was a typical exemplar of the new scientific spirit of the early nineteenth century, stated that it was his idea to present most of the conclusions of the *Recherches statistiques* in tabular form.[51]

We also, however, have an indication in the introduction that tables were more than a matter of clarity and convenience. "The reduction [of information] to tables has the advantage of excluding useless discussions and to guide all the research toward its principal goal which is the methodological enumeration of the facts."[52] Such a view would have the effect of closing debate on public policy, since the administration determined the research agenda that would be reduced to tabular form. Again, in the language of the introduction, "It is above all necessary to note that the real goal of these studies is to attain a degree of precision that administrative matters require."[53] Broadly speaking, what interested the administration, at least publicly, was "the hygiene of the capital," "industrial progress," and "the amelioration of the principal public practices."[54] Below the surface, there was also an issue of power. Foucault has taught us that knowledge and power are closely linked and, as I suggested in chapter 1, urban planning may be interpreted as an instrument of social and political control over the city by its administrators. The kind of knowledge that the *Recherches statistiques* collected, with all its scientific pretensions, was an important stage in the justification of a deep intervention into public life by political authorities.

In his memoirs Chabrol de Volvic reflected on the purpose of the *Recherches statistiques*. He had been prefect of the Seine Department from 1812 until, with a brief interruption during the Hundred Days, he left the office in July 1830. He remained in politics as a deputy from the Puys-de-Dôme until his death in 1843. Following his tenure as chief administrator of Paris he composed his memoirs both to explain his aims and as a guide to future Paris administrators.[55] Feeling freer perhaps to express himself in memoir form than in the tightly constructed statistical publication, Chabrol de Volvic wrote that his basic goal had been to "improve" Paris so that "there may be completed before the end of the century the realization of a general plan which would make Paris the most beautiful city in the world." He explained further that Voltaire had had such a plan, and by linking himself to the eighteenth-century philosophe Chabrol was calling attention to the need for infrastructural reforms in the capital and legitimizing that project.[56]

In his memoirs he also took special pride in the accomplishments of his administration, which, for him, consisted of the building of, or the planning for, slaughterhouses, canals, warehouses, and especially sidewalks. All these, he wrote, were central both to the health and commerce of the city.[57] He recorded, too, his impression of a study trip to London in 1823. It was London's infrastructural amenities that Chabrol chose to write about, praising the English capital for its public water delivery system, its sewers, its sidewalks, and its cleanliness.[58] While on the one hand he viewed Paris as "no less important than Memphis, than Rome or Athens," and as representing "the high point of Europe," on the other, he identified an important deficiency of his beloved city: Paris was inferior to other cities with respect to its streets and sewers, and Paris tended to neglect its exterior environment.[59] It was this aspect of the city's life that Chabrol de Volvic wished to address in *Recherches statistiques*.

As I suggested earlier, however, on the surface the work is more a compilation of statistics than a representation of a coherent vision of the city or a program of infrastructural reform. In terms of subject matter, volumes 1–4 consist mostly of tables on population, public welfare, agriculture, public instruction, fine arts (including theaters, public balls, concerts, and public gardens), coaches and transportation, water, meteorology, navigation, finances, topography, mineralogy, geology, commerce, and industry. Not every one of these categories is in each volume, but they represent the collective focus of the Restoration's *Recherches statistiques*. In addition, there are important individual narrative reports in the work. Volume 1 contains a highly theoretical piece by Fourier on population statistics and a short report by Chabrol de Volvic summarizing how the population data were collected, interpreted, and presented.[60] In the last three volumes there are additional essays on population statistics. Volume 2 contains an important study on street alignment in Paris by Chabrol, and volume 3 features a plan for a water-delivery system for the capital by the prefect and the report on housing in Paris by Daubanton.

Is there, however, a coherent vision of Paris or at least an intent to present an overarching view or plan of the city? I would suggest that a coherent vision of a new Paris does emerge in the *Recherches statistiques,* but that the work was not completed by the time Chabrol de Volvic left office and that its aim changed when he left the administration. The introduction to volume 1 makes it clear that its editors, following a "thorough discussion," had established a "general plan" for the presentation of their findings. They believed that there was an ideal order of presentation of statistical material in which information about the territory and climate would be followed by information on political institutions. In this kind of Braudelian vision before Braudel, the editors also posited the existence of connections among the mass of data they had collected but warned that their discovery was difficult and fraught with potential errors. The entire project, the statistical mapping of Paris, moreover, would take a great deal of time. In light of these difficulties the editors decided to publish data as they became available, rather than wait for completeness, as the information, even in its raw state, was an important tool for administrative action.[61] The first order of business, therefore, was that Paris administrators pay attention to the material foundations of Paris, its traffic and population patterns, soil, and climate. In short, of primary importance in the modern city was the relationship of the population to the topography and infrastructure of Paris.

Of major significance along these lines, given the prominent narrative space devoted to the subject, was Chabrol de Volvic's plan for water delivery to Paris. The prefect wanted Paris equipped with a circulatory water-delivery system that would address the health and safety needs of the city rather than its beautification. Such a system should assure the steady availability of water to all public establishments, like hospitals, prisons, schools, markets, and warehouses. An adequate supply of water would permit the administration to clean the city's streets and sewers, provide for its fountains, establish a reservoir for fire fighters, and, for a fee, provide water for homes. The prefect proposed a series of distribution reservoirs from which water would arrive in Paris through pipes connected to hydraulic pumps. Completing his circulatory water system, he also proposed a system of sewers for the removal of waste from Paris.[62] None of this could be accomplished without engineering science, which was becoming critical in urban planning.

We also glimpse a vision of a new Paris in the essays by Chabrol de Volvic on streets and by Daubanton on housing, even though they only treat individual limited topics. Daubanton's report on housing, for example, reinforced Chabrol de Volvic's on streets by focusing on the need for better circulation in Paris as a stimulus to housing construction in all its quarters.[63] Collectively, these essays saw Paris as a city equipped with efficient through-streets and sidewalks, linking all parts of the city with one another and the entire city with the provinces, a clean and healthy city center, an efficient water-delivery system, and adequate housing for its population. These amenities rather than monuments would make the city great, according to the *Recherches statistiques*.

Chabrol de Volvic's essay on streets, a tract whose subtitle summed up its major theme, "concerning the execution of a project for the alignment of the streets of Paris," is an especially significant representation of a new vision of Paris. It begins with a critique of past efforts at street reform, which, Chabrol complained, were always undertaken to meet individual problems as they arose. In his opinion the reform of Paris streets should follow carefully the outline of a comprehensive and fixed plan. It was his intent to establish just such a plan for his administration, and his essay was a fairly detailed outline of the plan. The aim of his reform was to extend, widen, and properly align every street of Paris. He established a prioritized agenda for this project. Work would begin first on those streets and avenues that he classified as the "great communication routes from quarter to quarter," the important through-streets of the capital. A second order of streets, whose reform was also urgent, were those important for reasons of "public security, of public health, [and of] the needs of commerce." The third, and significantly last, category of reform was directed to streets designated for "the embellishment of the capital."[64] He acknowledged the massive public-works nature of the project and anticipated that the government would support this undertaking financially in cooperation with private interests and that, under ideal circumstances, it would take about forty years to complete. The overall intent of the reform was to tie the city together through an efficient circulatory system in the interests of the city's public health and sanitation needs, commercial success, and public safety, as well as enhancing employment opportunities for workers throughout France.

Chabrol de Volvic's plan for street reform also addressed sidewalks. In his report on street alignment the prefect expressed a modest ideal with respect to sidewalk construction. He would build sidewalks simply where it was practical, following the principle that "it is . . . necessary either to renounce an imaginary perfection or resolve to perpetuate all the current inconveniences."[65] In several speeches to the Chamber of Deputies and budget reports for the Department of the Seine, however, he gave flight to his imagination and integrated proposals for sidewalk construction with a grand vision of free and unencumbered circulation throughout Paris and from Paris to the national territory. What he was interested in demonstrating through an experiment in limited sidewalk construction, he reported, was the possibility "for someone to go from whatever point in Paris to another by following an uninterrupted line of paved sidewalks, raised in wide streets and flush with the street in narrow ones." Following this system, "Paris would be divided into great squares by lines of sidewalks crossing the city in its length and its breadth."[66]

From the perspective of an engineer and an urban administrator seeking order and control, the grid system of street patterns was ideal. Chabrol de Volvic had already designed such a street system in 1805 in the newly founded town of Pontivy, a Napoleonic outpost in Brittany, and it was what he wished for Paris. Chabrol de Volvic, who had been a member of the scientific team that accompanied Napoleon Bonaparte to Egypt in 1798, had been subprefect in Pontivy from 1804 to 1806. The decision to build Napoléonville, as the town was called from 1805 to 1814 and from 1848 to 1871, was based upon the government's wish for better communication routes to Brittany and its wish to exercise greater control in the center of a region with an unruly past. Chabrol de Volvic, who produced the definitive plan for the new town, served Napoleon's political aim of imposing increased state authority and rational urban planning on peripheral and problem areas.[67] His interest in effective circulation through Paris, however, was also related to a recognition that the capital, for political and economic reasons, had to be integrated into a national system of highways and waterways. He therefore urged the undertaking of a national transportation public works program involving canals and highways as beneficial to commerce and agriculture, and he also called upon the French people to support the paving of Paris streets, the capital being the nation's largest market for provincial products.[68]

Although the theme of urban circulation resonates more powerfully in the 1840s, Chabrol de Volvic, in common with Saint-Simonians like Michel Chevalier and Stéphane Flachat, held a dynamic view of the city as a circulatory system related to a national system of movement and traffic. One of the principal characteristics of the modern Western city, namely, the utilization of the street exclusively as a conduit for free, uninhibited motion, rather than walking or socialization of any kind, is already in the making conceptually in the 1820s. It is a use of the street that Richard Sennett, in a critique of modern city planning, associated most strongly with mechanized urban transport, but the privileging of street vehicular over pedestrian movement had its origins, as we see again and again in this study, in the first half of the nineteenth century.[69]

Pierre Debofle, who made an exhaustive study of urbanism in Paris under the Restoration, concluded that "at the beginning of the [nineteenth] century and up until the beginning of the July Monarchy, one can hardly find any comprehensive plan for urban reforms."[70] This is true in a narrow technical sense. However, *Recherches statistiques* did aspire to a global view of Paris, and it was intended to serve as the foundation for a comprehensive material reform of the city.

THE SOCIAL QUESTION

On the level of statistical information, *Recherches statistiques* confirmed what contemporary observers had noticed, namely, that Paris was experiencing an increase in its population not matched by infrastructural or housing reforms. This partly accounted for the emergence of the "social question." Giovanna Procacci noted that it was during the first half of the nineteenth century that the social question, characterized largely by the poverty of so much of the working population, was constructed as an issue that political and economic elites and intellectuals had to address. Between the 1820s and 1840s, French social economy, which Procacci characterized as an orientation in studying the social question rather than a formal school, adopted, as an answer to poverty, a position falling between classic economic liberalism, on the one hand, and permanent rights for labor, on the other. The solution it offered was to turn to private philanthropy as a mechanism of intervention in the social order; it was one that would not, however, upset the property relations of that order.

This compromise, Procacci pointed out, broke down during the events of the 1848 revolution, when the claims for liberal use of private property clashed with the workers' demands for the right to work, demands that implied collective social control over property. At the time of the 1848 revolution the basic problem for authorities and intellectuals was that "the poor created a politically embarrassing issue: how to justify inequalities under a condition of basic equality." Auguste Comte had solved this dilemma with the notion of duty and public morality, characteristics to be instilled into all citizens by popular education, which would transcend the conflict between liberal and collectivist conceptions of social organization. Duty, therefore, creates social solidarity rather than conflict, and the social question is incorporated into the liberal society under this concept.[71] The year 1848 was also a critical moment in the attempt of government officials to come to grips with the social question because circulation in Paris became an urgent issue after February 1848, when the common people commandeered the streets of central Paris and blocked movement, so necessary to order, commerce, and modernization. The solution was to open new streets, especially in the capital's center, and the provisional government of 1848 advanced the argument that improved circulation would stimulate the economy and facilitate distribution, especially of bread—an obvious appeal to workers—throughout the city. Such an agenda would be realized by Napoleon III.[72]

If we examine proposals for the reform of Paris, however, it will be evident that there existed an important body of urban thinkers who examined the social question from the point of view of the spatial and material organization of the capital during the first half of the nineteenth century, not merely at times of intense crisis and well before Napoleon III, and that these writers had a broad definition of the spatial and the material, one that included not only infrastructural reforms, like longer and wider streets in central Paris, but also elements like barracks, schoolhouses, and a new architecture for the administration of welfare and the infrastructure. In all these projects urban planning related to the social question as a matter of control and order.[73]

The anonymous author of *Coup d'oeil sur Paris,* mentioned above, proposed a new type of apartment building that would house in the same structure, as owners of individual apartments, workers and modest members of the middle classes. Initial financing for construction would be provided both by private and by government capital. According to this plan, each individual building would be at least forty feet wide and long, with an interior courtyard. To the left and right of the main portal would be boutiques, with their own entryways. Built of stone, each apartment house would consist of six stories, and each story could be subdivided to include three separate apartments of five rooms each. Each occupant of an apartment would own the apartment. Some floors would consist of fewer apartments, and increased subdivision could make apartments affordable for the working classes. Members of the working classes, according to the author, could save enough to buy one of the smaller apartments. While no details were provided, this being simply a description of a model apartment building, the plan also called for water delivery to the building, gas lighting, and provisions for heating. The aim of the new housing, according to the text, was not merely to accommodate the increased Paris population in some comfort but also to affect "a decided improvement" of the morals of the workers and merchants, who would be drawn into the regime of property ownership.[74] There are many similarities in the above program to ideas then being worked out by Charles Fourier for an ideal housing unit, although it is impossible to determine a line of influence in either direction.

A far more extensive project to address the social question, revolving partly around housing, was devised in 1829 by Mirbel and A. Bareau. It is important to recall that Mirbel and Bareau represented a meeting of "property owners, architects, and builders." As president and secretary, respectively, of this meeting, they presented a report to the minister of the interior on the status of housing construction in Paris. There was a serious building slump in the capital at the time of their report, and their communication to the minister was mostly a brief for a governmental relaxation of building codes that would, they hoped, stimulate the building construction industry. Thus Mirabel and Bareau made a case for loosening height restrictions and rules on standards for building materials for new constructions as well as temporarily suspending land taxes for the same constructions. As part of their program of economic recovery they also called for important infrastructural reforms in the center of Paris and for government assistance in building cheaper housing for the less well-to-do outside the city center. The new vision of Paris they presented was not, therefore, neutral. Mirbel and Bareau represented well-defined economic and commercial interests in the city who stood to benefit by the reforms they espoused, reforms that were not, in the end, granted by the government.[75] What is interesting, however, is that the rhetoric employed in their argument drew upon well-known middle-class assumptions about workers and the space needs of the capital, all of them dressed up to appeal to the general welfare of both workers and the middle classes. Working-class housing especially was considered a main source of urban problems in the first half of the nineteenth century.[76]

This call for more housing was, therefore, in line with a larger discourse in Paris addressing the social question. Mirabel and Bareau began with a general critique of the government and builders for not being concerned enough with housing for "the working class, which is obliged to press itself, to crowd itself, in the unhealthy and airless streets of old Paris, at the expense of its morals and health"[77]—in addition to proposing more housing for workers, however, both men also suggested a policy that may be characterized as "social space engineering" and that would have great resonance at the time of Haussmann. They believed, for example, that the government had enough power in the laws of 1807 and 1810 concerning the expropriation of private property for "public utility," with financial compensation to owners, to continue the construction of the rue de Rivoli, even if this meant displacing a large portion of the working population from the center of Paris. Such "a rather considerable displacement of population" would be beneficial since it would facilitate the needs of urban circulation, the employment of huge amounts of capital, and the health of Paris center.[78] Mirbel and Bareau did not hide or apologize for their agenda, whose social and financial interests were apparent; as they wrote, "it is evident that, for public health and ease of circulation, the administration must vigorously [plan] that a part of the population of the center [of Paris] move toward the [city's] circumference." The government could engineer this outcome by the expropriations mentioned earlier and also through a positive policy of building roads from the center to the periphery of Paris and by cleaning up and thus making the extremities of Paris more attractive to those in the center (read: the poor).[79] Mirbel and Bareau also demanded the strictest order on Paris streets; they called for the removal of all commercial activities there, wanting the streets to serve only as efficient conduits of vehicular and commercial traffic.

It should be clear by now that Mirbel and Bareau were not primarily addressing the social problem. When it came up in their text, however, they suggested both a spatial method for taming it, in the form of better roads and order on the streets, as well as inexpensive housing for workers in the outlying districts of the city. That security and order were the key to the social problem for some planners is especially evident in Mirbel and Bareau's project for the Paris guard. They called upon the administration to provide a permanent headquarters in the center of each of the city's twelve arrondissements to house a police commissioner and his guard. At the time, police commissioners worked out of their own lodgings, and these were often difficult to find or maintain, given the nature of police work, and might not be conveniently located with respect to access to all parts of an arrondissement. A permanent police headquarters for each arrondissement, clearly marked as such, which included offices for the police commissioner, his secretary, and an inspector, room for the local police guard, as well as equipment for emergencies, like stretchers, lamps, fire-fighting provisions, and the like, would facilitate the surveillance of Paris, "the curbing of disorder, of misdemeanors, of crime" and thus ensure "order and public security." In addition, Mirbel and Bareau recommended building new barracks in Paris and establishing a new army corps to assist in the safety of the city.[80] Barracks already existed in the city, and they are mentioned in the eighteenth-century planning literature. During the nineteenth century, however, the concentration of the Paris population and two revolutions in which the common people claimed the streets made barracks appear all the more urgent, especially in newer districts, to the administrative forces of society. Such a program, moreover, would constitute additional construction projects for building entrepreneurs and architects, Mirbel and Bareau's clients.

The close relationship between order, the social question, and planning is even more apparent in the work of the architects P. Levicomte and F. Rolland, also mentioned earlier, who in 1833 proposed a model administrative center for Paris arrondissements. Here, once more, Foucault's insights may serve as a starting point in an analysis of Levicomte and Rolland's project. According to Foucault, architects never exercised the same kind of power over individual bodies that medical doctors, priests, or prison wardens did: they were not "people through whom power passed" and were not "important in the fields of power relations." Foucault allowed, however, that the architect "is not totally foreign to the organization, the implementation, and all the techniques of power that are exercised in a society," but he did not explain further how techniques of power are invested in architecture, at least for the nineteenth century, simply calling our attention to an element of social control that may be investigated further.[81] It is here that Levicomte and Rolland's project is instructive. Their major contribution to the discussion of space and order, it will be recalled, was a proposal for a Maison commune, which would provide infrastructural and welfare services to the Paris population. Let us explore in some detail how the Maison commune would also function as architectural and functional rationality at the service of urban order.

The context for Levicomte and Rolland's proposal for a Maison commune was the noticeable increase of the Paris population, the unhealthy state of many arrondissements, especially apparent during the cholera epidemic of 1832, and their belief that the administration should provide public work projects for the "laboring classes."[82] The first thing to notice is that the text presents a design for a model Maison commune consisting of a narrative description of all its services and architectural renderings of its interior and outer spaces. In other words, it is not merely a proposal for such a building, as in the texts of Mirbel and Bareau or of the many eighteenth-century planners discussed in chapter 1. It is a modern architectural blueprint of a building type for the urban environment. Levicomte and Rolland's goal was to persuade public authorities to construct a Maison commune as close as possible to the geographic and population center of each Paris arrondissement. Such a building would house offices and bureaus for a civil registry, a judiciary, national guard troops, the police commissioner and his force, welfare matters, popular education, streets and roads, financial services, public latrines, and apartments.

Facing page

In 1833 two architects, P. Levicomte and F. Rolland, proposed the construction in the center of each Paris arrondissement of a *Maison commune,* or city hall, to gather together and centralize all offices and functions specializing in urban services. Such a building would house a military guard, a police bureau, a charity office, a local savings bank branch, a fire brigade and provide rooms for popular education. Bibliothèque nationale de France

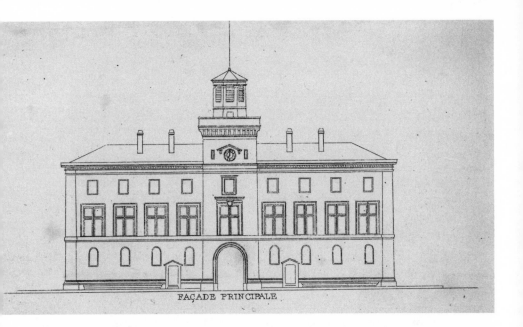

FAÇADE PRINCIPALE

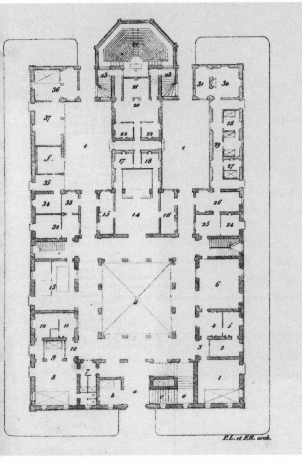

P.L. et F.R. arch.

Garde Nationale
- e. Cabinet de l'Officier
- 1. Corps de Garde
- 2. Dépôt d'armes
- 3. Anti-chambre
- 4. Cabinet des Adjudans
- 5. Cabinet du Major
- 6. Salle pour piquet &.

Police
- 7. Violon
- 8. Corps de Garde
- 9. Cabinet de l'Officier
- 10. Anti-chambre
- 11. Cabinet du Secrétaire
- 12. Cabinet du Commissaire

Grand bureau du Poste 13.

Justice de paix
- 14. Auditoire
- 15. Greffe
- 16. Secrétariat
- 17. Cabinet du Greffier
- 18. Cabinet du Juge

Instruction populaire
- 19. Salle de cours
- 20. Laboratoire
- 21. Dépôt
- 22. Cabinet de Professeur
- 23. Escalier conduisant à la bibliothèque et à la salle d'exposition.

Secours de Bienfaisance
- 24. Salle d'attente
- 25. Cabinet de consultations
- 26. Pharmacie et Laboratoire
- 27. Chambre de l'Élève Pharmacien
- 28. Infirmerie
- 29. Corridor pour les distributions
- 30. Cuisine
- 31. Dépôt

Caisse d'épargne
- 32. Salle d'attente
- 33. Caisse

Vérification des poids et mesures
- 34. Bureau
- 35. Hangard

Sapeurs-pompiers
- 36. Corps de Garde
- 37. Dépôt des pompes et ustensiles

Dépendances
- a. Vestibule
- b. Portier
- c. Escalier principal
- d. Cour principale
- e. Cours de service
- f. Écuries et hangard

Many of these services already existed in each arrondissement, and local *mairies* (town halls) already had civil magistrates, justices of the peace, and offices for charity. The important innovation here was the centralization of such services in each arrondissement in what would have to be a substantial government building. It is not fanciful to suggest that Levicomte and Rolland, as architects looking for an important commission, were advancing this reform in part to stimulate a substantial building program. The arguments they used, however, were designed to appeal to shared middle-class concerns about urban safety. Along these lines, the architects employed a rhetorical flourish, writing that the Maison commune would appear so useful and important to the urban setting that the government would pay for its construction, especially considering that it would save the money it dispensed renting out office space for the several services that would be combined in the Maison commune.

One of Levicomte and Rolland's paramount arguments for the construction of a Maison commune stressed the building's role in public security and safety. Its central location in each arrondissement might be compared to the panoptic function of a prison or to the circular architecture of Nicolas Ledoux in the eighteenth century. Ledoux had designed a model factory town, Chaux, in the form of an oval and placed its director in the middle, whence he could exercise power and surveillance. In addition to the presence of police and guards in the Maison commune, Levicomte and Rolland would have a platform above the building's belfry, with room for a night watchman and an alarm, which "could serve for nocturnal surveillance." It was comforting, they believed, that there is "during our sleep a man who is on the vigil for public security."[83] Levicomte and Rolland also provided lodgings in the Maison commune for the police commissioner and his family and attached to the building a municipal guard to assist the regular police, a "guard earmarked especially for repressive functions." The point of this, they argued, was not to replace the more conciliatory functions of the regular police but to ensure the supply of sufficient force for each quarter. A fire brigade, in their plan, was also attached to the Maison, and came under police control.[84]

Whether or not Levicomte and Rolland had a hidden motive in their proposal for a Maison commune, their design and project, which became part of the public record, addressed social control and safety in some detail. And if, on the one hand, their project for social control involved a rational organization of force in each arrondissement, on the other it comprehended a series of services designed to integrate the poor people into the state and its liberal economy. To this end Levicomte and Rolland would have an office of charity (*bureau de bienfaisance*) in the Maison commune. Intended to centralize the distribution of charity in each arrondissement, this office also had attached to it a pharmacy, two beds for emergencies—when someone from the quarter might be picked up from the street but was too ill to be transported to a hospital, for example—and an infirmary. In addition, a space in the Maison could serve as a "warming room" for poor people who could not otherwise find refuge during moments of extremely severe or inclement weather. Levicomte and Rolland added pointedly, however, that this emergency measure must not be considered permanent, as that would only encourage "idleness and corruption."

Charitable relief was not intended as a substitute for work, and the aim of the Maison commune was, they wrote, to instill in "the inferior classes . . . habits of order and of economy." Along these lines, they urged the establishment of savings banks for workers, locating individual branches in each Maison commune, setting thereby an example of thrift and making it easier for workers to deposit their savings. These banks would have the most beneficial effects upon workers, "making them simultaneously work harder and elevate their morals." The savings program would also contribute to "the social order and the public tranquility."[85] The same could be said of their charity. Note that savings banks, according to Foucault, were one particular "rational strategy" for fixing workers in their industrial occupations. So was education, as we shall see. These strategies were intended "to master a vagabond, floating labor force."[86]

Conceptualizing the control of social distress and its dangers in distinct levels beginning with surveillance and force, followed by charity and then savings (and presumably work, which was taken for granted), Levicomte and Rolland completed their agenda of social management through a program of popular education for the masses.[87] The architects believed that material aid to the poor had to be accompanied by an educational program, a position they adopted both for "ethical" considerations and reasons of "political calculus." The aim of education was to develop the "physical, intellectual, and moral faculties" of all the people. While France did not have universal education, people in all classes must share in common principles of "religion, of tolerance, and of ethics." While such a program would benefit the entire nation, it would be especially useful for the Paris population. Their intent was clear: to use a program of popular education to moralize the masses, to tame and draw them into a spirit of harmony with the upper classes. This was a program of Comtian solidarity, and education would "spread well-being among the masses by correcting their lewd vices, their impiety, their superstition" and "defend the weak against the seduction of parties, desirous of always dragging them into the circle of political agitation."[88]

The organization of Levicomte and Rolland's "popular education" for the Paris masses was similar to a program of worker education devised by revolutionary syndicalists later in the century. Like the revolutionary syndicalists, who housed worker courses in a workers' Labor Exchange (*Bourse du Travail*), Levicomte and Rolland set aside a room (*une salle de cours*) in the Maison commune for popular education. So important was popular education for the masses, the authors reported, that it needed the intervention of the municipality. They suggested, therefore, that the mayor of each arrondissement exercise direction over the program. The core of popular education consisted of night-time courses for adults, which focused on industrial education, and day-time courses for children, all "under the surveillance of the same magistrate [the mayor]." A library should be attached to the program, with books on industrial and commercial subjects. "This popular library, which will be open when the working class is off from work, and on Sundays and holidays, offers it a refuge against boredom, often even against debauchery." The library would also have "a permanent exposition room of industrial products and inventions or mechanical improvements," which workers could use as models in their own labor.[89]

The revolutionary syndicalists also complemented adult education courses with libraries and industrial exhibitions in their Labor Exchanges. For them, however, workers' education was conceived as a step in a revolutionary process against capitalism. The Levicomte-Rolland program was designed to capture the minds of workers and their children and lead them to cooperate with their masters. Their program of moralizing and controlling the masses extended to their personal habits as well, as Levicomte and Rolland called attention to the need for public urinals in the Maison commune as well as in all public buildings in Paris. This would address, according to them, one of the principal causes of the unsanitary condition of Paris, namely, "the constant public urination and the deposit of fecal matter against [public] walls," something quite prevalent "above all in the populous districts of the city."[90]

While Levicomte and Rolland did not respond to the social question in terms of the overarching physical characteristics of Paris, they did propose an architectural model for an individual building to be inserted into the center of each arrondissement, a building whose function was to centralize material and education services as a response to the great number of poor and workers circulating in Paris. This was a program of social control and moralization, even if it was part of a plan for an architectural commission, intended as an integral part of each quarter in Paris. It may also be seen as a forerunner of municipal playgrounds, free urban libraries, and sports facilities—all outlets for peaceful popular diversions.[91]

The Levicomte-Rolland plan constituted a relatively original manner of relating the organization of space to the social question. Far more frequent throughout the first half of the nineteenth century were planning proposals that addressed the condition of the center and streets of Paris. The great fear of nineteenth-century French middle-class intellectuals, including socialists or reformers, was the presence of large armies of poor people in the very heart of the capital, the old historic center on the Right and Left Banks. We encountered a hint of this in the Mirbel and Bareau proposal to push a portion of the population of central Paris to the city's periphery. Because fear of the masses—often indiscriminately characterized by the middle classes as the poor, migrants, criminals, revolutionaries, the unhealthy, and vagabonds—became a common theme in early-nineteenth-century planning literature, sometimes openly, often only as a subtext, we need to consider further what might be involved in this fear. We noted in chapter 1 Foucault's observation of the eighteenth-century's double conjuncture of population expansion and a growth in production and in the capitalist economy, which led to a kind of nomadism as more and more people moved from the countryside to the cities, a phenomenon especially noticeable in Paris. Such processes necessitated more effective disciplinary techniques to organize and control production and the floating population.

Foucault's insights are even more relevant for the first half of the nineteenth century, a time of dramatic population expansion and the continued expansion of production, when city planning may be regarded as a new disciplinary procedure for urban space. Paul Virilio and Gilles Deleuze and Félix Guattari deepened Foucault's insights with their own suggestive analyses of the dynamic between ruling elites and the masses and are especially suggestive for the nineteenth century. Revolutionary upheavals punctuated the early part of the century, 1830 following 1789 and 1848 following 1830. Circulation, according to Virilio, is essential for revolution, which does not occur at the place of production but in the street. Fear of the masses results from their unsettled nature; they do not reside in the city in the way the bourgeoisie does. State power, which establishes real estate as a principal value, seeks control over space for security against the potentially destabilizing "proletarian horde." As Virilo declared, state power is *"in other words highway surveillance."*[92] Deleuze and Guattari put the same matter slightly differently. Using the word *nomads* to describe the masses in history—a word, we should note, that runs through many nineteenth-century texts—these authors observed that the nomads' "war machine" (which may stand for revolutionary action in the modern world) required absolute speed and smooth space. The state, on the other hand, aimed to regulate movement and prevent any antistate action by establishing striated space. That is to say, the state always aims at the "capture of flows of all kinds, populations, commodities or commerce, money or capital," and it does so by regulating speed over its territory.[93]

With these insights in mind, we see a form of urban planning emerging in varied quarters which addressed the very real fear of revolution and the need for a disciplined work force that preoccupied the ruling elites of Paris. In addition to such material considerations, however, a further element may have been involved in proposed projects—and eventually in the reform of Paris under Napoleon III and Haussmann—for spatial forms that had the effect of social segregation. Richard Sennett observed that increases in population density in cities had the effect of making strangers more visible and that, moreover, this increase usually instigated a reorganization of the ecology of the city.[94] In the same vein, Zygmunt Bauman remarked, in a consideration of the psychological dimension of urban encounters, that strangers strike us as confusing and disturbing, that they are "socially distant yet physically close." In the city, "to live with strangers, one needs to master the art of mismeeting. The application of such an art is necessary if the strangers, for their sheer number if not for any other reason, cannot be domesticated into neighbors." The key for the urban dweller is to maintain his or her "social space" in such a manner as to avoid the stranger. Bauman suggested that the organization of modern city, "with its thoroughfares and urban motor ways, underground trains and air-conditioned and tightly sealed cars," which take people quickly from one place to another, facilitates the protection of social spacing. In addition, the organization of urban space has a "pronounced tendency to segregate classes, ethnic groups, or sometimes genders or generations—so that the techniques of mismeeting could be applied more concretely and with greater trust in their effect."[95] Although Bauman associated such strategies and planning with the twentieth-century city, similar considerations are quite apparent in the planning proposals for Paris during the first half of the nineteenth century.

One writer linked the cleaning of Paris streets to the "*extinction of begging*," because a program of urban sanitation would absorb a great deal of labor. Preference for an urban sanitation force, he added, should go to the ragpickers of Paris, people the established classes feared for their nomadic and unsanitary habits.[96] At least, according to Barrie Ratcliffe, this was the manner in which elite discourse viewed ragpickers, a marginal but numerically important and economically useful urban group, to further its aim of social control over urban space.[97] Another commentator, Amédée de Tissot, also suggested using beggars for cleaning streets, and he believed that a program of constructing sidewalks, paving streets, introducing public lighting, and improving sanitation would elevate French civilization.[98] In the mid-1830s, following the 1830 revolution and the 1832 cholera epidemic in Paris, an anonymous writer presented a petition from the electors of central Paris to the prefect of the Seine Department for the completion of a major street, the present-day rue des Francs Bourgeois (completed in 1868), which would establish an important connection between the Faubourg-Saint-Antoine and the center of the city, as well as a new approach to Les Halles food market. It is possible that this appeal, like that of Levicomte and Rolland, was partly designed to secure the commission for a public works project. One part of the petition noted that if the government approved of the completion of the street there would be a plethora of firms bidding to undertake the project. However, the arguments employed for a major street are so closely linked to disease and revolutionary actions in these central districts that they must be counted as real considerations. The author, informed no doubt by health reports following the cholera epidemic, observed of the present-day Third and Fourth Arrondissements that their streets were especially "narrow and sinuous," their houses densely packed together and unhealthy, and their residents crowded into "a small space." It was in such circumstances that cholera had made its greatest impact.

"All these conditions," the author wrote, "are without doubt sufficient to finally impel the authorities to act. But there is something else of an even higher order that should be incontestably decisive," namely, that these central quarters around the City Hall were the scenes of revolutionary intensity and upheaval. According to the anonymous text, it was imperative that officials finally begin opening wider streets through central Paris—the author referred approvingly to Alexandre de Laborde's project for new street constructions—both to admit air and sunlight but also to permit the national guard to manoeuver more easily.[99] Not only was the petition signed by electors of the old Seventh Arrondissement, which corresponded roughly to the present-day Fourth, establishing thereby the clearly elite status of the interested parties, but, where we can identify the profession of a signatory, the kinds of interests that lay behind the appeal become even more evident. Among those signing were three field-marshals and three generals of the army, the mayor of the adjoining Sixth Arrondissement, a member of the Chamber of Peers, and the director of the postal service—individuals interested in order, security, and rapid urban movement.

A final consideration with respect to this petition is that its author established a hierarchical classificatory scheme for public works projects which was directly related intellectually to Alexandre de Laborde and especially Chabrol de Volvic. In considering what public works projects should be undertaken "in a city where a large population is crowded together," and in what order, "one can divide them into a system of three classes." The first would be all those having to do with *"major communications from district to district"*; the second, no less indispensable, would be those reforms whose object was to insure *"public health, sanitation, and . . . commerce"*; and the third, "embellishment."[100] Infrastructural reforms at this time were now closely related to more basic matters than city beatification, as the reform of the city's health and the control of its populace had become the twin preoccupations of so many nineteenth-century elites and intellectuals.

Alphonse Esquiros addressed issues of urban space and the masses in a slightly more theoretical manner. Esquiros, according to Christopher Johnson, represented a spiritualist current in the communist movement of the 1840s. He identified with allusions in the Book of Daniel and the Revelations of St. John: "Foreseeing the sudden destruction of the world of sin, of the world controlled by the rich, and its replacement by an egalitarian New Jerusalem."[101] Esquiros nevertheless shared with the functionalists ideas about the relationship of the morphology of Paris to the social question, demonstrating the wide acceptance of such notions by a broad range of intellectuals. Esquiros observed that some luxury housing construction was taking place in parts of central Paris with the effect that poor people were being displaced, a significant number of whom were moving into the Arcis quarter of the old Seventh Arrondissement (today's Fourth).[102] From 1831 to 1846 this district, the single most densely populated in Paris, boasted some of the capital's worst housing stock and had one of the highest death rates in the city due to cholera.[103] Esquiros noted, too, that the death rate in the Arcis quarter had been ten times higher than the rest of the city's over the previous ten years (he published his book in 1847). Although he did not attribute this to a single cause, he did single out one element that contributed to the grim life in the Arcis quarter: "These narrow, obscure, dirty streets [of the district], where air remains continually immobile, where the pavement never dries, give asylum to a somber population whose character corresponds to the places where it makes its bed."

There was something more troubling than this, however. Esquiros noted that "below this useful class which attends to its subsistence by difficult work each day, there exists another recognizable everywhere by its absolute unraveling, by its profound degradation; a race without name which possesses only its misery and its vices."[104] H.-A. Frégier had used similar language in 1840 to describe workers and districts like the Arcis quarter, and Esquiros may have borrowed from the former's well-known work, which had received favorable mention by the Academy of Moral and Political Sciences.[105] Frégier, an employee of the Prefecture of the Seine Department, set out, in response to a contest sponsored by the Academy of Political and Moral Sciences, to study the most disadvantaged part of the Paris population, the very poor and criminal classes, whom he characterized as the "poor and vicious classes" or simply the "dangerous classes." These were the people who were worse off than the new industrial classes, people living in poor and unhealthy locales mostly in the central districts of Paris; he identified the quarters of Arcis, the Cité, and Saint-Honoré as having an especially large population of such types. Part of Frégier's solution to the social question was to have the government grant financial and legal assistance to building societies in order to construct new housing or convert old buildings and designate these for different classes of the working poor, preferably far removed from the center of Paris where, he argued, land was cheaper.[106] Healthier living quarters, he was convinced, would eradicate the bad moral behavior of the worse off in Paris.

Esquiros also made a useful distinction between employed labor and the group that had fallen out of the labor force, the body that Marx later identified as the lumpen proletariat. Esquiros, too, proposes a spatial and infrastructural solution to their situation. As he wrote: "It is the duty of the administration of society to rehabilitate these fallen beings; there is no doubt that the sordid milieu in which they live contributes to keeping them in their deplorable state."[107] The solution suggested had become by then a standard vision of how to transform space to meet social degradation: pave "the dirty and humid streets," "clean the popular quarters, build public water fountains," introduce "gas lighting to light up all eyes, like sunlight," and, "for the circulation of air in Paris," align houses and enlarge streets. The sense of movement which this program implied was, for Esquiros, the very essence of Paris, a city, wrapped "in its modern envelope," which had always transformed itself while preserving successive layers of its historic past.[108]

CIRCULATION AND A HEALTHY
AND PROSPEROUS CITY

If the social question could be addressed with spatial reforms so could matters of health and commerce, which, although separate issues, were frequently tied together in this literature, as two related themes. Concerning health, public anxiety about urban sanitation and hygiene had been present from the early part of the Restoration and did not have to await the coming of cholera to Paris in 1832. Typical of the link between health, commerce, and the infrastructure was the architect Devert's observation that "the current streets and squares [of Paris] are insufficient not only for the circulation of business but also for that of air, which is necessary for the . . . health of the people."[109] Chabrol de Volvic, as indicated above, reported that certain streets were important for "reasons of public safety, health, or for commerce."[110] Writing a few years earlier, Alexandre de Laborde devoted a major section of his planning text to Paris sidewalk development.[111] As in the case of Chabrol, there is in Laborde no overarching plan for a specific network of Paris roads, only the articulation of a general concept. There is, however, an acknowledgment that existing Paris streets should be equipped with sidewalks, a reform that would facilitate pedestrian movement, health, and the economy. As he observed,

> They [sidewalks] render the cleaning in front of houses as easy as it is today painful. One must live in a country where there are all sorts of sidewalks to sense their advantage; they are even, one can say, of great importance for the social order: indeed, anything that tends to diminish the loss of time and to augment circulation is of very great influence for commerce. One can easily arrive at the conclusion that activity is greatest in cities where communication is superior; everyone is one the move: women will go by themselves to shop at boutiques; a man can complete ten errands rather than one; as walking is easier one completes more business.[112]

Laborde's statement represents a very early and not so common acknowledgment that infrastructural reforms would have a beneficial effect on women. The transformation of the morphology of Paris on the ground level and its liberation of women in their daily rounds would become increasingly important as the century wore on.

Health and commerce formed two separate sections of Laborde's essay. His plan for a public wash house was partly motivated by his wish that authorities regulate the cleaning materials laundresses employed, something that "has recently attracted the attention of several of the capital's medical doctors."[113] And his proposals for water fountains, sewers, and a water-delivery system for all Paris houses were clearly related to the health of the city. As for the connection between commerce and the Paris infrastructure, Laborde referred approvingly to Arthur Dillon's plan for sidewalk construction, which, he also believed, would facilitate shopping and commerce. "Some corporation, some company of capitalists," he wrote, would also be interested in his public works projects, and would participate, to its profit, in their realization.[114]

Clearly grasping the link between circulation and economic development, Laborde proposed a classification of Paris streets that make it clear he regarded sidewalks, in tandem with streets, as an element of circulation throughout the city. It was also a means of reducing all Paris streets to some form of order. From a purely experiential perspective, Laborde believed, appealing to already established administrative norms, that one could distinguish three categories of Paris streets: those ten meters wide or wider, those eight to ten meters, and those less than eight. All, but especially the last two types of street, which were in the majority, should have sidewalks, he advised. The largest streets should too, although there were very few of these in Paris.[115] The similarity between Laborde's classificatory scheme and Chabrol's is obvious.

Laborde called for an additional street reform that would also impose urban order. In a variation of Louis-Sébastien Mercier's suggestion that all vehicles on Paris roads drive on the right side of the street, Laborde proposed that all pedestrians walk on the right side of sidewalks in one direction, so that all pedestrian movement would follow one direction on one side of the street and the opposite direction on the other.[116] Laborde put forth this suggestion, flowing perhaps from the engineer's habit of drawing straight lines on paper, in the larger context of forming a network of "great communication" routes, first, in the capital's most heavily traveled streets and then throughout the city.[117]

The anonymous author of the 1824 *Coup d'oeil sur Paris* also grasped the importance of sidewalks to a healthy capitalist economy. Unlike most reformers of the first half of the nineteenth century, however, who envisaged Paris bridges over the Seine River as free of any obstructions, thus making them purely functional conduits for traffic flow, this author would construct "elegant galleries" on the sidewalks over bridges, thereby stimulating an important commercial traffic. An additional benefit, he suggested, was that such shop stalls would block any suicide attempts from the bridges. As another antisuicide measure, he called for the construction of additional shop stalls at "the most dangerous points" along the quays—meaning, no doubt, where it would be easy to jump into the Seine. These stalls were intended for the sale of books, prints, and posters.[118] On the other hand, this writer did have ideas related to Paris circulation that were portentous both in their functionality and potential effectiveness. All revolved around public transit. He suggested, first, that all Paris regional stagecoaches be barred from the center of the city. These "rolling houses divided into apartments," as he characterized them, were not really "public coaches." His implication was that they were too expensive, even with second- and first-class compartments (hence the allusion to apartments), for the masses; they did not serve urban transit, being destined for trips outside Paris; and they were too large for the narrow streets of central Paris. Rather, such vehicles should be housed in large depots at strategic points in the city, and clients could take them from one of four locations, where they would be constructed: the new place de la Bastille, the esplanade of the Invalides, and the heights of the Faubourgs-Saint-Denis and Saint-Jacques.[119]

More important and sweeping than this suggestion, however, was the author's plan for a mass transit service in Paris, a proposal that preceded by four years the advent of mass public transit in the capital. Noting that Paris had experienced significant spatial growth over the last fifty years and that cabs, even with regulated fares, were too expensive for the common people, the author issued a call to government authorities to create a public transit system inside Paris destined primarily for the masses. "Let us occupy ourselves with the general mass; it is always the poorest while it is also the hardest working." Such a public transit system should have two essential characteristics: it should provide regular daily service, and its first lines should run north-south and east-west crossing at the center of the city. Secondary lines could be added, diagonally to the major ones, as demand warranted. Anticipating the "great cross" of Paris, the north-south and east-west boulevards traversing the city that Haussmann created, the point of his scheme was to connect the principal extremities of the city with its center.[120]

Others in this earlier period also saw Paris streets as the essential elements of a viable city and, as in the case of the architect, B. A. H. Devert, appealed to the authority of the abbé Laugier to lend authority to their proposals for new longer and well-aligned streets.[121] The important architectural writer and permanent secretary of the Royal Academy of Fine Arts, Antoine-Chrysostome Quatremère de Quincy, even though wedded to classicism, proffered an important definition of streets which spanned both an old and new ideals of street construction and thus may serve as a last example before we turn to the 1840s reformers. In his *Dictionnaire historique d'architecture,* published in 1832, Quatremère de Quincy defined the ideal street as made up of two elements, the functional and the aesthetic.[122] Premodern streets, like premodern cities, he observed, were not planned; they grew organically, by chance. As cities expanded, however, and new quarters formed, some form of planning became common. This applied to streets, and the most impressive modern streets were those planned to be long and well aligned—features that, in part, constituted "their beauty." Such streets existed in cities with considerable new building under way—he gave as an example Turin—or in a city like London, which had burned in 1666 and been rebuilt following certain planning principles. London's Oxford street was a model city street for Quatremère de Quincy. As for an ideal street system, he cited the case of Palermo, whose major streets formed a cross running through the city center. Quatremère de Quincy also regarded a certain gaiety, both in the form of new streets and in the architecture of the buildings and constructions on them, as a second key ingredient of their beauty. Thus, while the aesthetic aspect of street construction remains a central characteristic of Quatremère de Quincy's thinking, the essential form of the street—long and well aligned—was in keeping with what was becoming a modern vision of urban streets. And it was considerations of form, sometimes stripped of any aesthetic connotations or when aesthetic goals clearly became secondary to form and function, that came to dominate the thinking of the 1840s.

Those who focused primarily on health matters also observed a link between the city's material structure and health. In 1822 Claude Lachaise, an important medical statistician, ascribed the high mortality rates of some Paris arrondissements to their narrow and dirty streets, with tightly packed houses constructed on each side, streets that blocked the circulation of the air and sunlight considered at the time essential to health. His remedy was for all Paris to follow the model of well-to-do arrondissements—he used the Second as an example—where "the streets are aligned, and have above all a sufficient width, direction, and convenient slopes." Such streets, combined with gardens, "maintain the constant purity [of the atmosphere]."[123] This was also the time that important public hygienists like Alphonse Chevalier, Jean-Baptiste Parent-Duchâtelet, and Louis Villermé were beginning to discover the close connection between the physical environment and the health of the population.

In a report to the Paris Health Council in 1824, Victor de Moléon typified both the strengths and weakness of the medical community's approach to public health. Moléon also identified air and sunlight as the two most important agents in an individual's health. People, he reported, must always be placed in situations in which they can "habitually breath the purest air and receive for the longest possible time the invigorating rays of the sun." It was important, therefore, "that the construction of houses and the disposition of streets, of villages and of cities, be considered as an object of the highest interest for public health." He concluded his essay not with a blueprint for street or housing construction, however, but with a recommendation for deep administrative intervention into individual housing, its internal and external conditions, to determine its sanitary status.[124] This was a rather daring proposal, as it prescribed a vital government interest over individual property ownership rights. While it was beyond the competence of medical experts to do more than suggest street and infrastructural reforms, these writers were important in identifying the material environment as a key to health.[125] From here it was not a great step to calling for government intervention at all levels of municipal life to assure public health and tranquility.

Cholera was the major health issue in Paris after 1832. What is notable from the point of view of planning is that the disease did not add anything

The rue Chanoinesse, on the Île de la Cité. This street, which still exists today, was precisely the kind of narrow street that nineteenth-century urban reformers wanted to eliminate because it blocked air and sunlight from penetrating the urban fabric.
Charles Marville. Photothèque des musées de la ville de Paris

new to the understanding that the physical environment was critical to the health of the city. The disease was far more important in the planning perspectives of the Saint-Simonians and is therefore considered in chapter 4. Here one should simply note that cholera reinforced the belief of many functionalists that the key to the health of Paris was the reform of living and sanitary conditions in the disadvantaged areas of the city. Often the city's infrastructure, especially its street system, was seen as an entry into environmental transformation. Typical was the observation of the anonymous author of a plan to open a major street in central Paris that cholera had made it more obvious that authorities and builders had to construct larger streets and regulate the height of buildings so that air and sunlight could circulate more freely,[126] or the comment of Levicomte and Rolland that the surest means of preventing such diseases was to "enlarge the streets, open up squares, [and] increase the distribution of water."[127]

The general state of sanitation in Paris was closely related to health issues. The thinking on this subject of Guillot, the associate inspector general of sanitation and lighting mentioned earlier, is especially relevant, as it connects health, cleanliness, and public order in ways that are typical of many urban reformers during the first half of the nineteenth century. Mary Douglas's insights on dirt and disorder, discussed in the last chapter with respect to Arthur Dillon, are also relevant in understanding Guillot's project for dirt removal from Paris. For Douglas, the removal of dirt was understood as "a positive effort to organize the environment." "Pollution ideas," she explained, "work in the life of society at two levels, one largely instrumental, one expressive. At the first level . . . we find people trying to influence one another's behaviors." For those who hold political power, "the ideal order of society is guarded by dangers which threaten transgressors. These danger-beliefs are as much threats which one man uses to coerce another as dangers which he himself fears to incur by his own lapses from righteousness." At this level, according to Douglas, the "whole universe is harnessed to men's attempts to force one another into good citizenship. Thus we find that certain moral values are upheld and certain social rules defined by beliefs in dangerous contagion." At the second level pollution beliefs acquired a symbolic value, so "some pollutions are used as analogies for expressing a general view of the social order."[128]

Translating Douglas's understanding of pollution and dirt to Paris, Donald Reid observed that the great effort of Parisian authorities to control the elimination of urban refuse through the construction of an urban sewer system was related not only to fears of disease but also to the symbolic and metaphorical relationship for the middle classes of the underground, the site of refuse and dirt, to the lower classes, crime and pestilence. He wrote that "sanitation and sovereignty were never far apart" in the Paris of the Old Regime and the nineteenth century and that the politics of sanitation reform were linked to the belief that the state could impose order and its moral sensibilities on the lower classes.[129] With respect, moreover, to purely physical conditions in Paris, there was, from the mid-eighteenth century on, great concern on the part of the city, private entrepreneurs, and property owners, as Barrie Ratcliffe showed, with the removal of sewage—the elimination of the "fecal peril"—from the capital. Fecal peril, so called because it included noxious emanations from cesspools and the city dump and the fear of miasmas, appeared especially serious as the population of Paris continued to expand significantly over the first half of the nineteenth century.[130] It would appear from the language employed by Guillot that he was as much concerned with exercising moral control and influence over the common people of the city as with establishing cleanliness in Paris.

On one level Guillot addressed issues of sanitation. He advised public authorities to concern themselves with "the means to clear the cul-de-sacs, the passages, the narrow streets, the alleys and other places where sanitation wagons cannot enter but which are, however, precisely those places where Parisians prefer to leave their garbage."[131] He noted, too, the numerous complaints from people living in the quarter of Ménilmontant, in today's Eleventh and Twentieth Arrondissements, the rue Château-Landon, in today's Tenth, the rue de la Pologne, today the rue de l'Arcade in the Eighth, and other places of exceptionally filthy streets. To address such matters he proposed, first, that depots be established at several convenient points throughout Paris—exactly where was a detail to be worked out later—and that barges transport refuse from these locations to strategic sites just outside the city. Second, he counseled an increase in the number of sanitation inspectors, bringing their strength up to twenty-four. Part of his argument for this reform was that there were currently forty-eight police bureaus in Paris, and that somehow the establishment of twenty four sanitation inspectors was not unreasonable.[132]

This linkage of sanitation inspectors to the number of police offices brings us to a second level of importance in Guillot's plan. Guillot wanted the government to grant sanitation inspectors the right to issue legal warnings and fines to those who violated the sanitation code of Paris. Moreover, he also called for greater cooperation between the police and sanitation inspectors, and, at a minimum, easier and friendlier contact between the two groups. This amounted to granting some police power to sanitation inspectors. Guillot's aim was to "multiply surveillance, and have it in some sense present everywhere." To this end sanitation agents should have the right to issue written citations. Moreover, as his office was responsible for lighting the street lamps at night, Guillot hoped that a larger sanitation corps would be able to keep as many lamps lit at night as possible through a "surveillance exercised . . . in all directions."[133] That he imagined a harmony among sanitation, lighting, order, cleanliness, and finally, the moral behavior of certain classes is evident in the concluding statement of his proposal. This was the last argument in the concluding chapter of his plan, which aimed to demonstrate a compatibility between police and sanitation department functions. Both, he wrote, wished to eliminate "the hideous spectacle of those men, the shame of decent manners and of our civilization, men one finds at every moment relieving themselves in public and without shame of the most humiliating functions of human nature. . . . Sanitation is no less interested than morality in the repression of this disgusting abuse." As an aid to this (moral and sanitary) reform he would establish free public latrines at several places in Paris.[134] Though he appeared, perhaps, to consider that workers and others far from home might need public toilet facilities, his moral condemnation was typical of middle-class values and perceptions of the Other, in this case, the lower classes.

THE IDEOLOGY OF CIRCULATION

When we move from the 1820s and 1830s to the decade of the 1840s we notice an important new emphasis on the nature of the modern city. It was a decade dominated by an "ideology of mobility," a time when there emerged, in the words of Bernard Lepetit, "a current of thought which made circulation the key to spatial organization."[135] Like Lepetit, I too would characterize the 1840s as the decade when the ideology of movement and circulation came to dominate urban planning theory and Paris came to be perceived as a site of constant movement. I would add, however, that we should distinguish a two-step process in the emergence of this ideology. Writers during the Restoration and the early years of the July Monarchy also came to see movement and circulation as a vital element of life in Paris. The difference between the two periods was that the earlier writers were just beginning to see circulation as one of several factors related to the city's well-being. They had not yet reduced circulation so completely to the key underlying element of the city's life, nor had they developed systematic and theoretical texts that placed circulation at the center of their analysis—that was the hallmark of the later writers—but they were clearly heading in this direction. We have already seen the value that Chabrol de Volvic attached to this element of urban life. Moreover, alongside circulation in some texts, there is a second major theme of urban planning, namely, a recognition of the importance to successful city life of a vital and stable urban core of public space, activities, and services—the clearly recognizable heart of the city, as it were.

The circulatory system of Paris, its network of streets and boulevards, came to dominate planning texts in the late 1830s and remained the central characteristic of these texts through the great reforms of Haussmann and Napoleon III and beyond. While planners from the earlier part of the century imagined circulation and communication through Paris to be an important mark of the modern commercial and populous city, several issues of the late 1830s and early 1840s resulted in an intense rethinking of the functions and spatial configuration of Paris, as intellectuals and government officials tried to master the new forces impinging upon the life of the capital. The outcome of this speculation was the elevation of urban circulation and the formation of a powerful city center to central tropes in the writings of many urban intellectuals trying to understand the modern city.

In addition to pondering the significant demographic expansion at this time, with its resulting housing shortages, increased population densities, and the increased visibility of the lower classes in the central districts, authorities debated the siting of newly planned railway stations and the expansion and possible transfer of the central food market, les Halles centrales. But what is especially dramatic about 1840 and the years that followed was that, as Christopher Johnson noted, "suddenly and dramatically, the social question exploded the nation with a torrent of ideas and events the historical impact of which went far beyond her boundaries." Several powerful and influential works of social criticism were published in 1840, among them Louis Blanc's *Organisation du Travail,* Pierre-Joseph Proudhon's *Qu-est-ce la propriété?,* Étienne Cabet's *Voyage en Icarie,* and Louis René Villermé's *Tableau de l'état physique et moral des ouvriers employés dans les manufactures de cotton, de laine et de soie,* an investigation of the condition of textile workers. Communist literature also began to circulate widely, works by Alphonse Esquiros, Abbé Constant, and J.-J. Phillot. At the same time as this radical literature was being spread, violence threatened Paris as some twenty to thirty thousand workers struck in the region between June and September 1840.[136] Middle-class agitation for an extension of the suffrage also extended to the working class, and demonstrations in favor of this reform attracted some twelve hundred workers in Belleville, a suburb of Paris, on July 1, 1840.

Parisian and national officials also worried about foreign affairs, as France found itself facing a coalition of European powers over the Eastern Question and, fearing a possible foreign attack, launched a national debate in 1840 on whether to build a fortified wall and free-standing forts around Paris. The fortifications question, which added to a sense of crisis during the 1840s, potentially linked purely spatial issues—the effect a wall enclosing Paris would have on urbanism within the city—with national defense. What is interesting about the fortifications, about which there was considerable controversy while they were being constructed, is that purely spatial issues, such as their impact on the physical layout and structure of Paris, were not primary; proponents and opponents of the project focused for the most part on national defense and on the relationship of a possible wall to internal control over the mass of the Paris population, which also became linked with the fortifications debate. While the fortifications debate did not generate an important literature on the internal form and structure of Paris, it is worth exploring briefly for a sense of the sometimes subtle relationship between political questions and the dynamics of space.

The idea for a fortified wall protecting Paris goes back to at least 1689, when the famous military planner and engineer and Marshal of France, Sébastien Vauban, studied constructing a military wall around Paris.[137] The idea for a wall became an obsession with public officials, however, following the defeat of Napoleon I and the entry of foreign troops into the capital. A Commission de défense du royaume explored the issue from 1818 to 1820 and in 1821 recommended the construction of a system of fortifications around Paris. Nothing so bold was undertaken at the time, but debate on the topic continued into the 1830s. In 1836 a new government under Adolphe Thiers pushed for the construction of a wall, but it was not until the summer of 1840 that a decision was made to proceed with fortified defenses around Paris. Foreign affairs decided the issue. At that time the Egyptian Mehemet Ali revolted against Ottoman rule. Thiers, who had been in power only briefly as head of the government in 1836, was prime minister once more, and he committed his government to supporting Ali. England and Austria, however, backed the Ottoman Empire, and for the moment France found itself isolated diplomatically. Under these circumstances Thiers obtained support from his cabinet, while the legislature was on vacation, to begin work on constructing a wall as an emergency measure. Thiers fell from power in October 1840 because of his belligerent foreign policy stance, but his successor, Marshal Soult, put the fortifications issue up for discussion before the legislature in order to obtain funds for the completion of the project. Discussion began on January 13, 1841, and the project was approved on April 3, 1841. A fortified wall and a series of detached forts around Paris were completed by the end of 1845.

The discussion surrounding the construction of the wall is interesting for what is says and does not say about perceptions of space in Paris. François Arago, the scientist and liberal political activist, argued that a wall around Paris was, in effect, a means to oppress Parisians, because the government could bombard an unruly city. As for the military logic of a wall, he noted that, in case of war, a wall would inevitably draw the enemy to Paris, where a large portion of the French military would have been tied up in defense of the city. Alphonse Lamartine, the poet and another well-known political liberal under the July Monarchy, led the opposition to the wall, which he characterized as a "counter-revolutionary" construction. He too believed that a fortified wall around Paris would only concentrate an enemy around the capital, whose fall would thus assure the defeat of France. "France's force is not in its walls: it is in its people," he wrote.[138] Michel Chevalier, a prominent Saint-Simonian, adopted a broader perspective, pointing out that preparations for war would only lead to war. The regime, he opined, would be better off developing its commercial exchanges, its railroad system, and European unity, all better guarantors of peace than a defensive wall.[139] Similar arguments are found in Jéronyme Baissas, one of many independent intellectuals confronting the fortifications question, who pointed out that the French government could use the fortifications to subdue Paris and that an enemy at the city's walls would certainly do so. Fortifications would be a permanent threat to civilization and liberty, as "the anger of power would always be suspended over our splendid monuments, over the productions of genius, over the heads and homes of the citizens of Paris." In more practical terms, fortifications would permit an enemy that had advanced to Paris to cut the city's food source in a siege, would inevitably lead to an increase in armaments, and, as Paris would be cut off from the provinces, would adversely affect provincial industrial development.[140]

Patricia O'Brien, who studied the fortifications question, pointed out that those in favor of a wall around Paris saw it as useful precisely as a weapon against urban rebellion.[141] And Karl Marx, interpreting the meaning of the wall and its architect, Thiers, from the hindsight of class warfare in France in 1871, quoted a comment the prime minister had made to the Chamber of Deputies in March 1840 to counter republican suggestions that the wall could be used to suppress Parisian liberties: "What!" Thiers exclaimed, "to fancy that any works of fortification could ever endanger liberty! And first of all you calumniate any possible government in supposing that it could some day attempt to maintain itself by bombarding the capital; . . . but that government would be a hundred times more impossible after its victory than before." Marx concluded that "no government would ever have dared to bombard Paris from the forts but that government which had previously surrendered those forts to the Prussians," referring to what happened in 1871 when a provincial French army led by Thiers and supported by Bismark did attack and suppress a popular uprising in the capital.[142]

César Daly, the editor of the important architectural journal *La Revue générale de l'architecture et des travaux publics,* took a broad perspective toward the fortifications, which considered space as well as social issues. The wall, he wrote, was a colossally unproductive expenditure; the government would be wiser to invest its funds in the construction and improvement of its means of communication—roads and canals, for instance. Communication routes not only were productive for their use in commercial exchanges but could also serve the national defense, and he gave as an example the development of canals around Paris. These would stimulate and facilitate commerce while potentially serving as defensive trenches around the capital in case of war. The construction of a fortified wall designed to protect the capital, moreover, would create serious social dislocation within. It would attract a considerable number of workers to Paris, who, once the project was completed, would remain there, seduced by the city's attractions, but without employment—a situation that would not occur if the public works were directed toward productive enterprises. Daly also saw a relationship between the construction of the wall, the increased demand for stone, and the rise in prices of building materials—all of which would have a deleterious effect on constructions within Paris.[143]

Another intellectual outside the government, A. Rabusson, analyzed the relationship of the wall to purely spacial matters within Paris. Once it was constructed the wall did impinge upon the growth of Paris and did transform the capital into a physically closed rather than an open city.[144] Writing in 1841, Rabusson, however, did not believe that the wall would block the movement of the population of Paris beyond the fortifications. Addressing an observation by contemporaries that a significant portion of the Paris population was migrating in a westwardly direction, away from the city's central quarters, Rabusson, like many intellectuals of the time, wished to counter this trend. It was his suggestion that if a wall were to be erected—and he was not opposed to its construction—than it had to be done in tandem with a massive public works program inside Paris. Only a reform of the Paris infrastructure, especially in the city's center, would anchor the city's population, and a compact population, with little incentive to leave Paris, would be easier to defend than one that sprawled beyond its fortifications.[145] The special mark of Rabusson's analysis was his awareness that any massive construction ringing Paris had to take into consideration the future growth of the city's population and address that likelihood. The pseudonymous Fourierist Perreymond had a similar understanding of the spatial problems of Paris in relation to plans for fortifications.[146]

The older vision of Paris—the city as a site of magnificent monuments—did not disappear, however, even when it took into account the relationship

of the wall to the physical form and structure of the city. In 1849, Félix Pigeory published an appreciation of the contemporary monuments of Paris.[147]
His book represented an overarching view of the capital. Imagining the wall
from on high, he concluded that "the architectural bearing of this wall from a
bird's-eye view is admirable. Its regular and pure lines have an important cachet which astounds the senses. They envelop Paris in a worthy and noble
manner. They frame the city with a wonderful distinctiveness." The appearance of the wall, especially following the planting of grass, would be "majestic." As for the stated aim of the wall, Pigeory noted that if enemies did attack
Paris, "the fortifications [would] be their tomb."[148] His survey of Paris monuments was thoroughly superficial and laudatory and his analysis of the fortifications completely uncritical. It is instructive, however, as the opinion of
someone who clung to an older vision of Paris, of Paris as an outdoor mu-
seum, a city of beautiful monuments.

Closer to the ground, other intellectuals grappled with more modern urban concerns, among them the displacement question, alluded to earlier,
which refers to the observation by contemporaries by the late 1830s that the
well-to-do population of Paris, in a reaction to the overcrowding and the poor
condition of streets in the city's center, was moving in significant numbers to
the north and west, creating there new quarters with better housing, better
streets, wide boulevards, and easier access to the countryside. These districts
were generally the recipients of superior municipal services, such as street
cleaning and paving, and new public buildings, like the Stock Exchange, the
Opera House, and the new Lyric Theater. This phenomenon worried many
intellectuals, who identified a notable imbalance of municipal services between the Left and Right Bank quarters and the general neglect by the government of the infrastructure of Left Bank districts. Intellectuals and government insiders expressed the fear that the Left Bank could become deserted,
except for its poorer population and students. Social inequality was potentially beginning to assume, the argument went, a spatial dimension. Unlike
the fortifications debate, moreover, the displacement question generated a
considerable literature on the infrastructure and physical layout of Paris.

So significant did this expansion appear that, on November 20, 1839, the
Minister of the Interior created a commission to study it.[149] While a chorus of
public intellectuals and government officials adopted this perspective, not
everyone involved in the debate agreed that some form of government action
was required to redress the imbalance of the Paris population, nor did they
accept the main arguments given for displacement. An anonymous writer,
identifying himself as an "inhabitant of the Right Bank," questioned the very
notion that the population of a modern city had to be spatially balanced

through all its parts. He noted, too, that the Left Bank already had a large number of public buildings and that it was normal to construct new ones on the opposite side of the Seine. He concluded by observing that population movement throughout the city was a normal phenomenon in a time of population growth and should not be regarded in the negative terms implied by the expression "displacement of the population."[150]

Alphonse Chevalier, a member of the government commission studying the displacement question, did not doubt the phenomenon, but he believed it had nothing to do with the poor infrastructure of the center of Paris. Rather, the presence of factories with steam-driven machines in central Paris quarters and it was the latter that prompted the rich to leave the historic parts of Paris for newer neighborhoods. He gave as an example the introduction of factories with steam-powered machines in the Marais and the Faubourg-Saint-Antoine, both in the old Eighth Arrondissement of Paris, which extended as far as the present-day place de la Nation in the Eleventh. Characterizing the feelings of the well-to-do person, Chevalier wrote: "He is fleeing the noise; he fears the bad smells; he dreads the smoke produced by steam-driven machines; the incessant racket of machinery terrifies him and tires his ears." It was these machines and not narrow streets or overcrowding that were causing the affluent to leave central Paris. It would appear that Chevalier is a reliable contemporary eye-witness because, while it is true that traditional handicraft industries still dominated in Paris at this time, some large-scale mechanized industries, like machinery and metallurgy, were developing in central Right Bank districts. They were attracted to the central quarters because good means of transportation, including adequate roads, were still lacking in other parts of the city, and distribution of production would be easier from the center. The solution Chevalier offered was for government authorities to ban these new factories from central Paris and relegate them to the outskirts of the capital. This would address displacement and also benefit workers, he believed, by causing them to move closer to their employment beyond the city walls, where taxes were lower than within the city.[151]

Whether or not contemporaries accepted displacement as abnormal or accepted the major reasons offered to explain it, the issue generated a considerable amount of theoretical speculation, both within and outside the government, on what constituted the fundamental material nature of modern Paris. While details differed from thinker to thinker, a consensus emerged from this debate that a modern city needed a powerful central anchor and an efficient street system connecting all parts of the city and connecting the city to the national territory and beyond; that authorities must reject partial or individual urban ameliorations and devise a comprehensive plan for infrastructural reform and stick to it; and that the creation of a modern circulatory system and vital city center required a massive public works program. Furthermore, it was clear from these speculations that city planning was beginning to be seen, even if only dimly, as a potentially scientific enterprise. And all solutions addressed the need to maintain order and pursue rational efficiency and maximum use of time for production through the organization of the city and the construction of a collective infrastructure. That concern, expressed in fully developed theoretical urban planning texts, became a hallmark of early modern urbanism, although the program they espoused would have to await the coming of Haussmann to be realized.

The displacement-of-the-population debate took place over two relatively distinct periods. The first, and most important, was 1839–43, which produced the first cluster of mature pioneering texts of early modern urban planning in Paris. Among those producing representative texts, from the point of view of their theoretical insights, rigor, and contemporary recognition, were several members of the investigatory commission of 1839, notably Jacques Lanquetin, Alphonse Chevalier, and Ernest Chabrol-Chaméane. Independent intellectuals included, most prominently, A. Rabusson and Hippolyte Meynadier; Louis Daubanton, the former official of Chabrol de Volvic's administration; and the Fourierists, Victor Considerant and the pseudonymous Perreymond. The decade from 1843 to 1853, which constitutes the second period, was characterized by the acceptance among leading urban thinkers of ideas already worked out earlier, the addition of a few important fresh theoretical insights, and the integration of the new thinking in the conclusions of a study commission on the Paris infrastructure formed by Napoleon III in 1853, the Siméon Commission.

In order to impose some conceptual order on this material and also avoid unnecessary repetition, I will take the ideas of Chabrol-Chaméane and Hippolyte Meynadier as emblematic of the new urbanism of the functionalists of the period ending in 1843. Chabrol-Chaméane was a member of, and the reporter for, a subcommission formed within the 1839 government commission. His group was charged to study the condition of the three Left Bank arrondissements of the time, the Tenth, Eleventh, and Twelfth. Of the many writers dealing with Paris urbanism, Chabrol-Chaméane, while by no means unknown, has received the least attention by modern historians.[152] Yet his report, not as detailed or comprehensive as the analyses of Rabusson or Lanquetin, nevertheless announced several themes with a decidedly modern resonance, many of which are also found in their works and the projects of other planners, and he did so in a very concise manner.[153] Three themes stand out in Chabrol-Chaméane's analysis: the role of the center of Paris in the city's life, the significance of an urban communication-circulatory system, and the necessity of central and global planning. With respect to a theory of the importance of the center of Paris, its old historic locales around the île de la Cité and the île Saint-Louis, Chabrol-Chaméane assumed a Newtonian perspective common in this period, the acceptance of a gravitational metaphor that would receive, according to Bernard Lepetit, its most comprehensive development a year later in the writings of Jean Reynaud, a Saint-Simonian.[154] But while Reynaud imagined a capital city, any capital city, as the center of a gravitational field within the larger territory, Chabrol-Chaméane represented the historic center of Paris as a force of attraction for the entire capital. Extrapolating from Newtonian physics, Chabrol-Chaméane assumed that what had made Paris vital was its stable central anchor and that any destabilization of its position through urban sprawl would threaten its viability. This was the common assumption of all the thinkers named above, but what distinguished Chabrol-Chaméane was his theoretical understanding of why this was so.

The function of the historic center of Paris, according to Chabrol-Chaméane, was to provide the population with essential public services and public monuments. This part of Paris was the site of important churches, fountains, the central market, and the principal hospital of the city. He did not list other buildings or functions as examples, but his point was that the important administrative, ceremonial, judicial, and health services of the city were easily accessible to all because of their location in the geographic center of Paris. The creation of sprawl would necessitate the duplication of such services elsewhere, closer to the location of the population shift. Not only would this be expensive, but the process would also create a new city alongside the traditional one. It is not an exaggeration to suggest that Chabrol-Chaméane intuitively understood that the very urban nature of Paris would change and that the old historic city would decline and die if the sprawl continued. Chabrol-Chaméane also understood something about a city's center one hundred years before Richard Meier worked out a communications theory of urban growth and explained more fully the importance of city center services in attracting people to central urban locations.[155] According to Meier cities formed around central places because it was in these locations, easily accessible by efficient transportation, that one found a pool of services, institutions, talent, information, and the like which were essential to the effective functioning of the city. Communications of all kinds naturally coalesced around an urban core, according to Meier. This was the insight that Chabrol-Chaméane shared with people like A. Rabusson and the entire 1840s generation of planners.[156] One solution to the displacement problem, therefore, was for the government to recognize the role of the urban core in the life of the city and plan the construction of new buildings in its proximity.

The greater part of Chabrol-Chaméane's report focused on urban communication. He called for the development of better communication routes between the Left and Right Banks, including new bridges and the utilization of the quays as circulation routes, and for more efficient communication streets within the Left Bank, which did not, he believed, have as many large new streets as its sister bank. His guiding principle, also shared by the 1840s reformers, was that all parts of Paris, including its extremities, be linked with one another and with the center. Streets and boulevards, moreover, should be well lit for security, supplemented by a municipal guard. In addition to construction work on streets and boulevards, Chabrol-Chaméane proposed the building of more public schools—although largely for the middle classes—the relocation and construction of a new royal library on the Left Bank (close to the centers of learning), the delivery of water throughout Paris, and the utilization by the administration of unproductive property, such as convents and prisons, for the planning of new housing within the city. While not specific with respect to the role of the government and private entrepreneurs in these constructions, it was clear Chabrol-Chaméane envisaged cooperation between the two and significant government outlays. He did suggest, however, that the government grant tax rebates to building entrepreneurs who participated in publicly useful projects and, anticipating Haussmann's method of financing new constructions, proposed that the government borrow the funds necessary for public works projects.

Equally modern was Chabrol-Chaméane's conception of the requirements of a comprehensive plan of urban public works projects, beginning with the assumption that such a plan would govern the underlying reform of the city, which he designated as the establishment of "the public system of streets and boulevards in order to facilitate circulation and openings."[157] The need for global planning is a leitmotif that runs through the planning texts at this time. What was prescient about Chabrol-Chaméane's conception was his insight that all planning for new building constructions, especially new streets, anticipate future population growth in Paris. What this meant with respect to new housing was that the administration should develop old and new quarters equally. As for new streets and boulevards, he counseled that they be *"larger and more orderly even than the most recent ones."* He concluded his thoughts on planning and its relation to solving the displacement problem with these words: "The question that we believe to be most important and which governs the entire problem may be reduced in great part to a question of the public roads and their alignment [and] new constructions in the old quarters. "[158]

Other urban intellectuals had come to similar conclusions concerning the global requirements of modern Paris and differed only with respect to details or extent of exposition. A. Rabusson put the displacement question in a long historical context and called for the transfer of Les Halles from the Right to the Left Bank and an for extension of the wall surrounding Paris to accommodate the increased population, items not in Chabrol-Chaméane's program. Otherwise, he too placed great emphasis on a vital city center, communication routes throughout Paris, and monuments as important points of urban attraction, reminding his readers that Paris was simultaneously a commercial and a fine arts capital.[159] Jacques Lanquetin criticized Rabusson's projects as too "radical," but he also wanted the center of Paris reformed for better circulation, streets and boulevards to link all parts of the city, the construction of new housing and boutiques, and the establishment of a global plan that would guide the government in its direction and control of the large public works projects he envisaged.[160] Daubanton proposed public works projects not suggested by the others—for example, the decentralization of the central market to points near railway stations; the joining of the île Saint-Louis to the île de la Cité, linking thereby the quai de Bourbon with that of la Cité on the Right Bank side of the islands and the quai d'Orléans with the quai de l'Archevêché on the Left Bank side; and the construction of a bridge between the eastern end of the île Saint Louis and the île Louviers, establishing thereby a direct communication between the Faubourg-Saint-Antoine on the Right Bank and the Faubourgs-Saint-Jacques and Saint-Germain on the Left—but he likewise wanted the city to undertake the revitalization of its center with significant public works and a comprehensive program of street reform.[161] Hippolyte Meynadier stands apart from these others in the wide scope of his project for a new Paris and his influence on other planners, most notably the members of the Siméon Commission, established by Napoleon III in 1853 to plan, in part, a comprehensive reform of the Paris infrastructure.

In 1843 Meynadier, an official in the national Beaux-Arts Department at the time of the Restoration and a contributor during the July Monarchy to the *Revue générale de l'architecture et des travaux publics,* the leading nineteenth-century French architectural journal, published *Paris sous le point de vue pittoresque et monumental ou Éléments d'un plan général d'ensemble de travaux d'art et d'utilité publique.* Meynadier was not an architect—he had headed the office of theaters in the administration—[162]but his book covered architectural as well as infrastructural reforms. In this sense it represents, as Bernard Marchand observed, a transition between Old Regime concerns for architectural beauty and an urbanism attentive to infrastructural reforms.[163] His infrastructural reforms were remarkably forward looking, however. Lavedan characterized the book as the product of empirical research into the structure and appearance of Paris and a realistic assessment of what urban reforms and new constructions could be accomplished.[164] Meynadier's work, however, was also informed by a theoretical vision of Paris as a circulatory system of roads and an understanding of the close relationship of these roads to the city's monuments and public buildings. In its global vision of the city and attention to architectural and infrastructural details, the book represented an important moment in the planning literature on Paris.

Its two main goals, according to Meynadier, were to plan "a system of major new arterial roads [streets and boulevards]" and to examine and choose "the most favorable sites for [the city's] monuments of art and of public utility that will be built or reconstructed."[165] The treatise that follows this introductory statement is a rather detailed and comprehensive plan spelling out all the projects necessary to reform the Paris infrastructure and its important buildings. Meynadier's starting point, worthy of special note, was to assert forcefully the necessity for and the manner of establishing comprehensive planning for the modern city, especially its foundational road network. Moreover, no public buildings of any kind could be planned without first laying out a new system of major streets and boulevards in Paris, which would serve as both an aesthetic and a functional setting for buildings. Meynadier's insistence on planning the streets and boulevards of Paris as an integral part of the plan for buildings and the reform of the entire city is a core idea of the 1840s planning texts.

Meynadier's ideas were informed by a dynamic conception of the space needs of the capital. Unlike many twentieth- and twenty-first-century professional planners, who consider isolated or individual projects, Meynadier visualized Paris as a unity. Part of this premise, his starting point for city planning, was the principle that those responsible for Paris urbanism had to devise a "general comprehensive plan" for public works that considered every part of the city simultaneously. Lavedan pointed out that Meynadier's book "is not illustrated with any plan"; but this misses an important point. Meynadier, in a modern-sounding, scientific manner, outlined the requirements for constructing a comprehensive city plan. While this is the aspect of Meynadier's work that Lavedan characterized as "purely empirical," Meynadier's suggested *method* for devising a global city plan represented an important understanding of the requirements of urban planning.[166] His approach to constructing a general plan included the following elements: the urban planner must visit the different sites of urban projects at different hours of the day; examine "attentively" the daily flow in neighborhoods, its daily comings and goings; penetrate "the nooks and crannies of all the streets"; calculate the time it takes to move about different parts of the city; study "the back and forth movements of the plebeian masses on the public roads"; project the present and future needs of each quarter; and explore "the nature of the interests which are especially concerned with such and such a point of this great home [Paris] where all the questions of the social order are worked out."

In Meynadier's prescription to explore the daily life of a quarter as a requirement of urban planning, one can detect, even if faintly, an awareness of something that, according to Henri Lefebvre, modern urban planners under capitalism tend to overlook, namely, the requirements, in Lefebvre's terminology, of *"l'espace vécu,"* that is, the community of real human beings with their subjective needs.[167] Meynadier concluded by recommending not merely comprehensive planning for Paris but central planning as well, which would take into account "the community of insights and interests that it is necessary to establish between the State, the City, and the Civil List [the personal property of the sovereign] in order to have them operate . . . as if they were a single and unique master of a vast plan."[168] Obviously, however, planning Paris in this scheme was the preserve of elites, no matter how much research they undertook into the daily life of the city.

Meynadier's "system of major new communication routes," designed by him to bind the city together, as well as to improve its economic health, sanitation, and aesthetic quality, consisted of four new major roads in Paris on the Right Bank and two on the Left Bank.[169] The first he named the "grande rue du centre," a "monumental" street to be built between the rue Saint-Martin and the rue Saint-Denis and ending at the place du Châtelet. These were clearly the future boulevard de Sébastopol and the boulevard de Strasbourg. Also on the Right Bank he would construct the grande rue de l'Arsenal, which would start at the quai des Célestins and the rue Saint-Paul and end at the Bourse, thus vitalizing the southeast of Paris, and the grande rue du Nord-Est, a street that would extend from the barrière de Ménilmontant to the Louvre and form one line of a hexagon as it crossed over the grande rue du Centre and the grande rue de l'Arsenal. These streets were never constructed, but the last major road Meynadier proposed for the Right Bank was. This was the grande rue de l'Hôtel de Ville, the major east-west Paris street begun by Napoleon I, the (present-day) rue de Rivoli, with slight variations in its trajectory. Completing his grand circulatory scheme Meynadier proposed for the Left Bank a continuation of the grande rue du Centre from the pont Saint Michel to the barrière d'Enfer, a major arterial road that corresponds to the present-day boulevard Saint Michel, and another, perpendicular to the latter, which corresponds approximately to the current boulevard Saint Germain.[170] In a narrow sense, Meynadier's plan for new major and secondary Paris streets addressed the displacement question, which he believed would be redressed with a balanced circulatory system between the Left and Right Banks of the city. It also represented an awareness that major streets enhanced commercial values, created a healthier physical environment, and effectively showed off monuments and public buildings. Most of all, Meynadier's outline for a reformed Paris street system was his way of intellectually grasping and arguing for a Paris conceived of as one organic, dynamic entity tied together by its major streets and boulevards.

While urban circulation and public buildings are the great twin concerns of Meynadier's book, he raised other themes, some that he himself worked

The pont au Change, leading to the place de Châtelet, which connected the boulevard de Sébastopol on the Right Bank to the boulevard Saint-Michel on the Left Bank, formed an important link in the north-south "cross" bisecting Paris. Charles Marville. Bibliothèque historique de la ville de Paris

The boulevard de Sébastopol, which traversed the Right Bank in a north-south direction and connected to the boulevard Saint-Michel on the Left Bank. Planners before Haussmann had dreamt of such major through-streets to ease the circulation of people, merchandise, and troops throughout the capital. Charles Marville. Bibliothèque historique de la ville de Paris

out and others that his contemporaries had developed or would develop further. Meynadier outlined a project for a major park in the western part of the capital, which he named the Parc de Paris, modeled on London's Green Park. He also proposed the establishment throughout Paris of small parks, each with amenities like a fountain, benches, and public statues, which he labeled "green stadia."[171] He evinced, too, a sensitivity to historic preservation, arguing that even in the midst of new constructions some signs of old Paris be retained. He worried that history could be erased in programs of urban reform. To counter this he suggested that the city purchase historic mansions that might be marked for demolition with the purpose of guarding those buildings, "which still impart a particular cachet to several quarters of the capital."[172]

One last point is worth noting. Meynadier also observed somewhat critically but ever so briefly, that Paris still hid considerable poverty.[173] With the exception of his method for constructing a global plan, which appears to take into consideration the common people, and the acknowledgment of hidden indigence, it was the material structure and aesthetic appearance of Paris, however, its roads and public buildings, that interested him most. Given the sweep and concerns of his analysis of the physical structure of Paris, Meynadier, along with the Fourierists, represents the full flowering of comprehensive city planning, an important characteristic of early modern urban planning that has come under considerable criticism in the late twentieth century.

By the mid-1840s virtually all important planners, those working within the functionalist tradition as well as planners in the socialist camp, had come to accept certain basic tenets of planning for Paris. There was general agreement that modern Paris—the use of the term *modern* to describe Paris was a characteristic of this period, indicating that planners understood that their proposals and the transformations currently under way were creating a city that differed in its material organization and needs from Old Regime Paris—required a coherent well-aligned network of primary roads linking all parts of the city, a vital and stable city center, and a comprehensive plan to guide the execution of reforms. It was also commonly understood that the reform of the city center and the road system were essential to commercial success, health, and security, even more so following the revolution of 1848. What we see in the late 1840s and early 1850s, however, are some original planning proposals having to do with the concept of the organic city and with the social question, all articulated with reference to the above principles, which also form an important part of the functionalist intellectual planning legacy.

In 1847, Jean Brunet, a graduate of the École polytechnique, designed a comprehensive plan for a network of seven major boulevards that would serve the principal parts of the Paris.[174] He introduced his project with the self-confidence and certainty of the engineer-turned-planner by asserting that a comprehensive plan, "conforming to principles and rules of organization," would determine public opinion and also eliminate any chance, accidents, or errors in public works projects.[175] His originality in this domain lay in his respect for the successive boulevards already built over time in Paris. Equally important was Brunet's use of the term *organic* to describe Paris and its road system. As he wrote, "the flux of an always active population needs an integrated system of large organic arterial roads." In calling for such roads, however, Brunet rejected the notion of simply joining different points in Paris with straight lines.

Defining the principle of "the system of boulevards," he explained that "by this term I do not mean, as one does today, any long wide road planted with trees, but rather the series of concentric encircling arterial roads, which represent successive circles of the organic city during the different epochs of its development. This general system of boulevards is the foundation for the constitution, the connection, and the circulation of the body of the capital."[176]

The insight that modern Paris, in planning ideals as well as in the constructions of the July Monarchy, was an organic circulatory system was not in itself profound or original; the city as a body, as we have seen, was a common metaphor during the eighteenth century, and planning texts of the early 1840s implicitly represented a road system that would realize an organic city. What is significant is that Brunet, like Meynadier, represents a form of planning that respected tradition rather than breaking radically with it. However, the use of the word *organic* to describe a network of roads, whether straight lines or not, reminds us that the concept of the city as an organic circulatory system had become an integral part of the Paris planning tradition before the construction of Haussmann's road system, and before Maxime du Camp, writing between 1869 and 1875, would represent the Paris that resulted from Haussmann's reforms as a living organ, bound together by its infrastructural reforms.[177]

Planners also articulated important new variations on the relationship of space to the social question at this time. Françoise Paul-Lévy wrote that following the February 1848 revolution, at which time the insurrectionary movement "rendered visible for all to see the privileged knowledge that the Parisian people had over its territory," the dominant classes interpreted the presence of the common people on the streets of Paris as an impediment to order and modernity. For the elites, "it is necessary to break the connection between the road system and popular appropriation; it is necessary to transform the streets."[178] While such concerns were present from the beginning of the century, the events of February 1848 rendered the social question more pressing. A trio of planners, Grillon, G. Callou, and Th. Jacoubet, had designed a road system for the capital in 1840/41 that would address its security needs; they reintroduced their plan in August 1848, following the repression of the June Days of the 1848 revolution, because it so perfectly fit the current ideology of order. The "avenues of communication" in Paris, they argued, must be regarded as a complement to the fortifications wall surrounding the capital, so that "troops could move rapidly and en masse across Paris in order to direct themselves toward the points where their presence is necessary. Army units, in the interests of order, must also be able to travel through the center of the city in any direction."[179]

Unlike most nineteenth-century planners, however, who wished to transform the entire center of Paris, these men did not wish to see the city center emptied of its merchants and workers, forced to the periphery by current building programs. Pointing out that many industries required cold, damp conditions—they noted the leather, olive oil, and curing trades—Grillon, Callou, and Jacoubet proposed maintaining several streets in central Paris as relatively narrow, a sui generous proposition seemingly at odds with their suggestion that troops have easy access to this part of the city.[180] Another urban commentator, Théodore Vincens, simply proposed the transformation of Paris, especially its central anchor, as a means of absorbing workers in useful labor.[181] To finance such a program Vincens suggested that the government issue paper money against the value of real estate. He concluded optimistically that "social convulsions have given us the Republic. A convulsion is also needed to embellish Paris, but a shake-up directed toward the well-being and utility of everyone."[182] He published these words on June 15, 1848, nine days before the government began its repression of Paris workers enrolled in the National Workshops.

Another reform proposal following the 1848 revolution deserving mention is the one by Henri Lecouturier, also published in June 1848.[183] While not strictly speaking a reformist or functionalist proposal—Lecouturier, who subscribed to a democratic republican socialism, offered a substantial remaking of Paris—it represents a spatial program designed to address the disorder caused by the revolution. Its ultimate goal of peace, order, and urban stability, like that of the program of the communist, Esquiros, was not that far removed from many of the aims of the functionalists.

A short contemporary biographical sketch of Lecouturier indicates that he was born in 1819 in the Calvados region and that he moved to Caen in 1840, where he studied law, although he never practiced as an attorney. Far more interested in literature, he tried his hand unsuccessfully at poetry and a novel. In 1846, he moved to Paris, where he studied science at the university and then embarked on a successful career popularizing current scientific knowledge in journals. This sketch suggests that he was primarily interested in letters and that he was removed from the events of the 1848 revolution. The book he wrote on Paris had a modest success, according to his biographer, largely because of "the novelty of its ideas and the passionate nature of its critique."[184] Of special interest is the language Lecouturier employed to characterize the general populace and the city and his definition of Paris. Deeply concerned with the unhealthy physical condition of the capital and the extremes of wealth and poverty there, Lecouturier expressed a principle that could stand as the motto of all planners who follow in the Enlightenment tradition: "Moral order cannot be established in the midst of material disorder. One must accept matters as they arrive and organize the material order before turning to the moral order."[185] His description of the material condition of Paris formed the basis for his definition of the city.

Writing three years after Friedrich Engels had described conditions in Manchester and other English cities in *The Condition of the Working Class in England,* Lecouturier used remarkably similar language to represent Paris. Engels observed in 1844 that in Manchester, in an area known as Allen's Court, there was "everywhere heaps of debris, refuse, and offal; standing pools for gutters, and a stench which alone would make it impossible for a human being in any degree civilized to live in such a district." He concluded a portion of his portrait by advising that "if anyone wishes to see in how little space a human being can move, how little air—and *such* air!—he can breath, . . . it is only necessary to travel hither [Manchester]."[186] Lecouturier wrote that "the greatest number of the streets of this marvelous Paris are dirty passages, always damp with a pestilent water. Tightly pressed between two rows of tall houses, the sun never descends to the streets. . . . A pale and sickly multitude crosses there without respite, the foot in soggy gutters, the nose constantly breathing infection, and the eye hit at each street corner with the most repulsive filth." He added, as if for shock value, that "these streets are inhabited by the more well-to-do workers." In contrast to these conditions there were "other quarters more beautiful, better aerated, cleaner; but they are only occupied by those who do not live in Paris year round." The population of these districts, owners of beautiful mansions, usually live in the countryside for large parts of the year.[187] The point he wished to make was that such conditions threatened the very nature of Paris.

Lecouturier defined modern Paris—a definition that could easily apply to any modern city—as consisting essentially of its people rather than its particular monuments. In his view, the important characteristic of Paris was the presence, the constant meeting on the same soil over centuries, of the city's inhabitants. This constituted a community of interests which transmitted its legends, traditions, and ideas across time. In the present, however, the stability of Paris, he believed, was potentially undermined by the lack of housing for the population. The result was that Paris was becoming a "corridor city," a place where people gathered to make their "fortune" and move on "as soon as their dreams called them elsewhere." Evoking the nomads about whom Deleuze and Guattari theorized, Lecouturier fretted that in such a city there was "no stable population settled definitively on the Parisian soil and as a result no family; [and] without a family no morality [and] without morality no republican virtues." The outcome of this condition was revolution and, in language that was both concise and an expression of deep-seated psychological concern, "Each revolution is a new invasion of barbarians."[188]

Lecouturier's antirevolutionary stance, as well as his vision of Paris, sprang from his republican social-democratic ideology, which he explained at length in his tract *La Science du socialisme universel.*[189] In this work he defended, in a labored synthesis of pseudo-science, his own variant of Hegelianism and a measure of John Locke, his strong belief in progress as the fundamental law of history. Socialism, he explained, is the science of the principles that govern the universe. Two elements make up the universe, matter and the more perfect part, spirit, the domain of human beings. Spirit is the active principle, acting on matter, and both inevitably move in the direction of progress, in the direction of a world in which people increasingly cooperate so that eventually all humanity will be joined in a spirit of fraternity and mutual aid. Because he embraced the material world, which he believed should be both a source of production and meaningful play, Lecouturier was strongly anti-Christian. Moreover, although he referred to himself as a socialist, by which he simply meant anyone who believed in social betterment and reform, he employed the classic argument of John Locke that everyone who expended labor on an object must have the right to the product of that labor, most importantly a right to private property for personal use. From these beliefs also flowed his antirevolutionary stance. For Lecouturier revolution was a social sickness, as one oppressive class was replaced by another; the means to advance society was through education, specifically, knowledge of the laws of socialism. The republican form of government represented for him the embodiment of all these principles, and his tract on Paris was an attempt to translate democratic republican principles into a program of urbanism.

Lecouturier, therefore, troubled by the revolution of 1848, proposed two programs to address the instability engendered by masses in the city. First, he counseled a government program of increased housing at affordable rents for the general populace. Specifically, he suggested increased building as well as the conversion of many Parisian mansions, those "noble mansions large enough to house an army regiment" and only meet the luxury requirements of a single individual, into inexpensive apartment units. He took care to note that he did not want to eliminate private property but only to break up its concentration and its use as an instrument of control over the labor of others.[190]

His second, more radical plan involved an extensive reconfiguration of the space of Paris. It was not a totally utopian or fanciful notion, however, as it was rooted, as were other similar plans encountered here, in the physical structure and form of the real city. His plan, moreover, took Washington D.C. as its explicit model in the sense of dividing Paris into spacious avenues, distinct neighborhoods that resembled villages, with considerable plantings of trees and greens. What Lecouturier proposed was a division of Paris into four quadrants—the quarters of Saint-Honoré, Saint-Antoine, Saint-Germain, and Saint-Marcel—each demarcated by walkways, avenues, gardens, and fields. This was another spatial variant of the "great cross" principle and would be accomplished by a massive public works. Each of these four divisions, in turn, would be divided into four villages by two large avenues, also in the form of a cross. Buildings of public utility would be situated in the middle of this space. In a further reflection on the importance of circulation, Lecouturier would link the new Paris of his plan with a steam railway system.[191] Paul-Lévy interpreted Lecouturier's "cross" as a transitional form leading to Haussmann's similar plan for a system of Paris boulevards. It is transitional in that Lecouturier introduced elements of the countryside into the urban fabric and also incorporated the river Seine into the pattern of avenues, thereby situating the major north-south east-west crossings further south than Haussmann did. Haussmann's reform of the circulatory system of Paris, according to Paul-Lévy, was also characterized by a more resolutely urban design, the avenues and boulevards being primarily intended for vehicular traffic rather than for plantings.[192]

In Lecouturier's scheme the authorities would be careful, also, to preserve the great monuments of the city. Like Meynadier, Lecouturier was sensitive to the preservation and spatial siting of historic monuments, something not always respected by Haussmann. He also evinced an understanding of the potential violence of a form of rational planning that had emerged from the Enlightenment. His planning philosophy, cited in full, could stand as a corrective to the massive urban reconstruction to follow under the Second Empire:

> I do not pretend to strike indiscriminately, with a brutal and intelligent pickaxe, everything that stands on terrain destined to be cleared away. No, there are glorious national monuments, useful for France, that must rest intact on the soil on which they were constructed. These masterpieces were not raised to be buried among the formless hovels; they demand to be seen from every angle, admired from every perspective; their true location is in the middle of a level site, planted with superb trees. These marvels of nature must form a cortege for these marvels of art.[193]

Although Lecouturier would protect historic monuments he did not exhibit similar sensitivity toward displacing parts of the population of Paris. In his prescription for the housing problem he evinced a type of thinking which was typical of many thinkers steeped in the Enlightenment tradition and which we have met before and will meet again. Intellectuals in the Enlightenment tradition were so confident of the rationality and correctness of their beliefs that they ignored the subjective needs of entire classes of the urban population, preferring to impose their own plans and projects for the betterment of those subjects. Lecouturier, for example, suggested quite openly that one manner of lowering rents in Paris would be "to send individuals who were useless in Paris to the countryside." Le Corbusier, the twentieth-century heir of early modern progressive city planning, wrote in almost identical terms on one occasion.[194] Lecouturier did not explain the criteria for such individuals, but he imagined that in the countryside they and their families could easily purchase "a cottage which would bind them to the soil." They would fix up their cottage little by little, have a garden and a field that would yield all the basic necessities of life. Part of the family would engage in agricultural labor and the other part in "some honest industry useful and related to the work in the fields."[195] For those remaining in Paris rents would fall as the demand for housing declined. Lecouturier would also require the removal from Paris of all industrial and commercial establishments that did not directly serve the needs of the city, and this too would result in a decrease of the Paris population. He justified the forced displacement of industry and part of the populace by noting simply that governments had always had the right to "isolate workshops that were unsanitary or dangerous for the body; I would," he wrote, "even exile the workshops that were unsanitary and dangerous for the soul. It is important to remove from the cities the moral fever that they [the industrial workshops] engender and propagate by contact."[196]

Given middle-class fear of workers in the post-February 1848 period, Léon Marie's project to engineer the removal of the poor people from the center of Paris, through spatial reform rather than radical transformation of the city, was more in line with official thinking.[197] Marie proposed emptying central Paris of its "dangerous" population by having the government remove Les Halles from the city center, then divide the market into two, with one part located at some extreme point on the Right Bank and the other on the Left Bank. Then, through the "transformation of old Paris, the opening of new streets, the enlargement of narrow streets, the increased value of land, the extension of commerce and industry, the [new] apartment houses, the vast stores and workshops replacing each day the old cottages, the poor and working-class population finds itself and shall find itself driven to the extremities of Paris, with the result that the center would only be peopled by the well-to-do population." Marie celebrated the possible disappearance of "old Paris" as a measure of great security resulting from the removal around the central market of the "restless population," which "crowds [the streets] every morn-

ing, and which could become dangerous at moments of a strike or an insurrection." In any case, he remarked patronizingly, workers could find "more
cheerful, healthier, and less expensive lodgings" in the suburbs.[198]

Although Marie did not explicitly single them out, women were certainly a conspicuous part of the "dangerous" and "restless population" in and
around the market feared by the middle classes and closely associated with insurrection and immorality—a part of the population, as Victoria Thompson
pointed out, that had to be closely watched and regulated. We will encounter
again the suggestion that workers would be better off in the suburbs because
of better conditions there in proposals related to the construction of an underground passenger railway (see chapter 5), which would make it easier for
the poor to travel to and from the center of Paris. Marie concluded that public works in the center and throughout Paris were imperative, finally, as a
means to employ "the brave workers of the building trades industry, the hardest working, the greatest friends of order."[199] This statement was full of irony
and calculated thinking, given that the building-trades workers were among
the most militant of Paris.

Safety and order were also of great concern to L. Chambelland, who published his ideas on Paris urbanism in 1853, the year Napoleon III's regime began preparations for rebuilding the capital.[200] Chambelland's premise, which
harked back to Delamare, was that "in a well-policed state, municipal administration is the most useful of the various ministries, and the division of
public roads is the most important branch of municipal administration."[201]
In addition to calling for the usual program of improved traffic flow, road
cleaning, street paving, installation of sewers, and sidewalk construction,
Chambelland observed that "in order for circulation to be easy, free and convenient in a great city, it's not enough that streets be clean and well-paved; it
is necessary also that the public, and especially strangers, be able to easily find
their path, be able to direct themselves, day and night, in every direction,
without any guide other than an intelligent order of street names and house
numbers." He also counseled the lighting of all Paris streets, by gas lamps
equipped with reflectors or by electricity.[202] An important program of mod-
ifying house numbering, a goal of Paris authorities since the fifteenth century,
had been under way since 1847, and gas lighting, as we have seen, had advanced considerably in Paris under the July Monarchy.[203] Chambelland proposed a more original measure of safety and security in suggesting that da-
guerreotype portraits be attached to the Parisians' internal passports, or
identity cards.[204]

A measure of how extensive claims for public works had become before
Haussmann assumed office may be judged by three additional urban com-

mentators, Armand Husson, Ch. Gourlier, and Louis Lazare. In 1850 Husson, an employee of the prefecture of the Seine Department, issued a treatise on public works legislation and the public roadway of France, with important sections on Paris.[205] In it he laid out the legal basis upon which successive French governments would be able to expropriate property for the construction of roads and streets, a document that could serve as the basis for any future legislation on the subject. In 1856 he added his own voice to the program for reform in Paris by adopting virtually de novo Chabrol-Chaméane's project for the reform of the Left Bank, a proposal that also took for granted a global plan for Paris.[206] In 1852, Gourlier, a member of the Conseil général des bâtiments civils, published a survey of the successive measures taken since the earliest times to ameliorate the conditions of Paris streets and housing.[207] In it he praised the work of Chabrol de Volvic in introducing a significant number of sidewalks in Paris. He was especially generous, however, in his praise for Haussmann's predecessor, the Count de Rambuteau, who had begun important public works, especially the rue Rambuteau, "work that would be extremely desirable to see continued and finished."[208]

Of the three, Louis Lazare was the most important, by virtue of his finely detailed and wide-ranging publications on Paris, which were based on extensive first-hand investigations, and he must rank as one of the most astute urban commentators in mid-nineteenth-century Paris.[209] Unlike Baudelaire's casual *flaneur,* Lazare explored the city in the manner of an urban sociologist or urban anthropologist, long before such professions came into existence, using his observations and the enormous documentation on Paris he had amassed to try to affect public policy. Lazare entered public service as an archivist for the city in 1835, specializing in documents on Paris property holdings. He is perhaps best known for having produced, along with his brother, Félix, also a government employee, a massive dictionary of Paris streets and monuments in 1844.[210] Louis lost his post following the revolution of 1848, as the new administration removed many officials of the previous one. In order to support himself, Lazare founded *La Revue Municipale,* an urban affairs journal which he edited and for which he wrote from 1848 to 1862. While he cared deeply about urbanism in Paris, he also pitched the journal to industrialists and property owners, people of the "well-to-do classes" who could afford its subscription price.[211] As a result of his often severe criticism of Haussmann's reforms, officials of the Second Empire closed down the publication in 1862.

In 1850, however, before Haussmann had come to power, Lazare wrote a five-part series in *La Revue Municipale,* "The Creation of a Comprehensive Plan."[212] It is a forceful summation of the arguments of the planners of the first half of the nineteenth century, functionalists and socialists alike, on the necessity of comprehensive planning. For the most part synthetic rather than original, the series is nevertheless important because it points to the widespread circulation of ideas about comprehensive planning which were then being popularized in an influential journal. Addressing his articles to the general council of the Seine Department, which exercised administrative power over Paris, he pointed out that Paris was constantly growing. The city's fixed population posed no problem, but the railroad was bringing a "floating population" into the capital, a "mob attracted by the irresistible desire to know or see Paris again." As a result the city and the department needed a comprehensive plan," on which one could trace, following serious study, the projects which are indispensable to circulation."[213] He concluded his series with a nine-point program on how to construct such a plan—a distinguishing feature of his articles, as his contemporaries usually did not spell out in such detail the manner in which to establish a comprehensive plan. It is worth citing in full, as it underscores the importance of contemporary thinking on comprehensive planning. In order to create a new Paris, Lazare concluded that one should follow the following principles:

1. No new street openings to be made in Paris before the *adoption* of a comprehensive plan.
2. Borrow realizable projects from the Commission of Artists and transfer them to the new plan.
3. Group together crown property which could facilitate new street openings.
4. Have one person study plans for national cross-roads up to the fortifications.
5. In order to evaluate this operation, name a commission, to be presided over by the prefect [of the Seine department] himself, and whose members shall be chosen from within the Municipal Council, the administration of the city of Paris, and from among municipal engineers.
6. Once the fundamental principles of the comprehensive plan are agreed upon, the Departmental Commission shall be convoked, *in an extraordinarily session,* in order to judge and formulate a program.
7. The plan should then be deposited in the City Hall and submitted to a public inquiry for two months.
8. There shall be a register comprising all observations concerning new plans [for roads]. These observations must be signed.
9. The public inquiry over, the results are to be submitted to the General Council [of the Seine department] which would decree the work.[214]

As we can see from all the above, by 1853, the year Haussmann and Napoleon III began their preparations for the rebuilding of Paris, there was in place an extensive archive of proposals and plans for the reform of the capital.

The plans under consideration here fall into the functionalist camp insofar as the primary aim of the functionalist planning model was to impose order and control over the city and to regulate population and vehicular flow. None, save Lecouturier, aimed for a total reconstruction of Paris according to some abstract model of the ideal city or without consideration for property rights or existing structures. Although reformist, this current of planning required a comprehensive planning program, a principle it shared with other currents of pre-Haussmann planning. The functionalists took the basic material structure of Paris as it was and wished to open and align its existing streets and build new ones. They also focused on the center of Paris, which in these plans required more extensive urban renovation. It was a form of urban planning that paralleled the needs of political authorities for urban order and never questioned that authority. This form of planning stands in contrast in its ultimate aims, although not so markedly in its details, to a socialist form of planning that did question, at least theoretically, political authority and the social order. It is to the other major currents of pre-Haussmann planning to which we now turn.

CHAPTER THREE

The Saint-Simonians and Paris

LIKE THE FUNCTIONALISTS, Saint-Simonian engineers and intellectuals were critical agents in the emergence of new spatial conceptions of the city during the first half of the nineteenth century. Saint-Simonians were followers of Henri de Saint-Simon (1760–1825), a French intellectual whose writings on the newly emerging industrial society of the early nineteenth century proved both influential and prescient.[1] While Saint-Simon's ideas evolved and changed over time, an important current in his philosophy was the faith he placed in the power of industrialists and technocrats, advancing national and international programs of public works, to bring about a new order of social harmony and betterment. His disciples, the Saint-Simonians, also thought in terms of applying the scientific and technological knowledge of experts, for example, engineering projects like canal building or city planning, to the solution of society's problems.[2] With respect to city planning, even though Saint-Simonians frequently thought in terms of the city as an abstraction, Paris eventually came to occupy a central place in their writings. They regarded the city in general, and Paris in particular, as an open system, which was itself part of a larger territorial and even global network. Saint-Simonian thinking regarded the urban circulatory system—the network of roads that linked one part of urban space to another and to the national territory and beyond—as the fundamental underlying structure of the city. The city was a nodal point in a global network of cities. While their thinking resembled that of the functionalists and Fourierists of the 1840s with respect to space and movement, the Saint-Simonians' special contribution to a new understanding of Paris, or any major city, was a far deeper theorization about the city as part of a national and eventually global system. The ideal city they imagined contrasted with the baroque and premodern city, which was conceived as a closed system, in which emphasis was placed on linear perspective and monumental buildings grouped into a single coherent architectural style.

In addition to their vision of Paris as the center of an international system of trade and human intercourse, Saint-Simonians were also the apostles of a faith in the power of urban public works to usher in a new society of health, order, and cooperation among all the city's inhabitants, another major theme in their perception of the modern city. We need to consider as well the Saint-Simonian theory of and justification for the productive and constant circulation of capital through cities and the larger territory as a central feature of the modern industrial capitalist world. And, although engineers were an especially important element within the Saint-Simonian movement, not all Saint-Simonians were engineers nor all engineers Saint-Simonians.

Saint-Simonian engineers were interested in planning the territory and the city partly as a function of their professional profile but also because they believed that the social problems of the masses, increasingly apparent in cities, could be addressed with engineering solutions. Given the importance of engineering in a modern society, Saint-Simonians were an especially fertile and imaginative source of projects designed to address the urban social condition. Joseph Rykwert, writing of the École polytechnique, from which so many Saint-Simonians had graduated and which exemplified this spirit, and of the principles of Jean-Nicolas-Louis Durand, who taught there, noted that "the declared purpose of the whole Polytechnique project of social betterment through technology . . . required the rationalization of urban planning so that the whole building process could become the medium of the social engineer. In that sense, the enterprise was implicitly utopian. The methods that the Polytechnique taught were so clear, simple, and almost self-evident that they have remained the tacit and unquestioned assumptions of many planners and architects."[3]

Rykwert's characterization of the Saint-Simonians as utopian brings to mind Friedrich Engels' 1880 critique of the so-called utopian socialists.[4] It was Engels' position that Henri de Saint-Simon, Charles Fourier, Robert Owen, and, by extension, their followers adopted a form of social analysis that, for all its good intentions, was hopelessly out of touch with real economic and historical developments and conditions. Unlike Marxism, which Engels labeled scientific by virtue of its search for the "real" underlying economic causes of social problems, utopian socialists—which is how he famously characterized the French and English socialist reformers—sought the solution to all social ills and inequities in reason and in the establishment of models of a better society. The more deeply these reformers became invested in an ideal model the more their work drifted off into "pure fantasies."[5] In more recent times, Sébastien Charléty and F. A. Hayek faulted the Saint-Simonians, especially Saint-Simonian engineers, for an authoritarianism born of their mastery of scientific knowledge and space and the belief that this rendered any solutions they proffered, including social projects, superior to all others. Society, Saint-Simonians held, should be structured hierarchically, with experts, ideally engineers and other scientific experts, directing its affairs. Another critic, Paul Bénichou, on the other hand, placed great weight on the romantic and religious element in the Saint-Simonian movement.[6]

While there is an element of truth to some of these characterizations, it is possible to complicate these assessments. Recent interpretations, moreover, have challenged the negative portraits of the Saint-Simonians. In the first instance, Engels' judgment lumps together three distinct schools of socialist reformism: Saint-Simonianism, Fourierism, and Owenism. With respect to France, a distinction should be drawn between the followers of Saint-Simon and Fourier, without the implication, however, that either group was "utopian," a label employed here only as a convention. What we now see as central in the Saint-Simonian project is the importance of public works, including the reform of cities, with special emphasis on Paris, within a national program of infrastructural improvement.[7] Robert Carlisle also made it clear that the Saint-Simonians, whom he characterized as "bourgeois radicals," were socialists only in the pre-Marxian sense of the word, that is, they asked the broad question of how society should best function and answered it by calling for love, association, sharing, and organization.[8] Antoine Picon noted that Saint-Simonian engineers were pioneers in devising programs to reform cities like Paris within the context of a national program of improvement of communication routes, which would facilitate the production and territorial distribution of goods. In the Saint-Simonian manner of thinking, the city now became an open system, connected to the national territory, and not merely an entity whose primary markers were its history and monuments.[9] Bernard Lepetit, too, singled out the Saint-Simonians, along with the Fourierists, as devising a new spatial conception of the city in which circulation was the key to urban and national economic development and social progress and in which the city and the territory both existed as part of a new national and international commercial network.[10]

The most sustained critique of the "utopian" label applied to the followers of Saint-Simon and Fourier comes from Michèle Riot-Sarcey.[11] Riot-Sarcey studied some two thousand letters written to the editors of the Saint-Simonian journal, *Le Globe,* as well as the 1831 revolt of the silk weavers of Lyon and the significant strike movement in the Paris region during the summer and early fall of 1840. From these she was able to recapture the political dimension of the demands of the social reformers, the "real" in their program, and the sense of the flow of ideas that circulated among all social groups, socialist and nonsocialist, at moments of upheaval. Most tellingly, the social reformers proposed solutions to structural or immediate crises that involved a new political and economic organization, one that stressed a more equitable relationship between family members, a social hierarchy based on talent, and a new democratic politics. The social reformers refused to blame poverty on the character flaws of the poor or to moralize about workers and have them accept the social status quo. In the politics of the social reformers, privileges owing to birth had to be abolished and wealth distributed more evenly throughout society. Their entire program seriously challenged received notions of family, society, and power, and as a result, Riot-Sarcey concluded, political elites defined the social reformers as "utopian" purposely to exclude them from a national debate on social issues and politics.

The "reality" of the "utopian" Saint-Simonians may be seen quite vividly in their social and planning proposals. An important starting point in an understanding of Saint-Simonianism is the 1828 essay by Prosper Enfantin, *Mémoires d'un industriel de l'an 2240,* Enfantin's major contribution to the Saint-Simonian treatment of public works.[12] Enfantin (1796–1864), who, following the death in 1825 of Saint-Simon, emerged as the leader of Saint-Simon's followers, had begun his advanced schooling at the École polytechnique (1813). Financial difficulties, however, prevented him from graduating. Taking up the profession of wine merchant, he traveled throughout Europe, and, following his father's advice and financial assistance, went to work in a newly organized bank in Saint Petersburg from 1821 to 1823, where he joined a circle of Polytechnic engineers, including Pierre-Dominique Bazaine, Eugène Flachat, Émile Clapeyron, and Gabriel Lamé, on temporary service there. It was these men who typified the practical, public works school of Saint-Simonianism. With them he discussed economic and philosophical questions, and when he returned to France, he fell in with Olinde Rodrigues, who converted him to Saint-Simonianism.[13]

According to Robert Carlisle, the *Mémoires,* discussed within the inner group of Saint-Simonians and completed in the spring of 1828, is "the clearest projection of the Saint-Simonian vision." It "represents the culmination of the specifically technocratic ambitions first apparent in Saint-Simon and in *Le Producteur,*" a Saint-Simonian publication.[14] While this is perhaps an exaggeration—Carlisle also writes that the *Mémoires* "is far from being the most brilliant or insightful of the Saint-Simonian writings"—the work is important because it announced themes that are worked out more rigorously and elegantly in 1832 in two separate works, one by Michel Chevalier, and the other, collectively, by Gabriel Lamé, Émile Clapeyron, and the Flachat brothers, Stéphane and Eugène. It is instructive, too, that the *Mémoires* was published during the Restoration period, which saw the beginnings of a growing interest in public works in several important circles.

The title of Enfantin's essay, which imagined life in the year 2240, is reminiscent of Louis-Sébastien Mercier's *L'An deux mille quatre cent quarante,* which imagined Paris in 2440.[15] The literary device in both works projects a real space into some future time in order to criticize the present and suggest remedies. Two themes that stand out in Enfantin's work are especially relevant to thinking about space in the first half of the nineteenth century. The first is the centrality of public works, and the second the special role of France and Paris in his imagined new world order. Enfantin, like all the Saint-Simonians, began with the premise that contemporary society was being transformed by industry and technology, and, in a lesson learned from "the celebrated engineers," he wrote, there was an intimate connection between industrialization and science, especially concerning "the rules of *public hygiene* and the important public works of general utility."[16] While he did not identify "the celebrated engineers," he obviously meant to invoke the contemporary engineering advances in both England and France. Deeply impressed with the progress of technology and industrialization, represented dramatically by Watt's steam engine, Enfantin mentally registered the break in the equilibrium between production and consumption involved in the new industrial system. Industry, powered by the new machines, was transforming production but would also displace workers. It was incumbent upon industrialists, whom Saint-Simonians wished to invest with public policy concerns in the new society, to study new types of work in order to employ displaced labor.

France and Paris had a special role in this mission, according to Enfantin. The Saint-Simonians were internationalists who visualized a world order based upon industrialization. Enfantin imagined that he had been elected to a "European Congress," whose primary goal was to forge a confederation of Europe, the first step in the unification of the western and "oriental" worlds.[17] France, which already embodied a universalism in its language and civilization, at least according to Enfantin's projection, would lead this movement. And "one could say that the ancient power of the city of Saint Peter"—the allusion to the Rome of Saint Peter was related both to the new religiosity represented by Enfantin and perhaps to the goal of a new universal catholicism—would be "transferred to Paris, for all eyes were fixed on this capital while awaiting the dawning of a new age for humanity."[18] In this fashion, the social order that was threatened by the Industrial Revolution would be reestablished through production and new communication routes linking the entire world. The new society would be hierarchically arranged, with experts like engineers occupying the upper social and political ranks and everyone accepting their position, because it was based upon natural capacities. The key institutions of the new order would be a principal bank, to centralize the economy, and a "spiritual college," to take the initiative in ethical and moral decisions.[19] Harmony would reign because all would be based upon peaceful trade and production, all organized cooperatively. The civilizing mission would be led by Paris, conceived as a center of international communication—an idea that anticipated by more than eighty years the proposal of H. C. Andersen and E. M. Hébrard for an ideal city that would serve as a "world center of communication."[20]

Enfantin described a public works program only in embryonic form, starting with the improvement and expansion of communication routes, which essentially meant waterways and the railroad. Yet he was prescient given the developments in France and England at the time. The *Mémoires,* which does not discuss railways per se but only the need for effective national and international communication, appeared during a lively debate in France in the 1820s on how to add a railway system to the many French waterway routes that united the country geographically. François Caron showed that, contrary to popular belief, the French exhibited early on a strong interest in rail transportation.[21] That interest emerged first among mining engineers who saw rail travel as an effective addition to waterways for the transportation of coal between mining centers and neighboring cities. The advantages of metaphorically shrinking the national space were also recognized. In 1810, one Moisson-Desroches called upon Napoleon I to establish seven major railway lines in order to shorten the distances of the empire. In 1818, another engineer, Gallois, following a study-trip to Britain, reported on Stephenson's locomotive engine, and in 1826, Henri Navier, a pioneer in the construction of suspension bridges, proposed the construction of a rail line from Paris to Le Havre. In a treatise that connects with the Saint-Simonians' preoccupation with the social question, Joseph Cordier's *Considérations sur les chemins de fer* (1827) linked the resolution of social issues to the development of the railroad. With respect to actual railroad construction, work began on the first French railway line, the Andrézieux to Saint-Étienne line, in August 1825 and was completed in 1827, opening officially on October 1, 1828. Originally intended exclusively for mining products, the line accepted passengers in 1832. In this year, too, the Lyon to Saint-Étienne line, whose first section was opened in 1830, was completed.

Other events point to 1832 as a critical year in the transformation of mental attitudes with respect to a new, relatively untried, but potentially revolutionary mode of rapid transit. In 1832, Émile and Isaac Pereire, prominent bankers under Napoleon III and followers of Saint-Simonianism, argued for a partnership between the state and banks to develop French railroads and in the same year asked for the concession to construct and operate a rail line from Paris to Pecq. Also in 1832, Paulin Talabot, another prominent Saint-Simonian banker, in partnership with maréchal Soult, petitioned for a rail line to tie together mining regions of Alais and Grand-Combe. Caron characterizes all these developments as the emergence of a powerful railway lobby in France among prominent intellectuals, engineers, and capitalists.[22]

At the center of this lobby were the Saint-Simonians, for the year 1832 also saw the elaboration among Saint-Simonian thinkers of a sophisticated theory of railway development, an important component of the new mental perception of speed and space, the city, and the national and international territories. While the Saint-Simonians were not alone in favoring railway development, their writings had, according to Caron, a certain "emphatic character," even a "lyricism," which made them perhaps the single most effective group in the campaign for the railroad in France.[23] An eloquent and systematic expression of the Saint-Simonian brief for planning railways was Michel Chevalier's *Système de la Méditerranée*.[24] Chevalier had been a brilliant student at both the École polytechnique and the École des Mines. He converted to Saint-Simonianism shortly before the July 1830 revolution, and in October 1830 Enfantin called upon him to direct the journal, *Le Globe*, which was, from November 1830 until late April 1832, the leading forum of Saint-Simonian ideas.[25] The essay "Système de la Méditerranée" first appeared in *Le Globe* in January 1832. It was published separately from the journal, with two other essays, in March 1832.

The Mediterranean system was intended by Chevalier as the embodiment of a new politics of peace and cooperation between east and west through the material regeneration and advancement of all countries and regions surrounding the Mediterranean Sea. Chevalier began his analysis and explanation of this system by noting that the Mediterranean Sea formed the central boundary between the West and the Orient—the latter expression is Chevalier's—traditionally a space of political conflict and wars. A pacifist like most Saint-Simonians, Chevalier wished to see this territory become the center of a new world order, an idea already expressed by Enfantin. The key instrument of this transformation would be the development of communication routes ultimately linking the production centers of the entire world. While Chevalier acknowledged the continued importance of rivers, the sea, and canals in this mission, he placed great hope and emphasis on railroad development, as both the symbol and the reality of the universal association he wished to achieve. Railroads, he believed, should crisscross the entire Euro-Asian land mass. Not only would they unify hitherto politically fragmented nations— he used the Italian peninsula as an example, thus portending Cavour's scheme for an Italian railway network that would result in political unification in the nineteenth century—they would connect to the major ports of the Mediterranean Sea, to a new canal at Suez, and to the Atlantic Ocean, thus pulling the entire world—Europe, Africa, the Americas and Asia—closer together.

But there was more to railroads than a new physical means of transportation. Railways had become the symbol of all the hopes Saint-Simonians had for a peaceful, modern industrial society, a means to unite the peoples of the world in productive trade and social harmony. Chevalier likened the world railway network "to a system of veins and arteries along which civilization circulated."[26] Two critical ideas are contained in the last characterization. The body metaphor, so widely used during the nineteenth century, makes it appear that what is being written about is natural and therefore correct, and the idea of the railroad as the material instrument of the spread of civilization, which in Chevalier's thinking was uncritically associated with Western history and culture.

Although Chevalier did not devote much reflection to cities in the essay on the "Mediterranean System," cities were nevertheless an important component of the railroad network he planned. "The railroad," he wrote, "shall singularly multiply the connections between people and cities." Increased speed was becoming a characteristic of the modern world; the railroad was capable of transforming Rouen and Le Havre into Parisian suburbs, he remarked, and the time of travel between Paris and St. Petersburg had been halved. The natural result of the intense world development of railways would be a global communications system, by which Chevalier meant the political as well as material unification of the planet. The center of this communications system, which revolved around the Mediterranean Sea—"the pivot of the world"— with respect to the mission he had defined, was, in Chevalier's scheme, France. As Chevalier openly shared the legitimist view of a social hierarchy and embraced French centralization, one may infer that Paris would be at the center of his system, although he does not openly state this conclusion.[27]

If Paris is not explicitly at the center of the Mediterranean system, Chevalier's project established a general theoretical outline for an approach to city planning that would be especially relevant for Paris. First, the network of railroads that Chevalier proposed conformed to a preconceived master plan. Chevalier worked out the exact trajectory of the vast railway network that would cover the Euro-Asian continent.[28] Planning was also part of Chevalier's thinking when he issued a general call to engineers and the entrepreneurs of industry, commerce, and agriculture to provide the documents necessary for formulating a "comprehensive plan of works to execute and of industrial enterprises to establish in France, and to put this plan in harmony with the general plan for the Mediterranean project."[29] He also issued a call both for "a grand comprehensive plan" to exploit agriculture and the mineral resources of the Mediterranean world and for "a vast system of banks" to support such undertakings.[30] As Carlisle noted, the notion of planning projects of one sort or another, projects that involved the technical expertise of the engineer or scientist, was central to the Saint-Simonian approach to environmental reform.[31] Chevalier would soon apply planning principles to the French capital.

These ideas, which were essentially a brief for a government-sponsored public works program of vast proportions, embracing the national territory as well as cities, rested on a conception of politics quite at variance with the liberal political economy of the day. Chevalier proposed a new political administrative and economic order, one that combined elements of both reform and portentous innovation.[32] His starting point was his belief in the need for a social and political organization that would harness the maximum productive capacity of society. Inasmuch as France would lead this world movement, he used the French example as the model of the new order. First, he argued for a change in the traditionally excessive centralization in French political life—especially as it had emerged under Napoleon I. While making it clear that he favored political centralization, Chevalier proposed granting local administrative units, the departments in the French case, some measure of "spontaneity" in devising industrial programs suitable to their respective regions. In addition, under his administration the chief local official should combine the essential public services, "finances, highways and roads, public education, public health, [and] the different associations which address the needs of *work* and the welfare of *workers*." In a break with accepted wisdom, Chevalier suggested as a first principle of public policy that "the most thrifty government is not one that spends the least but the one that spends the most."[33] Coming about a hundred years before John Maynard Keynes, this represented an understanding that public spending, especially for public works and not war, would create jobs and stimulate the entire economy, a point he made quite explicitly throughout his writings.

In Chevalier's system, the greatest amount of capital would be expended on railroad construction. The source of that capital would be both public and private. He gave an example of how that might work. In peace time the French military budget was about 200 million francs. Transferring those funds to public works would produce "colossal results." He noted that about

100 million francs would be necessary to complete the Le Havre to Marseille railroad project, which was then being planned. Government funds and government credits and guarantees to private financiers would ensure the completion of this and all French railroads and their operation by private firms at healthy profits. Similar cooperation could be applied to the development of canals, the improvement of river ways, and, most importantly for cities, the distribution of water and the construction of sewers, essential requirements of public health.[34] Cities, in effect, occupied a vital place in a territorial network of production and distribution centers, all of which were to be developed by a giant public works program in partnership with private capital.

Two other elements, in addition to government planning and direction, were necessary to make this system operate successfully: the banking system and a workers' army. The French banking system during the Restoration was one of the most highly developed on the continent, although the organization of credit was still in rudimentary form, as it was in all countries at that time.[35] The Bank of France, with a monopoly in Paris, as well as departmental banks, made loans to the government, invested in insurance companies, and began to underwrite companies in canal building, metallurgy, mining, and especially railroad construction. At this time, too, some individuals in France recognized the necessity of capital circulation and the expansion of credit for industrial progress. Among the most important of these was the banker Jacques Laffitte.[36] In 1821, Laffitte proposed to the government the creation of an investment bank/holding company with a capital of 240 million francs, a huge sum for the time. The government, fearing too much financial power in the hands of one person, turned down the proposal. In 1825, it turned down another similar proposal by Laffitte for a smaller investment bank. While Laffitte was engaged in banking activities he also expounded on the importance of credit and the application of new technology in production in his 1818 book, *Développements de la proposition . . . relatif à un projet de la Banque de France.* The Saint-Simonians were greatly influenced by this work as well as by Laffitte's efforts to expand industrial credit.[37] Although not original in this regard, the campaign for the expansion of credit was not without importance.

Saint-Simonians were extremely effective propagandists for their position, and their vision of the global character of credit and industrial expansion was prophetic. Chevalier's work, which also called for the development of a system of credit banks to finance public works, including railroad construction, was an especially important text in the Saint-Simonian campaign for industrial progress. Credit, Chevalier observed, was the essential motor of industrial development. War, on the other hand, destroys or dries up investment credit. The entire political system should be structured to favor the expansion of credit and the conversion of the war machine to industrial development. The minister of finance, according to Chevalier, should direct the banking system, and the "wall that separates the public treasury from the bank, the general and particular receipts of the departmental and communal banks, should fall. The administration of public finances, considered as an institution of credit will become a colossal force."[38] Such a banking system would raise capital by borrowing. In Chevalier's plan, the entire banking industry, now supported by public funds and loans, was designed to accelerate the process of railroad construction and industrialization, and would involve the general public, capitalists, and the government treasury. In this scenario, the new man of the future, he predicted, would be the banker, who in Chevalier's project had a social role to fulfill. He also wanted bankers to combine to form "their holy alliance," a clear allusion to the diplomatic congress of European nations formed in 1815, nationally and across national boundaries, to achieve great material advances for all peoples.[39] In the twentieth and twenty-first centuries the banking industry would form such concentration, but mostly for profit rather than a social goal.

The second indispensable pillar of the new society, and just as important as capital, was labor. Chevalier proposed the conversion of army regiments into a workers' army. The model he had in mind was the École polytechnique, where military training was secondary to professional studies. For army recruits the regiment would become a school of industrial arts and trades. The government would direct the enterprise, which would cost nothing, as the regiments would become centers of industrial production. These centers, moreover, would be strategically located in parts of the country where the particular industry represented by a regiment was most advanced. The entire conversion process from a military army to a workers' army would be gradual, and the workers' army would keep its military uniforms, music, and celebrations. This system would also favor private industry in the long run, as soldier-workers leaving the army after their service could enter the private industrial sector as well-trained workmen.[40] One detects here an affinity to Louis Blanc's 1840 proposal for social workshops, also to be established by the government, although as competitors to private industry, the prelude to nationalization. Nor is it a very big step from Chevalier's project to the revolutionary syndicalist idea that production should be organized around the nucleus of the labor union. The three ideologies represented by the Saint-Simonian, the reformist socialist, and the revolutionary syndicalist plans also share the strong belief in some form of central planning. Chevalier was quite explicit about this: "Independent of an organization of workers," he wrote, "one must also have a plan of work." Such a plan would be an essential component of the larger project that went under the title the "Mediterranean System," whose first element was the construction of a European network of railroads. In France the first stage of this network would be the Le Havre to Marseille railroad, about which there was considerable discussion among French political leaders and Saint-Simonians at the time.[41]

Scattered throughout Chevalier's essays that make up the *Religion saint-simonienne,* of which the "Mediterranean System" occupies the last section, are justifications for the new order that focus not only on production and progress but also on internal peace and security. While this, too, was presented abstractly, the argument that the new productive system would guarantee social order and harmony had great relevance for Paris, the site of a revolution in 1830 and the terrible cholera epidemic in 1832. In his appeal to capitalists, industrialists, and the government to consider his proposals, Chevalier maintained that a productive economy, in which workers were gainfully employed in meaningful jobs and treated well in a system of universal association with capitalists, was the best bulwark against riots and sedition. Describing his Mediterranean system, he concluded that "it would be difficult to conceive of a measure which was a more powerful guarantee of public internal order and security."[42]

Another foundation against disorder, he believed, was private property, which he also defended,[43] owing to his belief in a class division quite at variance with Marx's: Chevalier held that society consisted of those who worked, owners and workers on one side, and those who do not, the idle rich on the other. He was also anxious to assure both liberals and legitimists that nothing in his project threatened public order or the hierarchical organization of society. In fact—and this forms a principal contribution of Saint-Simonianism to the modern world—Chevalier argued for a government run by elites, by individuals with technical and highly professional capacities. Moreover, bureaucratic elites should not come and go with each administration; rather, he proposed a permanent state bureaucracy, which, in addition to its professional qualifications and expertise, would accumulate and pass on its knowledge.[44] While a modern commentator like F. A. Hayek sees in such proposals the tyranny of reason, one should keep in mind that government in France at that time rested on a patronage system determined largely and arbitrarily by birth into the upper classes.[45]

Chevalier's Mediterranean system was informed and inspired by a remarkable realization on his part. He had exactly identified the historical forces that were beginning to shape the nineteenth century and that divided it from the previous century. He realized that his world—in effect, the modern world in formation—was being shaped by three principal elements: industrialization, urbanization, and significant population expansion. This was an exceptional observation, because these processes were in their infancy and Chevalier was able to step back from his own times, as it were, without the benefit of hindsight, and recognize and analyze the underlying material aspects of modernity. Even Marx and Engels grant that "Utopian Socialism," which appeared in the earliest stages of the industrial process, was nevertheless "full of the most valuable materials for the enlightenment of the working class."[46] Chevalier noted in 1832 that fifty years earlier the European industrial system had barely begun and the great manufacturing centers of his day did not exist. Since the peace of 1815, however, "the manufacturing industry has progressed prodigiously," in France giving birth to major urban centers, which had seen a doubling of their population since 1790. Cities such as Lyon and Rouen and their surrounding villages "are no longer recognizable: Saint-Étienne and Mulhouse, which were only small cities, have been transformed into great cities."[47] Chevalier consciously designed the Mediterranean system to shape and harness, for the benefit of the largest part of the population, its active working members, the new material forces of the nineteenth century.

CHOLERA

On March 26, 1832, two months after the publication of Chevalier's plan for the Mediterranean system, medical authorities positively identified the first four cases of cholera in Paris. The epidemic would turn the Saint-Simonians' attention to Paris and result in the formulation of a detailed agenda for the capital. Once it arrived, cholera, which public authorities had been tracing from its origins on the Indian subcontinent to Europe and England, spread rapidly through all neighborhoods in Paris. Despite earlier public attempts at a quarantine of France, the disease easily penetrated Paris and was responsible for about a hundred deaths by April 3. By April 9 more than eight hundred persons had perished, and by April 14 authorities had counted twelve to thirteen thousand persons infected and seven thousand deaths due to the disease. The epidemic lasted 189 days, from March 26 to September 30. This first invasion of the spring was followed by a second wave in June; the second cholera outbreak lasted about a month, from June 17 to July 18. Contemporary statisticians fixed the total number of deaths due to cholera at 18,402, or 13,901 during the spring and 4,501 during the summer. The population of Paris at that time was 785,862.[48]

Although the disease struck the poor and their neighborhoods more frequently than the rich and theirs, no social group or quarter was completely immune. The well-to-do classes, as Catherine Kudlick observed, were threatened simply by the realization of their close proximity to the abysmal living conditions of the poorer classes which, according to contemporary wisdom, were partly responsible for the epidemic.[49] One contemporary, Clavel, a Saint-Simonian, captured the nature of this threat when he wrote that "cholera always begins by attacking the poor, but soon passes over their bodies to invade the rich."[50] Foucault observed that urban space has its own particular dangers. Disease and revolution were the great twin anxieties of the urban middle classes throughout Europe from 1830 to about 1880.[51] In Paris the cholera epidemic had followed on the heels of the 1830 revolution. During the epidemic, in April 1832, Paris ragpickers demonstrated against a government decision to change street-cleaning procedures. Soon thereafter, riots broke out in several parts of the city, because many poor people suspected that cholera was the result of a government campaign to poison them. The fact that the epidemic also hit during a time of severe economic recession increased uneasiness among the well-to-do.[52] Cholera and revolution became linked in the minds of bourgeois Parisians, and the disease had to be brought under control and revolution averted.[53] For contemporaries cholera opened up, in an urgent manner, the issue of whether and to what degree public authorities should intervene in the space of Paris and the lives of its citizens to counter the disease.

The dream of an orderly public space on the level of an entire city—which was the program of the Saint-Simonians—was strongly hinted at by many health professionals confronting the cholera epidemic. On this issue it is instructive to differentiate between the Saint-Simonians and the public health officials to whom Parisians turned for guidance in dealing with the epidemic once it had struck Paris. If we look at the health officials first, those whose profession was seemingly the most appropriate for dealing with disease, it becomes apparent that hygienists, both in their epidemiological studies of cholera and in their prescriptions to fight it, also looked deeply into the environment as a contributory factor. They were not unanimous, however, about how much intervention was needed in public space in order to fight the disease. Ann La Berge explained that the French public health movement in the early nineteenth century was characterized by two competing ideologies, liberalism and statism.[54] The liberal ideology, represented by L. R. Villermé, essentially held that there was a high degree of correlation between disease and death in Paris and degrees of poverty. Reform, according to this school, should focus on the individual's moral and material status. Statism, represented by A.-J.-B. Parent-Duchâtelet, saw environmental factors as the key to disease and called upon the state to take the leading role in environmental reform.

The possibility of urban planning had been broached even before cholera arrived in Paris, as sanitation and dirt were usually associated with disease. In 1831, as the epidemic was making its way across the continent, a writer identified only as Leuret wrote an article for the official journal of the French public hygienists' profession, the *Annales d'hygiène publique et de médecine légal,* on preventive measures to be taken as cholera approached France.[55] The first requirement, he believed, was to establish, under the control of the army, a sanitary cordon around France to prevent, to the extent possible, contact with the disease. Should cholera arrive on French soil, then local sanitary cordons would attempt to isolate the affected region. At the same time, and as a first measure, quarantine stations should be established throughout. Inside France, the sanitary commissions of the public health councils—the Paris health council had been established in 1802 by the prefect of police and became a model for provincial health councils[56]—should organize to advise localities on treating the disease. All streets and other public spaces where people gather, Leuret advised, should be thoroughly cleaned and "purified." All wells should be sanitized and sewers and public latrines emptied before cholera arrived; Leuret especially warned against stagnant water anywhere.

With cities like Paris in mind, Leuret proposed government intervention deep into the urban fabric. All houses inhabited by individuals with professions that were, according to the perceptions of the time, especially dangerous to public health "should be visited with very special care." These included people who raised dogs, pigs, rabbits, chickens, or pigeons. Listed, too, were ragpickers, boarding-house keepers, public-bath attendants, tanners, and gut spinners. Casting his net widely, he would, finally, have inspected "workshops of any kind which could become noxious because they were ill-kept and because of the odors they vented." Connecting the social question to health, Leuret also urged the rich and the government to advise the poor on sanitary measures and to provide them with work. The rich could take care of themselves, he concluded, but society had to come to the aid of the poor, partly as a matter of "humane sentiment and in the interest of public health."[57]

Apart from calling for clean streets and public spaces, however, Leuret's program concentrated on public control over individuals thought to be dangerous to both public hygiene and public order: the members of the lower classes. Other reports, issued after the outbreak of cholera in Paris, also recognized the need for some kind of public works projects and a program that focused on individual care and control. Unlike Leuret's article, however, these reports had epidemiological information that linked the urban environment and cholera. H. Boulay de la Meurthe was the president of the public health commission of the Eleventh Arrondissement, the Luxembourg quarter in the present-day Sixth Arrondissement, a fairly affluent area in the 1830s. In August 1832, he issued a report on what his commission believed to be the likely causes of cholera.[58] The commissioners, following an analysis of their quarter, concluded that the primary cause of the disease was the foul air of Paris, which was brought about by the unsanitary conditions. The air was being contaminated, for example, by lack of ventilation on narrow streets, stagnant water on unpaved streets, and garbage in public spaces. Paris, Boulay reported, was in great need of a sewer system, public latrines and urinals, new and wider streets, and sidewalks.[59]

Instead of suggesting a massive public works program, however, the commission went on to observe that cholera affected the indigent more than the rich and that there was a moral dimension to this finding. Cholera attacked the poor more often because poor people were "beings debilitated by excess" who "neglect personal hygiene and cleanliness around themselves." In other words, the commission, despite its identification of environmental factors responsible for spreading cholera, concluded by falling back on the social dimension of the disease. It essentially blamed the higher incidence of cholera among the poor on the poor themselves, on their "ignorance" of sanitary practices. Cholera would be eradicated, Boulay concluded, by a program of sanitary education for all and an amelioration of the social condition of the poor, although he never explained how this was to be achieved.[60]

Another member of this commission, Dr. C. P. Tacheron, writing in a separate publication, admitted that the causes of cholera were unknown.[61] Nevertheless, statistical analysis demonstrated to him, as it did to others, that poverty, sanitation, and cholera were closely linked. He recognized that cholera affected unsanitary neighborhoods disproportionately and that there was a relationship between the physical structure of Paris—the height of buildings prevented the circulation of air and sunlight and Paris had many unsanitary streets—but he, too, fell back, to an even greater degree than did Boulay, on an explanation that put the burden of the disease on the poor. Cholera, he believed, was partly due to the excesses of the poor, to their moral failings. Aware of environmental factors, however, Tacheron hinted at some government regulation of workshops, not a contentious issue as it affected mostly the working poor. He also wanted a program of increased surveillance, including a program of police inspections of workers' housing.

The analysis of the cholera epidemic by M. F. Moreau is especially interesting as it connects quite dramatically with middle-class fears associated with the disease.[62] Moreau acknowledged poor urban sanitation in Paris as contributing to cholera. But poverty was a more important factor, and he explained the spread of the disease almost exclusively in terms of personal responsibility. He gave the example of the rue Neuve-de-la-Fidelité, in the fau-bourg Saint-Denis in the old Fifth Arrondissement (Moreau's study was based on the Fifth Arrondissement, today's Tenth). Public authorities had built a sewer on that street following the July 1830 revolution. Despite government attempts at cleaning the street, however, the rate of cholera was relatively high there. Moreau attributed this "above all to the indigence of the majority of the inhabitants whose flats are generally dirty and poorly laid out."[63]

More frightening to Moreau, however, was the condition of the area around the farmers' market of Saint Laurent on the rue Saint Laurent. From the twelfth to the seventeenth centuries the market had been controlled by different religious houses, which also operated a leper hospital nearby. Here is how Moreau, in a statement that perfectly sums up middle-class fears of the poor and the workers and their living quarters, described the area around the market:

> For several years some of the constructions built on this enclosure have been torn down; but the grounds they occupied were never sealed or paved, and have turned into muddy cesspools, impassable for pedestrians and ve-hicles alike. There is more: the people living nearby and those passing through have transformed the empty lots into public latrines, a kind of small dump in the district and one can say without exaggeration that in many places the soil is so covered with fecal matter as to be invisible. If one leaves the public road in order to penetrate into the dwellings one finds them in perfect harmony with the street. The hovels (and they cannot me-rit any other name), which still exist, old and dilapidated, fallen in ruins, are inhabited by ragpickers, day laborers, beggars, living as lodging-house boarders.[64]

Foucault, in one of his most penetrating and well-known insights, noted that by the eighteenth century leprosy and lepers had disappeared from the European landscape but that the mental and physical structures responsible for confining them, for excluding them from the general populace, remained. Writing about the confinement of the "insane," Foucault observed that "often, in these same places, the formulas of exclusion would be repeated, strangely similar, two or three centuries later. Poor vagabonds, criminals, and 'deranged minds' would take the part played by the leper."[65] Foucault's anal-ysis applied equally well to the urban poor, generally, especially at the time of the cholera epidemic. Consciously or unconsciously, without mention of the word *leprosy* and in a concentrated passage that equated the street with the condition of individual living quarters, Moreau linked the most marginal social elements of his day, the ragpickers, day laborers, and beggars, those re-

garded as the quintessential urban nomads, to the feared leper. Moreau's conclusion that increased deaths due to cholera were a result of poverty and unsanitary conditions, implying that these issues should be addressed, was mild
compared to the expression of his middle-class anxieties about the lower
classes. These fears were perhaps addressed when, in 1852, a good portion of
this market area was destroyed by the opening of the boulevard de Strasbourg.

While not advocating meaningful environmental reform, reports such as
Boulay's, Tacheron's, and Moreau's nevertheless were opening up the possibility of significant public intervention into the public space of Paris. Moreover,
not all reports on hygiene and sanitation reverted to an individual, as opposed
to an environmental, solution to the cholera epidemic. The government's official 1834 *Rapport sur la marche et les effets du choléra-morbus dans Paris* on
measures to take to combat the disease was more balanced and measured.[66]
Its conclusion represented thinking similar to the Saint-Simonians' program
for combating cholera. The author of the *Rapport*, Louis-François Benoiston
de Châteauneuf, concluded, as most hygienists did, that the higher incidence
of cholera among the poor was due to their poverty and ignorance of hygienic
measures, as well as to the unsanitary conditions of many Paris streets and
houses.[67] He also linked the disease, more metaphorically than scientifically,
however, to a stratum below the gainfully employed: "Without fixed domi-
cile, without steady work, this class, which has nothing of its own except its
misery and its vices, after wandering on the public thoroughfare during the
day, retreats during the night into the furnished boarding houses of the different quarters of the capital, which seem to have been forever reserved to receive them." This "mobile" and "nomad" population, which included old
people, women as well as children, consisted, the report estimated, of about
thirty-five to forty thousand people. Disease among these individuals was as
much a result of character as of the environment.[68]

On the other hand, the report also recognized the significance of environmental factors for health. It suggested the construction of workers' housing,
larger streets so that air could circulate easily, the installation of sidewalks, the
enactment of government building codes to limit the height of buildings, and
the suppression of the many courts and alleys in Paris. It also called for the
prompt cleaning of public space, especially streets, "in keeping with the needs
of the immense circulation of which Paris is the theater." A fundamental part
of the street reform program the report recommended was the unclogging of
central Paris, with new streets going in all directions, and the building of spacious public squares planted with trees. These new streets would become the
city's new promenades and also "finally spread light and life in those obscure
quarters where half the population vegetates so sadly, where dirt is so wide-

spread, the air so infected, the streets so narrow, and death so active that it hits these more often than elsewhere; where the population is so weak, pitiful, to such a point that one out of three called to military service is rejected."[69]

It is interesting, apropos of the connection between the environmental and the personal, that if the above program were instituted, as it would be during the Second Empire, workers and the unemployed poor of central Paris would be displaced from their living quarters. The report also advised on the necessity for better water delivery to Paris, the installation of fountains, and the construction of sewers throughout the city. The overarching need of Paris, as articulated in the report, may be reduced to "circulation"—of water, clean air, sunlight—and the construction of wide streets with houses whose height was in a correct relationship to the size of the street, which, in turn, would facilitate circulation. As we have seen earlier, however, the delivery of water and the construction of roads were not within the expertise of hygienists, but of engineers.[70]

ENGINEERS

Two elements, water management and public roads, gave engineers a special entree into planning urban space.[71] The delivery of water especially, essential to urban life, was so complex and scientific a procedure that it became the special provenance of the engineers of the Ponts et Chaussées. It was engineers, too, who thought out circulatory networks, like the railroad, and sought to link the territorial rail and highway roads, for which they had a special responsibility, to city streets and boulevards, especially in the capital. Both the circulation of water and the circulation of vehicular and pedestrian traffic were seen, as already noted, as the essential infrastructural reforms of the mid-nineteenth century.[72] It is also likely that the Saint-Simonians were familiar with Chabrol de Volvic's representation of Paris as an efficient circulatory system forming part of a national communications network in which speed and the exchange of products were central, and that such a program implied some kind of government intervention in the planning of the urban space as a requirement of the modern state.

Saint-Simonians were part of the engineering tradition represented by Chabrol de Volvic. Not being public officials, however, they could be far bolder than Chabrol was in proposing solutions to the space issues of Paris. They also did so within the context of the cholera epidemic, which made the topic of public space urgent. Given the severity of the cholera outbreak, the Saint-Simonians turned their attention to planning in Paris.[73] Between April 2 and April 16, 1832, four Saint-Simonians, Stéphane Flachat, Michel Chevalier, Henri Fournel, and Charles Duveyrier, addressed the issue of cholera in Paris in the pages of *Le Globe* and in so doing opened up a powerful argument in favor of comprehensive urban planning.[74] While in many instances the program of the Saint-Simonians resembled the suggestions of the hygienists and also mirrored eighteenth- and nineteenth-century reformist ideas about a healthy urban environment, the Saint-Simonians exhibited a more rigorous and consistent focus on the material, on the reform of the infrastructure, on a theory of public works as the key to social and health issues than all others at the time. Furthermore, they did not suggest half measures, and their program amounted to a call for the comprehensive planning of the urban infrastructure. This program did not blame the poor or poverty for the cholera epidemic, although Saint-Simonians recognized a social dimension to health issues. Saint-Simonians, however, also adopted a policy of social space engineering that was typical of reformers in the Enlightenment tradition.

Stéphane Flachet, a follower of Enfantin until, for personal reasons, he broke with him in the summer of 1832, was a civil engineer; with his half brother, Eugène Flachat, he was responsible for the construction of the Paris to Saint-Germain railroad line, which opened in 1837. Although only twelve miles long, this was the first French line designed for mechanical power and as a passenger carrier.[75] In Flachat's 1832 analysis of cholera in Paris, he laid out some of the main points of the Saint-Simonians, variations on which were taken up by his colleagues.[76] The first feature that strikes a reader of Flachat's piece is his confidence in the capacity of the "people" of Paris to overcome the disease. By "people" he meant the great mass of the working population, rich and poor alike. He acknowledged that cholera had "vividly struck the imagination of the people of Paris" but, unlike the hygienists, he blamed no special class or profession of the population for the spread of the disease.[77] Rather, the people of Paris were "capable of enthusiasm, gaiety, courage," essential characteristics for the "vast works" needed to fight the disease. Exhibiting the confidence of engineers in the power of science to solve social problems, Flachat believed that the common people of France and Paris could become an example to the world in fighting cholera and "a magnificent response to Asia," where the disease had originated. By this he meant that Paris would set the example that India and Asia could follow in fighting the disease that was also ravaging their societies. What was needed were "great works," that is, public works projects, which would simultaneously act upon the people's "imagination, satisfy its love for the majestic, its desire for the beautiful, and at the same time allay its misery."[78]

Flachat's projects, despite his use of terms like *majestic* and *beautiful*, consisted of plans for three important infrastructural reforms for Paris: (1) the abundant delivery of water to the city, (2) the completion of the rue de Rivoli, and (3) the cleaning and opening up of the crowded central Paris quarters near the Seine River. In these plans we see another instance of a unique focus with respect to Paris. The functional element replaced the aesthetic; the emphasis in this program of urban reform was on the circulation of water through the city, a new east-west through street, and greater mobility in the center.

While no one at the time knew what caused cholera, what seemed incontrovertible was the close association of the disease with dirt and poor sanitation.[79] For engineers the delivery of water to Paris was deemed essential to clean the city. Flachat, writing in almost poetic terms, imagined the elements of widespread and thorough delivery and circulation of water through Paris. "Water for the people of Paris!" he wrote; "water on the public squares, in the streets, in the houses, on each floor; fountains sprouting water everywhere, spreading a salutary freshness." In addition, he called for free "vast baths," public bath houses for everyone, rich and poor alike. For the workers such bath houses would provide needed respite and cleanliness following the workday. Abundant water in Paris would also permit the construction throughout of a "general system of sewers." The principle should be adopted, he wrote, that any new building erected in Paris be accompanied by the laying of pipes for sewers, an economical measure compared to deferring the job until some time in the future when buildings had already been sited.

The key to his project was the constant circulation of water in and out of the capital, above and below ground, movement that would guarantee health. He outlined the system thus: "Run water on the surface of the city, a great abundance of fresh and pure water for all the needs of hygiene and consumption, and, immediately after usage, collect this water in underground canals which will draw it away from the rapidly destabilizing influence of humidity and the atmosphere; to be complete this is what the distribution of water must look like in a city."[80] Flachat believed that the prime responsibility for the circulation of water, an element of the urban circulatory system in the minds of the Saint-Simonians, and other public works projects should be the city of Paris.

The second part of his program addressed the rue de Rivoli, which, between 1800 and 1835, had been completed between the rue Saint Florentin, at the northeastern part of the Tuileries gardens, and the rue Rohan, just west of the Palais Royal. The architects to whom Napoleon I turned to design this street, Charles Percier and P. F. L. Fontaine, achieved a monumental perspective through the plan for a system of architecturally unified arcades continuing along the length of the street. Anthony Sutcliffe declared that "the effect of continuity and perspective was unrivaled anywhere in the world."[81] Flachat was not unmoved by "this magnificent street, parallel to the Seine," as he described it, even though it was still under construction.[82] His main preoccupation, however, was not architecture. For him this street was an "opening which daily became more necessary for circulation which is so active in these quarters [near the street]." Government authorities envisaged this street extending further east, to the Bastille, but work stopped as Napoleon I became increasingly involved in foreign war. Another reason the project stalled was that the congested area west of the place du Louvre to the place du Châtelet consisted of some very narrow streets.

Construction of the rue de Rivoli was an important piece of unfinished business, according to Flachat, for the extension of this street as planned would traverse the unhealthiest and narrowest streets in the city, where houses were among the most poorly constructed. The rue de Rivoli as it existed already, Flachat believed, brought air and light to central Paris. It also passed close to the rue de la Mortellerie, today the rue de l'Hôtel de Ville, "which had furnished cholera its first and its most numerous victims."[83] The rue de la Mortellerie, moreover, fed into the place de Grève, where executions had taken place since the Middle Ages. Flachat's clear implication was that an extended rue de Rivoli would result in better health for central Paris, so long associated with crime and unsanitary conditions. The only "utopian" element in Flachat's proposal concerned the manner of completing the street. Noting how inadequate current laws of expropriation were and how landlords were able to block the purchase of land necessary to extend the street, Flachat suggested "associating" landlords with the extension rather than trying to "expropriate" their properties.[84] He provided no details, however.

Flachat was not in the least utopian, on the other hand, in his proposals for cleaning the central quarters bordering on the Seine River. He put forward a program for the material transformation of these districts and an accompanying social policy, which would have deep resonance at the time of the Second Empire. David Harvey pointed out that Georges Haussmann "appealed directly to the tradition of Enlightened rationality and even more particularly to the expressed desire of writers as diverse as Voltaire, Diderot, Rousseau, and Saint-Simon, and even to socialists like Louis Blanc and Fourier, to impose rationality and order upon the chaotic anarchy of a recalcitrant city." Armed with this intellectual tradition, in addition to the support of Napoleon III, Haussmann was able to impose his policy of "creative destruction," tearing down entire neighborhoods, especially in central Paris, with a great deal of assurance that his reforms were correct and necessary. As one contemporary observer of Haussmannization, Edmond About, wrote in the celebratory *Paris Guide* of 1867: "Like the great destroyers of the eighteenth century who made a *tabula rosa* of the human spirit, I applaud and admire this creative destruction."[85]

One of the important intellectual ancestors of Haussmann's policy of creative destruction was Flachat, who assumed, with respect to sanitation in the central quarters, that "the *quartiers* that border the river can only be cleaned by the destruction of almost all the buildings that make up the Cité, as well as the quays and all the small adjacent streets." The Cité referred to the île de la Cité, site of Notre-Dame Cathedral, the Palais de Justice, buildings of the Public Relief Administration, and old houses into which were crowded some fourteen thousand individuals, "making it," as David Pinkney remarked, "one of the worst slums of Paris."[86] Flachat typically failed to suggest what might happen to the inhabitants of all the destroyed buildings. Neither did Haussmann, who nearly succeeded in wiping out all residential housing on the island, leaving in 1870 only about a hundred people living there.

While Flachat wrote about tearing down old buildings in central Paris, he also targeted one specific part of the population of this area, those who were attracted to the various docking facilities along the Seine, as candidates for relocation. In Flachat's program all these facilities would be removed and boats banned from being stationed on the Seine in central Paris. Merchandise arriving by boat would be routed to newly constructed ports outside Paris, at the canal Saint-Martin, at Villette, at the Grenelle station, at Bercy, and at Saint-Ouen. In another example of social space engineering, Flachat wrote that "if this measure is finally taken the entire population of the ports, this population which is the weakest and the poorest of Paris, will be forced to seek new housing, and a good part of this population will even leave the interior of the city in order to live in the suburbs, where it will find for the same price it pays today more healthy and better ventilated lodgings." Since early modern times there was a concentration of commercial activities around the banks of the Seine River. Laundry boats, water mills, water sellers, charcoal peddlers, wood merchants, and dyers converged there. All these would be forced out by Flachat's social space engineering, and in their place would be an unobstructed river and newly beautified river banks. The "quays would become the most healthy and the most agreeable promenade of Paris," he concluded.[87]

It is impossible to know whether Flachat, in addition to wanting to see the Seine River within Paris free of all obstructions to river traffic, simply wanted members of the poorer classes removed from the center of the city because of the danger they posed in the imagination of the bourgeois, himself included, or whether he wished them to have better and healthier homes, as he wrote. What is clear is that his planning solution, in which he imagined ideal constructions, ignored the real lives of the people involved.[88] Flachat concluded his analysis by posing a clear opposition between the Saint-Simonian and the medical approaches to cholera. Prescriptions for medicine, the cleaning of streets "where the sun never penetrates," and medical visits to the poor had not been effective. His program, he was confident, would address the spiritual and material needs of the people, which was his manner of calling for massive public works in Paris.[89]

Henri Fournel, graduate of the École polytechnique and a mining engineer, articulated the Saint-Simonian program for Paris in the form of an open letter to the King of France, Louis-Philippe.[90] He too called for a public works program for Paris that consisted of water distribution, the construction of railroads and canals, an expanded central food market, and the completion of the rue de Rivoli. He added that public works should be accomplished by a workers' army, and he demanded the expropriation of private property where necessary for this program but did not explain how this would be accomplished. Michel Chevalier's contribution to this discussion applied some of the ideas found in his "Mediterranean System" to Paris.[91] He also demanded a huge public works program for the French capital and the establishment of a banking system to finance the new undertakings. Without explaining the link between poverty and cholera, he nevertheless expressed the Saint-Simonian conviction that the elimination of one would result in the eradication of the other. Public works, he wrote, would result in "confidence and hope, which is the best of all preventatives against cholera. This would be the end of misery that feeds the cholera; it will be the substitution of order for an industrial disorder more murderous than the cholera." Like all Saint-Simonians his program required urban cleaning and improvement "of the highest order, such as the establishment and distribution of abundant water, the construction of sewers, the cutting of a street from the Louvre to the Bastille [the rue de Rivoli extension]."[92] Unlike Fournel, however, Chevalier was more forceful with respect to expropriations, calling upon the government to pass enabling legislation, including the right to establish compensatory prices. Like Flachat, Chevalier explicitly criticized the medical approach to cholera for its focus on the individual rather than on comprehensive environmental reform.

Charles Duveyrier, the last of the four Saint-Simonians who collectively embody the Saint-Simonian shift of attention to Paris, differs from the others in several important respects. First, unlike so many Saint-Simonians, Duveyrier was not an engineer. Trained as a lawyer, he became a regular contributor to *L'Organisateur,* the first official journal of the Saint-Simonians, as well as to *Le Globe.* He also had a career as a successful playwright and businessman involved in railway construction. Duveyrier's thoughts on the new Paris are expressed in three articles, two of which, most likely inspired by the cholera epidemic and the intellectual ferment represented by his colleagues' reactions to the disease, appeared in *Le Globe* in 1832, and the third in a chapter written for a collective, multivolume work entitled *Paris, ou le livre des cents-et-un,* also published in 1832.[93]

In reading these essays on an ideal Paris, it is clear that Duveyrier acknowledged the cholera epidemic and health only briefly.[94] These topics functioned as spring boards for a highly imaginative projection of a completely reformed Paris, a portrait of the ideal capital city. The first two essays were more grounded in the reality of Paris than the third, which expressed a less restrained flight of imagination. Duveyrier recorded his own variation of the body metaphor as applied to Paris, adding to it a religious dimension. Paris, for Duveyrier, was the heart of France, which in turn was the principal center of Europe, and as such must animate all parts of the kingdom. "Paris," he wrote, "is going to organize itself as the metropolis of the globe." In this capacity it would serve as the apostolic center of a new world order, which it would inaugurate. The three great needs of Paris, where reforms would begin, were "sanitation, improvement, [and] communication." These would be accomplished by massive public works projects, directed by Paris and other capital cities, including regional capitals, all tied together in a territorial network revolving around the French capital. Thus Paris would become a "nucleus for the world, linking to itself, in a short while, the most perfectly functioning interior and exterior circulatory system in order to facilitate the centralization of all human progress, its diffusion, and its application to all the people of the world."[95] He called upon Parisians and the rest of the French populace to lead the first stage of "this colossal enterprise" of public works projects and also to participate in festivals that would impart a religious character to these works.

"Communication," "circulation," and "centralization" animated Duveyrier's thinking. In his program, the first stage of the process of translating these elements into public works would begin with the construction both of Paris streets and of a railway system emanating from the French capital, reforms to be accomplished by an army of workers. Chevalier had already discussed the significance of an international system of communications, with the railroad at its center and the army of workers, but Duveyrier provided elaborate detail on the organization of the workers' army. In a variation on Chevalier's plan, where army work battalions were organized according to the industrial specialty of the region to which they were attached, Duveyrier would have the different regiments of the Paris workers' army correspond to different trades, for example, companies of bridge workers, diggers, masons, carpenters, and blacksmiths. The initial organization and training of this "pacific army of workers" would take place at the four principal points in Paris where railroads would leave the city in different directions for the four provincial capital cities of Le Havre, Nantes, Strasbourg, and Marseille. Two corps of engineers would lay out the plans for these railroads, which would cover the entire national territory.

Duveyrier also included a social program to his linkage of a new form of industrial organization with the construction of railroads. In his plan, the workers' army, while waiting for plans to be drawn up for the national rail system, would begin work "on the demolition and reconstruction of the entire central part of Paris, consisting of the Cité, the quarters of Saint-Jacques, Saint-Marceau, the block of buildings between the rue Poissonnière and the vieille rue du Temple and the most crowded parts of the quarter of Saint-Antoine."[96] This was another instance of addressing the issue of the densely packed working-class sections of central Paris, which impinged so vividly on the imagination of the bourgeoisie. While the tradition of clearing central Paris was not new, Duveyrier, unlike those who went before him, proposed a unique strategy for population displacement and resettlement. He would have the first work battalions take charge of the orderly transfer of the population forced by demolitions from central Paris, "this muddy and unhealthy portion of the capital." The displaced persons would move to new lodgings built expressly for them by the work battalions "at the edges of Paris."[97] A strong tradition of urban renewal in central Paris was being elaborated during this period, and although Duveyrier took care to provide for new housing in his plan, a seemingly humanitarian gesture, the use of the workers' army to accomplish the population displacement may be interpreted not only as a matter of keeping order but as a matter of force being applied to a social issue.

Having planned the clearing of most residential buildings in central Paris, Duveyrier proposed the construction of new ports from Bercy to Charenton and from Passy to Sèvres. He would replace old ports in central Paris with a wide expanse of cleared land with plantings for shade. On this cleared terrain, too, he would have tracts constructed in a furrow for a railroad that would follow the course of the Seine from Bercy to Passy. This rail system would connect with the outer walls of Paris, which Duveyrier would replace with "a large and rapid communication roadway."[98] Between 1852 and 1866 railroad companies and the government did participate in the construction of a light-rail line around Paris, the Petite Ceinture, which corresponded to Duveyrier's plan for rapid transit around Paris. In addition to railway construction, Duveyrier also advised that authorities reform all muddy, dirty, blocked, or infected streets, those places "inhabited by the little people, which is the largest portion of the population."[99] This policy should replace individual reforms, he wrote, clearly implying that street constructions should follow a comprehensive vision or plan. Rounding out a public works program that focused on communication and circulation with street reform and railway building, Duveyrier proposed the building of canals, hospitals, and public schools, plantings, and the clearing of land—all part of what he characterized as the necessary "immense enterprises."[100]

As an accompaniment to and culmination of the public works projects, Duveyrier planned art festivals publicizing and celebrating the new constructions. Following in some measure the use of festivals during the French Revolution to mobilize the citizens and celebrate the new political order, and anticipating the employment of artists as part of public works projects in the United States during the depression of the 1930s, Duveyrier wished to mobilize artists—musicians, sculptors, actors, dancers, singers, and painters who had studied at the elite School of Rome as well as provincial "talents of the second order," representatives of all the arts—in order to call attention to, and glorify, the vast undertakings that he proposed. Art would aim to inspire workers, guiding them toward the accomplishment of the great public works projects. Workers, too, would participate in these festivals, organized, presumably, by the directors of the new order, the industrial elites. Art for the masses, art mobilized for political and propaganda purposes was Duveyrier's vision.[101]

In his plans Duveyrier not only significantly advanced Saint-Simonian thinking with respect to reforms to undertake in Paris but also established the infrastructural foundations and the outline of a newly imagined Paris. Once the second wave of cholera had passed, in the summer of 1832, Duveyrier submitted his essay "La Ville nouvelle, ou le Paris des Saint-Simonians" for publication in October of that year. In this essay he gave complete flight to his fancy and designed a completely new Paris. His vision derived from the same impulse that informed his earlier reformist suggestions, namely, the ideal of the city as a circulatory system.

Antoine Picon, reflecting on Duveyrier's essay "La Ville nouvelle" found in it a vision of Paris that combined aspects of the medieval city, its organic spatial formation, and the new advances of industrial society. As such, his dream of a new Paris differed from the typical projects of most engineers with respect to ideal cities, which were based upon more strictly geometric patterns. This was important partly because Duveyrier's ideas found resonance in the writings of Jean Reynaud, a former Saint-Simonian, who in 1841 advanced a highly theoretical piece on the development of Paris that is, in many respects, a forerunner of Walter Christaller's central-place theory of urban development. Duveyrier was significant too, as Picon observed, in that his ideas prefigured aspects of Adolphe Alphand's plans for parks and Eugène Belgrand's projects for water distribution in Paris under the Second Empire.[102]

Preceding the essay was a copy of Duveyrier's letter to the editor of *Le Livre des cents-et-un,* which serves as an introduction to "La Ville nouvelle." In it he followed a literary tradition exemplified by Louis-Sébastien Mercier, in which he described the architectural and social confusion and disorder that characterized Paris before moving on to offer a new image of the city. It is a rhetorical device found in the writing, among others, of the Fourierist Victor Considerant, who, in the 1840s, also characterized contemporary Paris in similar terms (see chapter 4). Looking at Paris, Duveyrier wrote that "we live in a confusion of houses, of temples, and of buildings of every type, which conveys an idea of the saturnalia of the ancients or of the primitive chaos of the world." As for the city's inhabitants: "And in the middle of this satanic dance, [were] the jumble of men and women, pressed together like ants, their feet in dirt, breathing an infected air, negotiating all the encumbrances on their streets and squares, thrust among the rows of high black or pale houses, without hope nor care of anything better." Duveyrier offered, in contrast to this negative representation of the city, a picture of the future of Paris as a city of "order, of convenience, and of beauty."[103]

Duveyrier was sensitive to the likelihood that his vision would be taken for "a dream, a fantastic hallucination" because he was projecting a radically restructured organization of space in the French capital.[104] Françoise Choay defined a purely utopian text—Thomas More's *Utopia* is the classic example—as one in which the model society is "opposed to a historically real society" and "is located outside of our system of spatio-temporal coordinates: it is *elsewhere.*" Later utopian texts, according to Choay, depart from More's paradigm in that they pay more attention to the spatial aspects of the utopia than More did.[105] Although Duveyrier's plan for a new Paris contains obvious utopian elements, it cannot be characterized simply as a utopian text. First, Duveyrier wished to be taken seriously, and he expressed an Enlightenment faith in the power of reason to accomplish the colossal reforms he had in mind. Furthermore, his ideal city was a real city—Paris—radically reorganized, as Picon pointed out, to combine traditional and rational spatial elements. In a sense, also, "La Ville nouvelle" may be interpreted simply as a model for which to strive.[106]

The essential feature of the new Paris was its organic shape, a clear allusion to the human body, an image employed, as elsewhere, to suggest something natural and, therefore, normative. Among its principal characteristics were communication and speed. To assure this combination Duveyrier called for a city of efficient communication routes either paved with stone or of iron, in other words, roads and highways as well as a railroad system.[107] While this vision embraced the science of his time he also visualized a Paris whose "streets are sinuous like rings that twist round each other." He envisaged a city that functioned harmoniously from a spatial perspective, united by its roads, a city that looked like "a single edifice."[108]

If Duveyrier's plan for streets was in keeping with the already existing forms of the city—its organic structure—his plan for social organization represented a radical break from traditional norms. Duveyrier imagined a concentration in different parts of the city of the various similar occupational groups and civic functions. For example, he would group around the Étoile, from the plain of Monceau to the Muette park, in the present-day southwestern part of the Sixteenth Arrondissement, all "the buildings consecrated to the pleasure of balls, of spectacles and of concerts; the cafés, the restaurants with their mazes, their kiosks and their carpets of grass with fringes of flowers."[109] Different sections of the city would be designated for schools specializing in the physical and applied industrial sciences, for men of action and force, for industry, for hotels, for pure scientists and academics, and so on. He was especially kind toward the old and the sick, whom he would house in special homes in the middle of the Bois de Boulogne. The bank would have its own magnificent building near the center of the new Paris. In the very center of the city he would have a temple in the shape of a woman, representing beauty, love, and hope for the new world, from whose highest point would flow a great beacon of light, meant to symbolize a new city of virtue.[110] Although romantic and fantastic themes are part of Duveyrier's project, a project that lacks a scientific language and method to express and achieve its goal, it is significant that planning, ideas about zoning, and a holistic treatment of space in Paris are at the heart of his entire vision and part of his legacy.

POSTCHOLERA SPATIAL CONCEPTIONS

Although the cholera epidemic shifted the attention of Saint-Simonians to Paris, it did not displace their priorities from public works conceived on a large territorial base. In fact, immediately following the cholera epidemic two major Saint-Simonian texts again took up issues of extensive public works projects. The first, a collective work by four engineers, Gabriel Lamé, Émile Clapeyron, Stéphane Flachat, and Eugène Flachat, entitled *Vues politiques et pratiques sur les travaux publics de France,* was obviously in preparation during the cholera epidemic, as it was completed in August 1832 and published the following month.[111] Michel Chevalier wrote the second text, *Des Intérêts matériels en France,* on the material interests of France, published in 1838, in which he turned from his overarching vision of a global communications system to a detailed agenda of public works projects to undertake in France.[112] A third work, a theoretical piece on cities by Jean Reynaud, an engineer also affiliated with the Saint-Simonians, was published in the *Encyclopédie nouvelle* in 1841. It represents the theoretical culmination, the very apex, of Saint-Simonian thinking on cities and space, with Paris serving as the model capital city.[113]

The first two works are important for their elaboration of four critical themes, all closely related, that run through so much writing on space during the first half of the nineteenth century: (1) circulation/communication through cities and the national and international territory, (2) Newtonian metaphors of attraction and centralization with respect to cities and beyond, (3) the planning of public works, and (4) the circulation of capital. Reynaud's text, which works out a central-place theory of cities in which cities are seen as forming interlocking territorial networks in hierarchical patterns following arithmetic and geographical laws, is an important, but unacknowledged, forerunner of Walter Christaller's central-place theory of southern German cities.[114]

One historian refers to the *Vues politiques et pratiques sur les travaux publics en France* as "the fundamental work of 'practical' Saint-Simonianism," although a similar characterization may be applied to Chevalier's 1838 treatise on public works.[115] It is certainly true that its four authors devoted not only their writings but also their careers to pragmatic and realistic engineering projects. All four were civil engineers and had participated together in the construction of the Paris to Saint-Germain railway line, among others. Like Chevalier, Lamé and company believed that the key to the material prosperity of France was the ability of people and products to circulate rapidly throughout the entire territory. In the Lamé and company plan, as in all Saint-Simonian speculations on circulation, all forms of territorial communication routes were essential: canals, waterways, and the railroad. The object of the railway routes could stand for the entire transportation network: "to establish the most rapid communication possible from the center [of the territory] to the borders."[116] Chevalier put the matter in more poetic terms: "All is ready so that the perfection of the viability of the territory by water and land can take rapid flight."[117]

There was already in Chevalier's earlier work on the Mediterranean system and Enfantin's essay an implied Newtonianism, which put Paris and France at the center of a new world civilization. Newtonian references were often used in the early nineteenth century by individuals analyzing space issues.[118] Nowhere is this more evident than in Lamé and company's and Chevalier's discussion of railroads. Both the *Vues politiques* and the *Intérêts matériels* planned a French railroad system that would revolve around Paris, and both embraced the increased political centralization that would result from the material unity of the country. Lamé and his coauthors also added that such a rail system could be useful militarily, as it could transport troops from the center to the borders of France quickly, making the railroad a central component of national defense.[119] Both sets of authors also laid out the principle of a rail hub system revolving around Paris, thus prefiguring the 1842 railway law, which planned a similar national railway network. Lamé's group envisaged seven major rail lines, five radiating from Paris and the other two covering the south and north territories, respectively: (1) From Paris to Valenciennes, Lille, and Calais, (2) from Paris to Le Havre, (3) from Paris to Strasbourg, (4) from Paris to Lyon and Marseille, (5) from Paris to Bordeaux with a branch to Nantes, (6) from Bordeaux to Lyon, and (7) a parallel route to the borders of the north.[120] Chevalier's plan also called for five major lines originating in Paris and two additional ones covering the south and north of France, respectively: (1) a line from Paris toward the Mediterranean via Lyon and Marseille, (2) a line from Paris toward England, Belgium, and the Rhenish provinces, (3) another line from Paris to Spain via Bordeaux and Bayonne with a branch to Nantes, (4) a line from Paris to central Germany, Vienna, and the Danube via Strasbourg, and (5) a line from Paris to the English Channel via Rouen. He called for two additional lines, one from the Bay of Biscay toward the Mediterranean, or from Bordeaux to Marseille, and another from the Mediterranean toward the North Sea, or from Marseille to the Rhine.[121]

Railway construction of this magnitude required planning by a central authority. Chevalier observed that France had, in the Ponts et Chaussées, in the Department of Mines, and in the army, an extraordinary resource of excellent engineers who could execute a public works program for France. All that was lacking was "a comprehensive plan." His book was intended as a model for such a plan. He noted, too, in a critical insight on the difference between eighteenth- and nineteenth-century thinking about planning a new society, that eighteenth-century visions of society and individuals were generally utopian while his own times reflected a more practical and realistic attitude by not trying to force society and individuals into some theoretical framework. He noted, for example, that engineers represented a new type with respect to planning, a type that attacked concrete spatial problems with scientific solutions.[122] He called, finally, for a commission centered in Paris and several other principal French cities to study the railway question. Lamé and company were equally insistent on overall comprehensive planning. In their project a tribunal would constitute an "industrial jury," which would advise the government and its national corps of engineers on all public works projects.[123] It would be accomplished by a partnership between the state and private entrepreneurs, with overall direction of any project resting with the state. Such a dual system, however, should be the first step, they stated, in a transition from private to complete state control for all public works projects.[124]

If the Saint-Simonians were throughly modern with respect to their projects for railroad construction and other public works projects and large-scale planning, they were equally so with respect to their insights into the nature of capital and capital circulation, the fourth major theme taken up in the texts under consideration. Writing more than a decade after the articulation of Saint-Simonian ideas about the centrality of rapid communication/circulation as the critical stimulus and precondition of material prosperity for the largest part of the population, Karl Marx analyzed the requirements of capital in terms similar to those of his "utopian" predecessors. In *Grundrisse: Foundations of the Critique of Political Economy* Marx wrote that "the more production comes to rest on exchange value, hence on exchange, the more important do the physical conditions of exchange—the means of communication and transport—become for the costs of circulation. Capital by its very nature drives beyond every spatial barrier. Thus the creation of the physical means of communication and transport—the annihilation of space and time— becomes an extraordinary necessity for it."[125]

Here Marx was writing about the structural necessity for capital to circulate if capitalism is to generate profit and about the connection between the communication revolution, itself a source of capital investment and therefore capital circulation, and the capitalist process. Like the Saint-Simonians, Marx and Engels recognized a cultural component to the circulation of capital and the transportation revolution. Writing in *The Communist Manifesto,* they observed that "the bourgeoisie, by the rapid improvement of all instruments of production, by the immensely facilitated means of communication, draws all nations, even the most barbarian, into civilization."[126] Marx and Engels were being ironic, as Marshall Berman observed, because the very success of the bourgeoisie and its capitalist mode of production would eventually spell its demise, while the spread of civilization was also a means whereby the capitalist would come to dominate the world.[127] The Saint-Simonians, however, were not being in the least ironic in their insights into the circulation of capital and the transportation revolution.

If the power of capitalism derives from the very magnitude of the process of capital accumulation and circulation in all its forms, including transportation investments, there is also an ideological component to its success. It is in this arena that the Saint-Simonians were critical agents in the diffusion of, to borrow an expression from Max Weber, a "spirit of capitalism." The pragmatic Saint-Simonians, like Chevalier, Lamé, Clapeyron, and the Flachat brothers, embraced, in all their writings, capitalist development as a means of improving the material condition of the largest part of the world's population. Chevalier, writing in *Des Intérêts matériels,* postulated three conditions essential to material progress: (1) the "means of communication by water and land, which bring closer together things and people"; (2) credit institutions, which multiply the power and movement of capital, and (3) special apprenticeship education for workers and industrial education for the bourgeoisie, by which he meant knowledge of sound Saint-Simonian economics. Chevalier took it as axiomatic that "the usefulness of communication is today universally recognized; it would be superfluous to pause to demonstrate its importance." On the other hand, he believed that the importance of credit institutions and industrial education were not so well appreciated. In order for industry to prosper, he advised, capital must be available both to producers and to consumers, who would acquire the products of the industrial system. Capital, in short, must circulate throughout the economy. Having identified the material requirements of the industrial society as the communications networks and the banks and other institutions of credit, Chevalier added to these a knowledge of the power of these instruments, itself a form of capital in his system, as the last condition for the successful operation of the industrial society.[128]

Lamé and company also accepted as a basic tenet of a successful industrial society the requirement that capital remain productive. In their view a workers' army and a massive public works program would generate the level of productivity necessary to insure the forward march of industry. Like Chevalier, who proposed credit banks, Lamé and his coauthors proposed an institutional means of achieving the accumulation and the circulation of capital, which they also regarded as the critical engine of the modern industrial society. Following up on their suggestion that the state and private entrepreneurs cooperate in a program of public works, Lamé and company insisted that the private firms be organized in the form of limited liability corporations (*sociétés anonymes*), corporations in the very modern sense of the word. This organizational form, because of its very structure, could, they believed, best accumulate capital and guarantee, through the circulation of stocks and bonds, its "easy circulation" throughout the economy. Such circulation, which favors the public and any particular industry participating in this process, would have "a powerful influence" on the entire economy.[129]

Limited liability corporations already existed in France at the time of these speculations but they were far from widespread. Between 1821 and 1833 there were 119 *sociétés anonymes* in France. The largest number, 29, were in the transportation sector and accounted for a little more than half the total capitalization of such firms. During this period, moreover, the average annual formation of new corporations was 9 per year. Far more common at this time were limited liability partnerships *(Sociétés en commandite par actions)*, of which there were 673 registered in the years between 1826 and 1837. A limited liability partnership was managed by an active partner or partners who were subject to unlimited liability, while the investors, or silent partners, did not participate in management and enjoyed limited liability. The right to issue shares made the limited liability partnership similar to a joint-stock enterprise. The largest number of limited liability partnerships were also in the transportation sector.[130] Not only were the Saint-Simonians quite forward-looking with respect to economic organization, but their ideas on modernization and railroad policy would find significant resonance during the Second Empire. As Alain Plessis observed, the Second Empire was the first regime in France to make economic policy a central goal of state policy. Napoleon III believed, along with the Saint-Simonians, that in order to be great a nation needed more than military might; it required an industrial revolution. The emperor also believed, once more borrowing from Saint-Simonian principles, that the state should not remain neutral in the industrial-economic sector but should create conditions favorable to the expansion of this sector. It is well known, too, that Napoleon III favored and fostered economic concentration and that bankers deeply influenced by Saint-Simonianism, like the Pereire brothers, became central players in economic matters during the Second Empire. In addition, urban reform, especially of Paris, and railroad construction marked two of the most dramatic accomplishments of this regime.[131] Thus the Saint-Simonians, as represented by the texts under review, emerged not merely as lobbyists for a railroad program, as noted above, but also as spokesmen for a great transformation in economic practices—credit banks, government involvement in economic matters, concentration of capital, central economic and urban planning, a railroad and transportation revolution—which characterizes the modern capitalist system.

If Saint-Simonian ideas had their greatest practical impact during the Second Empire, Saint-Simonian theorizing with respect to cities found its most sophisticated elaboration in 1841 at the hands of Jean Reynaud. A graduate of the École polytechnique, Reynaud (1806–63) was part of the generation of Polytechnique engineers deeply influenced by Saint-Simonian ideas. He practiced engineering only briefly, preferring to devote his time to editing, along with Pierre Leroux, the *Encyclopédie Nouvelle* (1836–42), to which he also contributed important entries. He was especially interested in the organization of space, and his article "Villes" for the encyclopedia summed up the Saint-Simonian theory of city development.[132]

There are several points to observe about this article before turning to its content. Let us begin once more, by way of contrast, with Françoise Choay's belief that a fully formed modern urban planning is characterized by a scientific language, and that only emerged during the last decades of the nineteenth century.[133] Reynaud's reading of the city, however, including his analysis of city planning, was driven by a self-conscious scientific approach and aspiration. Furthermore, while his speculations were largely theoretical and abstract, we learn at the end of the essay that the ideal capital city informing most of Reynaud's analysis is Paris. It is important to remember, finally, that the 1840s mark a decisive turning point in reflections about Paris because of the sense of urban crisis that was widely experienced. As indicated in the last chapter, this crisis had to do with issues such as the displacement of the population, the building of fortifications around the city in response to fears of foreign invasion, and an awareness of serious overcrowding in relation to the city's infrastructure. Reynaud's essay did not address any of these—or other—urban issues or problems that arise in the 1840s directly, in part because his theory of city development could apply to Paris or any city abstracted from any particular moment. But Reynaud's essay did represent a "conceptual continuity," according to Lepetit, with late-eighteenth-century perceptions of city and territory, to which I would add that it marked the culmination of Saint-Simonian speculations of the 1820s and 1830s rather than, strictly speaking, a response to specific issues associated with the 1840s.[134]

The scientific spirit of Reynaud's "Villes" is embedded in his approach and in the conclusions of central-place theory that are at the heart of the essay. Acknowledging the importance of capital cities to the destiny of nations—they are the progenitors of industry, science, philosophy, religion, and the arts, in short, the great fruits of civilization in Reynaud's characterization—he posed a series of theoretical questions regarding the nature of cities: Why do cities exist? Why do they grow? Why do sovereigns come and go? What governs the relations of cities to territories beyond their boundaries? How do cities subsist? How are they administered? What constitutes their general character? In other words, Is there a general theory of city development? In order to simplify the consideration of these complex questions Reynaud reduced his general list of topics to three, all related to the architecture of cities, which he considered at length in the essay: (1) the geographic position and grandeur of cities, (2) the circumstances of their site and the order of their buildings, and (3) the sources of variations among them. It was Reynaud's aim to gather as much data as possible with respect to his problematic and derive from his findings general laws of city development expressed insofar as possible by the principles of arithmetic.[135] Christaller asked almost identical questions in 1933: "We seek the causes of towns being large or small, because we believe that there is some ordering principle heretofore unrecognized that governs their distribution." And later, "How can we find a general explanation for the sizes, number, and distribution of towns? How can we discover the laws?"[136] Whether Reynaud succeeded in discovering these laws is less important than his fidelity to the critical approach of science and the rooting of his hypotheses in an analysis of constructed space rather than in preconceived foundational myths of city development.

Impressive, too, is the degree to which Reynaud succeeded in articulating a modern conception of the manner in which cities and towns are ordered in space and the degree to which this ordering conformed to specific laws of spatial development. For Reynaud, economic and social considerations shaped a town's location and were at the center of his analysis—as they were for Christaller. The first principle of agglomeration for Reynaud was sociability, the "natural" desire of like-minded people for mutual contact. To this he added economic considerations. In the countryside, where he began his examination, villages were formed as centers of social intercourse but were also situated near their fields. All other things being equal in the terrain, villages and their fields formed a system of hexagons with villages in the center. Cities and towns inserted themselves within these hexagons, being formed for the same reasons that determine the emergence of villages. In the case of cities and towns, for example, artisans congregated together to service the countryside. In Reynaud's words: "It is evident that, theoretically, in the case of a uniform territory, their [towns'] geometric position with respect to villages is exactly the same as that of the villages with respect to the neighboring fields; that is to say, given a territory divided into rural hexagons, one would assign the position of cities by new hexagons embracing a determined number of the first, and in which the cities would occupy the center." The extent of these hexagons—the hexagon is a favorite geometric metaphor for the geographical space of France—will be determined by the ease of communication between the villages and their cities. Therefore the position of cities as well as their grandeur, according to Reynaud, will be determined by the state of the roads and of the cultivation of the countryside.[137] These elements constituted, for him, a law of city and village placement.

In his own central-place model Christaller, as Lepetit observed, assumed city placement within "an environmentally uniform region."[138] Whereas Reynaud began his analysis with the same assumption, he pointedly qualified this first principle. In this he appears more subtle than Christaller and certainly more prescient in terms of recent scholarship with respect to situating preindustrial and early modern cities in a nonstatic geographical and cultural environment.[139] Reynaud observed that his general law of spatial ordering assumed uniformity of territory and conditions, which, he underscored, is never the case in reality. Other factors invariably come into play in the siting and hierarchy of villages and cities. These include the availability of water, which acts as a powerful factor in determining the position of villages, which require water for their fields, as well as cities, which require water for cleanliness and health; the presence of public administration in certain cities; the importance of industry and commerce in a certain territory; the strategic significance of a certain location; the availability of building materials suitable for the construction of the city; flatness of terrain to facilitate traffic circulation; effective air flow for the health of the city; or merely a magnificent aesthetic setting. Human sociability, the original impulse of village and city formation, is also reinforced by the church in early modern cities and by schools in more modern cities.[140] The key Saint-Simonian themes and concerns with respect to space are encapsulated in this list.

Two elements, alongside Reynaud's hypothesis on the distribution of cities and villages, need special mention; these are the Newtonian metaphors of the centrality of capital cities and their communications systems and the role of planning in cities. Lepetit wrote that in Reynaud "the gravitational metaphor receives its most comprehensive development."[141] This is significant because Reynaud used Newtonian or gravitational metaphors to highlight communication/circulation as the central feature of modern urban society. First, differences in communications networks are critical in the placement and hierarchy of cities. People, whether they have much in common or not, are attracted to places where the means of communications for them and their products is easiest. The most attractive cities are those that have easy access to other cities and to a capital city. Cities, and especially capital cities, have a pull, a force, as in gravity. The channel of this force consists of roads, canals, rivers, and, in modern times, the railroad. Every element in the nation revolves around its capital city, regarded by Reyaund as the very heart of the nation. In the real world this capital city is usually not in the geographic center of the territory, however, because one cannot assume a uniform spatial environment, but it achieves, nevertheless, an equilibrium between itself and all other cities in the territory. The central placement of the capital, therefore, refers to something cultural, political, economic, and historical rather than purely geographic. Communication/circulation, so important in the thinking of Saint-Simonians and all other groups and individuals thinking about space in the nineteenth century, was elevated by Reynaud to an integral part of a law of city spatial development.

Reynaud integrated his speculations about central places and circulation into his analysis of the interior of the city.[142] Keep in mind that the model for his theory was Paris. With respect to urban planning Reynaud balanced the need for some comprehensive planning, on the one hand, with the freedom of individual spatial decisions, on the other. He made the point that modern cities are generally unplanned. Some constructions and aspects of public space, however, affect the entire community. These involve health, safety, and circulation, over which the state, he believed, must have some control. Thus, the state should intervene to set basic rules for housing construction, like height and density in relation to public space, in order to permit the circulation of air and light. Public space must also be set aside for adequate streets and public gardens, further ensuring the circulation of air and thus guaranteeing the health of the city.

A key component of planning, according to Reynaud, must embrace the city's circulatory system, which he compared "to the vascular system of organisms."[143] Modern cities had one characteristic that elevated their circulatory system to the first rank of infrastructural considerations. Unlike medieval cities, which possessed one easily identifiable center, modern cities have several centers. In order for these centers to be integrated into a harmonious whole, the modern city needed a more complex circulatory system than previously. Its design was complicated, moreover, by uneven terrain, private interests, and the habits of each city center. There was only one method to achieve an effective urban circulatory system, which would bind all parts of the city: "This determination [of the circulatory system] can only be achieved by a power from on high, which has both a view of the totality and the details, and which therefore knows how to regulate harmony by a balance of all the particular tendencies and its perception of all general connections."[144] In this economical statement, Reynaud summed up both the aims of the modern planner and late-eighteenth- and early-nineteenth-century conceptions of the modern city. He identified circulation as the fundamental characteristic of the modern city, which he saw as a general, integrated system rather than as a collection of separate villages. The planner must have a comprehensive picture of the whole. Such ideas about center versus periphery and circulation were shared by virtually all progressive intellectuals who thought about Paris during the first half of the nineteenth century.

Although holistic considerations were important for certain aspects of city planning, Reynaud criticized the notion that a city could be planned de novo and remain aesthetically interesting or that all aspects of urban construction had to follow some general plan. His basic premise was that only God could construct the perfect city. All humans had faults, and therefore no one person should presume to lay out an entire city or comprehensive reform project. Considering the entire city as a single edifice, Reynaud hypothesized that the laws of its harmony were complicated, more complicated than any single construction. He would, therefore, permit individuals to design their own residences—reserving to the state the right to construct public buildings and set general construction standards—believing that an organic harmony would emerge out of the many individual designs. In other words, some underlying principle of order results in a harmony for the overall structure of the city. In this approach Reynaud differed both from the Fourierists, who are the subjects of the following chapter, and the many state engineers involved in the design and reform of cities during the nineteenth century. Concerning the latter group, Picon observed that Reynaud's concept of planning, in which the organic and individual in the city coexists with planning in certain spheres, represented a radical critique of the plans of state engineers for the construction of new cities.[145] One of the most famous of these new cities was laid out by Chabrol de Volvic—Napoléonville, whose most prominent feature was the grid pattern of streets. It was such a city Reynaud had in mind when he offered his opposite model of ideal planning, balancing spontaneous organic growth with central planning.

The architect Léonce Reynaud, Jean's brother, drew an important logical conclusion from Jean's imagining of the ideal city. Writing during the middle of the Haussmannization of Paris, Léonce aimed an ironic attack against the manner in which Paris was being transformed; he did not single out Paris explicitly, but it was clearly the model for his critique. The attack was ironic, as Picon observed, because Léonce, a professor of architecture, criticized those architects who planned ideal cities.[146] Building upon his brother's analysis, Léonce wrote that such cities or plans for cities violated a fundamental principle of urban development, namely, that the organic unplanned development of a city yields an underlying natural order. Architects, when planning cities, he noted, always think in terms of regularity and geometry where there is complexity. He summed up his critique as follows: "An ideal plan exercises a hideous influence."[147] The important point here is that both brothers recognized that urban planning is best not practiced by architects devising rational plans for an entire city without consideration for traditional and historic patterns of urban development. Of course, this was not the model Haussmann and Napoleon III followed in Paris. The kind of planning that emerged out of Saint-Simonian circles, when it addressed Paris and cities in general, would ultimately find great resonance in a postmodern critique of the kind of planning represented by a strict modernism. On the other hand, the Saint-Simonians also shared in the tradition that emerged from the Enlightenment with respect to city space, namely, a faith in the power of reason to guide the reform of the city and the elevation of its citizens. And they are particularly important in the emergence of modern urban planning to the extent that they insisted on seeing the city whole—Paris is their model—and as part of a territorial network that was both national and global.

CHAPTER FOUR

The Fourierists and the New Paris

THE FOURIERISTS' VISION of the nature of the modern city, and of
Paris in particular, was related in some respects to the Saint-Simonians'
dream of Paris. The Fourierists took their inspiration from Charles Fourier
(1772–1837), an important socialist of the first decades of the nineteenth century. Fourier's aim was to establish a society free from all repression and open
to the complete fulfillment of an individual's passions and appetites. In such
a society all classes would be reconciled and women liberated from their sub-
ordinate position. These ends would best be realized, he believed, in a rural
commune, the phalange, an autonomous democratic community of 1,620
people of different but harmoniously compatible physiological and emotional
profiles. Such a commune would be the model for the total restructuring of
society, something that would be achieved peacefully, as reasonable persons,
he held, would gladly subscribe to his vision. While Fourier believed that laws
governed social behavior, taking his inspiration from Newton's description of
the laws that governed the physical universe, his ideas were also rooted in his
intuitive understanding of human psychology. Fourier's followers during the
1830s and 1840s, largely under the influence of his major disciple, Victor Considerant, maintained the master's goal that all social classes cooperate harmoniously and that society be restructured with communes as its base. According to Fourierists, who would increasingly move away from Fourier's more
radical ideas and toward greater pragmatism, the communes would not be
centers of rural living but would exist in the heart of industrial life. Nor
would they have to be created de novo; they could be based upon already existing local political units. Unlike Fourier, his followers also came to stress the
role of technology in the future society, distanced themselves from discussions
of sex and free love, and adopted a religious posture as the ground of their so-

cial beliefs. Eventually they came to see the state as a critical agent of social change.[1]

Like the Saint-Simonians the Fourierists saw Paris as an important point in a network of national and international communication routes, a center of production, and a site for public works projects. Historians have also acknowledged that both Saint-Simonians and Fourierists mentally registered the radical changes in the structure of urban life taking place during the first half of the nineteenth century and, as Antoine Picon observed, both were in agreement that cities, especially capital cities, were in need of significant reform. According to Picon, there was, however, one essential difference between them. Fourierists focused on the ideal city and ideal housing, the Phalanstère and the Phalange, erected in a rural setting, as constituting the basis of a new society. The Saint-Simonians, on the other hand, focused more concretely on the real city as an industrial entity and on its problems.[2] Generally speaking, Saint-Simonian engineers are described as more pragmatic and more interested in public works than Fourierists, who are characterized as more inclined to theoretical speculations, guided, in the words of Bernard Marrey, by "the 'Idea' and by 'Reason.'"[3]

Two figures in particular stand as emblematic of Fourier's followers: Victor Considerant, the leader of the Fourierist school, and the pseudonymous Perreymond, a prolific and important urban writer of the 1840s. With respect to city planning, Fourier and the Fourierists, while indeed inclined to theory and speculating about the ideal society, were not as "utopian" as they are made out to be, either by Friedrich Engels in his celebrated assessment or by present-day critics.[4] Moreover, Considerant and Perreymond were both engineers, and Considerant was a member of the Paris Municipal Council—occupations that ideally suited them to reflections on the modern city, even while they took their initial inspiration from Fourier. While Fourier's followers did not adopt a scientific language or constitute or define a new discipline, they, like others in this period, did regard the urban milieu as a field governed by certain laws of spatial development, thus anticipating the application of scientific principles to urban studies and programs. They also contributed significantly to the new mental vision, which regarded the city from a comprehensive perspective in which the functioning of all its parts counted more than the magnificence of its individual constructions. And unlike the Saint-Simonians, moreover, the Fourierists paid more direct attention to planning Paris than to considering the capital as an abstract model of urban development.

FOURIER AND CITY PLANNING

Mention of the name *Fourier* immediately brings to mind the plan for a utopian rural community, the Phalanx, housed in a fantastic palace, the Phalanstery, where harmony and the full expression of natural passions would prevail. One view of Charles Fourier's utopianism with respect to community life notes that Fourier neglected the world outside the Phalanx, that he delighted in rural life, and that he offered "no counterbalancing enthusiasm for or interest in industry, urban life, technology, or science."[5] Jonathan Beecher, Fourier's biographer, however, corrected this view by pointing out that Fourier was attracted to urban architecture as a young man and in the 1790s had formulated some general principles concerning the ideal urban center. While it is true, as Beecher said, that Fourier's city planning became part of a larger theory of social transformation and that he did favor a rural setting for his ideal society,[6] Fourier's writings on the city, although not extensive and not essentially on Paris, did establish a broad approach to the city, one that subsequently inspired his important disciples when they proposed plans for a modern Paris.

Fourier drew up a plan for an ideal city sometime in the 1820s, a continuation of his 1790s speculations, which were first published in 1841 as a section of his *Théorie de l'unité universelle* and again in 1849, in a pamphlet entitled *Cités ouvrières: Des modifications à introduire dans l'architecture des villes.*[7] He was guided in his plan for the ideal city by some general principles. He began by observing that each historical stage of human development could be defined by the distinct style of its architecture and that in all periods up to the present buildings had been constructed without an overall plan for the city; consequently, they were "confusingly grouped among torturous, narrow, poorly laid out, and unhealthy streets."[8] Using the word *civilized* as a negative characteristic of his own age, Fourier noted that civilized cities had inherited the chaotic condition of the unplanned city.

Fourier's first principle with respect to the ideal city, which followed from this critique, was that cities follow a rational plan, and be constructed according to a conscious overarching vision of the whole, and, although he believed that such planning could be realized most effectively in new cities, comprehensive planning could easily be transferred to a contemporary city like Paris. His followers would do just this. Fourier's second principle was that architecture should satisfy both the visual sense and functional needs of rich and poor alike.[9] Finally, Fourier assigned the central role of planning to architects and to a body of town councilors. Of the two, Fourier placed the greatest hope in architects. For Fourier, the architect and architecture were the keys to urban reform, the elements that would establish the material foundations of the new social order. His ideal architect was "a man of taste, a political architect, [who] could, by simply reforming architectural customs, transform Civilization." This was an architect who could adopt *"le mode composé,"* or a unitary vision of architecture and the city, and thus could become "the savior of the social world."[10]

What becomes apparent here is that Fourier broadened the professional profile of the architect to make him into what we would today refer to as an urban planner. Architecture, he wrote, was eminently capable of cleaning up unhealthy neighborhoods and decorating avenues around the homes of the wealthy; it should do the same for an entire city.[11] It is noteworthy that Fourier insisted that the architect have "taste," an aesthetic consideration that he combined with the rational needs of planning. In this Fourier was much like the Saint-Simonian engineers who tried to balance reason and sentiment, science and art, in their city-planning schemes.[12] Shifting to a prescription of how to achieve city planning, Fourier proposed that "the plan or distribution of the city" not follow the design of any one architect, as this could lead to excess or, by implication, to some serious design error. Rather, he suggested the incorporation into a master city plan of the best elements of different contemporary architectural ideas and projects through architectural competitions.[13]

The only mention of some form of power in the ideal city was the Committee of Town Councillors (*comité d'édiles*) or, as Fourier referred to this group on another occasion, a Committee of Pomp (*comité d'apparat*), which would judge and control all city construction.[14] Fourier also expressed the wish that some enlightened sovereign, willing to construct a new city, might adopt his principles of urban planning.[15] Beyond this, however, he did not linger over the connection between political power and the construction of an ideal city. Writing in the late twentieth century, Henri Lefebvre pointed out that architects and urban planners always need to satisfy some master, either the state, a private developer, or a private client.[16] Fourier's failure to grapple seriously with power must be seen as a serious flaw in his speculations on planning. The question of power, however, would be addressed by his followers, who were quite cognizant of the need to interest the state in any plan for urban reform.

What follows in Fourier's exposition was an outline of the ideal city. This was, indeed, a purely utopian construction unrelated to Paris, but a sketch of Fourier's model provides an insight into the features and principles that he regarded as central to a rational city and that are reflected in the plans of his disciples for a new Paris. Fourier's ideal city was actually a plan for a central city surrounded in concentric circles by three suburbs.[17] Strict zoning structured the city: buildings in all sectors must have a designated amount of space around them, a volume that would increase in the outer zones; heavy industry and large roads were relegated to the suburbs, and lighter industry in the central city to nonresidential areas. Buildings in the central city and its suburbs should have varying degrees of ornamentation. In the central city, where land was expensive, all residential buildings should be relatively large to accommodate several households—a condition Fourier purposely built into his plan—and provide common services for its tenants, most notably the collective hiring of domestic service for a common kitchen. In another decided recognition of the importance of aesthetic considerations alongside the rational ones, Fourier proposed that streets and avenues conform to a baroque model, that is, according to him, that each end in some significant view, either a public monument or the countryside. Building styles along the neo-baroque streets, however, should vary so as to avoid monotony. The only regularity Fourier allowed was for monumental public architecture, like the gallery-street of the Louvre.[18] One can glean here an anticipation of Ebenezer Howard and Le Corbusier, although Robert Fishman noted that Utopian Socialism had been forgotten by the time Howard proposed his Garden City and Le Corbusier planned his Radiant city.[19]

Fourier was not original in his proposal to bring order and health to the city through the planning of wide and smooth-flowing streets and boulevards. We have already seen the growing awareness of eighteenth-century intellectuals of the importance of urban circulation to the life of the city, an appreciation that followed upon William Harvey's discovery of the circulation of blood through the body and Adam Smith's exposition of the easy circulation of capital through the economy, and these intellectuals had come to regard the ability of people and commerce, as well as of air and sunlight, to circulate easily through cities as a condition of their health.[20] Fourier also failed to acknowledge a likely intellectual debt to Pierre Patte (see chapter 1), whose work was based upon an important architectural competition and who articulated a comprehensive vision of the city and the importance of free circulation.[21]

The metaphor of the city as a circulatory system had become common by the nineteenth century, and this translated into programs to construct relatively wide and uncluttered urban thoroughfares. Fourier marked an important step in this direction by elevating the planning of an entire city, tied together by its road system, to the same status as monumental constructions. His followers also employed the concept of circulation, and, more specifically, speculations on the urban road system, not merely to suggest reforms of the urban infrastructure and also as a means by which to envisage the city whole. Reform of the urban road system to create a rational and overarching communication network through Paris and from Paris outward to the rest of France became the central element of Fourierist city planning, as it was of Saint-Simonian city planning. The essential difference between the two socialist camps was that the Fourierist line of reasoning and planning began with, and focused on, Paris rather than the global network of the Saint-Simonian program.

FOURIER'S FOLLOWERS:

CONSIDERANT

An important transition occurs when we move from Fourier to his disciples. In the plans and projects of Victor Considerant and Perreymond we see a shift in reformist socialist thinking from the purely theoretical to real city planning projects that combined theory with concrete suggestions for urban reform. This shift was not sudden, however. In 1834 Considerant published *Considérations sociales sur l'architectonique,* which he later incorporated as a section in the first volume of *Destinée Social.*[22] Characterized by Jonathan Beecher as Considerant's "major treatise," *Destinée Sociale* was published in three volumes between 1834 and 1844.[23] It was intended as a simple and clear exposition of Fourier's ideas generally, while the *Considérations* section articulated the Fourierist principle that architecture defines an age, critiqued contemporary unplanned or "civilized cities," called for a total social transformation, and provided a detailed description of the interior life of the Phalanx and the Phalanstère.

There was, however, one important link between this largely philosophical and utopian work and the world of real cities. Considerant rooted his critique and rejection of contemporary cities in an analysis of Paris. He began his examination by placing an imaginary observer on one of the towers of Notre-Dame Cathedral, thereby providing this critic with a view of the entire city from its geographic center. Seen from this vantage point the defining characteristic of Paris was its total lack of harmony and order; it was a city where "incoherence and fragmentation" reigned supreme. The underlying structural problem with Paris was "this absence of uniformity, of harmony, of all architectural foresight." Considerant found the disorder not only aesthetically offensive but dangerous. Reflecting typical eighteenth-century conclusions concerning the lack of free movement of air and sunlight and the spread of sickness in the city, and writing several years before Engels described conditions in Manchester in similar terms and Lecouturier employed comparable language to represent Paris, Considerant declared that "there are in Paris a million men, women, and unfortunate children who are crammed in a tight circle where the houses press against each other, rising up and superimposing their six overburdened stories; next, 600,000 of these inhabitants live without air or light, over somber, vast and viscous courts, in humid cellars, in garrets open to rain, to wind, to rats, to insects: and from the bottom to the top, from the cellar to the window tops, all is decay, stench, filth and misery." Considerant, like the public health officials of the time, recognized the close connection between urban form and disease and reminded his readers of the cholera epidemic of 1832, regretting that "the well-to-do have forgotten all that."[24]

Considerant outlined a critique of the confusion, social misery, and disorder inherent in Paris, but he also observed that the condition of Paris was also the condition of London, of St. Petersburg, and of Madrid; in short, it was characteristic of "all the great capitals; and of all the putrid dwellings of men, cities and villages, but above all of the great cities." Yet he observed, in a thesis that underlay his own efforts at practical urban reform in the 1840s, that all the urban "decay, stench, filth and misery" was "an expression of the human combinations which have produced [these conditions] and not the result of an absolute necessity and of the natural order." He was convinced that "permanent misery, periodic pestilence, and the poisoning of the atmosphere are the work of men: God had not made these things."[25] The implication was that people could plan their societies to avoid social distress.

Beecher interpreted Considerant's description of Paris from the Notre-Dame Cathedral tower as an example of the Fourierist's larger critique of French society as divided and in constant conflict. For Considerant and the "progressive" generation of the 1830s, the key to the social question, to the problem of extremes of poverty and wealth, and a major theme and section of Considerant's *Destinée Sociale,* according to Beecher, was a new social structure based upon organization, upon the unity of all social classes in the common work of production and consumption.[26] Michel de Certeau, writing in the late twentieth century, while not addressing Considerant's vision of Paris and French society, offered an interesting interpretation of the phenomenon of observing the city, any city, from a panoptical aerial perspective, which suggests an additional dimension to Considerant's manner of reading Paris. Certeau, whose observation of New York City from the 110th floor of the World Trade Center towers caused him to reflect upon the multiple ways of understanding a city, remarked that interpreting a city from on high "makes the complexity of the city readable" and represents a form of "optical knowledge" that has "the ambition of surmounting and articulating the contradictions arising from the urban agglomeration." It is a form of knowledge that values the geometric, the rational, the totalizing perspective,[27] a manner of comprehending space, moreover, that fits the "Enlightenment project," which held, according to David Harvey, "that the world could be controlled and rationally ordered if we could only picture and represent it rightly."[28] The creation of Paris as a city free of social conflict and constructed according to rationally planned spatial dimensions was a major aim of the Fourierists. But in the 1830s, Considerant's only suggestion in *Considérations sur l'architectonique* with respect to the lack of planning and disease and misery in Paris was to propose a utopian commune.

FOURIER'S FOLLOWERS:

PERREYMOND

During the 1840s, on the other hand, Considerant, like so many Parisians, addressed such issues of space as the siting of Les Halles and the fortifications question in the capital at that time. The Fourierist who first devised the most extensive plan for Parisian urban reform was not Considerant, however, but a close collaborator, Perreymond. The historical record is silent with respect to Perreymond's biography. He most likely studied at the elite French engineering school, the École polytechnique, but there is no record of a student there by that name.[29] Marcel Roncayolo speculated that someone named Edmound Perrey, a contributor to the *Revue générale de l'architecture,* whose writing style and choice of subject matter resembled Perreymond's, may have assumed the pseudonym Perreymond as his writings became more political, and while this is as good a speculation as any, we will never know for certain.[30] In the 1840s Perreymond collaborated closely with the Fourierist journals, *La Phalange* and *La Démocratie pacifique,* as well as with the *RGA,* where he was one of the editors. His closest intellectual ally, and obviously a personal acquaintance, was Considerant. On occasion both men wrote articles together on planning matters, and *La Phalange* records that once, on November 6, 1841, they jointly presented to the minister of public works a project for a French national railway system.[31] Perreymond was also a partisan of the democratic movements of the late 1840s. In 1846 Considerant helped found a Franco-Polish committee in favor of Polish independence and two years later formed a Society of the Friends of a Democratic Poland. Perreymond was undoubtedly close to these groups, as in 1847 he published *Cracovie, ou les derniers débris de la Monarchie polonaise,* in which he argued strongly for the freedom of Poland from tsarist control. Perreymond must also have been familiar with the Polish communist mystic Louis Krolikowski, who had arrived in Paris in 1839 to champion the cause of freedom for Cracow by presenting petitions to the French and English governments. Once in France, Krolikowski joined with Cabet and his followers and was instrumental in Cabet's seeing a connection between early Christianity and a communist society. As a result of his contacts with the opposition, however, Krolikowski adopted a pseudonym, Charles, so as not to lose the financial support he was receiving from the French government. In 1847 he began using his real name.[32] Whatever Perreymond's connection with Poland or to Krolikowski , we know that he was a member of the Spanish Democratic Committee and that he wrote in support of independence movements in both Spain and Portugal at this time.[33] In most of his writings, like those on Paris, Perreymond never used a first name or an initial. In 1854, however, one Charles Perreymond wrote a brochure examining Portuguese politics.[34] There is no way to determine if this is the same Perreymond who wrote about Paris. Given the style and subject matter of the study on Portugal, it could easily be, but this only deepens the mystery of why Perreymond used a pseudonym or only signed a first name on one occasion.

If we lack biographical information on Perreymond, we do have an extensive set of writings by him which appeared between 1841 and 1851 and fall into two broad categories: social, economic, and political treatises written from a Fourierist perspective and city-planning texts.[35] In political matters Perreymond shared Considerant's Christian socialism, which entailed a belief in nonviolence and the cooperation of all segments of society. Like many engineers in the first half of the nineteenth century, Perreymond also evinced a concern with technical mastery over the physical environment combined with an intense interest in social projects.[36]

Between December 1842 and November 1843 Perreymond contributed to the debate on urban sprawl in Paris by publishing a nine-part study, "Études sur la ville de Paris," in the *Revue générale de l'architecture,* on reforms to undertake in the French capital.[37] This is one of the fundamental documents in the transition in France from perceptions of the town as the site of magnificence and aesthetically pleasing architecture—in Donald Olsen's terminology, the "city as a work of art," or in Richard Etlin's more inclusive characterization, the city as "the space of magnificence, of hygiene, of clarity, and of emulation"[38]—to modern comprehensive urban planning, which elevates the functional arrangement of space on the ground to a status equal to that of architectural monuments. In the Perreymond text the overriding concern is with circulation and traffic flow and with the proper spatial relationship between the vital urban center of public services and attractions and the rest of the city. One context for this concern was the anxiety expressed by public officials and intellectuals during this time with overcrowded streets—streets teeming with vehicles of all kinds, people, and dense building construction.[39] Moreover, as we have seen in earlier chapters, concern with the city's central core and the focus on circulation and the city as a site of production linked to the national territory were among the central tropes in city-planning texts during the first half of the nineteenth century. Perreymond's study provides the fullest theoretical expression during the 1840s of such mid-nineteenth century ideas about the city. Moreover, Perreymond's profession is another signal of the importance of engineers, as opposed to architects, as the new managers of urban space by mid-century. Although the two professions were not yet sharply divided, engineers, as Picon noted, thought in more dynamic terms than architects and focused more on the total control and reorganization of urban space.[40]

Perreymond was not the first to speculate about the significance of communication flow and a stable city center as keys to urban planning in Paris. As we have seen, the eighteenth-century architect Pierre Patte had already argued for a Paris road and street system that linked all parts of the city.[41] Closer in time to Perreymond, in 1840 Ernest de Chabrol-Chaméane had identified a vital and stable city center and an overarching road system connecting all parts of the city to this center as essential to the efficient functioning of Paris—as Meynadier did in 1843.[42] Perreymond differed from these two writers, however, in working out such insights with greater rigor and theoretical sophistication. With respect to the importance of the city center, moreover, Perreymond went beyond Chabrol-Chaméane and Meynadier in the radical reforms he suggested for the reorganization of the city center.

Perreymond's hypothesis explaining the contemporary condition of Paris was informed by his conviction that the "vital principle" of successful urban development,[43] what had made the city viable and great in the past, was that Paris had originally had a compact center of vital public services in one location, the Cité; that additional centers of important public activity had remained close and in easy communication with each other and the historic center; and that the Seine River provided a principal communication route for the entire city, reinforcing the unity of the urban fabric. As Paris grew, however, centers of public services and activities multiplied and dispersed, forming within the political boundary of the city several centers with little relationship to each other. Paris, he believed, had lost the two essential qualities that had made it a well-functioning city: "*homogeneity and centralization.*"[44]

The major negative consequence of the lack of a powerful central anchor in Paris was the uneven economic and social development of the city. Commercial and entertainment activities were centered on the Right Bank, and as they became ever more important and concentrated there, the well-to-do moved in a westward direction along this part of the river, reinforcing its importance. In turn, the government favored this area with better communication routes and other services, which resulted in an even greater concentration there. The Left Bank was becoming a "desert" in the sense that public works and economic activity were passing it by, and the region was becoming increasingly poor. Collectively, Perreymond observed, Paris was a wealthy and great city, but it was spatially and socially fractured and divided, a condition that in the Middle Ages corresponded to the hierarchical beliefs of the time but in the modern world was untenable.

Perreymond then elevated these insights into two general principles that he believed were applicable to any city. First, for a city to be viable and healthy—by which he meant a city with even and equitable development and with easy access for all to public services—it must have one principle stable and vital center of commercial, judicial, political, and cultural services, and such a center must be linked to all secondary urban centers and to the periphery of the city by easily accessible and major urban communication routes. Moreover, Perreymond clearly meant that such a vital center was also the virtual geographic center of the city. A second principle, closely related to the twin themes of the vital center and efficient communication, was the notion, espoused especially by Saint-Simonian but also by Fourierist engineers, that the motor of modern society was commerce and industry and that these could be served well only in a territory, including its urban nuclei, where smooth communication throughout was the norm.[45] Later we will encounter Perreymond's project for a national rail system, which he believed was more spatially centralized that the one proposed by Michel Chevalier and the Saint-Simonians. Here we should note that rapid communication, movement, and circulation were absolutely central to Perreymond's conception of the modern world by pointing out that he also championed balloon flights as a potentially important mode of global circulation.[46]

Lepetit believed that Perreymond's theory of city development, with its discussion of the centrality and pull of an urban core, was inspired by the Newtonian law of gravitation, and was for Perreymond equally universal, that is, applicable to all cities as well as to regional space.[47] Fourier was also attracted to Newton's principles of order and harmony in the universe, and he believed "that the key to the right ordering of human affairs must lie in the discovery of some social or moral analogue to the principle of gravitational attraction."[48] For an urban planner, however, a principal difficulty in such an inspiration is that a Newtonian universe is rather mechanical and inflexible. The planner's ability to accept disorder in the city, to see little details—in short, to accept life as it is lived at the ground—is compromised by an Enlightenment faith in this model and the belief that it had a spatial equivalent in the city. Perreymond's design of a unified communications system in Paris was the urban spatial equivalent of the Newtonian universe.

Perreymond also had available to him another model of the importance of urban centrality and communication. Under Louis XIV France had become a highly centralized state politically and administratively. By the mid-nineteenth century it was also becoming evident, especially to an engineer like Perreymond, who had designed, with his fellow Fourierist engineer, Victor Considerant, an ideal national railway system,[49] that railroads would metaphorically shrink the national space, thereby adding spatial consolidation to political centralization. Not only did Perreymond not challenge the high degree of political centralization in France, as one might expect of a utopian socialist, but he faulted Louis XIV for not applying centralizing principles to Paris.[50] Perreymond embraced centralization as a principle that applied to the territory as well as to cities because it fit well with an ideology that equated commercial development with national unity and the easy circulation of capital and commerce, as well as with his belief in a universal law governing city development. Perreymond, building on Chabrol-Chaméane's insight, had also anticipated the Meier thesis on the attraction and centrality of a city center.

Beyond asserting general principles of city development, Perreymond was quite specific with respect to the exact public works projects necessary to reform Paris, devoting the third part of his study to a long list of these projects.[51] These he divided into three broad categories: reforms to be undertaken by the central government, those to be executed by the city, and those demanded by public opinion. In his first category were important public service buildings and constructions, a new national library, a new central post office, piers, a new national theater, a mint, royal archives, a ministry of foreign affairs office, a royal printing house, an exposition hall for arts and crafts, a residence for the archbishop of Paris, library buildings for the Arsenal and for Saint-Geneviève, and a building for the Institute of France. Circulation dominated the second and third categories: the need to improve navigation on the Seine River, the circulation of water in the city, the enlargement and improvement of the public roadway, and the siting of railway stations. What is important here is Perreymond's recognition of the role of the Seine as a major communication route through Paris, as well as its economic and commercial potential, and his integration of the river into a hierarchy of communication roads throughout Paris.[52] In this section of his work he also singled out the need to expand the central Paris food market.

Having established the importance of a powerful city center and communication routes throughout the city and having enumerated a list of specific projects, Perreymond, in the sixth and single longest section of his study, proposed situating the new constructions he identified, along with other improvements, in the historic center of Paris, whose radical spatial alteration he also envisioned. Pierre Lavedan characterized this section of Perreymond's work as an unbridled flight of imagination.[53] While this section is informed in some of its details by Fourierist conceptions and is a model of an ideal urban center, it is not, however, fanciful. The new Paris that Perreymond proposed, which was rooted in the spatial realities of old Paris, was a plan for a massive transformation of the city center and an important forerunner of Baron Haussmann's extensive renovation of that same center.

Perreymond's starting point for the transformation of the historic center of Paris was his call for the vast demolition of the contiguous quarters of the Cité, the Palais de Justice, and of the île Saint-Louis, with the exception of the great monuments there, such as the Cathedral of Notre-Dame and the Chapel of Saint-Louis. He would then fill in the left arm of the Seine River from the Austerlitz bridge to the Pont-Neuf on the Left Bank, thus creating one bed for the river. On this cleared terrain he would locate the new constructions and services he had proposed earlier. As a justification for massive urban renewal, he pointed out that the place of reform represented the geographic and traditional center of Paris, and massive new construction there would save the government the enormous expense of having to duplicate or create anew public services elsewhere.

Perreymond divided the open area into two large zones, Nouvelle Lutèce, which extended from the Pont-Neuf (Left Bank) to Notre-Dame, and the Bazar National, which comprised the territory from the Notre-Dame Cathedral to the end of the former île Louviers, which had been joined to the Right Bank in 1843 (today the space between the quay Henri IV and the boulevard Morland, and the rue d'Aubigné and the rue Schomberg). All the new establishments of public art, science, and administration that the city government was currently considering—the new libraries and the new theater, for example—would be constructed in Nouvelle Lutèce. Perreymond designated the Bazar National as the chief place of entry into Paris for people, commerce, and merchandise. There he would construct a new central food market, large warehouses, huge parking spaces for vehicles, and railway stations. He was particularly original in his insight that the siting of railway stations would be a powerful motor in the spatial configuration of Paris. In 1842 the central government had passed a railway law designating Paris as the hub of a future national railway system, thus making the issue of siting railway stations critical.

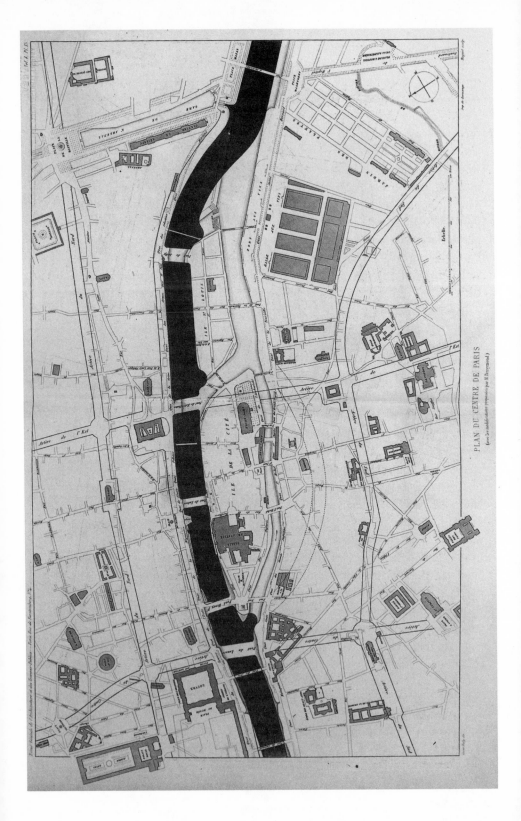

PLAN DU CENTRE DE PARIS

(avec les modifications proposées par M. Perreymond.)

Too many stations on the Right Bank, he correctly believed, would favor the concentration of people and construction there, so he planned new stations on the Left Bank. Moreover, he designated some stations for passengers only, and these would be located near the quays, from which points passengers could easily circulate through Paris. Rail stations for light merchandise would be located in the Bazar National. From there deliveries could be made throughout the city, while heavy merchandise would enter Paris at its periphery.

Perreymond was less original when it came to suggestions for new streets. He proposed major through streets perpendicular and parallel to the Seine River, but other writers were doing the same at this time.[54] What is important about Perreymond, however, is the strong case he made for easy and smooth circulation throughout Paris and his integration of the entire city into a network of streets and boulevards. He did have one original project for a new street, however, a forty meter-wide road, to be called the rue de Lutèce, running east to west in a southward arc from the Pont-Neuf to the quai de la Tournelle, thus traversing Nouvelle Lutèce. Perreymond incorporated Fourierist architectonic principles into this street; as in Fourier's commune, glass-covered galleries would connect public buildings and hotels, thereby facilitating "circulation throughout the interior of this first zone of the new center of Paris." Beyond this street, he also proposed that all public buildings in both zones of the new Paris center be connected "with large galleries and glass porticos in such a manner that one can go from one extreme to the other of the new center of the capital without having to suffer the inclemencies of the seasons."[55]

In the same decade that Perreymond was proposing an ideal Paris he also produced a series of important studies on the social question in the capital which offer insights into what his planning aimed to accomplish and in what sense his spatial conceptions might be linked to his Fourierist philosophy.[56] Perreymond subscribed to a Fourierist socialism as it was being articulated by Considerant.[57] Like Considerant, Perreymond believed that society at the time was fragmented and poorly organized with respect to labor and production and that egoism and individuality reigned, with the result that a small

Facing page

A project drawn up by the Fourierist Perreymond for a radical transformation of the historic center of Paris. The dotted arc represents a new east-west street, the rue de Lutèce, which would facilitate travel through central Paris. Avery Architectural and Fine Arts Library, Columbia University fraction of the population lived well while the large majority lived and toiled in misery. France possessed the resources to adequately feed and house its entire population, so a new social organization was called for. The new society would be one in which capital, labor, and talent combined in cooperative associations to increase production and its distribution. Such a society would be achieved through nonviolent democratic means—the expression most commonly used by the Fourierists was "pacific democracy"—brought about through the force and power of ideas. Like Considerant, Perreymond explicitly linked his social goals with the principles of early Christianity.

Perreymond worked out these ideals in meticulous detail—a characteristic of his writing—in two companion pieces, *Le Bilan de la France,* which he wrote in July 1848, a month after the closure of the National Workshops, and in *Paris monarchique et Paris républicain,* which he completed in July 1849 and published in 1849, the same year that *Le Bilan* appeared. National and Parisian authorities, in the days following the February 1848 revolution, had instituted emergency measures to solve the crisis of unemployment and social misery, which had contributed to the revolution. Among these was a declaration of "the right to work," which implied that public authorities had to create employment opportunities where none existed and that National Workshops should be instituted on the outskirts of Paris to absorb the city's huge unemployed population. By the end of June 1848, the government, opposed to the tampering with property rights and secure in its position, shut down the National Workshops. Workers, reaching a total of about fifty thousand, reacted by setting up barricades in their neighborhoods. Government troops confronted them and, in the ensuing battle, which began on June 25 (and lasted until the 27th), about three thousand people were killed and some fifteen thousand arrested, many of whom ended up in detention camps in Algeria. There is no direct reference to these events in *Le Bilan,* although Perreymond does address them in *Paris monarchique et Paris républicain.* Given the broad scope and extensive documentation of *Le Bilan,* Perreymond had probably already set down his ideas when the "June Days" took place. What we do have in *Le Bilan,* as well as in *Paris monarchique,* is an extensive documentation of the material condition of France at the time of the July Monarchy and the expression of a general philosophy of social organization.

Perreymond begins *Le Bilan* with an underlying assumption that the pressing reality of the times was "misery" and that, "from an ethical point of view, misery is the consequence of the antagonism, of the extreme individualism, of the fratricidal isolation in which men *still* live." Explicitly taking inspiration from scripture, he counseled "fraternity" and the destruction "of antagonism through the transformation and reconciliation of interests." The government was responsible for bringing this about since, as a consequence of the democratic principles of the revolution, "every man has the right to demand of society: *Let me live,* and society has the right to demand of him: *Give me your labor.*"[58] What was needed to achieve a new order was the cooperation and association of capital and labor in the spirit of Christian harmony. "Pagan egotism produces misery, revolts, wars, devastation, and death. Christian fraternity provides well-being, peace, work, and life." Society had to choose between the two.[59] He then devoted the greater part of *Le Bilan* to a detailed record of the material life of French people in order to identify precisely the nature and structure of this misery; he also offered an outline of how to overcome it. The solution was for society to replace the isolation of agricultural and industrial labor with cooperative production, which would increase output and lower the cost of living, providing the population with housing and workshops in which people could enjoy "pure air" and light, and guarantee everyone a free education, which would foster a love of justice and fraternity.

He incorporated Paris into this analysis—asking rhetorically, "What is Paris, this proud capital of French society?"—by offering a social definition of the capital as a place where *"five* out of six" people who had died over the prior ten years had been given a burial through charity, where statistical findings revealed "general misery" and "the profound evil of debts," the capital of a nation characterized by "continual destruction each day and every hour which renders society guilty of *suicide.*"[60] Paris and all French cities posed particular problems. There was in all French cities and their suburbs, he reported, a core of about three and a half million people who were perpetually poor. This was of great concern because "this nomad population of our cities is almost always forced to have recourse to public and private charity, and whenever it *can* or *wants to,* turns to stealing and prostitution in order to live."[61] Here Perreymond, though a social reformer, inadvertently betrayed a glimpse of the fear shared by the Parisian and French bourgeoisie of the urban poor. A reformation of society would not only eliminate misery and suffering, a biblical injunction for Perreymond, it would also tame the potentially dangerous urban masses. An even clearer sense of Perreymond's Christian socialism emerges in his post–National Workshops analysis of Parisian society.

On July 20, 1849, Perreymond completed a study in which he analyzed the social question with conditions in Paris serving as a model. In *Paris monarchique et Paris républicain* he grappled directly with the conservative shift in the political life of France. The movement in the direction of an antisocialist republicanism was represented by several major developments. A Constituent Assembly elected on April 23, 1848, was composed of a significant majority of conservative antisocialist representatives, and its first meeting, on May 4, marked the end, according to Maurice Agulhon, of the revolutionary period inaugurated in February.[62] It was this assembly that had dissolved the National Workshops in June 1848. Its choice of an Executive Commission composed of liberal republicans, also hostile to socialism, was another step in this conservative shift, as was the election on December 10, 1848, of Louis Napoleon, a man committed to Bonapartism and empire rather than republicanism, to the presidency of the Republic. Another decisive movement in this direction was the election on May 13, 1849, by universal suffrage, of the second major institution of the Second Republic, after the presidency, of a new Legislative Assembly. More than five hundred representatives in this assembly were conservatives, men favoring above all order and property rights. About one hundred were committed republicans, partisans of the newspaper *Le National,* while about two hundred of its members were democratic socialists. Perreymond's analysis of the transformation of French political life from February 1848, when workers had legally obtained lower working hours, the "right to work," a labor ministry, and National Workshops, to the summer of 1849, when conservative forces overturned these gains and were busy securing the unhampered use of private property, places him in the camp of the democratic socialists and, more specifically, in the ranks of Christian socialists, followers of people like Philippe Buchez and Considerant.

Perreymond believed that the great failure of liberal republicans was their inability to solve the social question, their failure to address in a successful manner "the *question of work.*"[63] The National Workshops had been poorly organized, and under Alexandre Marie, the man in charge of their operation, assisted by the engineer Émile Thomas, they had been engaged in socially useless labor. Perreymond defended the principle of organizing labor in National Workshops, but he would have had workers take part in public works projects aimed at housing construction, urban sanitation, and the manufacture of clothing and furniture, works that would serve the Republic and also "raise the population from the state of vileness in which it vegetates and wallows." Socially useful labor would benefit workers, who would in turn stimulate the economy, and all would prosper. Perreymond, a true child of the Enlightenment, believed that this idea had great and irresistible power. He fantasized an ideal outcome: "The great city was quieted: work ennobled and sanctified everything: the revolution of February had accomplished without discord its regenerative mission through work, its social mission by science and self-sacrifice."[64]

Beyond emergency measures like the National Workshops, Perreymond believed that a new permanent organization of labor was called for. All producers should form cooperative associations that would regulate labor, production, salaries, and distribution. Ideally formed in each trade, the workers' cooperatives, or mutual aid societies, would receive financial assistance and guarantees from the government, a debt they would repay over time. Using tailors, both masters and workers, as a model trade corporation, Perreymond suggested a federal structure in its organization. About twenty workshops of about twenty workers each would form in each arrondissement. These "salubrious workshops" would be distributed throughout Paris for "public convenience." Their size and cleanliness would "ameliorate immediately the unsanitary state of the corporation of tailors."[65] As a result, the state would obtain multiple benefits: increased production through a superior and harmonious organization of labor, lower prices for goods, a repayment of its loan, and social peace. The entire program was inspired by Perreymond's belief in Christian cooperation and mutuality. In this he resembled most closely the Christian socialist Philippe Buchez,[66] although Perreymond did not go so far as to call for the elimination of capitalism or of private property, merely their reorganization and incorporation into a regime of worker and owner cooperation.

Perreymond's goal for a reorganization of production in the form of cooperation was informed by an economic analysis directly tied to his vision of a new Paris. Circulation was the key to the economy as it was to the city. He began his analysis by translating the needs of the people in 1848 into the biblical expression *"Give us, Lord, our daily bread."*[67] This expression addressed Perreymond's main point, namely, that work is at the center of life. The essence of work for Perreymond was its dynamic nature: "Work reproduces work; multiplied by itself it continues to multiply." Work had no limits because "work is life, and life can only exist on condition that it renew itself, that it propagate itself without ceasing, without ever stopping."[68] It was therefore critical that society organize work efficiently for its own maximum benefit. For Perreymond this meant the recognition that, in terms of productive capacity, work performed in association was superior to work performed in isolation. Therefore, "the mission of society . . . consists in the art and science of grouping voluntarily, of uniting, of associating all human activities, of not permitting idleness, of utilizing all activities for the general interest and prosperity, in a word, to organize work." The point of this was to establish the organization of work on its "true foundations," so that "life shall circulate abundantly throughout the social body and with life the richness of production and the abundance of consumption." He summed up his entire philosophy concerning the importance of, and link between, circulation and work as follows: "In order to raise our country out of the misery in which it vegetates and languishes, it is necessary to utilize all the forces residing in men, women, children, in motors of all kinds, natural or artificial: to establish the electric current of work from the center to the periphery, from the periphery to the center."[69] Reducing work to human and machine motor force and energy, with the requirement that such work circulate abundantly in society in order to stimulate its own further circulation as well as that of capital, Perreymond's economic and work system had its spatial counterpart in a city whose infrastructure complemented the circulatory network of work and capital.

In practical terms he suggested that society give priority to useful work: to public and private sanitation projects in cities and the countryside, to the construction of clean housing, to the production of nutritious food, to the manufacture of clothing and useful furniture. All work, whether rural or urban, should be organized according to the principle of the division of labor. Echoing the Saint-Simonians, he called for the formation, in the departments of France, of work "battalions or communal groups of fifty, one hundred, two hundred workers, depending on the needs of the localities and the type of work."[70] In the cities and throughout France, corps of housing constructors, entrepreneurs, and workers should undertake the restoration of old and the construction of new housing for the masses. In all these projects Perreymond foresaw the financial assistance and cooperation of the central and local governments as well as local property owners, because the projects would increase the value of property and production throughout the society. He concluded his analysis by invoking the bold engineering spirit of the École polytechnique as a model for the totality of his projects. Openly parading his Enlightenment confidence in science and reason, he concluded that man's "moral, material, [and] intellectual" needs were known, that lack of such knowledge was no longer a problem. "To work, then," he wrote, "in the name of social regeneration through labor!" The result would be the eventual realization "of the superior harmonies of God, of Creation, and of humanity."[71]

If Perreymond had a positive and sanguine vision of what the future could be like he also expressed, even if in low voice, its opposite side. He rejected revolution and wished to see the social question solved peacefully in a society that harmonized opposing interests in the name of the higher goal of Christian unity. It is evident that he favored good housing for the masses, but it is not evident in his writing about Paris where exactly workers would live once they had been displaced from the city's center. Since a major point of his study was the issue of the displacement of the population, it is surprising that Perreymond never addressed this issue. Although his social analysis was worked out following his 1842/43 studies of Paris, he clearly held similar ideas when he proposed a new spatial organization for the capital. It might seem surprising at first that mention of residential housing was conspicuously missing in his project for a new Paris, although he drew up a list of streets whose houses should be demolished to accommodate his reform program.[72] People, too, hardly appeared in his analysis of the new Paris. The city in Perreymond's vision, as Marcel Roncayolo noted critically, was not a particular landscape or a place to live but rather a force field of movement.[73] When Perreymond mentioned people, as he did on one occasion, it was to note that his suggested reforms for the center of Paris would rid the center of Paris of its "dangerous, vicious, or miserable" population. In another section he advised that his design for the new Paris food markets on spacious grounds with adequate and generous roads would have a beneficial effect on morality and public safety because of the "material impossibility of making the environs of the markets a physical and moral sewer like that which surrounds these establishments today. The new placement [of the market] will no longer permit a particular population to congregate on a single point, and to create there a center of infection which is noxious to itself as well as to the health and morals of the general population."[74]

Only in one short section of the fifth part of the plan for Paris did Perreymond linger a while over the social question and its relation to space in Paris.[75] There he recorded, with some alarm, selective basic data concerning the lower classes of the capital. There lived in Paris, he wrote, some 330,000 people who were genuinely poor, who did not have, in his words, "twenty francs to their name." Of these, 63,000 "form the dangerous and brutalized class, and 55,000 the vicious class." This was in addition to "the frightening total of 84,000 indigents inscribed on the public rolls who receive *aid* from the hospice administration . . . without counting the shameful poor."[76] (He underscored the word *aid* to emphasize that the aid dispensed by the government was not sufficient to meet the real needs of the poor.) If the language was reminiscent of Frégier's negative portrait of the working poor in his book on the dangerous classes in Paris it is because Perreymond based his characterization of the lower classes on Frégier's work. The solution he suggested was that Paris be transformed into a "more and more desirable" city in order to attract a more well-to-do population. As for the very poor, whom he seemed to fear so much—and he did not distinguish between the working poor and those below this group—he found it necessary "through administrative measures skillfully combined, to lead the fathers of families of a certain fixed class of the population to understand that it is not in its moral and material interest to live in these poor infected lodgings, lacking in comforts and honest pleasures, that they could enjoy certain comforts of life if they would abandon the walls or the environs of the capital."[77] In other words, they should leave Paris to live in its suburbs and beyond. One means by which the government could ensure this result, he wrote, was to expend funds on public works projects in the provinces, rendering them more attractive to parts of the Paris population.

Given this kind of language, how does Perreymond's kind of planning relate to his socialism, to his concern for the social question found in his political writings? First, Perreymond's fear seems to have centered on a class of Parisians below the stratum of the working poor, although he does not clearly distinguish the two. With respect to workers simply, he did suggest a possible key to understanding how spatial reforms would advance a socialist agenda. As a preface to Perreymond's first article of the Paris study, César Daly published a letter from Perreymond to the journal introducing the series.[78] In it Perreymond observed that one consequence of the public works related to the roads and the center of Paris he was about to recommend would be to give "advantageous work to the laboring and suffering classes." The very nature of the work, the very execution of the projects, would itself provide immediate relief. As he elucidated no further, except by suggesting outmigration to suburbs for some classes mentioned above, these two remarks may be interpreted in two complementary ways. First, the public works projects would produce actual work of a large magnitude, employment with a salary for an extensive army of labor; thus gainfully employed, labor could aspire to improve its material social status.

The second possible meaning of Perreymond's remarks is, perhaps, more important. The nature of the projects Perreymond had in mind—the very subject of his entire essay—would result in a total transformation of Paris. It would be a cleaner and healthier city, one with an efficient distribution of water, an expanded market for more efficient food delivery, a vital city center, and, most of all, a modern system of streets and avenues to facilitate urban, national, and international commerce and production. The net result of the reform and transformation of Paris would be to create a city whose very spatial form would establish the material basis for the harmony of the social classes—although ideally the very poor would no longer live in the city—and guarantee happiness for all its inhabitants. It was as if the social question in Paris would be solved once the correct material and spatial framework for the city had been established. Presumably, too, Paris would serve as a model for other French cities, and such cities and the countryside, itself transformed through cooperative labor, would exist in a balanced and harmonious relationship. Perreymond did not so much ignore the social question in his plan for Paris as assume that the physical transformation of the capital would set in motion events that would, as a byproduct, alleviate if not go a long way toward solving social misery. In any case, his focus, his overarching concern in his plan for Paris, was the city's physical layout. Neither considerations of architecture, building aesthetics, or people figure prominently in his study, and his discussion of building projects was limited to public constructions. The omission, for the most part, of the people of Paris from his plan for the city seems especially surprising given Perreymond's Christian socialist beliefs, and must rank as a major flaw in his planning proposals.

Reading the corpus of Perreymond's writings creates the impression of someone with an enormous confidence in the power of reason to create a better social order and a rational city. While his essay on Paris was not completely unrelated to his socialism—the rationally arranged city is the material basis for a socialist order of harmony between the classes—he was largely concerned with getting the spatial dimensions right. In this domain he did work out the most rigorous theoretical, historical, and practical case for a new spatial profile for Paris of any of his contemporaries. The entire plan for a new Paris, he explained, was not only the product of his own research and ideas but was also intended as a synthesis of the many writings of his generation on space issues in the capital.[79] His contribution in this arena should not be minimized. His perspective on Paris was not that far removed from Considerant's, from the height of the towers of Notre-Dame Cathedral, but it was more sophisticated. It was as if Perreymond imagined Paris simultaneously from a bird's-eye perspective and from the ground in order to grasp the entire city at once, observing all the important spatial details of Paris without, however, losing sight of the whole. He had identified the importance of smooth and efficient communication as a feature of modern urban life, which led him to see the city as an integral organism with a coherent network of roads and traffic flow.

The new spatial form that Perreymond imagined for Paris was rational, coherent, and unified, so it formed the material basis for a harmonious organization of all classes. Progress in civic and social matters was the result, ultimately, of the march of reason and Christian principles. The city, moreover, was part of a national setting, and its spatial organization would contribute to the circulation of wealth and the productive life of the nation. Seeing the city as a unit he was also adamant that all urban reform had to conform to a comprehensive plan, that partial measures, while useful, were inadequate. After all, the original problem with contemporary Paris, he concluded, had been its growth without any central planning. The issue of urban reform was complex, but "it is necessary to find a general solution that satisfies each of the partial issues [of urban reform], according to the degree of their importance, and that coordinates all reforms in such a way as to harmonize them completely."[80] David Donald wrote that there is a belief in "high modernism" "that if you could get the space right, if you could organize all bits of the city in the right configuration, then the social problems would go away."[81] Donald was correct to criticize this vision as an oversimplification. I would add, however, that such an attitude toward space, as the example of Perreymond demonstrates, came into its own much earlier than the period of high modernism; it was the product of an Enlightenment tradition that reached its full flowering during the first half of the nineteenth century.

Perreymond was quite prescient in recognizing that reform in one part of the city could have unintended consequences elsewhere. Like so many reformers of his generation he understood the relationship of dense housing construction and narrow unsanitary streets to the health of the city, especially following the cholera epidemic of 1832, and he devoted the third part of his study to health and the city.[82] He understood, however, that "even the demolition and reconstruction of entire blocks of unhealthy houses, though dramatic, will only succeed in substituting well-planned and healthy quarters which are, however, like the Marais, uninhabited, in contrast to those with irregular and unhealthy constructions but which are full of animation, like the quarters of old Paris, if they are not combined with a view of the entire city."[83] Whether the example he chose was a good one or not is less important than his conclusion: all city planning had to follow a general plan. This focus on the interrelationship of all parts of the city must rank as a major contribution, by Perreymond and others of his generation, as we see throughout the early nineteenth century, to a theory of modern urban planning. While the comprehensive urban-planning vision frequently overlooked the real life of the common people and their neighborhoods, it also represented an intellectual advance over purely local or partial views of the modern city. In short, this form of planning had both positive elements and a potentially serious flaw, one that became more apparent as time went on. Comprehensive planning was a step forward in the understanding of the city as a unified entity linked to a larger territory, but, being the product of self-consciously elite intellectuals, if often failed to balance its vision with the subjective needs of the people or the neighborhood.

Although apparently deeply concerned with the social question, Perreymond also offered another example of what Michel Foucault identified as the increased concern in certain circles with social space engineering to maintain order. While this concern was especially characteristic of political authority in the nineteenth century, it is interesting to note that a political counter-current, the Fourierist, was also attracted, for reasons of its own commitment to rational planning, to principles of order in the city.[84] Moreover, the entire project of Perreymond and the Fourierists, although as socialists they were critical of unbridled capitalism and liberal politics, was consistent with what

Gilles Deleuze and Félix Guattari described as an essential requirement of state power—nonsocialist or socialist, one may add—namely, its "need for fixed paths in well-defined directions, which restrict speed, regulate circulation, relativize movement, and measure in detail the relative movements of subjects and objects."[85]

One more principle underlying Perreymond's text, a principle also shared by Considerant, needs mention. As indicated earlier, for Choay the adoption of a scientific language was one hallmark of modern urbanism. Perreymond and his cohorts did not develop such a language, but they did anticipate it. An implicit assumption of Perreymond's text is that city development is governed by underlying laws that can be discovered by reason. By investigating Paris Perreymond believed that he had come up with "an abstract formula which offers, as it were, the philosophy of the history of the successive population displacements of Paris. Moreover, this formula can be applied, with a few modifications, to the history of any city." The governing principle of healthy and balanced city development—that city growth depended upon all parts of the city having easy access to a "principal focus" that was "Singular, Stable, Central and Active"[86]—was one he had elevated to scientific certainty.

PERREYMOND, CONSIDERANT,

REGIONAL PLANNING, AND

POLITICAL OFFICE

Following his study of Paris planning Perreymond collaborated with Considerant to produce a series of articles on Paris urban reform for the journal *La Démocratie pacifique.*[87] While both men focused on individual projects they believed required the attention of public officials, projects that for the most part addressed the need for communication routes linking all parts of Paris, the other important characteristic of their approach to urban reform was to place the French capital within a regional context, that is, the greater Paris area of immediate suburbs, and to make an argument for what today we would call regional urban planning. On this subject Richard Sennett summarized the intellectual origins and trajectory of this form of planning.

> By the beginning of the Second World War, those concerned with the organization of cities had, by and large become ideologues of a peculiar sort. Their dogma was hardly an emotional one, nor an ideal of great intellectual depth, but these deficiencies were more than compensated for by a doglike faith in what has come to be called "metropolitan planning." This planning ideal, which gathered strength in the 1930s—although it was contained in

germ in the writings of Ebenezer Howard at the turn of the century—proposed to take the assumptions behind Haussmann's rebuilding of Paris one step further: city planners would design coherently the growth of whole urban regions, coordinate the physical, economic, and social efforts not only within the jurisdiction of one city, but also in relation to the needs of other cities around it. What was in Haussmann's work an assumption of the desirable power of one part of the urban complex to affect other parts became in the metropolitan planning ideology an ideal of *planning the parts from the nature of the whole.*[88]

Sennett's portrait is quite accurate, although the first insights into this form of planning belonged to Perreymond and his generation of city planners. As Parisians were moving north and west in greater numbers, Considerant and Perreymond noted that small centers of local activity—economic and artistic, for instance—were springing up both in and around Paris to the north and west without any thought being given to linking them spatially with each other or with the central city. The classic heart of old Paris, especially the three arrondissements of the Left Bank, were being drained of resources and people as a consequence. Beyond this, however, the expansion of Paris beyond its present fortifications was being severely threatened by the continuous buildup of areas outside the tax walls, which were being developed with no reference of their relationship to Paris, especially to a planned system of roads that could link the greater Paris area and accommodate the inevitable expansion of the capital. The solution both men offered is quite modern, seeing the city as part of a regional system. As they wrote, "What is needed is a plan of the whole, discussed by the delegates of the central government and by the representatives of the department, at the department's administrative headquarters. This plan should embrace the entire territory of the department and regulate the public works program of the state, the city and the communes, hitherto isolated and capriciously independent."[89]

In addition to their interest in regional urban planning, Perreymond and Considerant, as indicated above, joined the debate in the 1840s on France's railroad policy and thereby considered the position of Paris within the national territory. Their plan for a national railway network—one that differed radically from that of the Saint-Simonians—is interesting, moreover, because it represents another example of the translation of Fourierism into spatial terms. Considerant was initially opposed to all-out railway development in France, and he presented a reasoned case supporting his position.[90] Writing in 1838, he argued that current railroad technology was crude and that the enormous sums that would be necessary to build a national railway system would only serve to increase the power of the "High Barons" of the new "industrial feudal class."[91] The capital necessary for railroad construction would be better spent, he maintained, on addressing the social question at home, on investments in agricultural development, and on perfecting France's existing national highway and waterway system. By 1841 he had changed his mind, influenced most likely by Perreymond. In that year he wrote an introduction to an article Perreymond published in *La Phalange*.[92] In it he explained that a project for a national railway system proposed by Perreymond satisfied the aims of the Fourierist school for social justice and therefore he supported it. Jonathan Beecher wrote that Considerant had come to see the potential of the railroad for peaceful communication and to favor it as long as it was owned and operated by the state.[93]

What Perreymond proposed was an expression of his general ideology of communication. He accepted the need for a national railway system because it would intensify commercial exchange and passenger movement. What he opposed was the plan put forward by Michel Chevalier, a variation of which the government adopted in 1842. That is, he believed that a national rail network with Paris serving as the hub for a star-shaped track system left too many parts of the country without rail service. He proposed a vertebral system of tracks with the main line running north-south and passing through Paris and Châteauroux, the first representing the political and the second the geographic center of France. Secondary lines would branch off this central spine. Another feature of the Perreymond plan was its integration of France's waterways, which Perreymond believed should also be developed, into the rail system, producing thereby a balanced national transportation network. For Perreymond and Considerant this was a "system of centralization," which assured a fair spatial distribution of the riches of the country as well as greater geographic unity. Such a central north-south line, moreover, had strategic military advantages, as the occupation of the center meant that one could easily manoeuver to meet the enemy at any point in the country's circumference. This was the project both men presented to the minister of public works on November 6, 1841.[94]

In November 1843, the same year that Considerant and Perreymond collaborated with respect to Paris, Considerant won election to the General Council of the Seine Department from the Tenth Arrondissement of Paris. In April 1834 a new law had been passed on the administration of Paris. A small number of Parisian electors would choose thirty-six representatives for the General Council, three from each of the city's twelve arrondissements. In addition, electors in the neighboring arrondissements of Sceaux and Saint-Denis would choose eight for this body. The thirty-six representatives from Paris would also sit as a municipal council for Paris. It would be convoked by the prefect of the Seine Department and could only discuss matters submitted to it by the prefect. The law, however, contained two important innovations. For the first time since the Great Revolution, there would be a distinct body to pass on Parisian matters, and this was, even though based upon a narrow electorate of wealth and position, an elected body.[95] Considerant's victory on the second ballot, in a field of thirteen candidates, of which three were elected, was due partly to his favorable reception among the well-to-do electors of the Tenth Arrondissement for his "practical knowledge" and partly to support from various opposition groups to the July Monarchy, including legitimists.

Although public office might seem an unusual step for a Fourierist committed to the transformation of society into industrial communes, it was not, because Considerant and other followers of Fourier had been steadily moving away from the eccentric founder of their group and by the 1840s had transformed their program into "a broadly based social movement."[96] Considerant also wished to run for public office as a means of explaining and advertising Fourier's ideas. While never giving up the goal of establishing a successful commune, he aimed to establish social harmony among competing classes in the present. He was, moreover, like Perreymond, committed to a peaceful transition to social democracy, which was, for him too, an expression of the ideals of Christian brotherhood and fraternity. His November electoral success, finally, was not his first foray into politics. He had run unsuccessful campaigns for election to the Chamber of Deputies in 1839 and again in July 1842. Despite his losses, the experience of political activity, as Beecher observed, pleased him.[97]

It was not unusual, therefore, that as a representative of the Tenth Arrondissement to the General Council of the Seine Department, the administrative organ of Paris, Considerant would turn his attention to the contemporary problems of the capital. In January 1844, two months after his election, he published a reflective piece on the urban crisis in Paris in the *Revue générale de l'architecture*. In it he focused on the problems of the arrondissement he represented within the context of developments in greater Paris. This article, pedantically but accurately entitled "Note on the Interests of the City of Paris and Especially of the Tenth Arrondissement," was Considerant's most important contribution to the displacement-of-the-population debate of the 1840s. Here Considerant confronted the real city and its problems head on. Unlike Perreymond's major contribution on the same issue, "Études sur la ville de Paris," it contains no suggestion for radical or sweeping reform, although it shared with Perreymond's article a common theoretical perspective on the crisis.[98] Considerant's reform program is not only more modest and grounded

than Perreymond's, it had a hearing, given the former's position as a municipal councillor, at the highest level of power in the city.

If the overall problem identified by urban thinkers was a significant shift in
the population of Paris from the Left Bank center to the western and northern
arrondissements, Considerant concretized and humanized this problem by
comparing conditions and services in the Tenth Arrondissement and other
parts of old Paris, many of which resembled cesspools, with those in arrondissements on the Right Bank, which were characterized by the expansion of
luxury commerce. Taking streets alone, he noted that between 1831 and 1841,
fifty-eight new streets had been constructed on the Right Bank, at a cost of 15
million francs, while over the same decade the government had constructed
only thirteen streets on the Left Bank, at a cost of 2 million francs. He pointed
as well to the decline in prosperity of the villages surrounding the Left Bank
and compared those to the north, which were flourishing economically.[99]
Considerant concluded that a circular process resulted as the well-to-do
quarters attracted a greater share of public works projects, which only made
them more attractive.

To remedy this situation Considerant offered a proposal in keeping with
the engineering mentality of this time, whether socialist or not, that is, the
application of a field of knowledge about the form of the urban environment.[100] In addition to this impulse to redraw the city according to the dictates of reason, however, Fourierists like Considerant also had a strong sense
that principles of justice and equality should apply to the form of the city.
Simply put, Considerant demanded for the city "distributive justice and proportional equality."[101] He translated this general principle into a practical
program of urban reform that aimed to redress the imbalance between the
parts of Paris on both sides of the Seine. His first recommendation for urban
reform, which he shared with Perreymond, was that municipal officials adopt
a policy to maintain and revitalize the historic birthplace of Paris, the old
inner quarters of the Right and Left Banks, as a robust anchor and magnet
within the expanding city. Acknowledging his intellectual debt to the writings
of others who had theorized about the importance of the central urban core,
among them A. Rabusson, Jacques Lanquetin, Chabrol-Chaméane, and especially Perreymond, the first five parts of whose study of Paris had already appeared in the *Revue générale de l'architecture*, Considerant offered his formulation of "the true principle of the solution" to the displacement of the Paris
population. "The successive displacements of the centers of activity of the Parisian population," he stated, "will only cease on the day when the administration shall have understood the necessity of creating, along the banks of

the Seine, at the center of the face of the city, in the very cradle of Paris, a superior nucleus of life, of pleasures and businesses, endowed with an all-powerful attraction, and towering over all other points in the capital in its beauty, richness, vitality and grandeur." The spatial needs of Paris, therefore, revolved around the revitalization of the historic center of Paris, including the île de la Cité. The aim of public policy with respect to Paris, he thought, should focus on "the opening of communication routes going from the center to the circumference [of Paris], the complete navigation of the Seine, and the extensive and productive embellishment of its banks." Such a program was "alone capable of giving unity and force to the system of public administration which until now has been fragmented and incoherent."[102] These suggestions, it is obvious, hewed to the central idea being espoused by Fourierists and other urban intellectuals, namely, that a capital city must possess an effective communications network and a powerful urban core.

Like Perreymond, Considerant valorized the use of the Seine River as a natural communication route through the entire city, a project he integrated into his overall city plan. Thus, he suggested devoting an important part of the municipal and national budget to improving all-year navigation on the Seine, a measure that would counterbalance the construction of new canals on Right Bank Paris to the north and east and yield profits throughout France, as commerce circulated freely back and forth from the provinces to Paris. Both banks of the Seine River, moreover, should form "the two most powerful arteries of circulation of the city."[103] He also petitioned for the creation of a new through-street on the Right Bank that would link the rue de la Croix-Rouge to a point between the Pont-Neuf and the Pont-des-Arts. A new bridge built at that spot would lead this new street to the colonnade of the Louvre. As for tolls, they should be eliminated from all Paris bridges. Finally, authorities should distribute municipal water equally to all parts of Paris. Having identified the critical reforms Paris authorities should undertake, Considerant grounded his proposals by examining the municipal budget to demonstrate their feasibility.[104]

He concluded by calling for municipal studies of all urban planning issues and for the adoption of an overall plan for urban reform. Like Perreymond and other reformers of the 1840s, he understood perfectly well that city planning had to be comprehensive planning. Only when a "comprehensive plan" was adopted by municipal authorities should work begin on any individual projects, the most important of which he believed he had identified. A well-defined program for reform, articulated within the Fourierist camp, Considerant's project represents a significant part of early modern urbanism.

What emerges clearly from the writings of Perreymond and Considerant is that an organic comprehensive vision of Paris was articulated during the first half of the nineteenth century, and that the Fourierists were central to its articulation. The reconstruction of Parisian space was Haussmann's great accomplishment. Nothing said here is meant to suggest that theorizing about space should be confused with the construction of space, only that this theorization preceded Haussmann's reforms and is important in its own right as a new manner of looking at the modern city. Prominent Fourierists writing about Paris during the first half of the nineteenth century did consider Paris whole, did use speculations on the Paris roadway to tie the city together into an organic unit. They thus joined others, Saint-Simonians and functionalists, who also focused on circulation in order to project an organic city. It is interesting, too, considering the foregoing, that the perception that Paris was in crisis and that the reform of the communication/circulation network of the city was the key to its reform did not depend on a particular ideological stance. The Fourierists are particularly important in the debate on the modern city, however, in being consistently interested, as a group, in urban problems, and in their insistence, in tracts that combined theory with abundant data, that the modern city is a field of communication flows. That Considerant and Perreymond were engineers undoubtedly goes a long way toward explaining their perspectives and methodologies. In addition, the Fourierists did not merely respond to immediate urban problems but addressed issues of Paris urbanism throughout the decade of the 1840s and beyond.

One must not assume, however, that there is an inevitable progression from the Fourierists to Haussmann and Napoleon III. There were many varied influences on the prefect of the Seine and on the emperor. Napoleon III was probably inspired to reform Paris by his stays in London; by an eighteenth-century tradition of embellishment and improvement, exemplified by Voltaire and Pierre Patte; by the plan of the Commission of Artists during the revolution to bind expropriated lands into the fabric of Paris; by his uncle's ambitions for the capital; and by the realization that unproductive labor and capital desperately needed an outlet, which could be satisfied in a major public works program.[105] Haussmann, according to David Jordan, was partly motivated by a psychological abhorrence of disorder and an attraction for its obverse, the need for "the world to be ordered, its roads straight, its itineraries rational." Jordan also charted the important influence on Haussmann's thinking of his experience as prefect in the classical city of Bordeaux, where eighteenth-century reforms foreshadowed much of his work in Paris.[106]

It would not be an exaggeration, however, to add Fourierist concepts of the centrality of urban circulation, especially considering how widespread they had become in many circles, as an additional element to the making of the modern city. Beyond Haussmannization, moreover, there was in Fourierist thinking, as in modern urbanism, an emphasis both on the fundamental role of architects and experts in determining the design and reform of modern cities. In addition, there was a focus on the importance of a communication network linking all parts of Paris to each other and Paris to its suburbs, a principle that held for all cities. And there was an insistence on a comprehensive vision of the city, an appreciation of aesthetic considerations alongside rational plans, and, finally, a requirement that one discover the underlying principles of city development.

CHAPTER FIVE

Planning the Paris Underground

WHILE FOURIERISTS, Saint-Simonians, and functionalists were mentally constructing a new Paris above ground, others were looking forward to a circulatory city below ground. Visionary proposals to reform the circulatory system of Paris, including providing easier access to Les Halles, by creating an underground urban rail system for use by people and for the circulation of merchandise and provisions, were part of a lively debate among government officials, engineers, architects, and planners during the 1840s on the architecture of underground space in the French capital. The plans and projects proposed paralleled new views on the above-ground physical layout of the city. Discussion focused on four interrelated topics, the first three closely related to issues of urban circulation already encountered here: (1) the beginning shift of a portion of the well-to-do population to the western parts of the city, (2) the lack of access roads linking all parts of Paris, (3) the relationship of the several Paris railway stations to one another, and (4) the expansion and possible new location of the central market of Paris, Les Halles centrales.[1] Proposals for an underground rail system represent another example of the reduction of the space needs of Paris to its circulatory system at this time, with the innovation that the system could also be beneath ground, and the special role of engineers in the design of city space. As this subject obviously raises the question of the relationship of the 1840 plans to the opening of the Paris Métropolitain in July 1900, this chapter briefly projects into and beyond the Second Empire in order to clarify the relationship of these plans to the Métro.

Working within the broad framework of thinking about the city as a space that could be shaped and transformed according to rational, well-thought-out plans and visions, architects, engineers, and intellectuals in general produced pioneering proposals for the introduction of an underground railway in Paris in the first half of the nineteenth century which also involved a vision of Paris as a circulatory system for merchandise, pedestrian flow, and social control. In some of the plans a new urban rail system also addressed the issue of the ability of workers in particular to move about the city more easily, thereby alleviating social tensions caused by overcrowding in the city center, population shifts, and the lack, despite omnibus service since 1828, of effective and inexpensive mass transportation.[2] Reflected within these projects, moreover, were the interests and concerns of a growing capitalist economy. As Henri Lefebvre observed, space in a capitalist society is not neutral; it is capitalist space, space that needs to be productive, and most planners in this study, including underground railway planners, were very sensitive to capitalist considerations when presenting their projects.[3] Equally significant, the projects for underground rail travel also constituted an additional important intellectual underpinning for Haussmann's creative destruction and rebuilding of the French capital.[4] They did so by considering the city globally, at least with respect to circulation, and by projecting straight lines above and below ground in planning an urban rail system.

Before travel through a city by means of an underground railroad became common—beginning in 1863 in London, from 1900 in Paris, and from 1904 in New York—the idea of a journey below ground terrified the popular imagination.[5] Victor Hugo captured the fear of the subterranean by noting in 1862 that "Paris has another Paris under herself; a Paris of sewers, which has its streets, its crossroads, its squares, its blind alleys, its arteries, and its circulation, which is slim, minus the human form." The underground was the "intestine" of a Leviathan, where "the sewers alone form a prodigious dark network under both banks [of the Seine]." "All sorts of phantoms," he wrote, "haunt these long corridors, putrescence and miasma everywhere." He pointed to a significant contrast, however: "At the beginning of this century, the sewer of Paris was still a mysterious place." By the time he had completed *Les Misérables,* from which these lines are drawn, he could also write that "today the sewer is neat, cold, straight, correct. . . . The present sewer is a beautiful sewer. . . . Ultimately, if the geometric line is in place anywhere, it surely is in the stercorary trenches of a great city."[6]

A key to making the underground more hospitable, as Rosalind Williams showed, was the advent of the railway and tunneling technology. The railway, the new transportation system for the new industrial age, required straight or regular passages through irregular or difficult terrain. Consequently, railway companies, in addition to constructing bridges and viaducts, regularly began to build tunnels. The nineteenth century, building on eighteenth-century engineering advances in mining and canal building, became a great age of tunneling, as the underground was incorporated into the infrastructure of the city. It was a period when railway tunnels introduced the upper classes to the underground, an aquaintance the working class had already made.[7]

It should not be surprising, therefore, that one of the earliest serious proposals for some kind of underground means of communication in Paris was proposed by a railway engineer, Louis Léger Vallée.[8] Until recently, Vallée had not received much recognition in the historical literature as pioneer of underground urban travel in Paris. Histories of discussions and proposals leading to the opening of the Paris Métro in 1900 usually began with engineering projects proposed in the early 1850s. This upset Vallée's grandson, himself named Louis Vallée and also an engineer, who was prompted to try to right the historical record. In a letter to the important French engineering journal *Le Génie civil,* the younger Vallée stated that his grandfather, an engineer of the Ponts et Chaussées and in charge of studies of Belgian and British railways, had in 1835 proposed extending the North railway line into Paris up to the Hôtel de Ville and that he had suggested that railway lines coming to Paris from the north and the south could be linked underground. That "certainly originated the idea of the 'Paris Railroad.'"[9] The younger Vallée was mistaken with respect to the date of his grandfather's project—it was 1837—but correct in ascribing to him paternity of an early vision of the possibilities of underground travel in Paris.

The older Vallée's proposal fits within the general context of thinking about and planning for railroads by French state engineers at this time. Vallée, born in 1784, attended both the École polytechnique and the École des Ponts et Chaussées, which he left in 1803. He worked on canal and railway construction and by 1848 had risen to the post of inspector general of the national civil engineers corps (Ponts et Chaussées). He retired in 1850 and died in 1864.[10] Like the Saint-Simonian and Fourierist engineers who had graduated from the École polytechnique and worked for the state, Vallée evinced faith in the social power and benefit of engineering. In 1848 he proposed a change in the organization of examinations and the structure of the École polytechnique and the state engineering corps. His stated aim was that the national corps of civil engineers stress its commitment to "good public works, constructed with wisdom and genius," projects "well-calculated [and] perfectly adapted to the needs of the ports, of the rivers, of the canals, of the highways, [and] of the railroads," and that such public works be broad enough in conception to reconcile the needs "of the economy and convenience," as well as "stimulate commerce" and improve all parts of France.[11] He also expressed advanced democratic ideals. In 1839 he had corresponded with the socialist Louis Blanc and the democrat François Arago, proposing a liberal electoral law. On March 8, 1848, less than a month after the February revolution, he revisited this topic, proposing that elections for a constituent assembly be direct and by universal suffrage, that every citizen qualify to be elected as a deputy, and that deputies be paid.[12]

In a brief appendix to his electoral project he also addressed the workers' question. In this he revealed himself a partisan of a Christian social democracy. Three currents—early Christianity, the radicalism of Rousseau, and 1793, the most radical moment of the French Revolution—animated his position, which he expressed in highly condensed form: "Our governments have troubled themselves with the people for the longest time only to be able to repress them. The principle, worthy of the Bible, namely, that *society owes an existence to all its members,* has been forgotten as far as the masses are concerned, and because it emanated from the doctrine of J.-J. Rousseau, and because it had been proclaimed for the first time in 1793." The allusions to the Bible and Rousseau were clear to his contemporaries. He explained his preference for 1793, an especially militant time during the French Revolution, by citing a charter of that year which announced, as he put it, "the qualification of all Frenchmen to public employment." From this sprang his support for public government workshops performing useful labor and guaranteeing workers a minimum livable wage.[13]

Vallée's project for an urban railroad was only a brief for its feasibility, desirability, and placement, but it contained a democratic bent in his assumption that the state, not private entrepreneurs, would construct and operate the railways. What Vallée imagined was the extension into the interior of Paris of a major railway line. Recall that national authorities had decided in 1842 against the operation of French national railways by one company and that the different companies operating rail lines to Paris would site their stations at the periphery of the capital, not near its center. Vallée proposed the extension of one major line so that it would eventually link north and south railway lines within Paris. To accomplish this he suggested seven interior railway stations and a line running underground in the center of Paris under the Hôtel de Ville and from there above ground over arcades to two new bridges crossing the Seine, thereby bringing the line into the Left Bank arrondissements.

This line would not only carry passengers but could accommodate merchandise as well. This part of Vallée's plan also anticipated better-known plans for a Paris underground rail system, which followed in the 1840s and 1850s. Vallée observed that it would be more efficient and less costly for merchandise arriving in Paris to be delivered directly to its destination within the city. To facilitate this he suggested that shops, warehouses, and hotels be constructed along the new line. Thus, merchandise arriving in Paris "could be distributed, by means of cranes, to all the floors of shops."[14] Given the limited political will for major public works at this time, as well as the broad scope of above- and below-ground constructions necessary to realize an extensive urban railway, Vallée's proposal represented a flight of fancy, even though he presented it quite seriously and wrapped it in a cloak of scientific discourse.

Karen Bowie, a historian of French railways, remarked that Vallée's plan is interesting because "he expresses the thinking of that time on the relationship between the rail network and the capital."[15] His proposals were also part of the larger speculations during the July Monarchy on issues of traffic and pedestrian movement in Paris. He described the Paris circulation problem concisely: "If one considers that the streets of Paris are narrow and obstructed; if one considers that circulation, already very difficult on these streets, shall become more intense when railroads bring to Paris ten or fifteen times more travelers than arrive currently, that this will require more carts to supply markets, more omnibuses, more cabriolets, one will recognize at that time that railroads must penetrate deeply into the capital."[16] For all its interest as an early serious proposal for underground rail travel in Paris, however, Vallée's was not a plan for an urban railway system in the strict sense. His line was not intended for intracity travel or movement; it was only meant to facilitate movement of passengers and merchandise into and out of Paris. As such it belonged more precisely to projects for a national railway system rather than an urban one. Lastly, Vallée's importance as a precursor of an urban rail system, although it is an early part of the historical record, should not be exaggerated. His entire proposal for a Paris underground amounted to a little more than five printed pages, a mere outline, albeit with interesting suggestions. In 1838 another such early proposal for underground travel in Paris was put forward by André Bourla and Edouard Renaud, supporting a proposal by the firm of John Cockerill to bring three rail lines into Paris, to transport merchandise, animals, and people, one of which could travel underground at the place de Marais. This plan, too, was not meant for an urban rail system.[17]

It is from the 1840s, however, that we witness a proliferation of more mature plans for a Paris underground. If one of the earliest speculations concerning travel in subterranean pathways below Paris streets was advanced within a broad context of faith in the power of science and technology to shape space, a more immediate issue appeared in 1842, when the administration of Claude Rambuteau, prefect of the Seine Department, created a commission to study the construction, placement, and architectural form of an expanded central market for Paris.[18] The market was in the center of Paris and the site of an enormous concentration of carts, people, and food vendors.

Traffic around the market, where most of the food for Parisians arrived and was distributed throughout the city, had always been a problem. Discussion of the market's location and expansion, therefore, would necessarily involve planning for the circulation of people, merchandise, and vehicles. In 1845 the city and the prefecture of the Seine Department awarded the project for the design of new pavilions on the site of the old market in the Third Arrondissement to Victor Baltard, a former prix de Rome winner, who had submitted his proposal in July 1844.[19] In August, following the city's award, another architect, Hector Horeau, submitted a counter-proposal as part of a public debate on the soundness of Baltard's plans. In addition to suggesting a new location for Les Halles, which would be perpendicular to the Seine River at the quai de la Mégisserie in the Fourth Arrondissement, he outlined an imaginative use of space below the market as an element of city planning.[20]

The new pavilions of the central food market, les Halles centrales, designed by Victor Baltard. Quite spacious, each pavilion featured glass and iron as part of its construction materials. Charles Marville. Bibliothèque historique de la ville de Paris

Horeau, perhaps best known for his prize-winning entry for an exhibition hall for the London Great Exposition of 1851 (a commission he did not obtain),[21] planned an underground world below Les Halles largely out of his concern for integrating the market into an effective circulatory transportation network above ground. Traffic flow also dictated his placement of the market. Horeau objected to Baltard's plan because it sited Les Halles far from the banks of the Seine, where many coaches and carts were stationed; because it was not serviced by any major thoroughfare; and because the streets surrounding it were too narrow.[22] Horeau's first solution to the circulatory needs of Paris and the market, therefore, was to site the market in a poor, working-class section of the Fourth Arrondissement perpendicular to the river. His market would comprise six pavilions, two small ones placed between two sets of four large main buildings, all lined up in a rectangular plot bounded on the south by the quai de la Mégisserie and on the north by the rue aux Fers. The eastern boundary was the rue Saint-Denis and the western limit would be a new street running parallel to it. The Paris administration's planned expansion of the rue de Rivoli would bisect the market in an east-west direction. Key to effective surface circulation in and out of the market, therefore, were the five large through streets surrounding the market, the rue Saint-Denis and its parallel sister street going north-south, the rue aux Fers, the proposed rue de Rivoli and, most importantly perhaps, the Seine River, all providing east-west access to the market.[23]

In Horeau's scheme the spaces above and below ground constituted an organic unit. Each of the six pavilions was essentially "an immense covered courtyard, with vast galleries and covered sidewalks."[24] Below the entire complex Horeau envisaged a vast underground space to which he assigned functions related to the market above. This space, divided into cellars below each pavilion, would serve as a storehouse for unsold provisions and for goods destined for delivery. It could also act as a parking space for carts and a conduit for water and gas pipes. Ventilators and grills with shutters would regulate the temperature and also house lighting devices to illuminate the basement and the market above. Its most innovative purpose, however, was to accommodate an underground railroad system linking all parts of the market to the Seine and the greater Paris region.[25] The point of the railroad was twofold: to deliver produce that would enter Paris by way of the Seine River and to evacuate waste from the market. The important innovation here was not only the idea of an underground railroad but also its link to the river as part of a larger communication network combining river-boat traffic with the market.[26]

While our concern here is not with the arguments on the above-ground siting of the market, there is an aspect of Horeau's rationale that deserves special mention, for it represents a mode of thinking with reference to space, whether above or below ground, that was characteristic of all the planners discussed here. Horeau and his lawyer, J. Senard, who championed his client's proposal, assumed that the new market would simply displace an unhealthy and dilapidated section of Paris. Senard, anticipating Haussmann's and Napoleon III's creative destruction, pushed the argument further by coupling urban renewal with both strategic and economic considerations. He reminded authorities that this quarter had been especially troublesome during the revolutionary events of 1848 and that its reconstruction, especially the creation of large thoroughfares, would eliminate the possibility of "painful struggles" as well as being a wonderful investment opportunity. By labeling this section, the Chevalier-du-Guet quarter, and its inhabitants as physically and morally degenerate and potentially revolutionary, Horeau and Senard justified its wholesale destruction.[27]

Lefebvre noted that architects—and I would add engineers who function as city planners—do not deal with space in complete freedom, that behind any assignment there are interests and powers—a government authority or a developer, for instance. The architect reduces lived space, the space of real human beings with subjective needs, to a blueprint, to images with linear perspective, the enemy of lived space. The architect's discourse, like his blueprints, "too often imitates or caricatures the discourse of power," and at a minimum the architect's plan, "to merit consideration, must be quantifiable, profitable, communicable and 'realistic.'"[28] In his failure to consider the needs of the population of an entire quarter as it might have articulated them, and in his elaboration of an argument designed to win a public commission, an argument that replicated elite attitudes toward poverty, Horeau conformed to Lefebvre's architect. To complete his proposal and raise his appeal to authorities, Horeau took on as partners two public works entrepreneurs, G. Callou and M. Lacasse, who intended to develop the Chevalier-du-Guet quartier.[29] Horeau, along with Senard, also represented a concise articulation of the idea of imposing social order through the creation of effective communication routes and urban renovation, which, like the habit of drawing straight lines without always taking into consideration the subjective needs of the community, became an important element in the discourse and thinking of modern urban planners.

Despite Horeau's (and Senard's) crusade and determination, the administration steadfastly refused to consider moving the market. And it rejected an underground railway beneath the market tied to the main rail lines or the Seine—a rejection one modern critic considered a great error—even though Baltard recognized the value of such a system.[30] Despite losing the commission, partly because he was an outsider to the architectural establishment,[31] Horeau continued to speculate on the potential of underground space and an underground railroad as an element in city planning.

In 1868 he published a wide-ranging study on the public works needs of Paris.[32] Employing an analogy that goes back to the eighteenth century, his underlying assumption was that as "circulation in cities corresponds to the circulation of blood in the human body, it is therefore the essential foundation of life, of prosperity, of all immediate and future improvements."[33] Lacking both technical specificity and a systematic plan or project for the entire city, his study nevertheless envisaged a Paris where the smooth and efficient flow of people and merchandise would be accomplished not only through a transformation of the surface area of Paris but also through the creation of underground spaces at strategic points throughout the capital. He proposed constructing footbridges—fixed, turning, or mobile—and underground passages where traffic was most intense. He singled out the Seine River, over which he would place an aerial roadway or under which he would construct pedestrian tunnels equipped with carts; either system, he thought, would alleviate congestion. A telegraph system, he wrote, should exist underground and a basement be constructed under the poultry market. He revisited his plans for Les Halles, reiterating his belief in the superiority of placing the market perpendicular to the Seine. In the absence of this reform, he nevertheless campaigned for the construction of a grand space below the present market to accommodate traffic, to facilitate garbage disposal, and to house public water closets.

Horeau also featured the underground in several broader projects. In one he proposed the construction of tunnels beneath Montmartre hill. Lined with boutiques and equipped with wagons, these tunnels would transport people to their destinations on the hill—a somewhat fanciful suggestion perhaps. He also proposed transforming old quarries into vital public spaces with the planting of small trees, with coach stations, café restaurants, concerts, games, gymnasiums, luminous publicity columns (an obvious concession to commerce), and areas for diverse meetings, public festivals, and public lectures. Horeau suggested a similar transformation of underutilized or abandoned public spaces throughout Paris, proposing to "connect them by a general plan laying out an underground road that could accommodate a track for a horse-drawn railroad under the former exterior boulevard."[34] This was a passing suggestion, not supported by any detail, and it was the closest he ever came to imagining Paris serviced by an underground railroad for general passenger travel. By the time he mentioned this possibility, moreover, others had already devised rather elaborate underground urban railway systems. These plans for an underground railway, advanced by engineers, were more precise and scientific in nature than Horeau's. Nevertheless, Horeau, who went beyond the architect's usual emphasis on the placement and design of buildings to imagine the shape of the entire city, also contributed, along with engineers, to a shift in the perception of the city from a monumental architectural entity to a smooth functioning circulatory system.[35]

The first engineer to fully work out a new vision of the city with reference to an underground railroad was Fl. de Kérizouet (we do not know his first name) who, like Horeau, first published his plans for a partly subterranean urban railway in Paris in 1845. Little is known about Kérizouet. According to Norbert Lauriot, a geographer who studied the post-1872 Métro projects, Kérizouet was a student at the École des Mines de Saint-Étienne, where he learned about railway construction.[36] In his publications, Kérizouet is identified as a "civil engineer" and "former railroad administrator," with no further precision. What we do know about Kérizouet are his writings, which reveal a keen interest in a potential urban railway system in Paris and a sense that he fancied himself a kind of urban planner.[37] Writing a decade after Kérizouet, Karl Marx theorized that capital drives beyond spatial barriers and creates the means of communication and transport necessary for its circulation.[38] Kérizouet, like Marx, understood the pressing needs of a capitalist society to circulate goods and people, all central to the flow of capital, and these themes are reflected in his proposals for an urban rail system. In his first known work on the subject, he advanced arguments for, and designed the placement of, such an intraurban rail network.[39] Analogizing Paris, and especially the provisioning of its central market, to the exploitation of a mine, Kérizouet compared the many streets of the capital leading to the market to the galleries of a mine. He saw regular and efficient locomotion for the city, as for a mine, as the key to its successful functioning.[40] More specifically, a rail system within the walls of Paris would tie together the disparately placed stations of the national rail lines, expedite merchandise passing through Paris, simplify the delivery of provisions to the central market, and literally extend the space within the capital, as part of this line would be underground.

Kérizouet's placement of the Paris rail line provided the key to his urbanism. He envisaged an orbital railroad that tied together the terminal points of the Rouen, North, and Lyon railways. The line would descend into the center of Paris by way of terrain parallel to the rue Hauteville in the Tenth Arrondissement, basically follow the interior boulevards, turn into an underground line below the place de la Bastille, emerge above ground on the Saint-Martin basin, which it would then cross by way of a newly constructed bridge. A single branch of this line, also partly above and partly below ground, would go

along the rue Mondétour into the central market.[41] Kérizouet's project, therefore, completed the vital commercial communication network of Paris by
connecting the major rail lines, the canals, the customs headquarters near
which the new rail line was situated, the Seine River, and the central market.

Throughout his proposal Kérizouet equated an urban rail system with the
creation of a new and quite productive public space in Paris. Not only could
the underground directly link the rail lines of the west with those of the east
and north, it could also be the site of a common underground station, of
great benefit to the mutual financial interests of the separate companies that
operated these lines. The common station would receive merchandise in
transit from which it could easily be rerouted across Paris. The basic point of
the underground was to add a particular kind of space to Paris, one in which
merchandise and provisions could flow unimpeded and rapidly, not causing
traffic jams or necessitating any expropriations. Above ground, too, the urban
railway represented a new kind of space, that is, movement as a form of space.
Kérizouet noted, for instance, that on streets too narrow for the effective flow
of vehicular transit, an urban rail system, partly above or below ground, even
if it moved at a slow speed for safety, would assure steady and unencumbered
movement. In this proposal, finally, while Kérizouet observed that an underground rail system in Liverpool had provisions for passengers, he did not talk
about people, justifying the rail line in terms of its utility for the circulation
of merchandise, a neglect he would address in his next major publication.[42]

In 1847 Kérizouet, in *Rues de fer, ou locomotion dans les grandes villes,* joined
a discussion of an urban rail system to larger urban planning issues and to social concerns.[43] For the first time he also included passengers as a regular feature of an urban rail system. With reference to urban planning, he believed
that an urban rail network could solve the so-called shift of the population
question. In contrast, recall that for Perreymond the solution to the western
movement of the population along the Seine River was a government policy
of revitalizing the center, in particular, the Left Bank, through the establishment of better surface access routes, including the extension of railroads,
from the periphery of Paris to its center; inner-city slum clearance; and a
building program centered on, and radiating out from, the île de la Cité and
the île Saint-Louis, the geographic heart of Paris. Perreymond, however, was
not realistic in thinking that Paris authorities under the July Monarchy would
be bold enough to demolish the central slums, rebuild this part of the city,
and improve the capital's surface communication system—a program that
would have to await the authoritarian Second Empire.

Kérizouet differed from Perreymond in that he focused exclusively on the
efficacy of an urban rail system to address the displacement of the population

issue, a more realistic objective, as his proposal fell within current discussions among the large railway companies for the construction of a circular rail line outside Paris connecting their lines before they entered the capital. In *Rues de fer*, moreover, Kérizouet was primarily concerned with demonstrating the importance of an urban rail system per se, rather than arguing for an underground rail network, although the latter did figure in his proposal. He suggested essentially that the municipal government initiate the construction of a circular rail line linked to the great lines, but within Paris. Such a rail line, he believed, by providing easier movement between and within all parts of the city, would counteract the linear expansion of the population along the Seine, toward the west by the well-to-do and toward the east by the poorer classes. Intended as one element in an urban tram system for the capital, the circular rail line would also expand the existing space in Paris: "The capital of France, whose narrow streets do not suffice for its immense population, will then have a double system of circulation, each independent of the other, one at the level of the public roads, *the other below ground,* and thus the railroads will cross and run along the busiest streets."[44]

As for social issues, Giovanna Procacci's analysis (see chapter 2) of the importance of private philanthropy between the 1820s and 1840s as the "social economists'" preferred solution to the social question is also relevant here.[45] In *Rues du fer* Kérizouet envisaged the urban rail system as a "means of universal locomotion, simultaneously transporting men and things, with the combined advantages of economy, rapidity, and uninterrupted service."[46] Paris, he noted, was growing in population and space and as a consequence common people needed some instrument to "lighten the burden of living" in the capital, an urban rail system to permit them to leave their damp and overcrowded quarters, where mortality was greatest.[47] In what would become commonplace in the thinking of early urban planners like Kérizouet, issues of poverty and overcrowding were dealt with either by wholesale destruction of quarters, without concern for population displacement, or simply by providing for better travel to less dense areas, without, however, addressing the underlying poverty of certain segments of the population. Kérizouet did, on the other hand, confidently suggest that new housing could be constructed above newly created rail tracks, with the track essentially going through what would have been the basement level. Such housing would "fulfill a double use, namely, as lodgings and as circulation, both in harmony with the progress of science and with the needs of the population."[48] It is difficult, however, to imagine Kérizouet proposing that members of the bourgeoisie live in housing with a railroad going through their basement. He only broke with liberal political economy following the 1848 revolution by suggesting a government buy-out of the railroad companies and the creation of a single national state administration for their operation.[49] With the exception of this last point, however, all Kérizouet's proposals assume that capitalist and state development required the elimination of poor people and commercially unproductive enterprises from prime real estate districts and that the best one could accomplish for poor people was to transport them cheaply from the periphery to the center.[50]

Nothing came of Kérizouet's proposals during the July Monarchy or the Second Republic, but interest in an urban rail system for Paris intensified during the Second Empire. In addition to Horeau's speculations, discussed above, many additional projects of varying degrees of specificity were advanced during this time.[51] Not all were proposals for an underground railway. All, however, came within the context of heightened economic activity initiated by Napoleon III, including an especially active program of transportation reform, which included not only an accelerated agenda of railway building throughout France, constituting a veritable transportation revolution, but also sweeping changes in public transit in Paris. In 1854, ten private Paris omnibus companies, pressured by the government, combined to form a monopoly of public mass transport under the Compagnie Générale des Omnibus. The following year, again with government encouragement, virtually all cabs operating from public cab stations, the so-called *voitures de place,* combined to form the Compagnie Impériale des Voitures de Paris. In addition, construction of the Petite Ceinture, a circular rail line within Paris linking the disparate rail stations of the capital, began in 1852 and was completed by 1867. During 1867, moreover, Second Empire officials granted one company the right to operate steamboat service along both banks of the Seine River as far as the immediate suburbs. Traffic density in Paris, a major preoccupation of the 1840s, increased as the population of the city doubled, from 546,856, in 1801, to 1,053,261, in 1851.[52] The underground too came under increased scrutiny as Second Empire engineers began an extensive program of subterranean sewer construction, an underworld circulatory system that paralleled the one taking shape above ground.[53]

Of the several plans originating during the Second Empire for a Paris urban railway two are of particular interest here, the Brame and Flachet project, because it remains the best known, regarded in the historiography of Paris transport as the forerunner of the Paris Métro, and the Le Hir proposal, because of its broad scope as a transport planning document and its close conceptual relationship to the actual Métro. Like the earlier proposals, however, these projects, while rehearsing the by-now familiar arguments about economy of time and space, embody larger issues of urbanism and capitalism.

Fig. 4.

Ce double rang de magasins (que réuniraient de proche en proche des maisons transversales au lieu de passerelles) indique le produit que la Ville pourrait tirer d'un terrain de 875 mètres de longueur qu'elle possède près du canal Saint-Martin et qu'elle se prépare à vendre. — Cette disposition de constructions peu, sur d'autres points de la ligne de fer, remplacer des jardins qui sont aujourd'hui sans produit pour leurs propriétaires. — Les rues et les maisons formant façade sur la voie publique seraient traversées en tunnel.

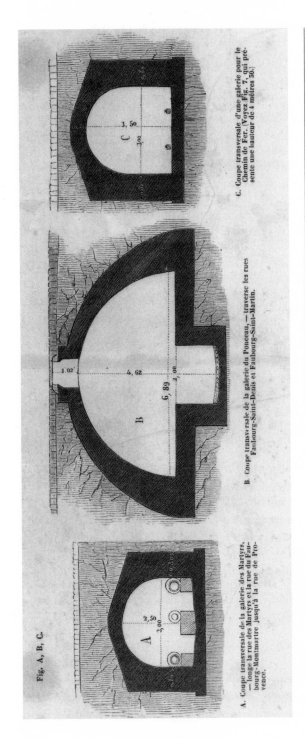

Fig. A, B, C.

A. Coupe transversale de la galerie des Martyrs, — longe la rue des Martyrs et la rue du Faubourg-Montmartre jusqu'à la rue de Provence.

B. Coupe transversale de la galerie du Ponceau, — traverse les rues Faubourg-Saint-Denis et Faubourg-Saint-Martin.

C. Coupe transversale d'une galerie pour le Chemin de Fer. (Voyez Fig. 7, qui présente une hauteur de 4 mètres 50.)

In the mid-1840s, Fl. de Kérizouet, an engineer with a keen interest in an underground urban railway system, proposed the construction of working-class housing outside the central districts of Paris. This housing would be built above railroad tunnels, which would increase circulation in the capital. Library of Congress

Two engineers, Édouard Brame and Eugène Flachat, are generally credited with having inspired the eventual Paris Métro. Lauriot demonstrated, however, that the attribution to them of the first serious and extended plan for an underground rail system for Paris was made by prominent engineers closely associated with the projects for an urban rail system in the 1880s, including Fulgence Bienvenüe, the future chief engineer of the Métro project, in apparent disregard of other existing plans. This was partly because Brame and Flachat, like those who eventually worked on the Métro, were government and establishment engineers and thus formed a relatively closed community.[54] Moreover, a simple reading of the Brame and Flachat proposal should disabuse anyone from ascribing the eventual architecture of the Paris Métro to these two men. Their significance was their ability, as distinguished government engineers in direct contact with the emperor, the Ministry of Public Works, and the Paris Municipal Council, to obtain a serious hearing at the highest political levels for the possibility of an underground rail system in Paris. A brief look at the careers of these two men and their famous proposal will clarify their contribution as well as open up the larger issues of capitalism and urbanism embedded in their project.

Brame's career path followed a traditional trajectory for a government engineer. Born in 1818, he graduated from the École polytechnique in 1839, whereupon he entered the service of the military corps of engineers. In the 1840s he worked on various provincial navigation and canal projects. In 1846 he became engaged in railway ventures, starting with work on the Paris to Saint-Germain line, and in 1847 he began work on the construction of the circular railway line ringing the periphery of Paris, the Chemin de Fer de la Petite Ceinture. His immediate superior on this assignment, Adolphe Baude, wrote to the minister of public works in 1851 that Brame had been steadily contributing ideas for the circular line since joining the project team on November 4, 1847—a letter intended, no doubt, to advance Brame's standing within the engineering corps. For his work on this and other engineering projects he was awarded the Legion of Honor in January 1854, rising to a chevalier of the order in 1881; before his retirement in 1888 he had risen to the rank of inspector general, second class, of the Ponts et Chaussées.[55]

Eugène Flachat, quite remarkably for one rising to the top of the French civil engineering profession, was essentially an autodidact. Born in 1802, he followed engineering courses at the École de Nîmes and also received engineering instruction from his older brother, Stéphane, a civil engineer and follower of Saint-Simon. Between 1823 and 1830 he and his brother worked on studies for a maritime canal between Le Havre and Paris. Thereafter, he spent several years in England studying with English engineers, among them

George Stephenson, the pioneer steam-engine builder. Back in France by the mid-1830s and strongly influenced by his brother's Saint-Simonianism, by the example of English railroad construction, and by his conviction that civil engineers had a critical role to play in initiating a program of national industrialization, Flachat deepened his involvement with the development of docks, canals, and railroads. He was preoccupied with introducing into France advanced English methods for producing iron, an interest that led him to a close association with the Saint-Simonian financier Émile Pereire and to join the project for the construction of the Paris-Saint-Germain railway line. It was there that Flachat, by then a thoroughly committed exponent of new modes of public transportation, especially the railway, met Brame. Following the revolution of 1848, he was elected the first president of the newly formed Société centrale des ingénieurs civils, a national society of civil engineers, and eventually became the chief engineer of the chemin de fer de l'Ouest. Like Brame, he received the Legion of Honor (1847), rising to the rank of officer in 1858.[56]

Evidence indicates that of the two men Brame initiated the plan for an underground rail line linking the Petite Ceinture and Les Halles centrales. He noted in a letter to the Minister of Public Works on June 30, 1853, that his work on the Petite Ceinture had convinced him of the need for a rail link between it and the central Paris market and that he had developed such a plan in concert with Flachat, who was currently engaged in the Les Halles project (another document notes that Flachat, on orders from Napoleon III, was studying the feasibility of a metallic cover for the market's pavilions). He believed that the prefect of the Seine Department and the Municipal Commission of the Paris City Council should be apprized of his work, and he wished to secure the permission of the minister to formally submit his and Flachat's proposal to these agencies. The minister granted Brame's request on July 7, after which the plan began to circulate at the highest levels of municipal and departmental authority. In addition to the public bodies mentioned above, the Brame and Flachat plan was reviewed by the chief engineer of the city, the prefect of police, and the inspector-general of the central market. All authorities welcomed the proposal. One record pointedly noted that other (unidentified) proposals for a similar link had been submitted for consideration but that the government chose to study only that of Brame and Flachat.[57] Closing this first phase of interest, the prefect of the Seine Department and the Paris City Council decided, even though the proposal was still in the review process, to grant a credit of one million francs for the construction of a subterranean gallery below Les Halles in case the authorities did approve an underground railway for the market.[58]

The first published version of Brame and Flachat's proposal was limited in scope.[59] The two engineers proposed that a rail line branch off from the Petite Ceinture at the plain of La Villette, travel above ground, approximately parallel to the Strasbourg Railway line (the present-day East Railway line), until it reached the rue de Nancy, where it would descend below ground. From this junction it would continue beneath the boulevard de Strasbourg to just above the rue Rambuteau (which intersects with the present-day boulevard de Sébastopol, a continuation of the boulevard de Strasbourg), where wagons from the rail line would connect with the central market by means of a system of turntables fitted with hydraulic machines to raise them. Traction for the train could be provided by a locomotive engine or by a fixed engine; Brame and Flachat preferred the latter, as such a machine could also ventilate the tunnel. This principal line, the two men wrote, could also connect with already existing underground tunnels, established by city engineers for sewers, to facilitate the removal of waste from the capital.[60]

Part of Brame and Flachat's justification for the project rehearsed what by now had become part of a standard discourse with reference to space and economy. Produce could arrive in the city center via the underground without adding to traffic congestion. The basement beneath the market could also serve as a new space for the construction of warehouses. An urban line, connected to the Petite Ceinture, would eliminate the need for many carts currently delivering goods to Paris, so delivery costs would drop. An urban rail line could also connect "with other public institutions," if the authorities wished.[61]

While never losing sight of their main goal—the linking of Les Halles to the urban railroad for the delivery of produce—Brame and Flachat proposed that merchandise and people could be accommodated on the underground line during the day, when it was not encumbered with produce for the market. With reference to merchandise and people, however, government officials had counseled Brame and Flachat to design their rail system so as not add to congestion around the market. Reports from the prefect of police and the inspector general of the market indicated that Brame and Flachat understood this and had agreed to plan for the arrival of merchandise and people into Paris at a central station some distance from Les Halles.[62] With this critique in mind, the two engineers nevertheless noted that their proposed rail line, in addition to serving Les Halles, had a "much more useful character," namely, that "the line, which during the night shall be used for the provisioning of Les Halles, can during the day receive cumbersome merchandise originating from the warehouses and stations beyond the fortifications. It can, *to a certain extent*, be used for the transport of passengers and especially workers who, as a result of the transformations going on in the central quartiers, will be obliged to travel to the outskirts of the city."[63] This comment referred to the well-known rebuilding of the capital's central districts by Napoleon III and Georges Haussmann and the displacement of the workers to the eastern and northern parts of Paris, often at some distance from their employment. Like Horeau and Kérizouet, Brame and Flachat did not address the underlying issue of poverty and its causes but suggested, rather modestly, an ameliorative measure of cheaper transportation for the poor. This was another example of using social space engineering to address the social question. Brame and Flachat devoted the most important part of their proposal to justifying the technical feasibility and the commercial potential of an underground railway linking Les Halles and the Petite Ceinture. They did, after all, and at a minimum, wish to satisfy their client, the state, and thereby secure the prestige of having planned a significant addition to the built environment of Paris.

Not only did the Brame and Flachat plan interest government officials, it also attracted French financiers and capitalists, who stood to reap great profits in the event of the construction of any urban rail system in Paris. Beginning in 1871, Blanchet, a former member of the Tribunal de Commerce de la Seine and a graduate of the École polytechnique, began to petition the prefecture of the Seine Department for the concession to construct the chemin de fer des Halles centrales, the Brame and Flachat rail link to the petite ceinture.[64] By 1870 Brame and Flachat, who had taken onto their team a third engineer, Grissot de Passy, had modified their plan slightly. Blanchet, also identified as a property owner, while working with Brame, Flachat, and de Passy, explained to Léon Say, prefect of the Seine, that "the metropolitan railway of Les halles centrales is only the first [line] of a vast underground network destined to place the center of Paris in direct communication with all the railway stations [of the city]." Such a line would be "of incontestable utility from the point of view of provisioning [the city]," would modify dramatically the delivery of produce and merchandise to the capital, and would thus solve a central issue "so important to economic life in Paris."[65] Blanchet, the spokesman for a consortium of capitalists who wished to construct the Brame-Flachat rail line, also made sure, especially in the infancy of republicanism, to make special provisions for workers on the chemin de fer des Halles. He suggested the creation of first- and second-class train compartments for the general populace and special morning and evening trains to accommodate workers. The first-class compartment would cost a rider ten centimes per kilometer traveled and the second-class six centimes; the price of a second-class ride would be reduced by half during the morning and evening hours when workshops opened and closed.[66]

Blanchet recited these by-then standard economic arguments as part of a proposal that his firm, the corporation Delahante et Compagnie, not only construct the chemin de fer des Halles but do so without government subvention. The whole point of his petition was to demand, in return for building the rail line, a ninety-nine year concession to operate it.[67] Other individuals who had submitted plans for an urban rail system for Paris to a special government commission formed in November 1871 to study this issue also stressed that they had the financial backing of entrepreneurs or financiers who would construct the line "without subsidy nor guarantee of interest." Among these were Alexandre Lavalley, the builder of the Isthmus of Suez, and Albert Rostand, an administrator of the Société du Crédit industriel et commercial, who, like the others, were attracted by their projections of ridership on the proposed rail system and the prospects for a significant financial return for their investment.[68] Engineers of the Ponts et Chaussées, however, rejected the Brame and Flachat plan, partly on the grounds that its principal line was burdened with too many functions and its projected central station beneath Les Halles too difficult to execute.[69]

Although the plan submitted by Louis Le Hir also was designed for intramural travel, it was far more inclusive and imaginative than Brame and Flachat's. First proposed in January 1854, it was the most extensive project to date for an underground rail system in Paris.[70] Perhaps more importantly, it articulated what would become the design theory behind the construction of the Paris Métro in 1900. Briefly put, Le Hir proposed the creation of six underground rail lines, comprising a total of about twenty-five thousand meters, each of which would follow the direction of the major streets and boulevards above ground. The idea that the Paris urban rail system, whatever the specific lines, would replicate below ground the flow of the major surface thoroughfares was, of course, exactly what planners and government officials established as the design principle for the eventual system.

Although Le Hir presented this proposal, he was not its technical designer. In 1860, Le Hir noted that in early 1853 he had conceived and prepared the general plan for an underground railway system in Paris. In 1854, Lacordaire,

Facing page

A map of the principal underground railway lines proposed by Louis Le Hir between 1854 and 1856. The novel feature of this design is that the six main lines of the system generally followed the major surface thoroughfares—the design principle followed in the eventual underground rail network. Library of Congress

RÉSEAU DE VOIES FERRÉES SOUS PARIS.

Prix 30 Centimes.

LÉGENDE

Chemin de Fer souterrain
Chemin de Fer variante
Chemin de Fer à fleur de Sol

Notice

a divisional inspector/engineer of the Ponts et Chaussées, had "worked out" the technical details of the project, which, in turn, were criticized by city engineers for potentially interfering with underground drains. In response, technical corrections were made by Mondot de Lagorce, a former chief engineer of the Ponts et Chaussées, whom Le Hir credited with being the principal technical architect of the definitive plan, which appeared in 1856. Le Hir, a lawyer practicing before the Imperial Court of Paris with a keen interest in railways and economic development generally,[71] wrote up the proposal and served as a spokesman for a consortium of engineers and notables who wished to develop the urban rail system.

Le Hir's project outlined an extensive array of services built into the rail system and its surface horse-drawn annex, including provisions for passengers, refuse removal, carting, and the delivery of letters, parcels, and rail passengers' baggage. As Le Hir wrote, the ultimate goal of the urban rail system was to "to connect the principal centers of commercial activity with each other and with the ports of the river and the canal, as well as with Les Halles centrales, to the great railway lines abutting on the capital." Moreover, by removing traffic jams the new railway system would "provide a rapid means of transport, at an especially moderate price, for passengers and goods." As with other similar proposals, Le Hir's consortium would build the urban rail network, at its risk and without government support, in return for a ninety-nine year concession to exploit it according to a schedule of tariffs for each of its services agreed to by the government.[72]

Like Kérizouet, Le Hir also evinced an interest in social issues and their relation to urbanism. Writing under the name L. Le Léonais a decade before his public concern with an urban rail system, he had celebrated the virtues of a society based on Christian principles of belief in God, love of neighbor, and charity. As he interpreted the modern community, it was a place where workers took great pride in their toil and accepted their place in the social order.[73] Immediately following the February 1848 revolution, he criticized the social workshops for being based upon a faulty social philosophy. He advocated a society based upon order, the family, pride in work, the sacredness of private property, equality of opportunity but not of rewards, and the people's acceptance of the complete independence of elected officials to establish social and political order.[74] He incorporated this socially conservative stance into the urban rail project. Even though, as in the preceding projects, the economy and commercial flow were given pride of place on the rail system, Le Hir insisted that people generally, and especially workers, would ride the urban railroad. The key argument he employed to justify a mixed use for the Paris underground was that "good order in the city" was linked to the "well-being of

workers." Like Perreymond before him, but for different reasons, he identified as the essential need of the workers their ability to move from the periphery of the city, where Haussmann's reforms were currently driving them, to its
center. Le Hir, therefore, simply took for granted the displacement of workers
because of market forces and integrated this dynamic into his proposed urban
rail system. Expressing this in positive terms he wrote that workers could find
healthier, cheaper, and larger quarters in "the outskirts of the city and beyond" and yet, by means of the underground railroad—he suggested a low
uniform fare of five centimes to attract passengers—still "travel through Paris
in every direction and from one extremity to the other."[75]

Le Hir's plan was not one of those considered by the special commission of
the Prefecture of the Seine Department to study proposals for an urban rail
system in 1872.[76] This angered Le Hir, who complained that for eighteen
years he had worked on the planning of an underground railroad and that "it
was not even the object of comment in the report of the prefectoral Commission." Yet it was not an obscure proposal. Le Hir wrote to the prefect of the
Seine Department about his project and published several editions of the plan
and brochures supporting it. In 1867 his plan was considered by municipal
engineers only to be dismissed on technical grounds, prompting Le Hir to re-
mark a few years later that "the author is used to such *scorn.*"[77] Moreover, one
reporter for an important Paris journal, *Le Siècle,* in a story on the Le Hir proposal, summarized its potential for creating a well-regulated city, a major
theme of urban planning discourse during the first half of the nineteenth century, and for the compression of time and space, a central focus of nineteenth-century urban commentators. He concluded: "Relieve Paris of the
congestion which obstructs it, change its appearance from that of a work site
in order to give it the appearance of a well-policed city, establish locomotion
for people and businesses, these measures are not only a good deal economically speaking but are beneficial from the purely human point of view."[78]

Despite its failure to attract official comment in 1872, Le Hir's proposal
was nevertheless significant for being part of the larger debate on the construction of an underground rail system in Paris dating from the July Monarchy, projecting the creation of new space within Paris that would solve the circulatory needs of the city in dramatic fashion. Public officials were keen to
explore this possibility and in November 1871, the general council of the Seine
Department invited the prefect to establish a special commission to study
plans for a new rail and tram network for the greater Paris region. The commission first met in January 1872 and published its report later that year. The
major requirement of this network, according to the commission's mandate,
was that it connect the different parts of the department with the Chemin de

Fer de la Petite Ceinture within Paris, connect the Petite Ceinture to the center of Paris, tie together the quays, link the interior boulevards, and join the major Paris railway stations either with the Petite Ceinture or the center of the capital.

Following its review of seven proposals, including that of Brame and Flachat, none of which satisfied it entirely, a majority of its members concluded that construction of a rail network should begin with only a few major lines to test their viability. Classed in this "first rank" was a line from the Bois de Boulogne to the Bastille by way of the interior boulevards, passing by or near the place de l'Étoile, and a major north-south line broken down into three sections: one going from Les Halles to the petite ceinture via the boulevard de Sébastopol, the second from the square Cluny to Montrouge following the boulevard Saint-Michel, and the last line a connection between the two. The commission also recommended against a surface urban rail system in favor of one underground, basing its decision on the belief that an underground rail system would not only protect property values and aesthetic vistas but would also have the greatest potential for future expansion. Finally, the report made clear that any urban rail and tram system for Paris and its greater region would be primarily for passengers. It explicitly set aside the question of the arrival of merchandise and produce on the system as too complex, a matter to be taken up at some future date.[79]

The argument is not being made here that there is a direct line of influence from Horeau, Brame, Flachat, and Le Hir to the 1872 report or the eventual construction of the Paris Métro. Horeau's proposals were either too closely linked to the central market or too general to be considered a true forerunner of the Paris Métro, Brame and Flachat's plan too narrow, and Le Hir's fell outside the government's serious consideration. Rather, what these and the several other plans studied by the special commission amounted to was the formation of a body of knowledge about the nature of the modern city and the design of one of its defining features, its circulatory system. With reference to the Paris Métro, Norma Evenson linked the proliferation of engineers' plans in the 1880s for an urban rail system to the political decision in 1872 to build such a system.[80] The argument here is the reverse, that the perception in the first half of the nineteenth century of clogged traffic arteries and population densities in Paris triggered speculations on an underground urban rail system as the key to the circulatory needs of the capital. In turn, these speculations attracted the attention of capitalists, who saw the potential for enormous profits in constructing and operating an urban rail system, and the government, which became convinced that an underground urban rail system would effectively circulate people (and perhaps merchandise and produce) throughout the city. The government decision in 1872 to consider an underground urban rail network grew out of the already numerous speculations by urban and transportation planners on the desirability and feasibility of such a system.

Plans for a Paris underground rail system addressed the concern with space and circulation in its broad sense that runs through so much of the planning literature of the nineteenth century. The underground urban railroad planners, if we may refer to them in this manner, were significant in that they began to speculate on alternative urban transport systems. Eventually visualizing the city whole from the point of view of its circulatory needs, they mapped out an underground railway system that addressed economic, social, and traffic considerations. They had enormous faith in the power of their vision and their technical expertise to regulate the city. They treated space, moreover, as a commodity that had to be put to productive use, and this involved speed and circulation as well as construction. While their proposals also ignored the lived community in order to designate the lines of traffic flow and urban development, their plans, quite public and extensive, were debated and studied by government officials and supported by capitalist entrepreneurs. Not only did this body of texts fit in with the well-known transformation of Paris during the Second Empire, speculation about underground circulation and its relation to above ground movement was another critical step forward in the emergence of modern urban planning.

CHAPTER SIX

The Siméon Commission

ON AUGUST 2, 1853, Napoleon III's minister of the interior, the count Fialin de Persigny, wrote to the count Henri Siméon, a senator and a former prefect in the administration of the July Monarchy, informing him that the emperor wished to appoint him to a commission to plan projects for urban improvement (*embellissement*) for the city of Paris. Napoleon III was prompted to form such a commission by the failure of the municipal council and of Haussmann's predecessor as prefect of the Seine Department, Jean-Jacques Berger, to undertake any bold urban reform. Napoleon III's decision to form an urban study commission represented his taking matters into his own hands. A note joined to Persigny's letter provides a window into the emperor's thinking concerning the rebuilding of Paris and is worth citing in full. "The Emperor wishes," it began, "to establish the following principles:

1. That all the great thoroughfares lead to the train stations;
2. That the height of houses always be equal to the width of the street and never exceed it;
3. That in the plans for large streets architects create as many angles as necessary in order to avoid monuments or beautiful houses, all the while maintaining the width of the streets, so that one does not become a slave of the tyranny of the straight line;
4. That a map indicating the totality of the urban projects be printed and made public;
5. That the project extend to the fortifications;
6. That public works be undertaken equally on the Left and Right Banks;
7. That the urban improvement projects begin: A, with the extension of the rue de Rivoli to the rue du faubourg Saint-Antoine; B, with the extension of the boulevard de Strasbourg up to the quai; C, with the boulevard Malesherbes;

D, on the Left Bank, with the extension of the rue des Écoles up to the place Sainte-Marguerite on one side and the platform of the Orléans railroad, intersecting with the Jardin des Plantes, on the other.[1]

This was, as is evident, an outline of the kind of street building, among other reforms, undertaken in Paris during the Second Empire, but with important variations, most notably Haussmann's failure to respect existing structures, except for those major monuments that became focal points through his urban clearance policy. On December 27, 1853, Siméon, who had agreed to serve and was the principal author of the final document, sent a copy of the results of the study commission's work to Napoleon III. In the final report Siméon and his collaborators offered a general philosophy of urban reform in line with Napoleon III's thinking, followed by data in the form of three appendixes (new roads proposed by the commission; a résumé of the data on new roads with total costs; new streets opened in Paris in the last twenty years), eight notes (dealing with bridges, parks, churches and cemeteries, barracks, public markets, monuments and public buildings, the administrative division of Paris, and successive public works before Napoleon III), and tables (outlining all public works projects in Paris by category and by regime).

In his *Mémoires,* Georges-Eugène Haussmann, who had become prefect of the Seine Department in June 1853 and thus the chief administrator of Paris, devalued and dismissed the report, whose existence he effectively suppressed. He then went on to claim credit for the plan of urban reform in Paris under Napoleon III, even while following in many respects principles laid down by the Siméon Commission. Recently, however, Pierre Casselle, the conservateur-général of the Bibliothèque administrative de Paris and a gifted historian, rediscovered the Siméon Commission report, in private hands at the time, as well as some archival material related to it. Historians are in his debt, for the report, which Casselle published in its entirety, is an extraordinary document on the material life of Paris and, in addition to being an expression of the emperor's ambitions for his capital, a kind of summation of the aims of urban intellectuals with respect to Paris that have been the subject of this study.[2] In this chapter I analyze the structure and work of the Siméon Commission and especially its vision of a new Paris. This image owes a great deal to the large archive of similar ideas about Paris readily available by this time, but it is particularly significant in being an official document generated by Napoleon III, the person ultimately responsible for the creation of modern Paris.

The work of the Commission des embellissements de Paris, to give it its formal title, was officially conducted by three individuals: Siméon, the duc de Valmy, and Louis Pécourt.[3] Siméon, in addition to his prefectoral service under the July Monarchy, had hoped to replace Berger, the prefect of the Seine Department in 1853, whom he found quite unimaginative with respect to the administration of Paris, only to see Haussmann gain that position. Haussmann respected Siméon's talent but also feared his ambition with respect to the Seine prefecture. Valmay had been a diplomat and Pécourt a magistrate. Neither had Siméon's administrative experience or political stature, and as a consequence it was Siméon who guided the commission's work and wrote its final report.

Siméon also counted on private advice in the work of the commission, and his behind-the-scenes advisors and collaborators are emblematic of the important intellectual link between the pre-Haussmann planners and the new Paris created during the Second Empire. Siméon received counsel and assistance in the preparation of his report from four important urban intellectuals: Théodore Jacoubet, Meynadier, and Félix and Louis Lazare. Jacoubet was best known for his publication in 1839 of an important atlas of Paris.[4] He was consulted by Siméon, according to Casselle, because of his knowledge of the topography of the capital. The Lazare brothers were even more important to the work of the commission. Félix Lazare was a government employee, having entered the Paris administration in 1834 as a member of the office of street plans; in 1842 he was named secretary of a government commission on street alignments. His brother, Louis, had been an employee of the archives of the Prefecture of the Seine Department and, from 1848 to 1862, the editor of *La Revue Muncipale*. Because of their knowledge of the city, both brothers were able to supply Siméon with data for many of the notes and tables of the commission's final report.[5]

Meynadier came to Siméon's attention, as the unpublished part of the Siméon archive indicates, partly through his own initiative.[6] In a letter to Siméon, Meynadier acknowledged that he had sent Siméon a copy of his book on Paris,[7] indicating that he "would be very pleased if you would look at it." And he expressed his pleasure at being so graciously received by Siméon.[8] There are also notes in the archive summarizing plans by Meynadier on streets, parks, slaughterhouses, cemeteries, the opera house, the national library, and a few remarks on the city hall.[9] Meynadier's influence is most apparent, however, with respect to ideas in the final report concerning parks and streets. The unpublished part of the Siméon papers contains a set of notes entitled "Project of M. Meynadier" and another entitled "Plan of the Emperor." Casselle speculated that the report's plan of primary and secondary streets were most likely based upon a more complete list of roads designed by Napoleon III and that the private written comments on these were by Meynadier.[10]

Certainly the broad principle of major roads crossing Paris in a north-south, east-west direction had already been laid down in 1843 by Meynadier in his book on Paris. The second note of the commission's report, calling for a major new park in western Paris, plantings, and the opening of small public gardens throughout the city, was unambiguously based upon the chapter in Meynadier's 1843 book on the same subject. And part of the report's sixth note, on the design of ceremonial steps on the Champ de Mars, declared that "the plan and the project of this idea has been prepared and designed by a man of taste, a man who has been very interested over the last ten years with all questions which concern the embellishments of Paris." The man of taste was Meynadier.[11]

Before turning to the report's text, note that, with respect to the foundational ideas that constitute its intellectual platform, the work of the commission, whose most important task was to plan a new circulatory system and infrastructure for the capital, also attracted the attention of the engineer Kérizouet, who had planned an urban railway for Paris (see chapter 5). In September 1853 he attempted to interest Siméon in his project for an urban railway in the capital. In two letters to Siméon, Kérizouet outlined the expropriations that would be needed for such a railway, recognizing that "today the difficulty is purely financial."[12] While the final report did not plan for any type of urban rail system, it did privilege movement within the capital.

The commission's report constituted a highly coherent text on urban reform and planning, more so than the *Recherches statistiques de la ville de Paris,* discussed in chapter 2. This is due in part to the narrative introduction by Siméon, a statement of the principles that should govern urban reform, and to the close integration of the notes and appendixes with this introduction. Virtually the same major overlapping themes that concerned planners during the first half of the nineteenth century also run through the entire document, namely, that the modern city requires an efficient circulatory system, comprehensive urban planning, security, social harmony, and a spatial design conducive to the expansion of capitalism. Only health was not a major topic in the report, it being taken for granted, probably, that wider streets and boulevards and the elimination of cemeteries and slaughterhouses within Paris, as it suggested, would create a more salubrious atmosphere. The report regarded the urban circulatory system as the foundation of the modern city, the reform upon which all other urban improvements would rest. This chapter focuses on the ideology and philosophy of planning in the report rather than the details of specific reforms.

CIRCULATION AND
THE MODERN CITY

It is evident from Napoleon III's initial charge to the Siméon Commission, published in its final report, as well as from the content of the report, that new streets and boulevards constituted the most important element in the emperor's Paris reform program. Siméon noted that "the following program, dictated by His Majesty, contains, in a few words, the thinking behind this undertaking." This referred to, and was followed by, the seven-point program sent to Siméon from the emperor quoted earlier, with minor editorial changes.[13] As Casselle observed, the new urban arteries planned by the commission would facilitate rail travel to and from Paris, open up the center of the city, and establish connections to the capital's periphery[14]—the same considerations earlier planners had privileged. I would add, too, that the reform of the Paris circulatory system expressed in the report was intimately bound up with creating an organically whole, safe, healthy, and prosperous city, aims that also run throughout the entire nineteenth century.

Apropos of communication/circulation, Siméon's introductory text offered a noncontroversial argument for an improved Paris street and boulevard system. Siméon observed that access from Paris rail stations to the city's interior spaces was cumbersome and difficult because of their placement outside the center and also because the July Monarchy had decided against a single major train station to service the different rail lines converging on Paris. The city was serviced at this time by seven train stations, four on the Right Bank (the Saint-Lazare, North, East, and Lyon stations) and three on the Left (the Austerlitz, d'Enfer, and Maine [today's Montparnasse] stations).[15] What the history of Paris demonstrates is that, in spatial terms, the railroads made it increasing necessary to design more rationality, control, and movement into space simply to be able to accommodate large numbers of people and great volumes of merchandise into and out of the capital. Siméon understood this point, around which he constructed an argument about new Paris roads. He remarked that hitherto no one had taken into account "the revolution that the establishment of railroads would bring to circulation." Before this time no consideration had been given to the "immense number of travelers that these new roads would wash into Paris from the departments and from foreign countries, or of the enormous quantity of merchandise and stock that they would be called to transport." Streets near railway stations, he reported, were clogged with vehicles that blocked circulation and commerce and caused dangerous accidents. He concluded that "travelers and merchandise must be able to arrive and leave [Paris] safely. The Commission has devoted itself with particular care to the accomplishment of this part of its mission."[16]

Siméon also advanced the argument that a major reform of Paris roads would help show off the capital's great public buildings, which had become less visible, often hidden behind successive constructions. He was thinking primarily of the densely populated île de la Cité, where the great monuments on the island, the Cathedral of Notre-Dame, the Palace of Justice, and the buildings of the Public Relief Administration, competed for visual space with a mass of private buildings, many, for example, pressing against the walls of the cathedral.[17] Siméon obviously meant that new roads would cut through such crowded districts resulting in a restoration of "the monumental character" of the île de la Cité. This was only a minor argument, however, and immediately thereafter Siméon returned to the larger issues that called for improved urban circulation/communication: "the growth of the population, the large number of travelers, the many business transactions, the increase in the number of vehicles circulating in Paris"—all these, as well as railroads, necessitated "new great roads" in Paris "in order to facilitate circulation which each day is becoming more difficult."[18]

From these general principles followed the commission's specific recommendations for a network of the most important roads to establish in Paris. It projected twelve communication arteries on the Right Bank and Four on the Left Bank.[19] The first, on the Right Bank, was to be a street connecting the Rouen (the present day Saint-Lazare) and North Railway stations. It was never constructed, but the other roads proposed for the Right Bank were. These consisted of the present-day rue Auber, the boulevards de Sébastopol, Magenta, Voltaire, and Malesherbes, a street prefiguring the avenue de l'Opéra, the rues Quatre-Septembre and Réaumur, streets prefiguring the rue Turbigo and the rue des Archives, the avenue de la République, and the extension of the rue de Rivoli. On the Left Bank the commission planned for the present-day rue de Rennes, the boulevard Saint-Michel and its extension, the avenue Denfert-Rochereau, and the boulevards de Port-Royal and Saint-Marcel. A street the commission planned crossing the entire Left Bank from the rue de Bourgogne east to the Jardin des plantes was never built. The plan, however, obviously anticipated Haussmann's Paris street projects. The commission, moreover, prepared a large watercolor map of the city on which it designated the "large thoroughfares" to be built, colored in blue, and the "railroad stations and barracks" to be built, colored in red.[20]

SECURITY AND THE
SOCIAL QUESTION

Embedded within the final text one can also detect a consideration other than traffic and urban movement. New streets and boulevards could be designed to facilitate urban security. Siméon hinted at this in his rationale for some streets the commission planned. Commenting on the future rues du Quatre-Septembre and Réaumur, which form a connecting road across today's Second and Third Arrondissements, Siméon opined that "this road will be one of the most important of Paris. It will penetrate some wretched quarters. . . . It's [the old Fourth Arrondissement around the Les Halles wholesale food market] a very active quarter," his euphemism for a space heavily populated with poorer people. Cutting through such a neighborhood would be "one of the greatest ameliorations that one can make in the interior of Paris."[21] He employed similar language to describe the projected boulevard Saint-Germain, which crossed the present-day Fifth, Sixth, and Seventh Arrondissements in an easterly direction, and the boulevards Port-Royal and Saint-Marcel, which crossed the same arrondissements in the same direction further south. Apropos of the Saint-Germain road, Siméon declared that "it shall be the only means to reclaim life in this part of Paris on the Left Bank, as well as to penetrate deeply and usefully the wretched quarters which extend from the rue des Saints-Pères up to the Jardin Des Plantes." As for the boulevards further south, they too would "penetrate a wretched quarter."[22]

According to Deborah Epstein Nord, nineteenth-century literary characterizations of the leading English industrial cities employed metaphors that evoked explorations to non-Western, "uncivilized" parts of the world as a way of trying to understand the new industrial city.[23] Siméon's use of such words as *penetrate* and *wretched* to describe the dreaded eastern parts of Paris, centers of working-class agitation and revolt, also suggest metaphors for colonial exploration and the taming of "uncivilized" peoples. Even absent such language, spatial planning for social control and security appear to have been an undeniable subtext of his program. Siméon suggested that the opening of a boulevard from the place du Trône to the boulevard du Temple, the current boulevard Voltaire, also in the eastern end of Paris, would give the government an opportunity to build clean and decent housing for people of modest fortune and workers in surrounding terrain that was not densely developed at the time. The lots he identified were in the present-day Eleventh Arrondissement. Casselle perceptively noted that the boulevard Voltaire would have the effect of separating the poorer classes to its east from the rest of the Paris population and that this may have been Siméon's intention.[24]

In considering Siméon's stated rationale for constructing different streets and his perhaps unstated wish for social segregation, one must keep in mind that statements like the above were relatively short and appear only at limited points in his text. It is almost as if they break through the text despite his aim to lay out a purely spatial rather than spatio-social justification for the new roads. This contrasts sharply, however, with the first draft of Siméon's introductory statement, which Casselle characterized as more radical than the final text and which I would describe as a more open expression of what remained somewhat hidden in the version he intended for public consumption.[25] In the rough first draft Siméon expressed quite candidly the relationship of street and other reforms to issues of security, beginning as follows: "The Emperor wishes that Paris become the most beautiful city in the world. He wants to clean the old districts where the population is crowded together and circulation impossible, render railroad arrivals easier, open in every direction great thoroughfares that abridge distances and which, in case of insurrection, assure an immediate repression of any violations of the social order."[26] Here, then, is an example of the kind of thinking Foucault may have had in mind when he suggested that during the nineteenth century, an age of new technologies and economic processes, planning space increasingly fell to people who "thought out" streets, bridges, and railroads, engineers rather than architects, for example, as a means of insuring order.[27] Siméon—a political person functioning as an urbanist— had planned a spatial organization of the city that would facilitate social control. In this he was not alone, because urban planners before him, whether as private individuals or government functionaries, thought in similar terms.

Unlike the public text, the draft was not an isolated or minor expression of the thinking behind the reforms that would reshape Paris and transform it into a fully modern city. The proposed extension of the boulevard de Strasbourg, the future boulevard de Sébastopol, would cut through a portion of the east end of Paris, linking the East Railway station to the place du Châtelet. Siméon noted in the final report simply that the extension of this boulevard had been decided upon as less costly than the widening of either the rue Saint-Denis or the rue Saint-Martin, which flanked its projected route on either side. In his initial reflections on this issue, however, he wrote: "This opening [of the boulevard extension] combines several advantages. It provides the heart of Paris an easy access to the great stations of the North and Strasbourg [the East Station]. It will render healthy a district that lacks air. It will beautify a part of Paris that has the greatest need for such a reform. *It will provide finally a strategic road of the greatest importance. All the important thoroughfares certainly have this advantage, but none to such a high degree as that one, because it crosses the theater of all the insurrections.*"[28]

Along these lines, Siméon, in the first draft of the report, also discussed his and the emperor's objectives for the rue Rambuteau. This street, a major project of the July Monarchy, had been decided upon in 1838 and most of it had been completed by 1845. It was supposed to cross over the rue des Archives, but the effective integration of these two streets would not occur until the late 1880s. Note, too, that Napoleon III and Haussmann had found the rue Rambuteau too narrow for the traffic needs of the capital.[29] Siméon, once more reflecting the aims of Napoleon III, addressed this issue, explaining that the extension of the rue Rambuteau from the rue des Archives to the place des Vosges, the present-day rue des Francs Bourgeois, "would be a measure of the greatest utility." In its current state, he observed, this street was "an impasse, and one reproaches it for being a failed enterprise." It was useful, however, for having already penetrated "some detestable *quartiers*." Its expansion and improvement, Siméon wrote, would "disencumber the Archives, the Mont de Piété [city pawn shop], the Saint-Gervais Market, the barracks of the departmental military police, the city hall of the Seventh Arrondissement, and the barracks of the fire department."[30]

While the completed reform of the rue Rambuteau project would improve traffic flow between Les Halles, the central Paris food depot, and the Marais, and also create a "corridor along which air and light could penetrate," it would also, as Anthony Sutcliffe observed, "split in two a centre of political unrest which had frequently been the scene of riot and revolt."[31] In discussing this and other street reforms under the Second Empire, Sutcliffe recognized the importance of strategic considerations in Napoleon III's street program but also warned against placing too high a value on this element. Also important in the overall project of street reform were considerations of traffic flow, aesthetic aims, slum clearance, and economic stimulation.[32] While Sutcliffe's balanced and comprehensive assessment of the rationale underlying Napoleon III's reforms is correct, what the Siméon papers also make clear is how fundamental strategic considerations were to Haussmann's program.

Another telling example of Siméon's linking of urbanism with security appears in his housing proposals. For public consumption he wrote that "the excessive elevation of houses is a very grave drawback for the sanitation and security of the city. Public health also suffers. Air does not circulate, the sun does not penetrate these streets dominated by buildings that are too high. One has built recently, in some narrow streets, veritable citadels which are two or three times as high as the streets are wide. A good rule for all new street construction would be to use the street width as a measure of the maximum height of houses."[33] The second sentence makes little sense because Siméon had edited the original version of his statement, eliminating two critical sentences that preceded it. Here is what he wrote immediately following his opening statement about sanitation and security in the city: "In case of sedition, troops, dominated by tall houses on narrow streets, lose a part of their power. One exposes them to great and useless losses by involving them in these dangerous roads."[34]

Siméon's introductory comments contained two more examples of spatial reform and security issues, both linked to roads and communication. One of the important features of his plan was that it championed comprehensive planning, planning that would extend beyond the tax wall surrounding Paris to include the city's immediate suburbs. Predicting that these suburbs would one day be incorporated into Paris, the report suggested that roads constructed in the suburbs be aligned with those in Paris. In his first thoughts on this matter he explained that, with new roads, suburbs would not "escape the surveillance" of the Paris administration, a phrase he did not employ in the final report.[35] He was quite prescient in this part of the first draft, pointing out that the territory between the city's tax wall and its fortifications was not under the control of the Paris municipal authorities but under the jurisdiction of eleven separate communes. He estimated, however, that logic dictated the eventual unification of this territory with Paris. In the meantime, political authority over the entire region should be placed under the prefect of the Seine Department and street constructions in Paris should be aligned with the larger Paris metropolitan region.

The second example, a short expression, may be taken as a metaphorical indicator of Siméon's concern with spatial control over the city and its masses. Charles Merruau, secretary general of the Department of the Seine in the administration immediately preceding Haussmann's, wrote in his memoirs that Paris railway stations had become the "true doors of the city."[36] This was a far more poetic manner of describing these new structures than Siméon's depiction of them as the "vomitories of circulation."[37] Characterizing train stations in this fashion betrayed a concern with the large number of people trains transported. New wide urban thoroughfares would assure crowd control in a strategic military sense and in the ability to absorb the crowds that descended into Paris from rail stations.

Siméon's concern with urban safety was also apparent in his inclusion of a separate note in the report concerning barracks.[38] The principle that governed his thinking on this subject—a reflection of Napoleon III's concerns as well as those of previous administrations and planners—was that "in a fortified city [Paris,] where tranquility is the best guarantee of the country's prosperity, and where convulsions are the ruin of France, the quartering of troops shall always be a question of the highest order."[39] He explained that the gov-

ernment had decided, rather than increase the number of barracks throughout Paris, to build or expand a few major barracks where many troops could
concentrate. An example was the Napoleon Barracks, constructed on the rue
de Lobau, behind the Hôtel de Ville, between 1852 and 1853. An ideal barracks, according to the report, it housed more than two thousand men. In the
section of his report on markets, Siméon also suggested the elimination of
five important slaughterhouses in Paris and their conversion into barracks
that could each house two thousand troops.[40] The total number of soldiers,
guards, and firemen securing Paris, both inside its fortifications and outside
in forts, he reported, was about forty-two thousand. This should demonstrate, he wrote, the government's resolve to guard against "insurrection" and
its ability "to assure in a certain manner the prompt repression of troubles."[41]

Barracks were not isolated structures, however, and Siméon understood
the close relationship between the construction of large barracks and new urban thoroughfares. "It is impossible not to provide the Hôtel de Ville and the
Napoleon Barracks," he wrote, "with a large thoroughfare going toward the
north of Paris."[42] An essential point of the presence of barracks in Paris was
the ability of troops to move from them deep into the city in order to repress
any uprising, which the linkage of barracks and new streets accomplished. If
we follow the insights of contemporary writers like Deleuze and Guattari and
Virilio, we can say that not only did the state wish to control the movement
of the masses, to regulate communication over space in order to keep in check
the potential revolutionary consequences of movement aimed against authority, it also needed to insure its own ability to move rapidly over space against
any disturbances.[43]

Siméon went further than most planners and urban intellectuals we have
encountered so far with respect to security in the city. In the note on barracks—which was meant for public consumption—he pointed to the truism
that many officers who commanded troops in the capital were often "strangers in Paris, living there only briefly, [and] generally are only familiar with the
quarters in which they reside." To counter this lack of knowledge, he proposed that selected officers, as part of their regular duties, survey each day
"the changes which are taking place not only on the streets but even in the in-

Facing page

The rue de Rivoli, facing west. On the left is the Napoleon barracks and behind it the
new city hall under construction. This street is a classic example of the new wide thoroughfares, which could easily accommodate normal circulation through the city as
well as the movement of soldiers. Charles Marville. Bibliothèque historique de la ville de Paris

terior of houses, courtyards, and the ground floor." He continued, in a radical proposal that combined spatial knowledge with urban military tactics, that "in this war of the streets, experience has proven that it was often necessary to attack the positions where the insurrection is fortified through the interior of houses. Well-informed officers would gain a great deal of time where any loss of time in these circumstances [the war of the streets] is a calamity."[44]

Again, insights by Foucault are highly suggestive in this context. Noting that politics is the "technique of internal peace and order," Foucault observed that the classical age had given birth, among a plethora of instruments of so-cial and political domination, to the "meticulous military and political tactics by which the control of bodies and individual forces was exercised within states."[45] In the city this control may be said to begin, at the most obvious vis-ual and material level, with the erection of the barracks and large thorough-fares. In nineteenth-century Paris, however, knowledge of the street, the clas-sic site of insurrections in the capital, was also necessary to insure order and security, and this is what Siméon's (and Napoleon III's) program addressed. Long before Foucault wrote about such matters both Siméon and Napoleon III had understood that, in Foucault's words, "space is fundamental in any form of communal life; space is fundamental in any exercise of power."[46]

Just how deeply government officials and planners like Siméon understood the security needs of the modern city is further illustrated by the concluding paragraph of Siméon's note on barracks. Before turning to it, however, let us refer once more to Foucault for a theoretical understanding of what might have been operative in the thinking of Second Empire officials concerning ur-ban reform. We have already had occasion to speculate about the extent to which disciplinary measures and technologies, about which Foucault the-orized with respect to the military, prisons, the factory, and the school, might have been extended at this time to city space. Central to these disciplinary technologies was the ability of authorities to maintain constant surveillance over their subjects, to keep a watchful gaze over the population, for example, again following Foucault, by such procedures as police regulations of city space, the architectural organization of internal space flows in buildings and factories to permit constant observation of their occupants, and the construc-tion of working-class housing estates. These are all aspects of what Foucault referred to as "a military dream of society."[47]

Siméon gives us another disciplinary strategy for controlling space, one that flows, as do city barracks, from the military model to which Foucault re-ferred. Following his suggestions that military officers have a familiarity with city streets and houses, Siméon wrote that for these soldiers to accomplish their mission "a map of Paris is necessary, one that represents all the houses [of Paris] and that is constantly brought up to date." He noted that such a map existed—, meaning, most likely, the plan for and map of Paris that Napoleon III had prepared and given to Haussmann when he became prefect of the Seine Department in 1853.[48] All that remained, he advised, was "to organize a permanent service to complete it officially day by day. Nothing is simpler or easier. It is when one is in a state of complete peace and total security that it is necessary to think about organizing the means of defense for the bad days. When they arrive there is no longer any time."[49] The equation of knowledge and power, therefore, following Foucault's formula, came together at the level of the city street in the production of a map whose purpose was not only urban but military planning as well.

CAPITALISM AND THE NEW PARIS

Napoleon III and the planners of the Second Empire were also mindful that social peace could not be secured exclusively by force. In 1848 France had been swept up in a revolutionary crisis that was partly political but also significantly economic. As David Harvey pointed out, France, like other European capitalist countries at that time, was experiencing a serious overaccumulation of capital and a huge surplus of unemployed labor. Conservative financial practices blocked the productive use of capital; jobs were lacking to absorb surplus labor. This situation, combined with political demands for more formal democracy and, finally, an insurrection, drove the Orléanists from power and ushered in the Second Republic. Three years after the February revolution, in 1852, the president of the republic, Louis-Napoleon Bonaparte, staged a coup that ushered in the Second Empire. The requirement to absorb excess capital and surplus labor now confronted Napoleon III. Historians are in general agreement that Napoleon III and his prefect of the Seine Department, Georges-Eugène Haussmann, intuitively understood that the great reforms of Paris would addresses the double crisis of capital and labor and also secure the health, security, and prosperity of Paris and consequently of France. Harvey summed up the problem neatly when, with respect to the needs of capitalism and the economy, he wrote that "the surpluses of capital and labor power had to be absorbed if the Empire was to survive. The absorption of such surpluses via the public works that so transformed the interior space of Paris entailed the free circulation of capital through the construction of a particular spatial configuration of the built environment."[50]

We should recall, too, that Foucault, who did not reduce the diffusion of power in society to economic structures, nevertheless acknowledged a critical link between them. The disciplinary society that he described as characterizing the modern world after the classical age corresponded to the conjuncture in the late eighteenth century of demographic expansion and increased production. "In fact, the two processes—the accumulation of men and the accumulation of capital—cannot be separated; it would not have been possible to solve the problem of the accumulation of men without the growth of an apparatus of production capable of both sustaining them and using them; conversely, the techniques that made the cumulative multiplicity of men useful accelerated the accumulation of capital."[51]

Closer in time to the reforms, Karl Marx, upon whose insights Harvey's analysis partly rests, had theorized about the central role of communication in the productive use of capital. In *Grundrisse: Foundations of the Critique of Political Economy*, Marx, as Adam Smith had done earlier, compared the circulation of blood in the human body to the circulation of capital in society, in a metaphorical association that differed significantly from the use of the same trope merely to designate the organic functioning of society, as became common in the nineteenth century. As we have seen, the Saint-Simonians also understood the importance of the circulation of capital as an aspect of the new industrial society, although they had not worked out a theoretical foundation for this understanding as deeply and broadly as Marx had done. It does not seem an exaggeration to suggest that the massive organization of a public works program satisfied the requirements both of a disciplined organization of labor, in a Foucauldian sense, and the circulation of capital, in a Marxist sense. As we will see, concerns for the free flow of capital and the absorption of labor haunted the work of the Siméon Commission.

What Siméon appreciated was that the planned reforms of the streets of Paris alone would require enormous sums of capital that had to be raised from private as well as public sources. He estimated the cost of all new road construction at 238,501,000 francs and concluded that it "would take a century to complete [the work] if municipal resources alone were used." This conclusion was not pure hyperbole, as the city budget for ordinary and extraordinary expenses for 1853 was about 77,000,000 francs.[52] Pointedly observing that the plan for new urban circulation originated with the emperor, Siméon wrote that an "important power" had been created that could assist in rebuilding Paris: "it is industry." Writing in terms that Marx and the Saint-Simonians would understand, Siméon, in language of great economy obviously intended as an appeal to finance capital, indicated that "peace [and] the accumulation of capital have given [industry] a force hitherto unknown" and that this economic sector "could easily invest annually twenty or thirty million francs" in the reform of Paris. As the "accumulation of capital" without sufficient investment opportunity would cripple the empire, as it had contributed to the demise of the previous government, such an appeal was an important signal to capitalists to join in the new public works projects in Paris for their own needs. "Industry," Siméon wrote, "in rendering great services to the population, would also find in that its profit." His summation on this point captured the entire range of benefits Napoleon III hoped to gain from the reform of Paris: capital investment, the absorption of surplus labor, and social peace: "The government of the Emperor does not know how to encourage enough these truly useful [financial] speculations which would profit everyone: the workers to whom they would provide permanent and lucrative work; the capitalists whose funds would find an advantageous employment; the men of art to whom one furnishes the occasion to exercise and utilize their talents; the population in general which always profits from that which brings to the great city new sources of amenities and prosperity."[53]

In the final report Siméon did not offer much detail about how the huge projects he proposed would be financed. He assumed that builders and financiers would understand the logic of investing perhaps as much as twenty or thirty million francs annually for about ten years in public works, given the resale value and rents they stood to gain from new constructions. The city treasury, he estimated, could invest about six million francs per year on these projects. Without giving any details, he also assumed that the country as a whole would be willing to support public works projects in Paris, as it would benefit as well. This implied the use of national tax money for the reform of the Paris infrastructure. In the first draft of the report, Siméon listed a few other possible sources of capital to finance public works in Paris. He suggested, again without any specificity, that railroad companies might be willing to invest in these projects, as they stood to profit from an improvement of the Paris street system, which linked their lines to the city. He suggested that the city and the state had been lax in collecting all they could from individuals who had purchased or were using crown lands and property expropriated from the Church after the Revolution, and that they could demand more of what was due to them. Pointedly, this suggestion, which could alienate the very class whose financial support was needed for the proposed reforms, was dropped from the final report, as was the vague suggestion that railway companies also contribute monies.[54] The commission, in other words, had no specific suggestions for the critical issue of financing the public works it had outlined, other than the faith that its projects would attract private capital investment, which would, in turn, be put to productive and profitable use.

In addition to addressing capitalists directly, even if briefly, Siméon devoted a large section of his report to workers and the social question, neatly tying together public works, especially new roads, with which the report opened, to security concerns, with which it ended. The intended audience, in terms of content and given the probability that workers would not read the report, was clearly the bourgeoisie. The report is interesting both for what it said and for what it neglected to say. Siméon noted, once more invoking the emperor as the motivating force behind the public works program, that the reforms in question would benefit "the laboring classes." The opening of new large thoroughfares, for example, would not only employ labor, it would bring "air, health, sun, and life" to workers' districts. These new thoroughfares, moreover, would presumably shorten distances between work and home for workers, who normally used "narrow, dirty, and encumbered" streets, which caused them fatigue and accidents. What he did not explain, however, was where workers would live once forced out of housing demolished for the new thoroughfares or faced with increased rents in new housing. As we have seen, failure to account for housing was typical of so many of the planners considered here. In light of Siméon's comments on new roads, on the shrinking of space, and on workers, it is ironic to note one overarching outcome of public works in Paris by the end of the Second Empire. As David Harvey observed, "much of the worker population was dispersed to the periphery (with longer journeys to work) or doubled-up in overcrowded, high-rent locations closer to the center."[55]

Siméon concluded this appeal to middle-class dreams of an orderly society by reminding his readers that the amelioration of workers' morals through the benefits of public works guaranteed that "public peace will be disturbed less often. A city where the artisans will be lodged in clean and airy houses, where they can find all the water necessary for their needs, where the rays of the sun will cheer their sad hearts, where, coming out of their workshops, they would encounter well-planted promenades, monuments, everywhere finally a beautiful spectacle to elevate their hearts [and] at the same time delight the eyes, such a city does not experience these unruly and dangerous populations which periodically compromise its tranquility."[56] What all this makes abundantly clear is that social stability and capitalist economic prosperity were the empire's central concerns—more so than considerations of the aesthetic value of public works—and that the empire's program did not originate with Haussmann but was in place before he assumed its direction.

Facing page

The boulevard Saint-Michel. An important example of the wide and relatively straight new boulevards that Haussmann and pre-Haussmann reformers wished to see in Paris. Bibliothèque historique de la ville de Paris

COMPREHENSIVE PLANNING

The final theme to consider is the commission's insistence on publishing a general comprehensive plan of all public works projects to be undertaken by the Second Empire. I noted in the introduction the common view of Haussmann as the "author" of a comprehensive vision of planning in the city, based upon his conception of space and his actual reforms. To this may be added Napoleon III's sense that, ideally, urban reform should be comprehensive. David Harvey noted that Haussmann's conception that all urban reforms had to be understood in a comprehensive relationship to each other was "already implicit in the sketch that the emperor passed to Haussmann, was step by step imposed upon the interior space of Paris as the public works took shape."[57] Napoleon III, who fancied himself quite knowledgeable about architecture, had created a color-coded map of Paris indicating in a prioritized order the streets he wanted built. He intended this map, which set the overarching agenda—details would be worked out by Haussmann—for the reform of Paris during the Second Empire.[58] While Haussmann did consider the public space of Paris as an organic entity, the idea of comprehensive planning under the Second Empire was not original with the prefect or with the emperor. Behind the Siméon Commission's reasoned justification for comprehensive planning lay the important and extensive archive of similar ideas about such planning that are the subject of this study and upon which the Siméon Commission's report rests.

The opening words of the commission's report are a simple expression of a modern view of the city combined with a shrewd practical consideration: "The Emperor has decided," Siméon began, "that a comprehensive plan indicating the successive embellishments with which he wishes to endow Paris shall be established by a commission. In this fashion the population may know the administration's projects in advance." Then followed a calculated sentence hoping to draw capitalists into this process: "Industry shall discover before it a vast field to exploit for the profit of its capital, the workers and the population."[59] The opening statement was followed by a seven-point program identifying the major communication routes that were planned, as well as the principle that should govern street width in relation to the height of buildings, and the avowal that new street construction should leave standing aesthetically pleasing homes and important monuments. The seven points were a general outline of the most important part of the Commission's plan. Siméon then explained the necessity for making such a comprehensive plan public. A public plan, he wrote, would habituate Parisians to the sweeping changes being proposed for the capital, changes that by their very scope would need to be executed in stages; it would eliminate all uncertainty with respect to where public works would be undertaken; it would minimize speculative guesses by property owners seeking to take advantage of rising property values; and it would prevent, especially in peripheral parts of Paris, unplanned and inappropriate constructions. Such a planning document would also consider the regional nature of the modern city and align the roads of Paris and its immediate suburbs. And it would consider both sides of Paris equally, the Right and Left Banks, treating them as parts of a single whole. Obviously, the ideas of Perreymond, Considerant, Chabrol-Chaméane, and Lanquetin, among others, are evident here.

These, then, are the major themes dealt with by the Siméon Commission: circulation, security and the social question, capitalism, and comprehensive planning. The focus of the report may be attributable to the commission's status as a government body—one primarily concerned with police and economic matters. In a narrow sense, the Siméon Commission's report is further evidence of Haussmann's lack of intellectual originality with respect to a certain conception of the kinds of reforms that eventually resulted from his administration. Haussmann, in delicate and diplomatic language, challenged the usefulness of the Siméon Commission and, while acknowledging that its report was well written, persuaded the emperor to disband it. He argued that the reconstruction of Paris would proceed more smoothly and quickly if there were no intermediary body between the emperor's wishes and their execution by the prefect of the Seine Department, in other words, if the entire public works program were centralized under the control of the emperor and Haussmann.[60] Napoleon III accepted this argument, ignored the commission, and let it die a bureaucratic death, its papers being lost until their discovery in the possession of Siméon's heirs in 1994. None of this, however, puts into question the enormous significance of Haussmann's accomplishments in reforming Paris. The reconstruction of Paris does remain his great legacy. It is only the originality of Haussmann's conception of space that is being challenged. Moreover, because Jacoubet, Meynadier, and the Lazare brothers figured in the preparation of the commission's report, Casselle warned of attributing the paternity of ideas contained in the report solely to Siméon. He also mentions Perreymond as a possible source of inspiration for ideas in the report, but without further explanation.[61]

There is much more at work here, however—much more to the intellectual origins of the commission's ideas than the individuals mentioned above. Studies of Haussmann and the reform of Paris in general also recognize some relation between ideas circulating from the eighteenth century and especially during the July Monarchy—Voltaire, the Plan des Artistes, and the Saint-

Simonians, for example, and Napoleon III's reforms.[62] What we have not had until recently, however, is a systematic and deep analysis of writings on space in Paris during the first half of the nineteenth century, an investigation covering not merely a few well-known figures but a wide range of urban thinkers, all of whom grappled with the pressing issue of the ideal form of Paris.[63] This is what is offered here, with a focus on the intellectual history of the extensive archive of ideas on space in the capital which constitute the collective plan for the transformation of Paris. What becomes apparent from such an investigation is that the Siméon Commission, as well as the reforms of Haussmann and Napoleon III, rested on a conception of the modern city that was in the making from the eighteenth, and especially throughout the first half of the nineteenth, century, a conception that had become widespread and the common intellectual property of most urban commentators before the Second Empire.

What emerged from the planning models of the first half of the nineteenth century and constituted one of the important intellectual advances of that time was the treatment of city space as an organic unified whole, a concept whose full consequences, both negative and positive, would become apparent as time went on. City space was seen, in addition, as a comprehensive space that was part of larger territorial units, the immediate suburbs, the national territory, and the global arena, also regarded as parts of a comprehensive network. By the time Haussmann came to power, moreover, urban intellectuals had already defined city space as a unified field for commercial exchanges, for better health, for security, and for visual magnificence, and had reduced these to the structure of its circulatory/communications system. The Siméon Commission's report, because of its official status, because it came at the end of the period we are studying, and because of its closeness to Napoleon III's thinking, represents, in a sense, the assimilation of this conception of the city by public officials, who would construct the new Paris. More important than the particulars of any single reform suggested by the report—the placement of an individual street, for example—was the report's treatment of Paris space as a single entity, the conviction that planning for such space had to be comprehensive rather than partial, and that this vision should be incorporated into a public global planning document. The new Paris that would emerge out of this plan would produce order and discipline, health, security, and a productive capitalist economy, the collective dream of modern urban planners throughout the first half of the nineteenth century. It was a dream that has served as the foundation of modern urban planning in the Western world.

CONCLUSION

A PARTICULAR VISION of Paris, and of the nature of the modern city, began to emerge in the mind of intellectuals in the eighteenth century. That vision became more fully developed and articulated during the first half of the nineteenth century, the foundation years of the large city in the age of capitalist industry. It held that a densely populated, modern, industrial city absolutely required order, safety, health, and efficient means of circulation for its populace, its police and armies, its manufactured goods, and its commercial trade. The new city, moreover, by virtue of its rational forms, would elevate the moral and physical condition of all its inhabitants—by which the planners meant, whether consciously or not, the subordination of popular culture to middle-class values, thus creating social harmony or at least social control and hegemonic order. Perhaps the single most important element in the understanding of the modern city that emerged at this time was that the city must function as an organic unit, a unified whole, and that any planning for such a city had to begin from the comprehensive vision of all its parts. This new vision of the city combined a classic Enlightenment ideal, namely, the belief that human perfection was possible and that such perfection could be achieved through rational comprehensive planning of city space, with a police function, which reflected the need of the state and civil society for social order, regulation, and control.

Paris intellectuals and planners began to envision such a city and devise plans to realize it. For the most part—there were some exceptions—these plans did not represent flights of fancy but a determined intellectual effort to shape the real space of Paris to fit the planners' ideal of a modern city. Planning ideas have great power. Referring to planning in the Western world, James Donald wrote that the planners' cities, which are grounded in a response to a material city, are neither real nor, strictly speaking, representations. Rather, they are "immaterial cities," "ideas or ideals that have played a powerful role in shaping the spatial organization and architectural design of cities." Much earlier the French modern architect, Le Corbusier, had written of the ideal city he designed: "The Radiant City already exists on paper. And once a technological project has been designed on paper (calculations and working drawings), it does *exist*." Commenting on utopian city plans, Jonathan Raban observed succinctly that "bits and pieces of ideal cities have been incorporated into real ones."[1] Le Corbusier's plans for the creation of apartment blocks as a key feature of the Radiant City, or his earlier planned Contemporary City, were a common feature of much contemporary urban renewal, and Raban's observation was certainly true with respect to the many plans and ideals for Paris that came out of the first half of the nineteenth century. The city dreamed of by these early planners came into existence, more or less, with Georges-Eugène Haussmann's and Napoleon III's reforms of Paris during the second half of the nineteenth century.

Paris, moreover, became a model for a form of planning that was comprehensive and for the most part rational (or geometric) and that privileged circulation, safety and surveillance (two sides of the same coin), and capitalism. Its intellectual underpinnings ran directly from the first half of the nineteenth century, which itself rested upon eighteenth-century planning traditions, to the early twentieth century; or, to express this differently, from Patte to Perreymond to Le Corbusier. The ideals of this form of planning have been ascribed, for the most part, to Haussmann and those planners who followed in his footsteps with respect to the global refashioning of city space, among them Ebenezer Howard and Patrick Geddes. What I have argued here is that this form of planning, inspired by a vision of the efficient and well-ordered modern city, was born, in almost all its manifestations, during the first half of the nineteenth century. The only element lacking at that time was the existence of the formal profession of planner. In all other respects, including a scientific approach and method, the planning proposals of the first half of the nineteenth century may be regarded as modern.

It was not, however, a monolithic form of planning, so I have attempted to nuance its development, dividing it into three models, the functionalist, the Saint-Simonian, and the Fourierist. The distinctions among these models were not rigid, however, and much of this planning coalesced around several common themes: global/comprehensive planning, circulation, order and security, health, and capitalism, each, either alone or in combination, being treated by planners in each model slightly differently or with varied emphasis. The three models, moreover, were shown to have passed through different stages. If I speak of a certain form of planning that emerged during the first half of the nineteenth century, therefore, it is to point to the collective intellectual force of the diverse archive of planning ideas that became common at that time. And it was a form of planning, no matter what its initial impulse or stated aim, that lent itself to the establishment of hegemonic order throughout the city.

The kind of planning that I have shown was born in the first half of the nineteenth century has come in for a great deal of criticism in the late twentieth century, much of it focused on the intellectual flaws of, and assumptions behind, rational comprehensive city planning, both with respect to its Enlightenment ideals and its subsequent elaboration in the twentieth century. Richard Sennett pointed out—quite correctly, I believe—that modern planners imagined that the city plan was more "real" than the lives of city people and that the plan was "the projection of a rigid group self-image." Plans that treat the city globally, he continued, tend to deny history and are too mechanical, as so much of the local and unexpected in the life of the city never makes it onto a plan. This is so, according to Sennett, because planners represent a particular psychological mode of thinking that seeks to deny and avoid "the dissonance and unexpected conflicts of a society's history."[2]

Closely related to this overarching psychological impulse at the heart of so much modern planning is that, at least in the nineteenth century, the planner's aims revolved around open class divisions and the fear of revolution and political upheavals. Perhaps this fear also lurked in the recesses of the modern planner's mind, as political or social dislocation are an extreme form of disorder that would play out in the streets of a city. Le Corbusier, for one, although famously preoccupied with the ill effects of motor cars on city streets (streets that he aimed to eliminate as obsolete in the high-speed motor age), pointed out that past revolutions had been hatched on the crowded streets and alleys of cities—he used as examples the spread of Christianity and the French Revolution. This changed when "one day, Napoleon III said: 'this can't go on, it's too dangerous. I want all this cleared up; I want this impenetrable warren sliced up into sections; I want straight avenues opened up that my cannons can fire along. Then we shall see if they can still get up these revolutions of theirs.' Haussmann obeyed those instructions. Napoleon's cannons brought new speed into city life. Seventy years later—now!—the automobile age owes to itself a monument in gratitude to Napoleon-Haussmann."[3]

The failure of modern planners to consult with, observe, or take into consideration the lives and opinions of the common people in their planning analysis is a leitmotif in the critiques of modern planning. Sennett's critique is similar to that of Henri Lefebvre, which we have encountered throughout this study, with respect to the habit of planners to ignore the subjective lives of people in the city.[4] Along the same lines, David Harvey wrote that "by treating certain idealized conceptions of space and time as real, Enlightenment thinkers ran the danger of confining the real flow of human experience and practice to rationalized configuration. It is in these terms that Foucault detects the repressive turn in Enlightenment practices towards surveillance and control."[5] This observation applies equally to the nineteenth-century planners, all of whom were very much children of the Enlightenment project of social betterment, a project that became even more pressing and complicated in the new heavily populated city in the age of industrial capitalism. Jane Jacobs did not disguise her anger with such modern planning assumptions, writing simply that "there is a quality even meaner than outright ugliness or disorder, and this meaner quality is the dishonest mask of pretended order, achieved by suppressing the real order that is struggling to exist and to be served." For Jacobs, modern city planning with its elitist bent of assumptions about the real subjective life in the city was a "pseudoscience" full of "familiar superstitions, oversimplifications, and symbols," a discipline that had "not yet embarked upon the adventure of probing the real world."[6]

Jonathan Raban attacked modern planning from an openly postmodern stance. In his book *Soft City*, Raban declared that the city is fundamentally unknowable and unquantifiable, a site for the interplay of a wide range of subjective and nonconformist behavior, so much so that no amount of planning could erase it.[7] Writing about London in the early 1970s, Raban embraced the subjective and quirky variety of real city life acted out in different neighborhoods where subtle signs are the markers for negotiating the city:

> The city I live in is one where hobos and loners are thoroughly representative of the place, where superstition thrives, and where people often have to live by reading the signs and surfaces of their environment and interpreting them in terms of private, near-magical codes. Moreover, these people seem to me to be not sports or freaks, but to have responded with instinctive accuracy to the conditions of the city. It seems worthwhile—at least as a corrective measure—to stress and explore some of the magical properties of city life at the expense of the customary rational ones, and to treat the evidence on this issue not as a vestige of some inferior pre-city stage of human development, but as a possible organic constituent of urban experience.[8]

In contrast to this real city that no narrative can capture accurately or totally, the planner, according to Raban, is fundamentally mistaken in the assumption that there is a rational city structure that will be brought to the surface in planning proposals and texts. Worse even than this falsehood, perhaps, "behind all these strategies [of modern planning] lies a savage contempt for the city and an arrogant desire to refashion human society into almost any shape other than the one we have at present."[9]

Raban was thinking here primarily of modern planners like Le Corbusier. He was also, however, like Sennett, Jacobs, and other critics, inveighing against a general model of planning which has its origins in the early nineteenth century. As some of the worst excesses of this form of planning are quite apparent in the modern world—one need only mention Haussmann's "creative destruction" of so much of Paris' historical patrimony or the failure of the Le Corbusier-inspired Pruitt-Igoe project in Saint Louis, Missouri—this form of planning is an easy target.[10] With these critiques in mind, the efficacy of early modern progressive urban planning must nevertheless be evaluated with reference to the values and problems of the first half of the nineteenth century, whose collective vision gave rise to modern planning. After all, the world of the early modern planners, the new city in the early years of industrial capitalism, was quite different from the early-twentieth-century city, as were the social sensibilities of the nineteenth century. One major concern of nineteenth-century urban dwellers was disease, which on two occasions assumed the form of cholera in Paris. Unsanitary conditions and disease haunted the imagination of the bourgeoisie throughout the first half of the nineteenth century, as did fear of political disturbances and the potential for social unrest among significant population densities in the city center. Another general problem was the inability of people, vehicles, and merchandise to travel freely from one end of the city to the other, or even to cross from one bank of the Seine to the other on unobstructed and toll-free bridges. Lack of easy urban circulation also posed special problems for the state and for capitalists. For the state the great concern was one of crowd control, rendered more complex by the increased population in Paris. For the capitalists, the ability of production and capital to circulate freely was a requirement of their success.

The early modern planning projects that addressed these problems were characterized by both beneficial prescriptions and inherent defects. There is no question that early modern planning projects would create a healthier, safer, more easily navigable, and wealthier city. Françoise Choay, who described Paris before Haussmann as a dysfunctional city in matters of circulation, social peace, and hygiene, celebrated the creation of a healthier, safer, and efficient city under Haussmann.[11] On the other hand, what appears to be dysfunctional from one class perspective may not appear so from another. Barrie Ratcliffe's writings raise serious questions regarding received notions of Parisian workers as a "dangerous class" or of the lower classes as being in a state of constant social and economic crisis.[12] And studies by David Garrioch and W. Scott Haine documented the presence of powerful neighborhood affiliations and an active social life among workers throughout the city from the eighteenth through the nineteenth century.[13] Nevertheless, in light of the particular problems of early-nineteenth-Paris—crowding in the city center, difficulty of circulation, insalubrious streets, and the like—as well as the expansion of commercial and industrial capitalism and the sheer physical growth of the city and its population, the elaboration by early modern planners of a theory of comprehensive planning, of an understanding that reforms and changes in one part of the city affect space relations in another, must rank as one of the intellectual achievements of early modern planning.

There was, however, another side to this achievement. Early modern planners' conceptions of the city had at least one serious shortcoming, judged by the standards of the time. There was no consistency among early modern progressive planning models with respect to housing for the poorer classes; some planning proposals designed housing for workers, while others simply ignored this question, even though their proposals would, if realized, result in considerable social dislocation for masses of city inhabitants. Moreover, in the one instance where one would expect a great deal of empathy with the common people and their problems, namely, in the planning model of the reformist socialists—those intellectuals who expressed great concern with the social plight of the masses—one finds just the opposite. The planning solution they recommended amounted to social space engineering that, for the most part, merely aimed to remove the poor from the central districts of the city without even providing a suitable alternative to their housing needs beyond general statements that life would be better in the suburbs. The early-nineteenth-century planners shared, whether consciously or unconsciously, the openly negative attitudes of the nineteenth-century middle classes toward popular and lower-class life. Therefore, the wish to control and dominate, the need for order and neatness, the fear of the working classes, were all either apparent or not far from the surface in early-modern-planning literature. Sensitivity to working-class neighborhoods and life was, generally speaking, not a consideration of the early modern planners.

The influence of early modern progressive city planning can be felt beyond Haussmann and the planning model he legitimated. Indeed, this form of planning found its ideal exemplar in the person of Le Corbusier, the Swissborn architect who became French in 1931. Le Corbusier may be taken as the modern city planner par excellence, the very culmination of the progressive planning tradition that is the subject of this study. In the first instance, as Anthony Sutcliffe showed, Le Corbusier exhibited the same Enlightenment faith in the efficacy of rationally planned space to achieve human betterment that lay at the heart of the early modern planning project.[14] And Norma Evenson opined that "Le Corbusier's most influential work epitomizes that optimistic peak of the modern movement marked by confidence in the splendors of a dawning new age, and a faith in advanced technology as a prime contributor to the solution of human problems."[15] This is certainly the manner in which Le Corbusier portrayed his project. Like the early modern planners, Le Corbusier had a deep belief in the necessity of global, comprehensive planning for cities, and he admired forceful urbanism led by an authority figure or a planning commission. Like his ancestors he, too, decried traffic problems, was concerned about unhealthy urban conditions, and generally disliked the disorder and confusion of modern cities.

To solve the problems of the modern urban world, Le Corbusier produced a plan and a model for a new "Contemporary City," which was similar in its outlines to the city the early modern urban planners had dreamed about, translated, as Robert Fishman observed, to the twentieth century and its needs and perceived problems.[16] Within the context of planning an ideal contemporary city, Le Corbusier turned his attention to a real city, Paris. His plan for the reconstruction of Paris, the famous Voisin Plan (1925), resembled Perreymond's similar project for the capital more closely than any Saint-Simonian urban ideals. Like Perreymond, Le Corbusier attacked the center of Paris, planning both a residential and a commercial city there. Concerned as much as nineteenth-century planners with the flow of traffic from one part of Paris to the other, Le Corbusier designed a street that would cut through the center of Paris east to west, from Vincennes to Levallois-Perret. The effect of this surgery was to gain "possession of the entire center of Paris." He continued: "The plan makes a frontal attack on the most diseased quarters of the city, and the narrowest streets: it is not 'opportunist' or designed to gain a yard or two at odd points in over-congested roads. Its aim is rather to open up in the strategic heart of Paris a splendid system of communication." He concluded that while his plan would rescue many of the great historical monuments of Paris, whole districts, like the Marais, the Archives, and the Temple, "would be demolished."[17] We should recall that these were the centers of working-class life in the nineteenth century that planners of that time also wished radically to transform.

Le Corbusier revealed himself as an heir to classic early nineteenth-century social space engineering ideals when he wrote, in the tradition of reformers like Léon Marie or Lecouturier, that "during these years of research, I have been forced to the conclusion that our cities are bulging with human detritus, with the hordes of people who came to them to try their luck, did not succeed, and now are huddled together in crowded slums. I knew we should have to say to them one day: there is nothing more for you to do in the city; there is no place for you here; go back where you came from, back to the country. And in that way, the cities could be cleaned up."[18]

On the whole, however, Le Corbusier represented a considerable advance over the early modern planners in this respect, that one primary focus of his ideal city was the mass of the population and its housing accommodations. The slab and zig-zag towers he designed for his ideal city were meant to provide clean and efficient apartment flats for all city dwellers, apartment units—he referred to them as cells—all of which faced green spaces, with sporting facilities, special nurseries for young children, and schools located just outside in parks surrounding the apartment complexes. Yet there is something terrifying about the scale of the residential buildings in Le Corbusier's vision, even in its ideal form, and not merely when it went wrong, as in the Pruitt-Igoe project. Robert Fishman summed up an especially negative estimation of Le Corbusier when he said that "the Plan Voisin still arouses the same horror it did at its original showing. It has to bear not only the burden of its own audacity but also its status as the archetype for so many disastrous plans that others subsequently carried out. For better or worse, the concepts embodied in the Plan Voisin represent Le Corbusier's contribution to the practice of planning."[19]

The forceful comprehensive planning favored by the early modern planners was epitomized by Le Corbusier's suggestion that the street itself be eliminated. Observing that the automobile had rendered streets overly crowded with traffic and dangerous, as vehicles moved at speeds far in excess of human biological rhythms, Le Corbusier concluded that "our streets no longer work. Streets are an obsolete notion. There ought not to be such things as streets; we have to create something that will replace them." As an alternative, "in the plans for the Radiant City, I have proposed that the pedestrian should quite simply be given sole possession of the entire ground surface of the city, the e-n-t-i-r-e ground surface, as though he were living in the heart of the countryside. And I have put the roads up in the air, 5 meters above ground level."[20] Concerning this proposal, Jonathan Raban opined—and I agree—that Le Corbusier's proposal to do away with the street was "the most radical and frightening of all. Take away the street, and one cuts out the heart of cities as they are actually used and lived in."[21]

Le Corbusier shared additional characteristics with early modern planners, and these provide a strong clue to what lay behind their form of planning: all regarded planning as a purely rational enterprise in the hands of the expert and were also deeply offended by disorder. While Le Corbusier did not wish to create monotony, recognizing that one could be "driven to despair by the uniformity of everything," he did express a deep love for the straight line and the right angle. Of the one he wrote, "a modern city lives by the straight line, inevitably; for the construction of buildings, sewers and tunnels, highways and pavements. The circulation of traffic demands the straight line; it is the proper thing for the heart of a city. The curve is ruinous, difficult and dangerous; it is a paralyzing thing." And "the right angle is, it may be said, the essential and sufficient instrument of action because it enables us to determine space with an absolute exactness. The right angle is lawful, it is part of our determination, it is obligatory."[22] With the exception of Charles Duveyrier, the Saint-Simonian who embraced curved lines, most of the early modern planners also thought in terms of straight lines or of bold arcs cutting paths through the center of Paris. And they, too, did so, they inform us, to create a better city for all its inhabitants.

In addition to the love of order that both the early modern planners and Le Corbusier expressed, to one degree or another, in their plans and writings, we need to add a final insight, again offered by Le Corbusier. Like the early modern planners, Le Corbusier offered his plans for a totally transformed Paris, or for an ideal city, as an expert, as someone convinced that he possessed the key to solving the spatial problems of the modern world. "By a strictly professional route," he once wrote, " I arrive at revolutionary conclusions. Since I am a professional man, I make plans according to my professional concepts; this is where my judgment is good." His opinion on planning, he believed, was "quite a dispassionate one."[23] Anthony Sutcliffe warned us that projects inspired by Le Corbusier's plans and writings were distortions of his intentions, quick solutions that "helped harassed local authorities to justify high-density slum redevelopment schemes that almost always lacked the amenities and social mixing which Le Corbusier considered essential." Sutcliffe also acknowledged that Le Corbusier may have had an "over optimistic view of human motivations and behavior." He believed, for example, "in the strength of man's communal instincts, which led him to maximize communal space and facilities, to reduce private space to a bare minimum, and to raise residential densities." Furthermore, "Le Corbusier's environmental planning system was inspired by the noblest of motives, and it is above criticism."[24]

If we grant this judgment then we are left with what amounts to the most serious flaw both in Le Corbusier and the early modern planners. While not denying their good intentions, one inevitably returns to the critique of Lefebvre, Jacobs, Sennett, Raban, and others. The early modern planners and their spiritual heir, Le Corbusier, did not, for whatever reason, either care about or have confidence in the needs and expressions of the ordinary person who lives and struggles in the modern city. Louis Mumford had an especially harsh criticism of this quality as it applied to Le Corbusier's plan for a Contemporary City:

> He [Le Corbusier] paid no more attention to the nature of the city and to the orderly arrangements of its constantly proliferating groups, societies, clubs, organizations, institutions, than did the real estate broker or the municipal engineer. In short, he embraced every feature of the contemporary city except its essential social and civic character. . . . Le Corbusier wiped out the complex tissue of a thousand little and not so little urban activities that cannot be economically placed in tall structures or function efficiently except at points where they are encountered at street level and utilized by a multitude of people going about their business at all times of day.[25]

The early modern planning tradition aimed to shape space as a matter both of social betterment and of social control and hegemonic order. All early modern planners shared an Enlightenment faith in the power of reason and science and the expert's uncritical self-confidence in his ability to interpret, plan, and prescribe the forms of the modern city, following only the dictates of his own vision. While the impulse behind early modern and modern urban planning may have been the betterment of humanity, the needs of state power, an elitist middle-class impulse to moralize, order, and control, and the requirements of the capitalist economy were integral aspects of this planning tradition, even when they were below the surface. Early modern and modern planning has had its triumphs and, in its elitist and immodest mode, its disasters. Like the Enlightenment project itself, early modern and modern planning left a mixed legacy.

Notes

INTRODUCTION

1. Benjamin, *Paris,* 35–59.

2. See, e.g., Le Moël and Descat, *L'Urbanisme parisien;* Pinkney, *Napoleon III;* Sutcliffe, *Autumn of Central Paris;* Gaillard, *Paris, la ville;* Evenson, *Paris;* Harvey, *Consciousness and the Urban Experience;* Ferguson, *Paris as Revolution;* Prendergast, *Paris;* See also Rabinow, *French Modern,* for a general discussion of planning in modern France.

3. An exception is a recently published collective work: Bowie, *La Modernité avant Haussmann.* See also Willms, *Paris, Capital of Europe,* which has some information on the material condition of Paris during the nineteenth century; Paul-Lévy, *La Ville en croix,* an interpretive essay on aspects of strategic planning; and Garrioch, *Revolutionary Paris,* which has a short section on urban planning in Paris during the eighteenth century. Victoria Thompson's article "Telling 'Spatial Stories'" appeared after the manuscript of this book was completed.

4. Choay, *L'Urbanisme,* 7–83; and idem, *The Modern City.* The second book, essentially an extended essay, published originally in English translation, recapitulates ideas Choay presented in the first.

5. Choay, "Pensées sur la ville, arts de la ville," 158–271; idem, introduction to *Mémoires du Baron Haussmann.*

6. Choay, introduction to *Mémoires du Baron Haussmann,* 10; idem, *The Modern City,* 16, 17 (her emphasis).

7. Choay, introduction to *Mémoires du Baron Haussmann,* 12, 30.

8. Sennett, *Uses of Disorder,* 89; Donald, *Imagining the Modern City,* 46; Harvey, *Consciousness and the Urban Experience,* 74.

9. Choay, *The Modern City,* 15–19.

10. Ibid., 19.

11. Choay, *L'Urbanisme,* 15–26.

12. See, e.g., Benevolo, *The European City,* 160–88.

13. Loyer, *Paris,* 326–27, 232.

14. For a discussion of this tendency in modern planning, see Lefebvre, *Production of Space,* 360–62.

15. Thompson, *Virtuous Marketplace.*

CHAPTER 1

Eighteenth-Century Roots of Modern Planning

1. For some recent studies of planning during the eighteenth century, see Etlin, *Symbolic Space*; Braham, *Architecture*; Harouel, *L'Embellissement des villes*; Leith, *Space and Revolution*; Le Moël and Descat, *L'Urbanisme parisien*; Garrioch, *Revolutionary Paris*.

2. Garrioch, *Neighborhood*, 221. For population statistics for the year 1801, see Pouthas, *La Population française*, 98, and a much earlier work, which gives the same figures: Say, *Études sur l'administration de Paris*, 474–75.

3. Farge, "L'Espace parisien au XVIIIe siècle," 123, col. 1; and idem, *Vivre dans la rue*.

4. Leith, *Space and Revolution*, 27–28, 115.

5. Harvey, *Condition of Postmodernity*, 27–28.

6. Etlin, *Symbolic Space*, 1.

7. See Sutcliffe, *An Architectural History*, 65–66.

8. An overview of architecture and urbanism in Paris during this period is in Lavedan, *Histoire de l'urbanisme*, 201–322.

9. Sutcliffe, *An Architectural History*, 22–23.

10. Ibid., 48; for a summary of the important constructions from the seventeenth to the nineteenth centuries and their impact on architectural style and urban planning, see ibid., 24–82; the section that follows relies heavily on this material.

11. Etlin, *Symbolic Space*, 1–29; Fleury and Monnier, "L'Urbanisme éclairé à Paris," 58–68; and Lavedan, *Histoire de l'urbanisme*, 271.

12. Diderot and d'Alembert, *Encyclopédie*, 17:277.

13. Cited by Etlin, *Symbolic Space*, 3.

14. Roche, *France in the Enlightenment*, 202–6.

15. Le Roy Ladurie with Quilliet, "Baroque et Lumières," 293.

16. Demangeon and Fortier, "The Politics of Urban Space," 10.

17. Etlin, *Symbolic Space*, 1–2. Although I expand Etlin's categories and change focus, I am indebted to his approach, which makes manageable a rich set of ideas that fall under the term *embellissement*.

18. Ballon, *The Paris of Henri IV*, 253.

19. For a discussion of Blondel, see Lavedan, *Historie de l'urbanisme*, 302–4; Bardet, *Naissance*, 197–218; Bernard, *Emerging City*, 26–28; and Sutcliffe, *An Architectural History*, 25–27, 48, 51–52.

20. The above section is based largely on Harouel, *L'Embellissement des villes*, 148–86.

21. Voltaire [François-Marie Arouet], "Des Embellissements de Paris," in *Oeuvres complètes*, 9: 163–74.

22. For a summary of all these constructions, see Sutcliffe, *An Architectural History*, 24–47.

23. For an analysis of Rousseau's attitudes toward Paris, see Grimsley, "Rousseau's Paris."

24. Voltaire, "Des Embellissements de Paris," 164.

25. Roger Mercier believes that Voltaire's trip to London may have prompted the poet to reflect about the condition of Paris; see Mercier, "Voltaire et Paris."

26. Voltaire, "Des Embellissements de Paris," 164.

27. Ibid., 173–74.

28. Laugier, *Essay on Architecture.*

29. Wolfgang and Anni Herrmann in ibid., xvii. For a detailed discussion of the relationship between public opinion and art in the eighteenth century, see Crow, *Painters and Public Life.*

30. Laugier, *Essay on Architecture,* 121.

31. Ibid., 122.

32. Ibid., 136 (quotation) and 134–45 (section on the gardens of Versailles).

33. Merriman, *Margins of City Life,* 35–40.

34. Sutcliffe, *An Architectural History,* 70.

35. Laugier, *Essay on Architecture,* 130.

36. Voltaire, "Des embellissements," 171.

37. Poncet de la Grave, *Projet des embellissemens.*

38. Ansquer de Londres, *Variétés.*

39. Jaillot, *Lettres.*

40. Fleury and Monnier, "L'Urbanisme éclairé à Paris," 58–68.

41. For this insight see Le Moël, "Urbanisme et lumières," 44–46.

42. Patte, *Monuments érigés;* idem, *Mémoires.*

43. Descat, "Pierre Patte," in Le Moël and Descat, *L'Urbanisme parisien,* 62; Picon, *French Architects and Engineers,* 192.

44. On this point see Picon, *French Architects and Engineers,* 187; for an extensive analysis of Patte, see Mathieu, *Pierre Patte.*

45. For a discussion of this project, see Lavedan, *Histoire de l'urbanisme,* 243–51; Herrmann, *Laugier,* 134–35; and Papayanis, *Horse-Drawn Cabs,* 31–32.

46. Patte, *Monuments érigés,* 120, 212.

47. Ibid., 213.

48. Picon, *French Architects and Engineers,* 195.

49. Patte, *Mémoires,* 6–20.

50. Ibid., 11.

51. Ibid.

52. Dussausoy, *Le Citoyen désintéressé.*

53. On Dussausoy, see Le Moël, "Urbanisme et lumières," 43–44.

54. For what follows, see Dussausoy, *Le Citoyen désintéressé,* 182–210.

55. Ibid., 202.

56. Ibid.

57. Ibid., 203.

58. Ibid., 11, 197, 201–4.

59. Ibid., 10.

60. Mittié, *Moyens,* 9–10, 12–13, and Tissot, *Paris et Londres,* 31.

61. Mittié, *Moyens,* 11–14, 21.

62. Louis-Sébastien Mercier, *Tableau de Paris,* and idem, *L'An deux mille quatre cent quarante.*

63. Popkin, "Preface," in Mercier, *Panorama of Paris,* 1–19.

64. Darnton, *Forbidden Best-Sellers,* 118; see also Ferguson, *Paris as Revolution,* 52.

65. The expression "thought experiment" is Darnton's; see Darnton, *Forbidden Best-Sellers,* 115.

66. For these insights, see Trousson, in Mercier, *L'An deux mille quatre cent quarante,* 45–47.

67. Mercier, *L'An deux mille quatre cent quarante,* 233, quotation at 237.

68. Prendergast, *Paris,* 34.

69. Mercier, *L'An deux mille quatre cent quarante,* 23–26; Backo, *Utopian Lights,* 248.

70. Lavedan, *Histoire de l'urbanisme,* 311–12.

71. Ibid., 316–17, and Descat, "Pierre-Louis Moreau et la Seine," in Le Moël and Descat, *L'Urbanisme parisien,* 79–92, quotation at 85.

72. See Sutcliffe, *Autumn of Central Paris,* 12, and Hall, *Capital Cities,* 61–62.

73. Hall, *Capital Cities,* 61.

74. See Pronteau, *Edme Verniquet;* idem, "La Commission et le Plan des Artistes," in Le Moël and Descat, *L'Urbanisme parisien,* 205–17, quotation at 208; and Sutcliffe, "Architecture and Civic Design," 90.

75. Le Moine, *La Parallèle du Paris.*

76. Cointeraux, *Plan de Paris,*1; *Paris tel qu'il est aujourd.hui ou embellissemens de Paris,* 14; on Cointeraux's program, see Leith, *Space and Revolution,* 292–95.

77. Houard, *Plan de Paris.*

78. Ibid., 34, 36.

79. Choay, *The Modern City,* 17.

80. Delamare, *Traité.*

81. Roche, *France in the Enlightenment,* 72.

82. Delamare, *Traité,* 4:1.

83. Ibid., 1:226.

84. Ibid., 4:168.

85. Ibid., 4:10.

86. Ibid., 4:10–11.

87. Ibid., 4:9–10.

88. Jordan, *Transforming Paris,* 51.

89. Rabinow, *French Modern,* 9.

90. Poncet de la Grave, *Projet des embellissemens,* 1:75, 77; 2:85, 95–101.

91. Jaillot, *Lettres,* 1:4.

92. Cointeraux, *Paris tel qu'il est aujourd'hui ou embellissemens de Paris,* 3–5.

93. Ibid., 9–10, and Leith, *Space and Revolution,* 292–95.

94. Garrioch, *Neighbourhood,* 211–16.

95. Farge, "L'Espace parisien au XVIIIe siècle," 123, col. 2–124, col. 2. See also Pétonnet, "L'Espace," cols. 1–2.

96. Patte, *Mémoires,* 19–25.

97. Cointeraux, *Paris tel qu'il est aujourd'hui ou embellissemens de Paris,* 4.

98. Mercier, *Tableau de Paris* (Paris, 1783–89), 1:32, 68–70; see also 5:162–63.

99. *Projet sur l'établissement de trottoirs,* and Dillon, *Utilité.*

100. Porter, *London*, 104, 125; Olsen, *City as a Work of Art*, 13.

101. *Projet sur l'établissement de trottoirs*, 4.

102. Ibid., 6.

103. Leith, *Space and Revolution*, 15–16.

104. *Projet sur l'établissement de trottoirs*, 7–8.

105. Ibid., 8, 11–12.

106. Ibid., 10.

107. Ibid., 9–10.

108. Dillon, *Utilité*. On church matters, see, e.g., idem, *Lettre de M. abbé Arthur Dillon, à M. de Cazalès;* and idem, *Projet d'un atelier de charité;* on political matters, see, e.g., idem, *Pétition de M. Arthur Dillon à l'Assemblée nationale.*

109. Douglas, *Purity and Danger*, 2. My use of Mary Douglas was suggested by my reading of Reid's *Paris Sewers and Sewermen.*

110. Dillon, *Utilité*, 13–14.

111. Ibid., 19–20.

112. Roche, *France in the Enlightenment*, 42.

113. Benjamin, *The Arcades Project*, 31 (quotation cited by Benjamin), 14–16.

114. Schivelbusch, *Disenchanted Night*, 143–54 (on shop windows).

115. Roche, *Everyday Things*, 119–20; see also Schivelbusch, *Disenchanted Night*, 85–86, 97–114, and Williams, *Police of Paris*, 190–93.

116. For Dillon on sidewalks and commerce, see Dillon, *Utilité*, 15–18.

117. Ibid., 16.

118. Ibid., 21.

119. Roche, *France in the Enlightenment*, 46–48.

120. Dillon, *Utility*, 31–33.

121. Etlin, *Symbolic Space*, 10–13; and Etlin, "L'Air dans l'urbanisme," 123–34.

122. This information is in Reid, *Paris Sewers and Sewermen*, 10–12.

123. Ibid., 12–15.

124. Alphonse L., *De la salubrité*, 9, 11, 13.

125. Ronesse, *Vues.*

126. M. de G** [Henri de Goyon de la Plombanie], *Projet d'utilité et d'ornament.*

127. Tournon, *Moyens.*

128. For a history of the building of the French canal system, see Geiger, *Planning the French Canals.* See also Lavedan, *Histoire de l'urbanisme*, 349.

129. Bruyère, *Rapport du 9 Floréal an X*, 44–45.

130. Lambert, *Paris tel qu'il a été.*

131. On the importance of engineers for city management, see Barles, *La Ville délétère;* Lepetit, *The Pre-Industrial Urban System;* Picon, *L'Invention de l'ingénieur moderne;* and idem, *French Architects and Engineers.*

132. Ronesse, *Vues*, 98 (his emphasis).

133. Tournon, *Moyens*, 44.

134. Guillaumot, *Considérations*, 8, 12–13.

135. Jaillot, *Lettres*, 19–21 ("Lettre sur [le] quartier du Luxembourg).

136. Sedillez, *Discours,* 4–7.

137. See Green, *The Spectacle of Nature.*

138. Dussausoy, *Le Citoyen désintréssée,* pt. 2:151; Patte, *Monumens érigés,* 213–14.

139. Reid, *Paris Sewers and Sewermen,* 15–16.

140. Patte, *Monuments,* 213–14; Poncet de la Grave, *Projet des embellissemens,* 193–205, quotations at 197 (on slaughterhouses), 205–11 (on cemeteries).

141. Ronesse, *Vues,* 86–87, quotation at 98.

142. Foucault, *Discipline and Punish,* 137–38, 221, and idem, "Space, Knowledge, and Power," 239–42, quotation at 239.

143. Poncet de la Grave, *Projet des embellissemens,* pt. 3:135–57.

144. Dussausoy, *Le Citoyen désintéressée,* pt.1:91–101, quotation at 94.

145. Ibid, pt. 1:15, 25–67.

146. Williams, *Police of Paris,* 190–93.

147. Schivelbusch, *Disenchanted Night,* 96–97, quotation at 97; 114–20.

148. Poncet de la Grave, *Projet des embellissemens,* 153.

149. Williams, *Police of Paris,* 283.

150. Poncet de la Grave, *Projet des embellissemens,* 209–14.

151. Jaillot, *Lettres,* 29–30.

152. Procacci, "Sociology and Its Poor," 115–62, and idem, *Gouverner la misère.*

153. Delamare, *Traité,* 4:435.

154. Voltaire, "Des Embellissemens de Paris," 171.

155. *L'Anti-Radoteur,* 196–204, quotation at 197.

156. *Projet* (1784), 12 (emphasis in original).

157. Goulet, *Observations;* and *Almanach des embellissemens.*

158. Goulet, *Observations,* 1–2.

159. Cited in *Almanach des embellissemens,* 32. See also Tulard, *Le Consulat et l'Empire,* 181.

160. Goulet, *Observations,* 2.

161. Leith, *Space and Revolution,* 186–89.

162. Goulet, *Observations,* 1–5, quotations at 1, 2, 4–5.

163. Ibid, 20–21.

164. Ibid., 10–11, 18.

165. For what follows, see ibid., 359–77.

166. Lavedan, *Histoire de l'urbanisme,* 327–29.

167. See Hènard, *Etudes; Almanach des embellissemens,* 58–63.

168. *Almanach des embellissemens,* 48–49.

169. Ibid., 53–54.

170. Ibid., 85–86.

171. Bertier de Sauvigny, *La Restauration,* 56.

172. *Almanach des embellissemens,* 85–86.

173. Etlin, *Symbolic Space,* 1–29, quotation at 19.

174. *Almanach des embellissemens,* 96–97.

175. For all that follows, see *Almanach des embellissemens,* 102–5.

176. Ibid., 103.

177. Ibid., 104.

178. For a summary of imperial urbanism, see Tulard, *Le Consulat et l'Empire*, 181–97; also useful is Sutcliffe, *An Architectural History*, 67–74.

CHAPTER 2

"Functionalist Planners" before Haussmann

1. For population statistics, see Pouthas, *La Population français*, 98; for quotation, see Chaussinand-Nogaret, in *La Ville classique de la Renaissance aux Révolutions*, edited by Emmanuel Le Roy Ladurie, 586. Vol. 3 of *Histoire de la France urbaine*. Edited by Georges Duby. Paris, 1981.

2. See, e.g., Choay, *The Modern City*, and Benevolo, *Modern Town Planning*.

3. Shapiro, *Housing the Poor*, 6.

4. Fuchs, *Poor and Pregnant*, 54–55.

5. Despite this popular perception, their does exist an important French doctoral thesis on urbanism during the Restoration. See Debofle, "La Politique d'urbanisme," and also idem, "Travaux publics," 42–77.

6. Bertier de Sauvigny, *La Restauration*, 53–54.

7. See Préfecture de la Seine, *Recherches statistiques sur la ville de Paris*, 1 (1821), Table 55, and Papayanis, *Horse-Drawn Cabs*, 61–67.

8. Bertier de Sauvigny, *La Restauration*, 54, and Lavedan, *Historie de l'urbanisme*, 366–77.

9. Lavedan, *Historie de l'urbanisme*, 364–65.

10. Morizet, *Du Vieux Paris*, 86.

11. For a survey of urbanism under the Restoration, see Debofle, "La Politique d'urbanisme," 3:508–685; see also Lavedan, *Historie de l'urbanisme*, 364–65.

12. Coleman, *Death Is a Social Disease*, 49–50.

13. Merriman, *Margins of City Life*, 42, quotation at 43.

14. Marchand, *Paris*, 39.

15. Ibid., 35–36.

16. Préfecture de la Seine, *Recherches statistiques sur la ville de Paris*, 4 (1829): Table 51, and ibid., 5 (1844): Table 64. See also L. Chevalier, *Laboring Classes*, 183.

17. Piette and Ratcliffe, "Les Migrants et la ville."

18. For a study of migrants in Paris, see ibid.; on the concentration of population and industry in the center, see Gaillard, *Paris, la ville*, 10–14, quotation at 13, and Daumas and Payen, eds., *Évolution de la géographie industrielle de Paris*, 3: pls. 6, 7.

19. Guillot, *Réflections*, 5–6.

20. Ibid., 7–8.

21. Préfecture de la Seine, *Recherche statistiques sur la ville de Paris*.

22. Information on this important figure may be found in Papayanis, *Horse-Drawn Cabs*, 39–53.

23. Lavedan, *Historie de l'urbanisme*, 361.

24. For information on Villot and the gathering of statistics in Paris, see Coleman, *Death Is a Social Disease,* 142–44; Lavasseur, "France," 200; Barbier, *Dictionnaire,* 4: 26–27; Cole, *Power of Large Numbers,* 56–58; and Papayanis, *Horse-Drawn Cabs,* 44–45.

25. Villot, introduction to *Recherches statistiques* (1821), 1:iii–vi.

26. Lepetit, *Chemins de terre.*

27. L. Chevalier, *Laboring Classes,* 45.

28. On the manner of conducting the census, see Préfecture de la Seine, *Recherches statistiques,* 1:99–102.

29. Chabrol de Volvic, report of Paris, Aug. 19, 1824, in Archives nationales (hereafter AN), F/5 (II) Seine/21.

30. Daubanton, "Rapport relatif aux entreprises de construction dans Paris, de 1821 à 1826," Préfecture de la Seine, *Recherches statistiques,* 4:5–73.

31. Ibid., 17–18.

32. Ibid., 22–23.

33. *Coup d'oeil sur Paris* (Paris, 1824), 6–7.

34. Mirbel and Bareau, *Mémoire,* 3–7. Note that Mirbel was identified by his family name only and Bareau by his family name and the initial of his given name. Florence Bourillon writes that the term *crisis* with respect to urban questions was generally not employed during the nineteenth century; however, its usage was not completely uncommon. See Bourillon, "Changer la ville," 11–12.

35. On the importance of engineers for city management, as indicated in chap. 1, n. 129, see Barles, *La Ville délétère;* Lepetit, *The Pre-Industrial Urban System;* Picon, *L'Invention de l'ingénieur moderne,* and idem, *French Architects and Engineers.*

36. Picon, *L'Invention de l'ingénieur moderne,* 578.

37. For what follows, see Picon, *French Architects and Engineers,* 99–105.

38. Laborde, *D'embellissemens,* i–ii.

39. Jacquemet, "les Porteurs d'eau" and Papayanis, *Coachmen.*

40. Devert, *Tableau indicateur,* 1 and 9 (plan for crossroad).

41. Legrand and Landon, *Description de Paris,* 2:5–6.

42. Mirbel and A. Bareau, *Mémoire.*

43. Leblanc de Ferrière, *Paris et ses environs,* 489–96 (section on public works).

44. Levicomte and Rolland, *Mémoire,* 16–17. For press accounts of their proposal, see *La Propriété,* no. 20 (Apr. 20, 1833), 2–3; and *Édile de Paris,* June 5, 1833, 10–20.

45. A consideration of the *Recherches statistiques* and of its principal animator, Chabrol de Volvic, from the point of view of urban planning is presented in Papayanis, *Horse-Drawn Cabs,* 39–53.

46. See Coleman, *Death Is a Social Disease,* 145, and Cole, *Power of Large Numbers,* 59.

47. For a discussion of the "author function" in relation to texts and discourse, see Foucault, "What Is an Author?" 101–20.

48. Chabrol de Volvic, in *Statistique des provinces,* 1:1. See also Boudard, "Un Préfet napoléonien," and Papayanis, *Horse-Drawn Cabs,* 42–44.

49. Lavasseur, "France," 200.

50. Préfecture de la Seine, *Recherches statistiques,* 1:iii and 3:v.

51. Chabrol de Volvic, "Mémoires," in Papers of Gilbert Joseph Gaspard de Chabrol de Volvic, pt. 1:5.

52. Préfecture de la Seine, *Recherches statistiques,* 1:v and vii. For a critique of the relation of statistics to "true" knowledge, see Scott, *Gender.*

53. Préfecture de la Seine, *Recherches statistiques,* 1:ix.

54. Ibid., 3:vi.

55. Chabrol de Volvic, "Mémoires," 7, 24–25.

56. Chabrol de Volvic, "Statistique générale de la ville de Paris et du Département de la Seine," manuscript, 5–6, in Papers of Gilbert Joseph Gaspard de Chabrol de Volvic, and "Mémoires," 23.

57. Chabrol de Volvic, "Mémoires," 40–41.

58. For the part of the "Mémoires" dealing with the London trip, see Debofle, "La Politique d'urbanisme," 350.

59. Chabrol de Volvic, "Mémoires," 7, 44–45.

60. Préfecture de la Seine, *Recherches statistiques,* 1: 1–113.

61. Ibid., 1:v–vii.

62. Chabrol de Volvic, "Rapport . . . sur les moyens d'amener et de distribuer les eaux dans la ville de Paris et sa banlieue," in ibid., 3:1–39.

63. Daubanton, "Rapport relatif aux entreprises de construction dans Paris," in Préfecture de la Seine, *Recherches statistiques,* 4: 1–73; and Chabrol de Volvic, "Mémoire présenté par M. le comte de Chabrol . . . concernant l'exécution du projet d'alignement des rues de la ville de Paris," in ibid. (1824), 2:1–23.

64. Chabrol de Volvic, "Mémoire . . . concernant . . . des rues . . . de Paris," 10–11.

65. Ibid., 20.

66. Chabrol de Volvic, in Paris, *Budget . . . pour l'exercice 1823,* 14.

67. Much of this information may be found in Papayanis, *Horse-Drawn Cabs,* 38–53. See also Morachiello and Teysot, "State Town," 24–39; Demangeon and Fortier, "The Politics of Urban Space," 8–13; and Picon, *L'Invention de l'ingénieur moderne,* 579–583.

68. Papayanis, *Horse-Drawn Cabs,* 50–51.

69. Sennett, *Fall of Public Man,* 12–14.

70. Debofle, "Travaux publics," 71.

71. Procacci, "Sociology and Its Poor," 115–62, quotation at 175.

72. For a discussion of this theme, see Paul-Lévy, *La Ville en croix,* 111–23.

73. For some interesting insights on space and order, see Foucault, "Space, Knowledge, and Power," 239–56.

74. *Coup d'oeil sur Paris,* 42–47.

75. Mirbel and Bareau, *Mémoire,* 25–48. See also, Sutcliffe, *An Architectural History,* 74.

76. Shapiro, *Housing the Poor,* 15.

77. Mirbel and Bareau, *Mémoire,* 7.

78. Ibid., 22–23. The law of Sept. 16, 1807, empowered all French towns to submit plans to the prefect of the department and the central government showing the alignment of streets and important public buildings, including those yet to be constructed.

The law of March 8, 1810, clarified that of 1807 in some details but also limited the discretionary power of the government with respect to expropriations; see Sutcliffe, *Towards the Planned City,* 128–29, and Tulard, *Paris et son administration,* 324–26.

79. Mirbel and Bareau, *Mémoire,* 60.

80. Ibid., 86–87, 91–93.

81. Foucault, "Space, Knowledge, and Power," 244, 247–48.

82. Levicomte and Rolland, *Mémoire,* 10–14.

83. Ibid., 18–19.

84. Ibid., 24–26.

85. Ibid., 26–30; quotations at 28, 29.

86. Foucault, "The Confessions of the Flesh," 202–4.

87. Levicomte and Rolland, *Mémoire,* 30–34, for an outline of their educational program.

88. Ibid., 30, 31, 31–32.

89. Ibid., 33–34.

90. Ibid., 38.

91. André-César Egron also combined spatial reform with an educational program to address the social question. In 1838 he proposed new fountains, new museums, and the restoration of churches in order to make Paris "the most beautiful and the most agreeable city of Europe." For the working poor and "indigent class" he suggested an increase in the number of benches along the quays and on the boulevards so that "the artisan can breath the air and rest from his daily fatigue," and the delivery of purified or filtered water. For adult workers he suggested educational courses as a means of keeping them away from cabarets and bars. For the children of the common people he proposed courses in music education, which would "develop in the young souls religious ideas, fill hours badly employed, and contribute in an unconscious manner to the amelioration of public morals." See Egron, *Embellissements,* 12, 16–18.

92. Virilio, *Speed and Politics,* 8–14 (his emphasis).

93. Deleuze and Guattari, "Treatise on Nomadology: The War Machine," in Deleuze and Guattari, *A Thousand Plateaus,* 351–423; see esp. 385–87, quotations at 385–86.

94. Sennett, *Fall of Public Man,* 53–56.

95. Bauman, *Postmodern Ethics,* 154, 157–58.

96. Chaumette, *Résumé,* 1 (his emphasis).

97. Ratcliffe, "Perceptions and Realities," 197–233.

98. Tissot, *Paris et Londres,* 11–12.

99. *Mémoire sur le projet d'une grande communication,* 2–4.

100. Ibid., 1 (author's emphasis; note that "embellishment" was not emphasized).

101. Johnson, *Utopian Communism,* 70–71.

102. Alphonse Esquiros, *Paris,* 1:21–22.

103. Vigier, *Paris pendant la Monarchie de Juillet,* 82, 234, 315–16.

104. Esquiros, *Paris,* 22.

105. For information on Frégier, see La Berge, *Mission and Method,* 162, 172–73.

106. Frégier, *Les Classes dangereuses,* 125–53.

107. Esquiros, *Paris.* 22.

108. Ibid., 20, 26 (the introduction outlines the argument about the nature of Paris).

109. Devert, *Tableau,* 3.

110. Chabrol de Volvic, Mémoire . . . concernant . . . des rues . . . de Paris," 11.

111. For what follows, see Laborde, *D'embellissemens de Paris,* 26–34.

112. Ibid., 28.

113. Ibid., 16.

114. Ibid., 27–28, quotation at iv.

115. Ibid., 31.

116. Ibid.

117. Ibid., 32.

118. *Coup d'oeil sur Paris,* 54.

119. Ibid., 58.

120. Ibid., 109–12, quotation at 111.

121. Devert, *Tableau indicateur,* 2; and idem, *Précis historique des,* 4–5. See also Tissot, *Paris et Londres,* 6–12.

122. For what follows, see Quatremère de Quincy, *Dictionnaire historique,* 2:396–97.

123. Lachaise, *Topographie médicale:* see, e.g., 120–21, 132, 148–49, quotation at 149, 203.

124. Moléon, *Rapports généraux sur les travaux du Conseil de salubrité,* 309–11.

125. Barles, *La Ville délétère,* 15–115.

126. *Mémoire sur le projet d'une grande communication,* 3.

127. Levicomte and Rolland, *Mémoire,* 13–14.

128. Douglas, *Purity and Danger,* 2–3.

129. Reid, *Paris Sewers and Sewermen,* 1–24, quotation at 17.

130. Ratcliffe, "Cities and Environmental Decline," 189–222.

131. Guillot, *Réflections,* 13.

132. Ibid., 24–68.

133. Ibid., 46, 50–51.

134. Ibid., 74–75.

135. Lepetit, *The Pre-Industrial Urban System,* 412–13; see also Pinon, "Les Conceptions urbaines," 44–50, esp. 46–50. I have treated the question of circulation in the context of the formation of a public transit system in Paris in *Horse-Drawn Cabs.* Three writers exemplified this ideology: Constantin Pecqueur (*Economie sociale.*), Andrieux, (*Études*), and Leblanc de Ferrière *(Paris et ses environs).* See also Boyer, *The City of Collective Memory,* 287–88, where Boyer also identifies circulation as a central element in the planning proposals of the nineteenth century.

136. Johnson, *Utopian Communism,* 66. The strikes are covered in Aguet, *Les Grèves.* For an important interpretation of these strikes, see Riot-Sarcey, *Le Réel de l'utopie,* 205–29.

137. For what follows, see Cohen and Lortie, *Des Fortifs au perif,* 17–38. See also Fernandez-Leveau, "La Dernière enceinte de Paris"; O'Brien, *"L'Embastillement de Paris,"* 63–82; Picon, "Les Fortifications de Paris," 213–21, and Vigier, *Paris pendant la Monarchie de Juillet,* 220–27.

138. For the information on Arago and Lamartine, see Cohen and Lortie, *Des Fortifs au perif,* 25–29.

139. M. Chevalier, *Les Fortifications de Paris,* esp. 6–8, 14–16.

140. Baissas, *Danger,* 1–15, quotation at 8.

141. O'Brien, "*L'Embastillement de Paris,*" 75–76.

142. Marx, *The Civil War,* 40.

143. Daly, "Des Fortifications de Paris," 1: cols. 601–5.

144. Picon, "Les Fortifications de Paris," 220.

145. A. Rabusson, *Si le mouvement de déplacement.*

146. Perreymond, "Études sur la ville de Paris," 4: cols. 81–82.

147. Pigeory, *Les Monuments de Paris;* see 324–43 for his discussion of the fortifications.

148. Ibid., 330, 344.

149. This question has been studied in Lavedan, *La Question du déplacement.*

150. *Réponse d'un habitant de la Rive Droite.*

151. A. Chevalier, *Du Déplacement de la population,* 6–10, quotations at 8–9, 19–22; for a discussion of industrial development in Paris during the nineteenth century, see Daumas and Payen, eds., *Évolution de la géographie industrielle de Paris,* 1:40–70.

152. Lavedan has one paragraph on Chabrol-Chaméane, and Pinon, in a short essay on urban theory in the first half of the nineteenth century, does not mention him; see Lavedan, *La Question du déplacement,* 23–24, and Pinon, "Les Conceptions urbaines." For an assessment of Chabrol-Chaméane, see Papayanis, "L'Émergence de l'urbanisme," 82–94.

153. Chabrol-Chaméane, *Mémoire.*

154. Lepetit, *The Pre-Industrial Urban System,* 420.

155. Meier, *A Communications Theory.*

156. For a brief treatment of several of the more important planners of this period, see Lavedan, *La Question du déplacement de Paris.*

157. Chabrol-Chaméane, *Mémoire,* 8.

158. Ibid., 10 (his emphasis).

159. Among Rabusson's several publications on the displacement question, see the following: Rabusson, *Éclaircisseueurs;* idem, *Affaire du déplacement;* and idem, *Note.* For information on Rabusson, see Lavedan, *La Question du déplacement de Paris,* 26–27.

160. See Lanquetin, *Question du déplacement,* as well as Lavedan, *La Question du déplacement de Paris.*

161. Daubanton, *Du Déplacement,* 29–34.

162. For this brief biographical information, see *Révue généale de l'architecture,* 5:453. There is some information on Meynadier in Papayanis, "L'Émergence de l'urbanisme."

163. Marchand, *Paris,* 60.

164. Lavedan, *La Question du déplacement de Paris,* 54–55.

165. Meynadier, *Paris,* 1.

166. Lavedan, *La Question du déplacement de Paris,* 54 (my emphasis).

167. Lefebvre, *The Production of Space,* 417–18.

168. Meynadier, *Paris,* 7, 12.

169. Ibid., 15–28.

170. For a discussion of each of these streets, see ibid., 15–43. For an analysis of Meynadier's proposals, see Lavedan, *La Question du déplacement de Paris,* 54–55, and Marchand, *Paris,* 56–60.

171. Meynadier, *Paris,* 105–13, 138–40.

172. Ibid., 147, 230–31, quotation at 230.

173. Ibid., 148.

174. Brunet, *Paris.*

175. Ibid., 7–8.

176. Ibid., 11–12.

177. Du Camp, *Paris.*

178. Paul-Lévy, *La Ville en croix,* 113–14, 122–23, and 178.

179. Grillon, G. Callou, and Th. Jacobet, *Études,* 16.

180. Ibid., 26.

181. Vincens, *Mémoire.*

182. Ibid., 10; for his discussion of paper money, see 7–9.

183. Lecouturier, *Paris incompatible avec la République.*

184. *Notice biographique sur Henri Lecouturier,* 5.

185. Lecouturier, *Paris incompatible avec la République,* 105.

186. Engels, *Condition of the Working Class,* 63, 65 (his emphasis).

187. Lecouturier, *Paris incompatible avec la République,* 20–21.

188. Ibid., 63, 73.

189. Lecouturier, *La Science.*

190. Lecouturier, *Paris incompatible avec la République,* 66–67.

191. Ibid., 88–106.

192. Paul-Lévy, *La Ville en croix,* 180–184.

193. Lecouturier, *Paris incompatible avec le République,* 98.

194. Le Corbusier, *Radiant City,* 321.

195. Lecouturier, *Paris incompitable avec le République,* 98.

196. Ibid., 94.

197. Marie, *Décentralisation.*

198. Ibid., 7–8, 12.

199. Ibid., 23–24; Thompson, *Victorious Marketplace,* 86–103.

200. Chambelland, *Réformes.*

201. Ibid., 3.

202. Ibid., 8–11, quotation at 8–9.

203. For house numbering, see Pronteau, *Les Numérotages.*

204. Chambelland, *Réformes,* 19-20.

205. Husson, *Traité.*

206. Husson, *Régénération.*

207. Gourlier, *Des Voies publiques.*

208. Ibid., 7 n. 2, 14–15.

209. For Lazare's extensive publications, see, e.g., his *Bibliothèque municipale.*

210. Félix and Louis Lazare, *Dictionnaire administratif.* For a brief biographical

sketch of the Lazare brothers, see Fleury, "Les Frères Lazare," ix–xix. I am currently completing a larger study of Louis Lazare.

211. See Lazare, "Prospectus."

212. Lazare, "Création d'un plan d'ensemble."

213. Ibid, no. 61 (Nov.1, 1850), 495.

214. Ibid., no. 66 (Jan. 16, 1851), 540 (his emphasis).

CHAPTER 3

The Saint-Simonians and Paris

1. For the standard biography of Saint-Simon, see Manuel, *The New World*. For a history of the Saint-Simonian movement, see Picon, *Les Saint-Simoniens*.

2. Carlisle, *The Proffered Crown*, 1–3.

3. Rykwert, *The Seduction of Place*, 51.

4. Engels, "Socialism: Utopian and Scientific," 683–717.

5. Ibid., 687.

6. Hayek, *Counter-Revolution*, 263–320; and Charléty, *Saint-Simonisme*, 355; Bénichou, *Temps des prophètes*.

7. Carlisle, *The Proffered Crown;* Gallice, "Les Ingénieurs saint-simoniens"; idem, "Les Ingénieurs saint-simoniens: le mariage"; Picon, "Le Paris des ingénieurs," 37–43; Lepetit, *The Pre-Industrial Urban System;* Ratcliffe, "The Economic Influence of the Saint-Simonians," 252–62; and Marrey, "Les Réalisations des utopistes," 193–215.

8. Carlisle, *The Proffered Crown*, 73, 127.

9. These ideas are worked out fully in Picon, *L'Invention de l'ingénieur moderne*, and idem, "Les Modèles de la métropole"; see also idem, *Les Saint-Simoniens*.

10. Lepetit, *The Pre-Industrial Urban System*, 409–419.

11. Riot-Sarcey, *Le Réel de l'utopie*.

12. Enfantin, *Mémoires d'un industriel*, 17:147–214. Robert Carlisle points out that a printing error gives the date of publication as 1838; see Carlisle, *The Proffered Crown*, 72 ff.

13. For a short biographical note on Enfantin, see Régnier, *Le Livre Nouveau*, 327–28.

14. Carlisle, *The Proffered Crown*, 72, 76, 78.

15. Mercier, *L'An deux mille quatre cent quarante*.

16. Enfantin, *Mémoires*, 154 (his emphasis).

17. Ibid., 180.

18. Ibid., 182.

19. Ibid., 155–60.

20. For information on the twentieth-century version of the world capital, see Sutcliffe, *Towards the Planned City*, 167–68.

21. This section draws heavily on Caron, *Histoire des chemins de fer*, 79–121.

22. Ibid., 93.

23. Ibid., 82, quotations at 98. For a summary of Saint-Simonian ideas and policies on railroads, see also Picon, *Les Saint-Simoniens*, 226–39.

24. Michel Chevalier, Stéphane Flachat, Charles Duveyrier, and Henri Fournel, *Religion saint-simonienne. Politique industrielle. Système de la Méditerranée* This work consisted of articles, by each of the authors, that had originally appeared in *Le Globe* between January and April 1832 and. They were then combined into this single volume. The essay *Système de la Méditerranée*, written by Chevalier, forms the last part of this work.

25. For a biography of Michel Chevalier, see Walch, *Michel Chevalier;* for information on *Le Globe* see D'Allemagne, *Les Saint-Simoniens*, 178–81.

26. M. Chevalier, *Système de la Méditerranée*, 136–37.

27. Ibid., 36–40, quotation at 36; 120–21 (social hierarchy), and 85 (centralization).

28. Ibid., 135–45.

29. Chevalier, "Politique d'association," in M. Chevalier et al., *Religion saint-simonienne*, 35.

30. M. Chevalier, *Système de la Méditerranée*, 146.

31. See, e.g., Carlisle, *The Proferred Crown*, 3, 39, 235–36.

32. M. Chevalier, "Aux hommes politiques," in M. Chevalier et al., *Religion saint-simonienne*, 83–100.

33. Ibid., 91 (his emphasis).

34. M. Chevalier, "Politique industrielle et système de la Méditerranée," in M. Chevalier et al., *Réligion saint-simonienne*, 11.

35. Cameron, *France,* and Gille, *La Banque en France*, 105–6.

36. For what follows, see Gille, *La Banque en France*, 105–24.

37. For this information, see ibid., 112–13. In 1837, Lafitte was able to found the Caisse générale du Commerce et de l'Industrie, a bank that in effect accepted deposits and made long-term loans to finance industrial and railroad development. And in 1852, Isaac and Émile Pereire founded the Crédit Mobilier, a bank with a huge capital base organized to make low-cost industrial loans, especially railway loans, and issue short-term bonds for the average person as well as the largest capitalist.

38. M. Chevalier, "Aux hommes politiques," in M. Chevalier et al., *Religion saint-simonienne,* 92.

39. M. Chevalier, *Système de la Méditerranée*, 108.

40. For a summary of this plan, see M. Chevalier, "Politique industrielle. Organisation industriel de l'armée," 12–13, and "Aux hommes politiques," 92–93, in M. Chevalier et al., *Religion saint-simonienne.*

41. Caron, *Histoire des chemins de fer*, 122–32.

42. M. Chevalier, "Politique d'association. Politique de déplacement," in M. Chevalier et al., *Religion saint-simonienne*, 38.

43. M. Chevalier, "Aux hommes politiques," 98.

44. Ibid., 96–97.

45. Hayek, *Counter-Revolution.* See also the recent essay on Hayek by Minoque, "The Escape from Serfdom," 11–13, and another by Cassidy, "The Price Prophet," 44–51.

46. Marx and Engels, *The Communist Manifesto*, 41–43, quotation at 43.

47. For his analysis of these elements, see M. Chevalier, *Système de la Méditerranée*, 104–5, quotation at 105.

48. Littré, "Le Choléra à Paris en 1832," 187–90.

49. Kudlick, *Cholera*, 64.

50. Clavel, "Le Choléra," 366.

51. Foucault, "Space, Knowledge and Power," 243.

52. The reaction of the upper classes to the cholera is covered very well in Kudlick, *Cholera*; see esp. 176–211.

53. Ibid., 64, and Delaporte, *Disease and Civilization*, 59.

54. La Berge, *Mission and Method*, 1–2.

55. Leuret, "Mémoire," 6:313–440.

56. See La Berge, *Mission and Method*, 113–27 (for the organization of the Paris health council).

57. Leuret, "Mémoire," 431–32.

58. Boulay de la Meurthe, *Histoire du choléra-morbus*.

59. Ibid., 25–28; 31; 41–42; 93.

60. Ibid., 101; 112–13; 116–18, quotation at 116.

61. Tacheron, *Statistique médicale*, 51–52.

62. Moreau, *Histoire statistique*.

63. Ibid., 42–43.

64. Ibid., 40–41.

65. Foucault, *Madness and Civilization*, 6–7.

66. Benoiston de Châteauneuf, *Rapport*.

67. Ibid., the report's conclusions are summed up on pp. 187–205.

68. Ibid., 191–96, quotations at 191, 192.

69. Ibid., 201, 202.

70. Barles, *La Ville délétère*, 212; Picon, *L'Invention de l'ingénieur moderne*, 584.

71. For a discussion of engineers and the management of water, see Barles, *La Ville délétère*, 136–38, 210–11; Lepetit, *The Pre-Industrial Urban System*, 410–11; and Picon, *L'Invention de l'ingénieur moderne*, 584–86.

72. Lepetit, *The Pre-Industrial Urban System*, 412.

73. This point is also stressed by Carlisle, *The Proffered Crown*, 204.

74. M. Chevalier et al., *Religion saint-simonienne*, 51–81.

75. For information on the Paris to Saint-Germain line, see Pinkney, *Napoleon III*, 16–17, and Caron, *Histoire des chemins de fer*, 137–38, and Picon, *Les Saint-Simoniens*, 229–30.

76. Flachat, "Le Choléra: Assainissement de Paris," 41–49; virtually identical ideas are in Flachat, *Réligion saint-simonienne: Le Choléra à Paris*.

77. Flachat, "Le Choléra: Assainissement de Paris," 43.

78. Ibid., 44.

79. Evans, "Epidemics and Revolutions," 144.

80. Flachat, "Le Choléra: Assainissement de Paris," 45.

81. Sutcliffe, *An Architectural History*, 71.

82. Flachat, "Le Choléra. Assainissement de Paris," 46.

83. Ibid.

84. On the expropriation laws, see chapter 2, note 78.

85. Harvey, *Consciousness and the Urban Experience*, 177–78 (for quotation by Harvey); 178 (Edmond About cited by Harvey).

86. Flachat, "Le Choléra: Assainisement de Paris," 47; Pinkney, *Napoleon III*, 87–88.

87. Flachat, "Choléra: Assainissement de Paris," 47–48.

88. This point is developed at length in Lefebvre, *Production of Space*.

89. Flachat, "Le Choléra: Assainissement de Paris," 49.

90. Fournel, "Au Roi," in M. Chevalier et al., *Religion saint-simonienne*, 75–81 (originally published in *Le Globe*, 13 Apr. 1832).

91. M. Chevalier, "Le Choléra-morbus," in ibid., 51–65.

92. Ibid., 53.

93. Duveyrier, "Paris," and "Le Pouvoir nouveau," in M. Chevalier et al., *Religion saint-simonienne*, 57–65 (originally published in *Le Globe*, Apr. 11, 1832); 67–74 (originally published in *Le Globe*, Apr. 16, 1832); idem, "La Ville nouvelle." For the original letter Duveyrier wrote to the publisher of "La Ville nouvelle," which is reproduced in the chapter, see Charles Duveyrier, " La Ville nouvelle," letter of Oct. 6, 1832, in Bibliothèque de l'Arsenal, FE 7825.

94. Duveyrier, "Paris," 62, 64.

95. Ibid., 59.

96. Ibid., 61

97. Ibid., 62.

98. Ibid.

99. Duveyrier, "Le Pouvoir nouveau," 68.

100. Ibid., 69.

101. For a discussion of the relationship of art to the social criticism of the French Left at this time, see McWilliam, *Dreams of Happiness*.

102. Picon, "Le Paris des ingénieurs," 38–42; see also idem, *Les Saint-Simoniens*, 253–58.

103. Duveyrier, "La Ville nouvelle," 316, 317, 318.

104. Ibid., 320.

105. Choay, *The Rule and the Model*, 34 (her emphasis), 222–23.

106. Picon, "Le Paris des ingénieurs."

107. He put this in completely metaphorical terms, comparing the city to a statue of a man, writing that "my city is in the posture of a man ready to march, with feet of bronze; they rest on a double road of stone and iron." See, Duveyrier, "La Ville nouvelle," 327.

108. Ibid., 328.

109. Ibid., 326.

110. Prendergast, *Paris*, 34.

111. Lamé et al., *Vues politiques*. For the completion date, see introduction, 5.

112. M. Chevalier, *Des Intérêts matériels*.

113. Reynaud, "Villes," in *Encyclopédie nouvelle*.

114. Christaller, *Central Places*.

115. Gallice, "Les Ingénieurs saint-simoniens,"22.

116. Lamé et al., *Vues politiques*, 103.

117. M. Chevalier, *Des Intérêts matériels*, 20.

118. Lepetit, *The Pre-Industrial Urban System*, 430.

119. Lamé et al., *Vues politiques*, 104. According to Picon, the Saint-Simonians grasped more clearly than most of their contemporaries the potential strategic and tactical importance of the railroads; see Picon, *Les Saint-Simoniens*, 233–34.

120. Lamé et al., *Vues politiques*, 104–5.

121. M. Chevalier, *Des Intérêts matériels*, 270.

122. Ibid., 20, 173–76.

123. Lamé et al., *Vues politiques*, 24.

124. Ibid., 236–66.

125. Marx, *Grundrisse*, 524.

126. Marx and Engels, *The Communist Manifesto*, 13–14.

127. Berman, *All That Is Solid Melts*, 93–96.

128. M. Chevalier, *Des Intérêts matériels*, 11, 13.

129. Lamé et al., *Vues politiques*, 290–92.

130. Freedman, *Joint-Stock Enterprise*, 27–28, 52.

131. Plessis, *Rise and Fall*, 58–97.

132. For a short introduction to Reynaud, see Robic, "Cent ans avant Christaller," 11; Reynaud, "Villes."

133. Choay, *The Modern City*; see also idem, *The Rule and the Model*, 233–56.

134. Lepetit, *The Pre-industrial Urban System*, 418.

135. Reynaud, "Villes," 670, col. 2–671, col. 1.

136. Christaller, *Central Places*, 2.

137. Reynaud, "Villes," 671, col. 1–674, col. 1 (for the entire discussion of the "principles of the aggregation of houses.")

138. Lepetit, "Event and structure," 17.

139. Ibid.

140. Reynaud, "Villes," 671, col. 1–684, col. 1.

141. Lepetit, *The Pre-industrial Urban System*, 420.

142. For the section that follows, see Reynaud, "Villes," 677, col. 1–684, col. 1.

143. Ibid., 680, cols. 1–2.

144. Ibid., col. 2.

145. Picon, *L'Invention de l'ingénieur moderne*, 586.

146. Ibid., 587–88.

147. Reynaud, *Traité d'architecture*, 573–601, quotation at 582.

CHAPTER 4

The Fourieriests and the New Paris

1. For a recent introduction to French socialism during the first half of the nineteenth century, including Fourierists and Saint-Simonians, see Pilbeam, *French Socialists*.

2. Picon, "Le Paris des ingénieurs," 38.

3. See, e.g., Marrey, "Les Réalisations des utopistes," 193–215, quotation at 195; Picon, "Le Paris des ingénieurs," 37–43; and Saboya, *Presse et architecture*, 134.

4. See note 6 and Friedrich Engels, "Socialism: Utopian or Scientific," 683–717.

5. Riasanovsky, *Teaching,* 81, 200.

6. Beecher, *Charles Fourier,* 54–74.

7. Fourier, *Oeuvres complètes* (hereafter cited as *OC*), 4:298–313. Idem, *Cités ouvrières.* An editor of *La Phalange* indicated that *Cités ouvrières* was written around 1820 and intended as part of the *Théorie de l'unité universelle.* See *Cités ouvrières,* 4. The text of *Cités ouvrières* is also in *OC,* 12:683–717. For the *Théorie,* see *OC,* vols. 2–5.

8. *OC,* 12:695.

9. OC, 12:697–98, and *OC,* 4:299.

10. For the first quote see, Fourier, *OC,* 12:695; for the second, see Fourier, *OC,* 4:299.

11. *OC,* 4:312

12. Picon, "Le Paris des ingénieurs," 41.

13. Fourier, OC, 12:706.

14. For the first, see Fourier, *OC,* 4:300; for the second, see Fourier, *OC,* 12:697.

15. Fourier, *OC,* 12:696.

16. Lefebvre, *Production of Space,* 360.

17. For what follows, see Fourier, *OC,* 12:696–702.

18. Ibid., 705.

19. Fishman, *Urban Utopias,* 13–15.

20. Beecher, *Charles Fourier,* 60–61; see also Etlin, "L'Air dans l'urbanisme," 123–34; Sennett, *Flesh and Stone,* 255–81; and Papayanis, *Horse-Drawn Cabs,* 8–35.

21. Patte, *Mémoires,* and idem, *Monumens érigés.*

22. Considerant, *Considérations,* and idem, *Destinée sociale.*

23. Beecher, *Victor Considerant,* 124.

24. Considerant, *Considérations,* 7–9,12–19; quotations at 8–9, 13.

25. Ibid., 9, 17.

26. Beecher, *Victor Considerant,* 124–38.

27. Michel de Certeau, *Practice of Everyday Life,* 94–110, quotations at 92–93.

28. Harvey, *Condition of Postmodernity,* 27–28.

29. Marielle, *Répertoire;* see also Fourcy, *l'École polytechnique.*

30. Marcel Roncayolo in a conversation on June 28, 2001.

31. *La Phalange* 4, no. 37 (Nov. 24, 1841), 593.

32. Krolikowski, *Mémoire historique;* Johnson, *Utopian Communism,* 93–94, 94 n. 88. I would like to thank Chris Johnson for calling my attention to Krolikowski.

33. Perreymond, *L'Espagne démocratique,* 5.

34. Perreymond, *Le Portugal.*

35. His major publications appeared between 1841 and 1851 autonomously or in the leading Fourierist journals, *La Phalange* and *La Démocratie pacifique,* as well as in the *Revue générale de l'architecture et des travaux publics (RGA),* which, although not a political journal, was edited by César Daly, whose sentiments were Fourierist.

36. Picon, *L'Invention de l'ingénieur moderne,* 81.

37. Perreymond, "Études."

38. Olsen, *City as a Work of Art,* 3–6; Etlin, *Symbolic Space,* 1–2.

39. See Papayanis, *Horse-Drawn Cabs,* 36–86.

40. Picon, *French Architects and Engineers,* 1–15.

41. See chapter 1 and Papayanis, *Horse-Drawn Cabs,* 31–34.

42. Chabrol-Chaméane, *Mémoire* and Meynadier de Flamalens, *Paris.*

43. For the quote, see Perreymond, *RGA* 3 (Dec. 1842): col. 552. Perreymond was very generous in his citation of Chabrol-Chaméane, quoting from the latter's report at length; see ibid., cols. 575–76. He also used the work of other individuals interested in the displacement-of-the-population question, notably Jacques Lanquetin and A. Rabusson; see ibid., cols. 575–78.

44. Perreymond, *RGA* 3 (Dec. 1842): col. 542 (his emphasis).

45. Lepetit, *The Pre-Industrial Urban System,* 430.

46. Perreymond, *Notions élémentaires.*

47. Lepetit, *The Pre-Industrial Urban System,* 430.

48. Beecher, *Charles Fourier,* 67.

49. Perreymond and Victor Considerant, "D'un Système national"; the study appeared under the same title in *La Phalange* 4, no. 37 (24 Nov. 1841): cols. 593–600.

50. Perreymond, *RGA* 3 (Dec. 1842): col. 550.

51. Perreymond, *RGA* 4 (Feb. 1843): cols. 72–79.

52. For an important treatment of the Seine River and its place in the planning history of Paris, see Backouche, *La Trace du Fleuve;* for an appreciation of Perreymond on circulation, see also Moret, *Les Socialistes et la ville,* 244–56.

53. Lavedan, *La Question du déplacement,* 56–57.

54. One major project for a north-south street was drawn up by Léon de Laborde in his *Projets.* Perreymond analyzes this work at length; see Perreymond, *RGA* 4 (Sept. 1843): cols. 524–25.

55. Perreymond, *RGA* 4 (Sept. 1843): col. 418 (for the first quote), and col. 419 (for the second).

56. The most important of these texts are: Perreymond, *Le Bilan de la France;* idem, *Le Pain du prolétaire;* and idem, *Paris monarchique et Paris républicain.*

57. See Beecher, "Fourierism and Christianity," 391–403; and idem, *Victor Considerant,* 148–49.

58. Perreymond, *Le Bilan,* 3–4 (his emphasis).

59. Ibid., 45.

60. Ibid., 42 (his emphasis).

61. Ibid., 45 (his emphasis).

62. Maurice Agulhon, *The Republican Experiment,* 22–23.

63. Perreymond, *Paris monarchique et Paris républicain,* 69 (his emphasis).

64. Ibid., 70–71, 72.

65. Ibid., 97.

66. See Pilbeam, *Republicanism,* 163–65.

67. Perreymond, *Paris monarchique et Paris républicain,* 99 (his emphasis).

68. Ibid., 100.

69. Ibid., 101.

70. Ibid., 102–3.

71. Ibid., 106–7.

72. Perreymond, *RGA* 4 (Oct. 1843): cols. 459–63.

73. Roncayolo, "Le Modèle haussmannien," 95–96.

74. Perreymond, *RGA* 4 (Sept. 1843): cols. 415, 421.

75. Ibid., 4 (Feb. 1843): cols. 85–86.

76. Ibid., col. 85 (his emphasis).

77. Ibid., col. 86

78. Perreymond, "Lettre de M. Perreymond à M. César Daly," *RGA* 3: cols. 540–41.

79. Ibid.

80. Perreymond, *RGA* 3 (Dec. 1842): col. 574.

81. Donald, *Imagining the Modern City*, 60–61.

82. Perreymond, *RGA* 4 (Jan. 1843): cols. 25–37.

83. Ibid., 3 (Dec. 1842): col. 579.

84. Foucault, "Space, Knowledge, and Power," 239–56.

85. Deleuze and Guattari, *A Thousand Plateaus*, 386.

86. Perreymond, *RGA* 3 (Dec. 1842): col. 554 (his emphasis).

87. Considerant and Perreymond, "De l'unité administrative," 1, no. 82 (Oct. 21, 1843), 1, and ibid., 1, no. 103 (Nov. 11, 1843), 1; and idem, "De la grande circulation dans Paris," 1.

88. Sennett, *Uses of Disorder*, 91–92 (his emphasis).

89. Considerant and Perreymond, "De l'unité administrative," 1, no. 103 (Nov. 11, 1843), 1.

90. Considerant, *Déraison et dangers*.

91. Ibid., 24.

92. [Victor Considerant], "Système national des chemins de fer," cols. 593–600, and Perreymond, "De La Locomotion rapide," in ibid., cols. 600–612. A summary of the Perreymond study also appeared in the *RGA*; see "D'un Système national des chemins de fer," cols. 581–88.

93. Beecher, *Victor Considerant*, 117–18.

94. [Considerant], "Système national des chemins de fer," col. 593.

95. Vigier, *Paris pendant la Monarchie de Juillet*, 125–38; see also 153 for a short discussion of Considerant's election.

96. Beecher, *Victor Considerant*, 103.

97. Ibid., 115–16.

98. Considerant, "Note," cols. 22–29.

99. Ibid., col. 23.

100. Rabinow, *French Modern*, 9.

101. Considerant, "Note," col. 23.

102. Ibid., 23.

103. Ibid., col. 29.

104. Examining the budget for Paris over the years 1797–1840, Considerant noted that the city had spent 11 million francs for work on quays, street paving, sidewalks, and underground quarries, while over the same years it had dispensed 16 million francs for fireworks and public festivals. It was urgent, he warned, that authorities not sacrifice

"sanitation and circulation, these two first needs of an immense population concentrated on a small space." The current municipal budget was 42 million francs, he reported, and his statistical analysis was intended to permit the reader to conclude that a greater portion of that budget should be expended for infrastructure reform; see ibid., col. 29.

105. See Pinkney, *Napoleon III,* 25–48, and Harvey, *Consciousness and the Urban Experience,* 63–64.

106. Jordan, *Transforming Paris,* 51 and 149–163. I would like to thank David Jordan for calling my attention to the importance of Haussmann's Bordeaux experience.

CHAPTER 5

Planning the Paris Underground

1. See Lavedan, *La Question,* and idem, Histoire de l'urbanisme; Des Cars and Pinon, eds., *Paris-Haussmann;* Loyer, *Paris.*

2. In the first half of the nineteenth century, omnibuses began to operate too late in the morning for workers to arrive on time for work and their zoned fare system made them too expensive for the average worker; see Papayanis, *Horse-Drawn Cabs,* chap. 2.

3. Lefebvre, *Production of Space,* 360–63.

4. On "creative destruction," see the discussion in Harvey, *Consciousness and the Urban Experience,* and Marshall Berman, *All That Is Solid Melts,* 98–105, where Berman discusses this theme under the rubric of capitalist "innovative self-destruction."

5. For an excellent treatment of the subject of the underground in literature and technology, see Rosalind Williams, *Notes on the Underground.* For Paris sewers, see Reid, *Paris Sewers and Sewermen,*

6. Hugo, *Les Misérables,* 1256–70; quotations at 1259, 1260, 1261, 1264, 1269–70.

7. For a discussion of the underground experience, see Williams, *Notes on the Underground,* 51–81; see also Schivelbusch, *The Railway Journey,* 16–32.

8. I would like to thank Sheila Hallset Baumair for calling my attention to Vallée. For an appreciation of Valée's importance, see Bowie, ed. "Polarisation," 1:19–21.

9. L. Vallée, *Génie civil* 21 (July 2, 1892). My thanks to Sheila Hallsted-Baumert for passing along this reference.

10. AN, F/14/2333/2.

11. Vallée, *Changements,* 3.

12. Vallée, *Une Loi,* 1–7.

13. Ibid., 15–16 (his emphasis).

14. Vallée, *Exposé générale,* 13.

15. Bowie, "Polarisation," 19.

16. Vallée, *Exposé général,* 12–13.

17. See Bourla and Renaud, *Mémoire.* I would like to thank Karen Bowie for calling this plan to my attention.

18. Boudon, "Horeau et les Halles centrales," 152. On the development of Les Halles and its quarter, see Boudon et al., *Système de l'architecture urbaine.*

19. Dion, "Horeau," 18–19. See also Broussel, ed., *Victor Baltard,* 5–8.

20. This underground space has been characterized by Françoise Boudon as "rather audacious" and by Pierre Lavedan as "outside of the sewers, the first attempt at underground urbanism." Boudon, "Horeau et les Halles centrales," 155; Lavedan, *Histoire de l'urbanisme*, 385. For Baltard's final plan and retrospective opinion on the placement, see Baltard and Callet, *Monographie des Halles Centrales.* See also Broussel, ed. *Victor Baltard,* and Préfeture du Département de la Seine, *Commission des Halles.*

21. On Horeau's life and work, see Dufournet, "Quelques Aspects," 145–51, and Choay, "Pensées sur la ville, arts de la ville," 174–78.

22. Horeau, *Examen critique*, 5–6.

23. For drawings of the plan, see ibid., 13–14.

24. Ibid., 7.

25. Ibid., 7–12.

26. Pierre Lavedan has written with reference to Horeau's 1845 scheme for an underground railroad that "it represents the origin of the Paris Métro" (Lavedan, *La Question,* 41). This is an exaggeration, however, as the 1845 plan was tied closely to the central market, and there was no suggestion that it could serve passengers.

27. See Horeau, *Examen critique,* 10, 11; Horeau, *Nouvelle observations,* 6; Senard, *Halles Centrales de Paris,* 15, 25, 27–28. For an overview of the rebuilding of Paris and the considerations behind this process, see Pinkney, *Napoleon III.* See also Boudon, *Système de l'architecture urbaine.*

28. Lefebvre, *Production of Space,* 361, 362. See also Harvey, *Consciousness and the Urban Experience,* 31, for a discussion of the state's need for the expert knowledge of the architect in order to legitimize its power over space.

29. Horeau, Callou, and Lacasse, *Note sur un projet de Halles Centrales,* 1 p. Senard, in his brief, noted that Callou and Lacasse were experienced public-works contractors with enough capital on hand to execute the project; see Senard, *Halles Centrales de Paris,* 39–40.

30. Dion, "Horeau," 20–21; Baltard and Collet, *Monographie des Halles Centrales,* 20–21.

31. Baltard referred to Horeau as an "architect who was unknown to the administration," and the Commission municipal pronounced the following harsh opinion of Horeau's lawyer: "Bad causes need to be defended by skillful defenders: to make a case for the Horeau project one has chosen a famous lawyer, but one who is a stranger to the city of Paris, to its needs, to its municipal needs." See Baltard and Collet, *Monographie des Halles Centrales,* 13; and *Halles centrales d'approvisionnement. Examen comparatif,* 9.

32. Horeau, "Assainissement, embellissements de Paris: Édilité urbaine," hereafter cited as "Édilité." This is also reproduced in Boudon and Loyer, *Hector Horeau, 1801–1872,* 7–22.

33. Horeau, "Édilité," 47, col. 2.

34. Ibid., 45, col. 1.

35. Horeau was not the only architect to go beyond the mere design and placement of buildings to imagine the city as a circulatory system. He was preceded in this outlook most notably by the eighteenth-century architect Pierre Patte. On Patte, see Papayanis, *Horse-Drawn Cabs,* 31–34, and Picon, *French Architects and Engineers,* chap. 8. For a dis-

cussion of the special role that engineers played in a shift in the perception of the city as a closed space, with its own history and monuments, to a vision of the city—and this applied especially to Paris—as a dynamic space, one in which movement and flow were essential to its economic and physical well-being, see Picon, "Les modèles de la métropole," 137–42.

36. Lauriot, "L'Adaptation géographique," 6–7.

37. See, e.g., Kérizouet, *Un Dernier Mot.* For Kérizouet as an urban planner, see the discussion below.

38. Marx, *Grundrisse,* 524.

39. Kérizouet, *Projet d'établisement d'un chemin de fer.*

40. Ibid., ix.

41. For details on this line, see ibid., 5–6 and accompanying notes.

42. For a justification of the project, see ibid., iii–xi. The issue of movement and space is found throughout the pamphlet; for the above example, see ibid., 5, and for Liverpool, 11–12.

43. Kérizouet, *Rues de fer, ou locomotion,* was first published on October 25, 1847, as an article in *Revue Indépendante* (Oct. 25, 1847) and then as a pamphlet.

44. Kérizouet, *Rues de fer, ou locomotion,* 30 (my emphasis).

45. Procacci, *Gouverner la misère.* See also idem, "Sociology and Its Poor," *Politics and Society* 17, no. 2 (1989): 168–69.

46. Kérizouet, *Rues de fer, ou locomotion,* 8.

47. Ibid., 28.

48. Ibid., 30; see also Kérizouet, *Projet d'établissement d'un chemin de fer,* fig. 4, for an illustration of what he had in mind for housing above railroad tracks.

49. Kérizouet, *Le Rachat.*

50. See, e.g., Kérizouet, *A Messieurs les membres du Conseil municipal.*

51. See J. Zambeaux d'Ambly, "Projet de chemin de fer atmosphérique"; [J. Tell], *Chemin de fer*—Tell first proposed his plan in 1855–56 and brought it up to date in 1882; Chemin de fer Métropolitain de Paris, *Mémoire: Avant-projet,* a modified version of a plan announced in 1853 by one Laurent Mouton, a public works entrepreneur, for an above-ground line linking Paris to its suburbs and modified in 1862 to include an underground network; Vautier, *Chemin de fer circulaire intérieur . . . Avant-Projet. Carte d'ensemble* (Archives de Paris, D1059/2); and the several reports from August and September 1854 on a plan by M. Savary and Alfred Férot for an above-ground rail system connecting the central market with the circular rail line ringing Paris (Archives de la Préfecture de Police, D/b 404). A note submitted on December 26, 1855, to the secretary general of the Prefecture of the Seine Department indicated that numerous projects tying together the circular rail line outside Paris and the central Paris market had been proposed since 1853; see AN, F/14/2180/2.

52. For the transportation revolution in Paris, see Papayanis, *Horse-Drawn Cabs.* For the Paris population, see Pouthas, *La Population française,* 98.

53. See Pinkney, *Napoleon III;* Reid, *Paris Sewers and Sewermen;* and Laroulandie, "Les Égouts de Paris," 107–40.

54. Lauriot, "L'Adaptation géographique," 4–6.

55. Biographical information is in AN, F/14/2180/2, dossier Brame; for the evaluation by Baude, see ibid., note of March 3, 1851. An unsigned note of December 26, 1855 (in ibid.), submitted to the secretary general of the Seine Department, indicated that Brame had been working on a proposal for an underground rail link to Les Halles in hopes of earning a promotion. See also the *Dictionnaire de biographie française* (Paris, 1956), 7:139–40.

56. On the Société centrale, see Picon, *L'Invention de l'ingénieur moderne*, 602; for biographical information on Flachat, see the clippings file of the Bibliothèque historique de la ville de Paris, Actualité 125, chemise biographique, esp. Émile Trélat, "Biographies scientifiques: Eugène Flachat," *Revue Scientifique* 9, no. 26 (June 25, 1898): 801–4, and a dictionary entry (655), unidentified, on Flachat. See also the notice in the *Dictionnaire de biographie française* (Paris, 1971), 8: 1429–30.

57. AN, F/14/2180/2, "Copie d'une note soumise au bienveillant examen de Monsieur le Secrétaire-Général" [de la Préfecture de la Seine], Dec. 26, 1855. On June 1, 1853, J. Zambeaux d'Ambly, associate mayor of Saint-Denis, submitted an outline for an underground railroad in Paris to the minister of the interior and the prefect of police that was quite similar to Brame and Flachat's plan, albeit lacking in details. He complained that although his proposal preceded the latter by two months it had received no recognition or acknowledgment. See Zambeaux d'Ambly, "Projet," and manuscript letter to the *Journal des Débats*, dated Feb. 20, 1854, clippings file, Bibliothèque administrative de la ville de Paris.

58. AN, F/14/2180/2, letter of Paris, June 30, 1853; dossier Brame, two-page handwritten letter, no title, no date (post-1863); and "Copie d'une note."

59. For what follows, see Brame and Flachat, *Chemin de fer*, 19 pp. + map.

60. Brame and Flachat provided a rudimentary drawing of their proposed line in the 1856 edition of *Chemins de fer*. That same year the engineer Dupuit joined Brame and Flachat to draw up more detailed projections of the line (see *Nouvelles annales de la construction* [Oct. 1855]: 65–66, and pls. 39–42).

61. Brame and Flachat, *Chemins de fer*, 12–16, quotation at 15.

62. Archives de la Préfecture de Police, D/b 504, report of Paris, Dec. 26, 1853, and report of Dec. 30, 1853.

63. Brame and Flachat, *Chemin de fer*, 14 (my emphasis).

64. For information on the Blanchet project, see Archives de Paris (AP), D10S9/4 (dossier Blanchet). No first name is given for Blanchet.

65. On Blanchet's relation to Brame's team, see AP, D10S9/4, Blanchet to Léon Say, 1871, 3p.AP, D10S9/4, letter of Oct. 16, 1871; see also Préfecture de la Seine, *Rapport de la commission spéciale*, 5–6, and Ponts et Chaussées. Direction des Travaux de Paris: Service des chemins de fers municipaux. "Rapport de l'Ingénieur en chef [Paul Haag]," Paris, Oct. 30, 1876 (unpaginated), in AP, D10S9/4.

66. See esp. AP, D10S9/4, Blanchet to Léon Say, 1871, 3p.

67. See, e.g., AP, D10S9/4, Blanchet to Léon Say, Oct. 16, 1871, and Blanchet to Ferdinand Duval, July 6, 1874.

68. Préfecture de la Seine, *Rapport de la commission spéciale,* 13, 15, 26, and 28.

69. The published evaluation is in Préfecture de la Seine, *Rapport de la commission spéciale,* 5–11; see also an untitled evaluation report of engineers of the Ponts et Chaussées, "Direction de la voie publique et des promenades, Service de la voie publique," in AP, D10S9/3 (mandate for report issued on May 31, 1870).

70. The Le Hir plan was first broached in three letters, one dated January 5, 1854, and the two others January 9, sent to, respectively, the minister of public works, the prefect of the Seine Department, and the prefect of the Paris police. It was published in 1855, under the title *Entreprise générale du transport des personnes et des choses dans Paris,* and revised slightly in 1856 with respect to placing the lines beneath underground sewers. The 1855 edition is used here: Le Hir, *Réseau des voies ferrées sous Paris;* for the information on the letters, see ibid., 5, and for the placement of the lines, 6.

71. For the retrospective details of 1860, see Le Hir, *Réseau de voies ferrées souterraines dans Paris* (1860), 3. For Le Hir's associates see, Le Hir, *Réseau des voies ferrées sous Paris* (1856), 3–4; for Le Hir's interest in economic matters and railroads, see Le Hir, *Des Chemins de fer de Paris,* and *Forces et institutions;* for his social ideas, see Le Hir, [untitled article], in *L'Harmonie universelle,* and Le Léonais [Le Hir], *Harmonies sociales.*

72. Le Hir, *Réseau des voies ferrés sous Paris* (1856), 33 (quotation), 18, 33 (request to operate the system).

73. Le Léonais, *Harmonies Sociales.*

74. Le Hir, in *L'Harmonie universelle,* 91–94.

75. Le Hir, *Réseau des voies ferrées* (1856), 10–11.

76. Préfecture de la Seine, *Rapport de la commission spéciale,* 4–5.

77. Le Hir, *Réseau des voies ferrées dans Paris: Oberservations,* 10–11, 11 n. 1 (his emphasis).

78. Jourdain, "Les Chemins de fer souterrains," 1–2.

79. Préfecture de la Seine, *Rapport de la commission spéciale,* esp. 1–2, 29–33, 52–53. The final decision to build an underground system was not reached until 1883, and the ruling that it would be operated by the city and not department officials only in 1895. For an introduction to the history of the Métro, see Daumas et al., *Analyse historique;* Mairie de Paris, *Métropolitain;* and Gasnault and Zuber, eds., *Métro-Cité.*

80. Evenson, *Paris,* 92–93.

CHAPTER 6

The Siméon Commission

1. Casselle, *Commission,* 5–6, 11; the official report starts on page 47, beginning with the seven-point program, with a slight editorial change at the end.

2. For a summary of the report, see Casselle, "Les Travaux:" 645–89. See also Bourillon, "A Propos de la Commission des embellissements:" 139–52.

3. This section, on the organization of the commission, rests heavily on Casselle's introduction to the commission's report cited in note 1. For what follows immediately, see Casselle, *Commission,* 9–11.

4. Jacoubet, *Atlas général de la ville*. For an analysis of this atlas, see Michel Fleury in Fleury and Pronteau, *Petit atlas pittoresque*, 12–15.

5. Casselle, *Commission*, 17–19.

6. The archives of the Siméon papers contain, in addition to the manuscript copy of the final report and its accompanying data, a draft copy of Siméon's introduction and unpublished private letters and notes for the report. The private correspondence is in the Bibliothèque administrative de la ville de Paris (BAVP), MS 1782.

7. Meynadier, *Paris*.

8. BAVP, MS 1782, f. 147–149.

9. BAVP, MS 1782, f. 207–11 (streets), 211–19 (street plan by Napoleon III), 220–22 (parks), 222–23 (town hall, slaughterhouses, cemeteries, opera, library). Casselle believed that notes concerning the emperor's street plans were by Meynadier. See Casselle, *Commission*, 24–25 n. 39.

10. See BAVP, MS 1782, and Casselle, *Commission*, 24, and 24–25 n. 39.

11. Siméon, *La Commission*, 111 and 111 n. 120.

12. BAVP, MS 1782, ff. 118–21; f. 120 (quotation).

13. Siméon, *La Commission*, 47.

14. Casselle, *Commission*, 23.

15. On the siting of railway stations, see Ratcliffe, "Urban Space," 224–34.

16. Siméon, *La Commission*, 48.

17. Pinkney, *Napoleon III*, 87–88 ff.

18. Siméon, *La Commission*, 51.

19. The list and justification for these roads is the subject of the commission's first appendix; see Siméon, *La Commission*, 55–60. What follows rests on Casselle's notes to this appendix.

20. Casselle, *Commission*, 40–41 (for a copy of the map).

21. Siméon, *La Commission*, 57.

22. Ibid., 60.

23. Nord, "The Social Explorer," 122–34.

24. Siméon, *La Commission*, 58; Casselle, *Commission*, 20.

25. Casselle, *Commission*, 19.

26. Siméon, *La Commission*, 172.

27. Foucault, "Space, Knowledge, and Power," 243–44.

28. Siméon, *La Commission*, 178 (my emphasis).

29. Sutcliffe, *Autumn of Central Paris*, 15, 17, 22–23, 59, and 67, quotation at 23.

30. Siméon, *La Commission*, 178.

31. Sutcliffe, *Autumn of Central Paris*, 15.

32. Ibid., 27–33.

33. Siméon, *La Commission*, 48.

34. Ibid., 173.

35. Ibid., 172, 174, 48–50.

36. Merruau, *Souvenirs*, 364.

37. Siméon, *La Commission*, 174.

38. Ibid., 94–98.

39. Ibid., 94.

40. Ibid., 101–2. He was referring to the slaughterhouses of Grenelle, Ménilmontant, Roule, and Villejuif, which he would replace with two new slaughterhouses near the fortifications and the railroad line ringing Paris; see 101 n. 103.

41. Ibid., 95.

42. Siméon, *La Commission*, 58.

43. See Deleuze and Guattari, *A Thousand Plateaus*, 351–423; Virilio, *Speed and Politics*.

44. Siméon, *La Commission*, 95.

45. Foucault, *Discipline*, 168; see also 171–72.

46. Foucault, "Space, Knowledge, and Power," 252.

47. Foucault, *Discipline*, 169.

48. For a discussion of the plan and map, see Pinkney, *Napoleon III*, 25–48.

49. Siméon, *La Commission*, 95–96.

50. Harvey, *Consciousness and the Urban Experience*, 63–66, 76.

51. Foucault, *Discipline*, 218–221; see also 84–85, 174–75.

52. Siméon, *La Commission*, 51–52, 52 n. 8, and 66–67.

53. Ibid., 51–52.

54. Ibid., 197–99.

55. Ibid., 53; Harvey, *Consciousness and the Urban Experience*, 95.

56. Siméon, *La Commission*, 53–54.

57. Harvey, *Consciousness and the Urban Experience*, 74.

58. Haussmann, *Mémoires*, 469; see also Pinkney, *Napoleon III*, 25–27, 40.

59. For this and what follows, see Siméon, *La Commission*, 47–50.

60. Haussmann, *Mémoires*, 468–69.

61. Casselle, *La Commission*, 5, 30.

62. See, e.g., Pinkney, *Napoleon III*, 25–48.

63. Recent exceptions are Bowie, *La Modernité avant Haussmann*, and Garrioch, *Revolutionary Paris*.

CONCLUSION

1. Le Corbusier, *Radiant City*, 94 (his emphasis), and idem, *City of To-Morrow*; Donald, *Imagining the Modern City*, 8; Raban, *Soft City*, 13–14.

2. Sennett, *Uses of Disorder*, 7–8.

3. Le Corbusier, *Radiant City*, 120.

4. Lefebvre, *Production of Space*, 360–62.

5. Harvey, *Condition of Postmodernity*, 253.

6. Jacobs, *Death and Life*, 15, 13.

7. For an appreciation of Raban as a postmodernist urban commentator, see Harvey, *Condition of Postmodernity*, 3–9; Raban, *Soft City*.

8. Raban, *Soft City*, 156,

9. Ibid., 15–22, quotation at 22; 156.

10. See, e.g., Von Hoffmann, "Why They Built Pruitt-Igoe," 180–205.

11. Choay, introduction to *Mémoires du Baron Haussmann,* 11.

12. For a summary of Ratcliffe's views and a bibliography of his writings on this subject, see Ratcliffe, "Visions et (ré)visions," 41–55.

13. Garrioch, *Neighbourhood;* Haine, *World of the Paris Café.*

14. Sutcliffe, "A Vision of Utopia," 216–43.

15. Evenson, *Le Corbusier,* 110.

16. Fishman, *Urban Utopias,* 194.

17. Le Corbusier, *City of To-Morrow,* 277–78, 279, 287.

18. Le Corbusier, *Radiant City,* 321.

19. Fishman, *Urban Utopias,* 207.

20. Le Corbusier, *Radiant City,* 121, 123 (his emphasis).

21. Raban, *Soft City,* 20.

22. Le Corbusier, *Radiant City,* 108–9 (on uniformity), and *City of To-Morrow,* 10, 21.

23. Idem, *Radiant City,* 8, and *City of To-Morrow,* 96.

24. Sutcliffe, "A Vision of Utopia," 237–40.

25. Lewis Mumford, "Yesterday's City of To-Morrow," *Architectural Record* 132 (Nov. 1962), 141, cited by Evenson, *Le Corbusier,* 18.

Bibliography

ARCHIVES

Public Archives

École Normal Supérieur

Fonds Considerant

Bibliothèque administrative de la ville de Paris

Commission des embellissements de Paris: MS 1779: rapport général définitive; MS 1780: documents préperatoires; MS 1781: rapport général, annexes, et notes, 3e expédition; MS 1782: correspondance, June 1853–May 1854; MS 1783: plan aquarellé.

Archives nationales (AN)

The F/14 series contains information on railways and railway engineers.

Archives de la Préfecture de Police

The D/B series has information on the Paris underground.

Archives de Paris (AP)

Series D1059/3–4 has dossiers on the Brame project.

Bibliothèque de l'Arsenal

Fonds Enfantin

Bibliothèque historique de la ville de Paris

The Série Actualités is a treasure-trove of information on the Paris underground, the fortifications of Paris, and other nineteenth-century subjects.

Private Archive

Papers of Gilbert Joseph Gaspard de Chabrol de Volvic: "Memoirs," manuscript, and correspondence.

PRIMARY WORKS

Newspapers and Journals

Annales d'hygiène publique et de médecine legale. 1829–53.

Annales des Ponts et Chaussées. 1831–50.

L'Architecte: Notions sur l'art de bâtir et de décorer les édifices. 1832–33.

L'Édile de Paris: Journal des propriétaires. Feb. 5, 1833–July 5, 1833.

Le Globe: recueil philosophique, politique, et littéraire. 1824–32.

Journal des Bâtiments, des arts relatif à la construction de la voirie, de la police, de la salu-brité de la jurisprudence, et de tout ce qui concerne la propriété. 1830–31.

Journal des Bâtiments et des arts et métiers qui on rapport à la construction. 1831–32.

Journal de l'industrie et du capitaliste. 1836–37.

Moniteur des architectes. 1847–1900.

Le Nouveau monde. 1849–51.

Nouvelles annales de la construction. 1855–1913.

L'Organisateur. 1829–31.

Le Populaire. 1833–47.

Le Producteur: Journal de l'industrie, des sciences, et des beaux-arts. 1825–26.

La Propriété: Journal d'architecture civile et rurale, des beaux arts, et d'économie sociale. 1832–34.

Revue générale de l'architecture et des travaux publics. 1840–90.

La Revue municipale [title changes: *Gazette municipale; Revue municipale et gazette ré-unis*]. 1848–62.

Revue du progrès politique, social, et littéraire. 1839–42.

Anonymous Works

Almanach des embellissemens de Paris ou exposé des travaux au moyens desquelles la capitale surpassera les villes les plus célèbres. Paris: A.-G. Debray, 1808.

Almanach de la Rive Gauche. 1842. Paris, 1842.

L'Anti-Rodateur, ou le petit philosophe moderne. London: Chez Emsley, 1785.

"Bicétre." *La Phalange: Journal de la Science Sociale* 1, no. 4 (1836): cols. 112–15.

[B.R.] *Paris historique et monumental depuis son origine jusqu'à nos jours.* Paris, 1855.

Coup d'oeil sur Paris, ou premiers moyens d'indemnité disponibles offrant plus de 20 million de rente à accorder de suite aux émigrés, sans sacrifice pour l'embellissement du palais du roi et de la capitale. Paris, 1824.

Chemin de fer, ligne du Nord. A Messieurs les Députés. Mémoire adressé par les 3e, 4e, 5e, 6e, 7e, et 8e arrondissements, au conseil général municipal de la Seine. Paris, 1842.

"Enlargissement des voies publiques. Halles." *Revue générale de l'architecture et des tra-vaux publics* 1 (Oct. 1840): cols. 625–26.

Halles Centrales d'approvisionnement. Examen comparatif du projet de l'administration ap-prouvé en 1845 et du projet de M. Horeau. Réponse au mémoire de M. Senard. Paris, Apr. 30, 1850.

Halles centrales d'approvisionnement. A messieurs les membres de la commission municipale de Paris. . . . Paris, 1850.

Histoire du Choléra Morbus dans le quartier du Luxembourg. Paris, 1832.

Mémoire sur le déplacement de Paris. Paris, 1840.

Mémoire sur le projet d'une grande communication à établir entre les quartiers du Faubourg Saint-Antoine, du Marais, et la Pointe Saint-Eustache. [Paris, 1834]. In *Projets pour la ville de Paris: Halles, Hôpitaux, et Ponts.*

Moyens d'améliorer le commerce et d'augmenter la valeur des propriétés de plusieurs fau-bourgs et quartiers de Paris. Paris, 1826.

Notice biographique sur Henri Lecouturier. Caen, 1861.

Notice sur la place de la Concorde et observation de plusieurs artistes sur les embellissemens adoptés pour cette place. Paris, 1836.

Paris à vol d'oiseau, son histoire, celle de ses monuments et de ses accroissements successifs depuis l'époque de sa première enceinte jusqu'à l'achèvement de ses fortifications actuelles. Paris, 1845.

Paris-Guide par les principaux écrivains et artistes de la France. 2 vols. Paris, 1867.

Le Pariséum moderne. Paris, 1816.

Précis historique des agrandissements et embellissements de Paris depuis Jules-César, 56 ans avant J.-C., jusqu'à ce jour. Paris, 1826.

Précis historique des canaux de l'Ourcq, de Saint-Denis, et de Saint-Maur, à Paris. Paris, n.d. [1820s].

Projet sur l'établissement de trottoirs, pour la sureté des rues de Paris, et l'embellissement de la ville. Paris, 1784.

Projets pour la ville de Paris: Halles, Hôpitaux, et Ponts. Paris, n.d.

Recueil de quelques artciles publiés dans le Sentinelle de l'Armée sur les fortifications de Paris. Paris, 1841.

Réponse d'un habitant de la Rive Droite à un mémoire au Roi sur le déplacement de Paris. [Paris, 1843].

Résumé des observations de plusieurs artistes sur les travaux et embellissemens adoptées pour la place de la Concorde. Paris, 1836.

"Sur la discussion, à la chambre des députés, au projet de loi relatif aux fortifications de Paris" [Mar. 1, 1841]. In *Recueil de quelques articles publiés dans "La Sentinelle de l'Armée" sur les forttifications de Paris.* Paris, 1841.

Tableau indicateur des rues, places et carrefours de Paris. Paris, [1825].

La Veillée de Thétis, pièce de vers présentée au concours sur les embellissemens de Paris. Par A . . . Paris, 1811.

Victor Baltard: Projets inèdits pour les Halles Centrales. Paris, [1978].

Author(s) Listed

Alphand, A[dolphe]. *Les Promenades de Paris.* Paris, 1867–73. Reprint, Princeton, 1984.

Ambly, J. Zambeaux d'. "Projet de chemin de fer atmosphérique à établir sous le Boulevard Napoléon depuis la gare de Strasbourg jusqu'à la place du Châtelet." Saint-Denis, June 1, 1853. Manuscript in Bibliothèque historique de la ville de Paris.

Andrieux, Paul. *Études et solutions nouvelles sur la viabilité à grande vitesse et les travaux publics.* Paris, 1844.

Ansquer de Londres [le P. Théophile-Ignace]. *Variétés philosophiques et littéraires.* London, 1763.

Arago, François. *Sur les fortifications de Paris.* Paris, 1841.

Arcet, Adelon d', Deyeux et al. "Rapport général des travaux du Conseil de salubrité de la ville de Paris pour l'année 1828." *Annales d'hygiène publique et de médecine légale.* 2 (1829): 307–46.

Arcet, Adelon d', Hazard fils, and Parent-Duchâtelet [Alexandre]. "Rapport fait au conseil de salubrité sur les nouveaux procédés de MM Salmon, Payen et compagnie, pour la dessication des chevaux morts et la désinfection instantanée des matières fécales, précédé de quelques considerations sur les voiries de la ville de Paris." *Annales d'hygiène publique et de médecine légale* 10, pt. 1 (1833): 35–65.

Aucoc, Léon. *Voirie urbaine. Des alignements individuels délivrés par les maires en l'absence de plan généraux. Limites du pouvoir des maires.* Paris, 1862.

Aude, Louis de l'. *Paris, doit-il être fortifie? Examen historique de cette question.* Paris, 1840.

Baissas, Jéronyme. *Danger des fortifications de Paris pour la civilisation, l'industrie, nos finances, et nos libertés.* Paris, 1844.

Baltard V[ictor], and F[élix] Callet. *Monographie des Halles Centrales de Paris: Construites sous le règne de Napoleon III et sous l'administration de M. Baron Haussmann.* Paris, 1863.

Barthèlemy. *Le Vieux Paris et le nouveau: Dialogue en vers.* Paris, n.d.

Bayard, Henri. "Mémoire médicale des Xe, XIe et XIIe arrondissemens de la ville de Paris." *Annales d'hygiène publique et de médecine légale* 32 (July 1844): 241–315.

———. *Mémoire sur la topographie médicale du IV arrondissement de la ville de Paris.* . . . "*Annales d'hygiène publique et de médecine légale* 28, pt. 1 (July 1842): 5–46; pt. 2, 241–309.

Beaudemoulin, L.-A. *Assainissement de Paris: Applications agricoles.* Paris, 1856.

———. *Assainissement de Paris: État de la question.* Paris, 1855.

———. *Assainissement de Paris: Examen du projet de traité entre la ville de Paris et M. Williams Scott.* Paris, 1856.

———. *Assainissement de Paris: Solutions pour les vigandes, les cabinets, les égouts, etc., comparées avec celles que propose la commission nomée par S. Ex. Le Ministre de l'intérieur.* Paris, 1858.

———. *Assainissement de Paris: Supression des ruisseaux, des viganges, de la boue, etc. Résumé général.* Paris, 1856.

———. *Assainaissement de Paris: Voies et moyens.* Paris, 1855.

———. *La Guerre s'en va.* 2nd ed. Paris, 1868.

———. *Hygiène publique: Londres et Paris.* Paris, n.d.

———. *Question monétaire.* Paris, 1864.

Beauregard, Testude de. *Comparaison des deux principaux pour projets de chemin de fer métropolitain parisien.* Lille, 1883.

Benoiston de Châteauneuf, Louis-François. *Rapport sur la marche et les effects du choléra-morbus dans Paris et les communes rurales du département de la Seine. Année 1832.* Paris, 1834.

Bères, Émile, Dronsart, and Hector Horeau. *Mémoire sur l'embellissement des Champs-Élysées et les avantages que le gouvernement et la population parisienne doivent en retirer.* Paris, 1836.

Berlier, J., and X. Janicot [Compagnie des tramways souterrains Nord-Sud]. *Notice sur la ligne de la Place des Abesses (Montmartre) à la Gare Montparnasse.* Paris, 1900. In Série Actualité 125, Bibliothèque historique de la ville de Paris.

Bidault, J.-H. *Notice sur les accroissements et embellissements successifs de Paris et indication de quelques travaux propres à augmenter la beauté ce cette ville.* Paris, Jan. 20, 1846.

Blanc, Louis. "De l'embastillement de Paris." *Revue du progrès politique, social, et littéraire.* 4 (Oct. 1, 1840): 160–71.

———. "Organisation du Travail." *Revue du progrès politique, social, et littéraire* 4 (Aug. 1, 1840): 1–30.

———. "Organisation du Travail: Réponse à diverses objections." *Revue du progrès politique, social, et littéraire* 6 (Oct. 1, 1841): 129–47.

———. "Travaux publics: Questions des Chemins de fer." *Revue du progrès politique, social, et littéraire* 2 (Nov. 1, 1839): 341–67.

Blondel, J. F. *Cours d'architecture.* 3 vols. Paris, 1771–77.

Boulay de la Meurthe, H. *Histoire du Choléra-Morbus dans le quartier du Luxembourg.* Paris, Aug. 1832.

Boullée, Etienne Louis. *Treatise on Architecture.* Edited by Helen Rosenau. London, 1953.

Bourla, André, and Edouard Renaud. *Mémoire pour servir à l'appui des demandes de la Cie John Cockerill.* Paris, 1838.

Brame, Édouard, and Eugène Flachat. *Chemin de fer de jonction des Halles centrals avec le chemin de ceinture: Rapport à l'appui du projet.* Paris, 1854.

Broussel, Patrice. *Victor Baltard: Projets inédits pour les Halles Centrales.* Paris, [1978].

Brunet, Jean. *Paris, sa constitution générale.* Paris, 1848.

Bruyère, L. *Rapport du 9 Floréal an X: Sur les moyens de fournir l'eau nécessaire à la ville de Paris, en particulièrement sur la dérivation des rivières d'Ourcq, de la Beauvronne, de l'Yvette, de la Bièvre, et autres.* Paris, 1804.

Burgy, Jules. *Du Nettoiement de Paris et moyens pour désencombrer cette capitale.* Paris, Dec. 25, 1840.

Buquet, J., Hector Horeau, and Ernest Luce. *De L'Organisation des ateliers nationaux, et de leur application à divers travaux d'utilité publique et à la colonisation de l'algérie.* Paris, 1848.

Byerley, J. *Mémoire sur les routes anglaises dites Routes de M. Mac Adam.* Paris, 1824.

Cabet, Etienne. *Six lettres sur la crise actuelle.* Paris, 1840.

Callou, G. *Lettre à M. Horace Say sur quelques questions de grande voirie, se rattachant à l'hygiène publique.* Paris, 1848.

Cantagrel, F. *De l'Organisation des travaux publics et de la réforme des Ponts-et-Chaussées.* Paris, 1847.

Carème, A. *Projets d'architecture pour les embellissements de Paris de de Saint-Petersbourg.* Paris, 1821.

Cartier, Eugène. "De l'unité des langues." *La Phalange: Journal de la Science Sociale* 1, no. 44 (Dec. 11, 1840): cols. 759–76.

———. "Politique. France. Faiblesse des corps de l'État et de la presse en face du choléra." *Le Globe,* no. 103 (Apr. 12, 1832), 409, cols. 1–3.

Chabrol de Volvic, G. J. G. *Description de l'Égypte.* Paris, 1826.

———, ed., *Recherches statistiques de la ville de Paris et le département de la Seine.* 4 vols. Paris, 1821–29.

Chabrol de Volvic, G. J. G. *Statistique des provinces de Savone, d'Oneille, d'Acqui, et de partie de la province de Mondori, formant l'ancien département de Montenotte.* 2 vols. Paris, 1824.

Chabrol-Chaméane, E[rnest] de. *Mémoire sur le déplacement de la population dans Paris et sur les moyens d'y remédier, présénté par les trois arrondissements de la rive gauche de la Seine (10e, 11e, et 12e) à la commission établi près le ministère de l'interieur.* Paris, 1840.

Chambelland, L. *Réformes et améliorations à introduire dans quelques parties du service de l'édilité parisienne.* Paris, 1853.

Chambray, Georges de. *De la Transformation de Paris, ville ouverte, en place forte.* Paris, 1843.

Chambre des Deputés. Session 1836. *Exposé des motifs et projet de loi portant demande d'un crédit de 4,580,000 fr. Pour l'achèvement de monumens.* Paris, 1836.

Chaumette, [Pierre-Gaspard]. *Résumé du système de nétoiement de la ville de Paris.* Paris, 1829.

Chemin de fer Métropolitain de Paris. *Mémoire: Avant-projet; Projet Mouton, modifié.* Paris, 1876.

Chevalier, A[lphonse]. "Assainissement des villes." *Annales d'hygiène publique et de médecine légale* 24 (July 1840): 283–91.

———. *Assainssement des villes.* Paris, 1840.

———. *De la Nécessité de bâtir des maisons pour loger les classes moyens et les ouvriers; de la possibilité de faire ces constructions en retirant un intérêt raisonable de son argent.* Paris, 1857.

———. *Du Déplacement de la population, de ses causes, de ses effets, des mesures à prendre pour y mettre un terme.* Paris, 1850.

———. *Hygiène publique. Note sur de nouveau moyens employés pour la désinfection des matières fécales dans les fossés.* Paris, [1835].

———. "Mémoire sur les égouts de Paris, de Londres, de Montpellier." *Annales d'hygiène publique et de médecine légale* 19 (Jan. 1838): 366–424.

———. "Notice historique sur le nettoiement de la ville de Paris, depuis 1184 jusqu'à l'époque actuelle pour servir à l'histoire de la salubrité et de l'hygiène publiques des grandes villes." *Annales d'hygiène publique et de médecine légale* 42 (1849): 262–319.

———. *Notice historique sur le nettoiement de la ville de Paris, depuis 1184 jusqu'à l'époque actuelle pour servir à l'histoire de la salbubrité et de l'hygiène publiques des grandes villes.* Paris, 1849.

———. "Notice historique sur la police et la dustribution des eaux dans Paris, depuis 360, jusqu'à l'époque actuelle, pour servir à l'histoire de la salubrité et de l'hygiène publique des grandes villes." *Annales d'hygiène publique et de médecine légale* 45 (1851): 5–71.

———. "Rapport à M. le préfet de police sur l'envasement du canal Saint-Martin." *Annales d'hygiène publique et de médecine légale* 7 (1831): 59–74.

Chevalier, Michel. *L'Exposition universelle de Londres. . . .* Paris, 1851.

———. *Les Fortifications de Paris: Lettre à M. le comte Molé.* Paris, 1841.

———. *L'Industrie et l'octroi de Paris.* Paris, 1867.

———. *Des Intérêts matériels en France: Travaux publics, routes, canaux, chemins de fer.* Paris, 1838.

———. *Lettres sur l'organisation du travail. . . .* Paris, 1848.

————. "Politique. France. Le Choléra-Morbus." *Le Globe,* no. 100 (Apr. 9, 1832), 397, cols. 1–2.

————. "Politique. France. Fin du choléra par un coup d'état." *Le Globe,* no. 102 (Apr. 11, 1832), 405, cols. 1–2.

————. *De la Question de l'intervention dans les travaux publics du gouvernement fédéral et des gouvernements particuliers d'États dans l'Amerique du Nord.* Paris: Journal des Économistes, 1842.

————. *Religion saint-simonienne: Fin du choléra par un coup d'état.* Paris, 1832.

————. *Religion saint-simonienne. La Guerre et l'industrie. Grands travaux à établir.* Éverat, [1832].

————, Stéphane Flachat, Charles Duveyrier, and Henri Fournel. *Religion saint-simonienne. Politique industrielle. Système de la Méditerranée.* Paris, Mar. 1832.

Chevalier, Michel. *Statistiques des travaux publics sous la monarchie de 1830.* Batignolles, [1848].

————. "Les Voies de communication aux États-Unis." *Journal de l'industriel et du capitaliste* 2, no. 5 (1836): 245–92.

Clavel. "Le Choléra." *Le Globe,* no. 92 (Apr. 1, 1832), 365, col. 3–366, col. 1.

Clerget, C.-E. "Du Nettoyage à la mécanique des voie publique. *Revue générale de l'architecure et des travaux publics* 4 (June 1843): cols. 265–74.

Cointeraux, [François]. *Embellissemens de Paris.* [Paris, 1795?]

————. *Paris tel qu'il est aujourd'hui ou embellissemens de Paris, d'aprèun système raisonné et impartial.* Paris, [1798].

————. *[Plan de] Paris tel qu'il était à son origin, plan de Paris tel qu'il est aujourd'hui.* Paris, an 7 [1798].

————. *Réflections impartiales sur l'Odéon.* Paris, [1795].

Colin, Auguste. "Communication de la méditerranée et de la Mer Rouge par un canal maritime et du chemin de fer." *Revue générale de l'architecture et des travaux publics* 6, no. 4 (1845–46): cols. 155–65.

————. "Les Fortifications de Paris." *La Phalange: Journal de la Science Sociale* 1, no. 52 (Dec. 30, 1840): cols. 873–75.

Commission de Métropolitain. *Rapport de la Commission Spéciale sur l'étude des chemins de fer et tramways d'intérêt local à établir dans le département de la Seine.* Paris, 1872.

Conseil municipal de Paris. *Embellissements de la Place de la Concorde et des Champs-Élysées.* Paris, Oct. 1834.

Considerant, Victor. *L'Avenir: Perspective du Phalanstère, ou Palais Sociétaire dédie à l'humanité.* Bordeaux, n.d.

————. *Considérations sociales sur l'architectonique.* Paris, 1834.

————. "Déclaration de principes." *La Phalange: Journal de la Science Sociale,* 1, no. 1 (Sept. 2, 1840): cols. 1–30.

————. *Déraison et dangers. De l'Engouement pour les chemins en fer. Avis à l'opinion et aux capitaux.* Paris, 1838.

————. *Descriptions du phalanstère et considerations sociales sur l'architectonique.* 1848. Reprint, Paris, 1979.

————. *Destinée Sociale.* 3 vols. Paris, 1837–44.

————. *Exposition abrégée du système phalanstérien de Fourier.* Paris, 1845.

————. "Fortifications de Paris." *La Phalange: Journal de La Science Sociale* 1, no. 7, pt. 1 (Sept. 16, 1840): cols. 121–24; pt. 2 (Nov. 1, 1840): cols. 465–69.

————. "Note sur les intérêts généraux de la ville de Paris, et spécialement du dixième arrondissement." *Revue générale de l'architecture et des travaux publics* 5 (Jan. 1844): cols. 22–29.

————. *Principes du socialisme: Manifeste de la démocratie aux XIXe siècle.* 2nd ed. Paris, 1847.

[Considerant, Victor]. "Système national des chemins de fer en France." *La Phalange: Journal de la Science Sociale* 4, no. 7 (1841): cols. 593–600.

Considerant, Victor, and Perreymond. "De la grande circulation dans Paris." *La Démocratie pacifique* 1, no. 110 (Nov. 18, 1843): 1.

————, and Perreymond. "De L'Unité administrative du département de la Seine." *La Démocratie pacifique* 1, no. 82 (Oct. 21, 1843): 1.

————, and Perreymond. "De L'Unité administrative du département de la Seine." *La Démocratie pacifique* 1, no. 103 (Nov. 11, 1843): 1.

Corps législatif. *Discours prononcé par Sedillez . . . sur le projet de loi relatif à des embellissemens dans les environs du palais et du jardin des Tuileries. Seance du 30 Pluvioise an 12.* Paris, an XII [1803].

Courtier de Vienne, F. A. *Paris moderne. Plan d'une ville modèle que l'auteur a appelée novutopie.* Paris, 1860.

Cramouzaud, Eugène. *Études sur la transformation du XIIe arrondissements et des quartiers anciens de la Rive gauche.* Paris, 1855.

Daly, César. "Des Fortifications de Paris." *Revue générale de l'architecture et des travaux publics* 2 (Jan. 1841): cols. 26–29.

————. "Fortifications projetées pour Paris." *Revue générale de l'architecture et des travaux publics* 1 (Sept. 1840): cols. 572–74.

————. Halles Centrales de Paris." *Revue générale de l'architecture et des travaux publics* 12, nos. 1–2 (1854): cols. 5–34.

Dameth, Henri. *Mémoire sur la fondation de cités industrielles dites cités de l'Union pour 600 familles de toutes conditions.* Paris, Nov. 1849.

Dantès, A. *Grandeur et décadence des travaux de Paris.* 2nd ed. Paris, 1869.

Daubanton, L.-J.-M. *Code de la voirie des villes (y compris la ville de Paris), des bourgs, et des villages.* Paris, 1836.

————. *Du déplacement de la population de Paris.* Paris, 1843.

————. "Rapport relatif aux entreprises de construction dans Paris, de 1821 à 1826, et à l'interruption des travaux depuis cette dernière année." Préfecture de la Seine. *Recherches statistiques sur la ville de Paris et le département de la Seine,* 4:1–73. Paris, 1829.

————. *Journal de la voirie.* Paris, 1832.

Davenne, H.-H.-B. *Législation et principes de la voirie urbaine ou traité pratique à l'usage des fonctionnaires chargés d'assurer l'execution des lois et réglements sur cette matière.* Paris, 1849.

Debussy. *De L'Emplacement des gares dans Paris et de la nécessité de les relier entre elles.* Paris, 1846.

De Fogères, Alf. Henry and L. *Chemin de fer des halles centrales et du Louvre aux chemins de fer de Lyon et de Ceinture Bercy, Saint-Mandé, Vincennes.* Paris, 1855.

Delamare, Nicolas. *Traité de Police.* 2nd ed. 4 vols. Paris, 1719–38.

Département de la Seine. Commission centrale de la salubrité. *Instruction populaire sur les principaux moyens à employer pour se garantir du choléra morbus. . . .* Paris, 1831.

Descauriet, Auguste. *Histoire des agrandissements de Paris.* Paris, 1860.

Devert, B. A. H. *Précis historique des agrandissements et embellissements de Paris.* Paris, 1826.

————. *Tableau indicateur des rues, places, et carrefours de Paris.* Paris, 1825.

Dézamy, Th[éodore]. *Almanach de la communauté, 1843 par divers écrivains communistes.* Paris, 1843.

————. *Code de la communauté.* Paris, 1842.

————. *Conséquences de l'embastillement et de la paix à tout prix: Dépopulation de la capitale. Trahison du pouvoir.* Paris, 1840.

Diderot, Denis, and M. d'Alembert. "Ville." In *Encyclopédie; ou Dictionnaire raisonné des sciences, des arts et des métiers,* 17:277–80. Paris, 1751–65.

Dillon, Arthur. *Lettre de M. abbé Arthur Dillon, à M. De Cazalès, compte rendu de l'état des finances, des titulaires ecclésiastiques; sous le régime de la liberté française. . . .* N.p., 1791.

————. *Pétition de M. Arthur Dillon à l'Assemblée nationale. . . .* Paris, [c. 1792].

————. *Projet d'un atelier de charité, proposée au gouvernement et aux administrateurs de la ville de Paris.* Paris, 1802.

————. *Utilité, possibilité, facilité de construire des trottoirs dans les rues de Paris.* Paris, 1803.

Du Camp, Maxime. *Paris, ses organes, ses fonctions, et sa vie, dans la seconde moitié du XIXe siècle.* 6 vols. Paris, 1869–75.

Duchesne, E. A. *Histoire statistique du choléra-morbus dans le XIe arrondissement de Paris, pendant l'épidémie de 1849.* Paris, 1851.

Dussausoy, Maille. *Le Citoyen désintéressé, diverses idées patriotiques, concernant quelques établissemens et embellissemens.* 2 vols. in 1. Paris, 1767–68.

Duveyrier, Charles. "Le Choléra. Réponse." *Le Globe,* no. 106 (Apr. 15, 1832), 423, col. 2.

————. "Lettre à l'avocat [Oct. 6, 1832]." MS FE 7825, Bibliothèque de l'Arsenal.

————. "Paris. Travaux publics. Fêtes." *Le Globe,* pt. 1, no. 102 (Apr. 11, 1832), 407, col. 3; pt. 2, no. 107 (Apr. 16, 1832), 425, cols. 1–3.

————. "Paris." In Michel Chevalier et al., *Religion saint-simonienne. . . . ,* 57–65. Paris, Mar. 1832.

————. "Politique. France. Politique industrielle." *Le Globe,* no. 52 (Feb. 21, 1832), 205, col. 1-2-206, col. 1; pt. 2, no. 55 (Feb. 24, 1832), 217, col. 1-218, col. 1.

————. "Le Pouvoir nouveau." In Michel Chevalier et al., *Religion saint-simonienne. . . . ,* 67–74. Paris, Mar. 1832.

————. *Religion saint-simonienne: Travaux publics, fêtes.* Paris: Éverat, 1832.

————. "La Ville nouvelle, ou le Paris des Saint-Simoniens [Ménilmontant, Oct. 1832]." MS FE 7.825/5, Bibliothèque de l'Arsenal.

————. "La Ville nouvelle, ou le Paris des Saint-Simonians." *Paris, ou le livre des cents-et-un.* Vol. 8 (Paris, 1832).

Egron, André-César. *Embellissements de Paris. Deuxième article.* Paris, [1838].

Eichthal, Gustave d', and Stéphane Flachat. *Religion saint-simonienne: Rapports adréssés aux pères suprêmes sur la situation et les travaux de la famille.* Paris, [c. 1831].

Emmery, H. C. *Ville de Paris: Égouts et Bornes-Fontaines.* Paris, [1834].

Enfantin, Prosper. *Les Mémoires d'un industriel de l'an 2240,* in Henri Saint-Simon and Prosper Enfantine, *Oeuvres de Saint-Simon et d'Enfantin,* 17: 143–214. Paris, 1868.

Engels, Friedrich. "Socialism: Utopian or Scientific." Reprinted in *The Marx-Engels Reader,* edited by Robert C. Tucker, 683–717. 2nd ed. New York, 1978.

————. *The Condition of the Working Class in England.* Translated by Florence Kelley-Wischnewetsky. Oxford, 1993.

Esquiros, Alphonse. *Paris les sciences, les institutions, et les moeurs au XIXe siècle.* 2 vols. Paris, 1847.

Flachat, Eugène. *Les Charbonnages et les chemins de fer.* Paris, 1858.

————. *Les Chemins de fer en 1862 et en 1863.* Paris, 1863.

————. *Établissemens commercieux. Docks de Londres. Projets de docks à Marseille.* Paris, 1836.

————, and Jules Burat. *De la Police du roulage considéré par rapport aux routes, au roulage, et aux messageries.* Paris, 1836.

————. *Voies de communications intérieures. Législation nouvelles. Chemins de fer d'intérêt local.* Paris, 1869.

Flachat, Stéphane. *Du Canal maritime de Rouen à Paris et des perfectionnements de la navigation intérieure.* Paris, 1829.

————. "Le Choléra. Assainissement de Paris." *Le Globe,* no. 93 (Apr. 2, 1832), 369, col. 3–370, col. 3.

————. "Le Choléra. Assainissement de Paris." In Michel Chevalier et al., *Religion saint-simonienne. . . . ,* 41–49. Paris, Mar. 1832.

————. *L'Industrie. Exposition de 1834.* Paris, [1834?].

————. "Politique. France. Politique Industrielle. Du canal maritime de la Seine." *Le Globe,* no. 64 (Mar. 4, 1832), 254, cols. 2–3.

————. *Religion saint-simonienne. Le Choléra. Assainissement de Paris.* Éverat, [1832?].

Fourcy, A[mbroise]. *Histoire de l'École polytechnique.* 1828. Reprint, Paris, 1987.

Fourier, Charles. *Cités ouvriers: Des modifications à introduire dans l'architecture des villes.* Paris, 1849.

————. *Oeuvres complètes de Charles Fourier.* 12 vols. Paris, 1966–68.

Fournel, Henri. "Au Roi." *Le Globe,* no. 104 (Apr. 13, 1832), 413, cols. 1–3.

————. *Bibliographie saint-simonienne, de 1802 au 31 décembre 1832.* Paris, Mar. 1832.

————. *Ce qu'on voit dans les rues de Paris.* Paris, 1858.

————. *Communications des deux mers.* Marseille, Sept. 3, 1833.

————. *Examen de quelques questions de Travux Publics.* Paris, 1837.

Fournel, Victor. *Paris nouveau et Paris futur.* Paris, 1865.

Frégier, H.-A. *Des Classes Dangereuses de la population dans les grandes villes, et des moyens de les rendre meilleures.* 2 vols. Paris, 1840.

————. *Fortifications de Paris*. Paris, 1844.

Gachet, Stéphane. *Paris tel qu'il doit être: L'Île de la Cité*. Paris, 1856.

Gastine, M. *Les Embellissemens de Paris*. Paris, 1811.

Girard, Pierre-Simon. *Des Eaux de Paris, depuis l'établissement des pompes à feu de Chaillot et du Gros-Caillou*. Paris, n.d.

Girard, P[ierre] S[imon]. *Simple exposé de l'exposé de l'état actuel des eaux publiques de paris et considerations succinctes sur le meilleur emploi à faire au revenu qu'on en retire*. Paris, 1831.

Girardin, Delphine de. *Lettres Parisiennes du vicomte de Launay*. 2 vols. 1860. Reprint, Paris, 1986.

Girardin, Émile de, and Louis Lazare. *Études municipales: Le Point de Mire*. Vol. 7. Paris, 1865.

Goulet. *Observations sur les embellissemens de Paris et sur les monumens qui s'y construisent. . . .* Paris, 1734.

Gourlier, Charles, J.-E. Biet, Grillon, and Eugène Tardieu. *Choix d'édifices publics projetés et construits en France depuis le commencement du XIXe siècle*. 3 vols. Paris, 1825–36.

Gourlier, Charles. *Des Voies publiques et des habitations particulières à Paris*. Paris, 1852.

[Goyen de la Plombanie, Henri de]. *Observations sur les grands chemins, sur les inconvéniens des corvées, et sur ceux des voitures ordinaires, avec les moyens d'y remédier*. Paris, [1775].

————. *Projet d'utilité et d'ornament pour la ville de Paris, proposé au public*. Paris, 1775.

Grillon, G. Callou, and Th. Jacoubet. *Études d'un nouveau système d'alignements et de percemens de voies publiques faites en 1840 et 1841*. Paris, 1848.

Griolet, Eug., et al. *Chemins de fer: Lignes du Nord et de l'Est. Entrée dans Paris. . . .* Paris, Apr. 19, 1842.

Guillaumot, C. A. *Considérations sur l'état des beaux arts à Paris, particulièrement sur celui de l'architecture, et sur la necessité d'y élever plusieurs monumens importans*. Paris, an X [1801].

Guillaute. *Mémoire sur le réformation de la police de France*. Paris, 1749. Reprint, 1974.

Guillot. *Réflections sur la malpropreté des rues de Paris, sur ses causes, et sur les moyens d'y remédier*. Paris, Dec. 1824.

Guyet. "Embellissements de la ville de Paris." In *Archives curieuses de l'histoire de la France depuis Louis XI jusqu'à Louis XVIII*, edited by F. Danjou. Vol. 6. Paris, 1838.

Halles Centrales d'approvisionnement. *A Messieurs les membres de la commission de Paris. Nouvelles observations présentées par les intéressés à l'achèvement du projet approuvé en 1845*. Paris, July 1850.

————. *Examen comparatif du point de l'administration approuvé en 1845 et du projet de M. Horeau. Réponse au mémoire de M. Senard*. [Paris], Apr. 30, 1850.

Les Halles de Paris: Projets et critiques. Baltard et Horeau. Paris, 1845–46.

Haussmann, Georges-Eugène. *Mémoires du Baron Haussmann*. 3 vols. in 1. 1890–93. Reprint, Paris, 2000.

Hénard, Eugène. *Études sur la transformation de Paris*. Paris, 1903–9. Reprint, 1982.

Hennequin, Victor. *Les Amours du Phalanstère*. Paris, 1847.

————. *Programme démocratique.* Paris, 1851.

Horeau, Hector. "Assainissement, embellissement de Paris: Édilité urbaine mise à la portée de tout le monde." *Gazette des architects et du bâtiment,* pt. 1, no. 6 (1868), 41, col. 1–48, col. 2; pt. 2, no. 7 (1868–69), 49, col. 1–57, col. 1.

————. *Examen critique du projet d'agrandissement et de construction des halles centrales d'approvisionnement pour la ville de Paris, soumis à l'enquête publique en août 1845. Description et avantages d'un nouveau projet de Halles centrales d'approvisionnement.* Paris, 1845.

————. *Halles centrales: Contre-rapport et comparaison entre le projet amendé et le projet Horeau [8 juillet 1851].* Paris, [1851].

————. *Mémoirs sur un projet de Halles Centrales d'approvisionnement pour la ville de Paris.* Paris, [1846].

————. *Nouveaux égouts purificateurs de la France.* London, 1858.

————. *Nouveaux égouts proposé à la ville de Paris.* Paris, 1831.

————. *Nouvelles observations sur le projet d'agrandissement et de construction des Halles Centrales d'approvisionnement pour la ville de Paris.* Paris, Apr. 1846.

[Horeau, Hector]. "Projet d'un nouveau pont sur la Seine." *Revue générale de l'architecture et des travaux publics* 7, no. 7 (1847–48): cols. 315–16.

Horeau, Hector. *Projet de salles d'exposition pour les produits des arts et de l'industrie.* [Paris, 1835–36].

————. *Rapport sur le projet d'un édifice déstiné aux sociétés savantes de Paris.* Paris, 1846.

————, G. Callou, and Lacasse. *Note sur un projet de Halles Centrales, proposé pour la ville de Paris, et présenté à M. le Préfet de la Seine par MM. Horeau, architecte, G. Callou et Lacasse, entrepreneurs de Travaux publics.* Paris, [1849].

[Horeau, Hector, Lusson, and A. Couder]. "Le Nouvel Opéra de Paris: Examen des Projets proposés." *Revue générale de l'architecture et des travaux publics* 7, no. 4 (1847–48): cols. 153–72.

[Horeau, Hector, and Hippolyte Meynadier]. "Jardins d'hiver de Paris et de Lyon." *Revue générale de l'archtecture et des travaaux publics* 7, no. 9 (1847–48): cols. 410–12.

Houard, B. A. *Plan de Paris, avec le détail de ses nouveaux embellissemens projetés, et en partie exécutés depuis le règne de Napoléon I.* Paris, 1807.

Hugo, Victor. *Les Misérables.* Translated by Lee Fahnestock and Norman MacAfee. 1862; New York, 1987.

Husson, Armand. *De la Régénération de la Rive Gauche de la Seine.* Paris, June 1856.

————. *Traité de la législation des travaux publics et de la voirie en France.* 2nd ed. Paris, 1850.

Huzard, Jean-Baptiste. *De L'Enlèvement des boues et des immodices de Paris considéré sous le double rapport de la salubrité et de l'économie dans les dépenses.* Paris, 1826.

Jacob, P. L. *Promenades dans le vieux Paris.* Paris, 1837.

Jacoubet, Théodore. *Atlas général de la ville, des faubourgs, et des monuments de Paris par Th. Jacoubet.* Paris, 1839.

Jaillot, J.-B.-M. *Lettres sur les embellissements de Paris.* Luxembourg, 1778.

————. *Recherches critiques, historiques, et topographiques sur la ville de Paris.* Paris, 1778–79.

Janin, Jules. *Un Hiver à Paris.* 2nd ed. Paris, 1845.

Joanne, Adolphe. *Les Environs de Paris illustrés.* Paris, 1856.

———. *De Paris à Saint-Germain à Poissy et à Argenteuil.* Paris, 1856.

Jouffroy, Charles-Th. *Projet de chemin de fer métropolitain de Paris. . . .* Paris, 1872.

Jourdan, Louis. "Les Chemins de fer souterrains." *Le Siècle,* June 19, 1855, 1–2.

Julliot, F. *Notice sur le nettoiement des rues de Paris.* Paris, 1830.

Kérizouet, Fl. de. *À MM. les membres du Conseil municipal et départemental.* [*Projet de rues de fer à établir dans Paris.*] Paris, 1848.

———. *Projet d'établissement d'un chemin de fer dans l'intérieur de la ville de Paris.* Paris, 1845.

———. *Le Rachat des chemins de fer, sa corrélation avec la question du travail.* Paris, 1848.

———. *Rues de fer. Examen de la question suivante. Supprimer les octrois de Paris sans surtaxer l'impot et sans réduire les recettes municipales.* [Paris, 1847].

———. *Rues de fer: Locomotion dans les grandes villes.* Paris, 1847.

———. *Un Dernier Mot sur les chemin de Lyon et sur les lignes inachevées.* Paris, 1850.

Krantz, J.-B. *Projet de création d'une armée des travaux publics.* Paris, 1847.

Krolikowski, Louis. *Mémoire historique et politique sur l'état actuel de la ville libre de Cracovie.* Paris, 1840.

Labarraque, Chevalier, Parent du Chatelet. *Rapport sur les ameliorations à introduire dans les voiries, les modes de vidange, et les fosses d'aisances de la ville de Paris.* Paris, 1835.

Labédollière, Émile de. *Le Nouveau Paris: Histoire de ses 20 arrondissements.* Paris, 1860.

Laborde, Alexandre de. *Les Monuments de la France classés chronologiquement et considérés sous le rapport des faits historiques et de l'étude des arts.* 2 vols. Paris, 1816–36.

———. *Paris municipe, Tableau de l'administration de la ville de Paris, depuis les temps les plus reculés jusqu'à nos jours, pour servir à l'examen du nouveau projet de loi municipale pour la ville de Paris.* Paris, 1833.

———. *Projets d'embellissemens de Paris et de travaux d'utilité publique, concernant les Ponts et Chaussées.* Paris, 1816.

Laborde, Léon de. *Projets pour l'amélioration et embellissement du 10e arrondissement.* Paris, 1842.

Lachaise, C. *Topographie Médicale de Paris.* Paris, 1822.

Lahautière, Richard. *Deux sous pour les Bastilles s'il vous plaît.* Paris, 1840.

Lambert, Ch. (De Bélan). *Paris, tel qu'il a été, tel qu'il est et tel qu'il sera dans dix ans.* Paris, 1808.

Lamé, Gabriel. *Notice sur É. Clapeyron.* Paris, 1864.

———, Émile Clapeyron, Stéphane and Eugène Flachat. *Vues politiques et pratiques sur les travaux publics de France.* Paris, Sept. 1832.

Lanquetin, Jacques. *Question du déplacement de la population. État des études sur cette question. A mes collègues du Conseil Municipal.* Paris, [Apr. 15] 1842.

Laugier, Marc-Antoine. *An Essay on Architecture.* Translated by Wolfgang and Anni Herrmann. Los Angeles, 1977.

Lazare, Félix and Louis. *Dictionnaire administratif et historique des rues et monuments de Paris.* Paris, 1844, 1855. Reprint, 1994.

Lazare, Louis. *Bibliothèque municipale: Publications administratives.* 12 vols. Paris, 1862–68.

———. "La Cité et les embellissements de Paris." *Bibliothèque municipale. Publications administratives* (Paris) (1862) 2: 73–III.

———. "Création d'un plan d'ensemble." *La Revue Municipale,* no. 61 (Nov. 1, 1850), 495–98; pt 2., no. 62 (Nov. 16, 1850), 502–5; pt 3, no. 63 (Dec. 1, 1850), 509–II; pt. 4, no. 65 (Dec.12, 1850), 528–29; pt. 5, no. 66 (Jan. 16, 1851), 540.

———. *Paris: Son Administration ancienne et moderne.* Paris, 1856.

———. "Prospectus." *La Revue Municipale,* no. 1 (June 1, 1848). 4 pp.

———, and M. Rigaud. *1760–1860: Paris sous le rapport de la salubrité à ces deux époques.* Paris, 1861.

Leblanc de Ferrière. *Paris et ses environs: Description historique, statistique, et monumental.* Paris, 1838.

Lechevalier, Jules. *Exposition du système social de Charles Fourier, de Besançon.* Paris, 1832.

———. *Qu'est ce que l'organisation du travail.* Paris, 1848.

———. *Question sociale. De la réforme industrielle, considérée comme problême fondamental de la politique positive.* Paris, 1833.

Lecouturier, Henri. *Paris incompatible avec la République: Plan d'un nouveau Paris ou les révolutions seront impossibles.* Paris, 1848.

———. *Le Paris des rois et le Paris du peuple.* Paris, 1850.

———. *La Science du socialisme universel.* Paris, 1850.

Legrand, J. G., and G. P. Landon. *Description de Paris et de ses édifices.* 2 vols. 2nd ed. Paris, 1818.

Le Hir, L[ouis], et al. *Entreprise générale du transport des personnes et des choses dans Paris. . . .* Paris, 1855.

Le Hir, Louis. *Des Chemins de fer de Paris à Brest à Caen et à Cherbourg.* Paris, 1845.

———. *Forces et institutions productives de la France. . . .* Paris, 1860.

———. [L. Le Léonais, pseud.] *Harmonies Sociales.* Paris, 1844.

———. [Untitled article]. *L'Harmonie universelle,* no. 45 (Apr. 9, 1848), 91–94.

Le Hir, Louis. *Réseau de voies ferrées souterraines dans Paris. Chemin de fer souterrain de Londres.* Paris, Nov. 1861.

———. *Réseau de voies ferrées souterraines dans Paris. Observations sur le Rapport de la Commission préfectorale chargée de l'examen des projets de chemins de fer dans Paris et le département de la Seine. Paris,* [1872].

———. *Réseau des voies ferrées sous Paris. Transports généraux dans Paris par un réseau de voies ferrées souterraines desservant les principaux quartiers et les mettant en communication avec les gares des chemins de fer et par un service complémentaire de voitures à chevaux Paris:* 1856.

———. *Réseau des voies ferrées sous Paris. . . .* Paris, 1857.

———. *Réseau de voies ferrées souterraines dans Paris. . . .* Paris, 1860.

———. *Réseau de voies ferrées souterrains dans Paris. . . .* Paris, 1866.

———. *Réseau des voies ferrées sous Paris. . . .* Paris, 1872.

Le Moine, P. J. *Le Parallèle du Paris de la république, avec le Paris des rois.* Paris, 1793.

Lenoir, Albert, and Pierre Landry. "Théories des villes: Comment les villes sont formés." *Revue générale de l'architecture et des travaux publics* 12, nos. 10–11 (1854): cols. 292–98.

Le Normand [Louis-Sébastien], and [Jean-Gabriel-Victor de] Moléon. *Economie publique: Travaux et embellissemens de Paris.* Paris, [1825].

Leroux, Pierre, and Jean Reynaud. *Encyclopédie nouvelle, dictionnaire philosophique, scientifique, littéraire, et industriel.* . . . 8 vols. Paris, 1836–41.

———. *Enclycopédie nouvelle.* . . . 8 vols. in 6. 1836–42. Reprint, Geneva, 1991.

Lescot, Alphonse. *De la Salubrité de la ville de Paris.* Paris, 1826.

Lester, Martin. *An Account of Paris at the Close of the Seventeenth Century.* Shaftesbury, 1698.

Le Sueur, C.-P. *Projet d'utilité et d'embellissement pour la ville de Paris, addressé aux sections.* Paris, 1790.

Leuret. "Mémoire sur l'épidémie, designée sous le nom de choléra-morbus." *Annales d'hygiène publique* 6 (1831): 313–440.

Levicomte, P., and F. Rolland. *Mémoire sur un projet de construction de maisons communes, ou nouvelles mairies, dans la ville de Paris.* Paris, 1833.

Littré, E. "le Choléra à Paris en 1832." In E. Littré, *Médecine et médecins,* 84–197. Paris, 1872.

Lurine, Louis. *Les Rues de Paris: Paris ancien et moderne.* 2 vols in 1. Paris, 1844.

Marie, Léon. *De la Décentralisation des Halles de Paris.* Paris, May 1850.

Marielle, C.-P. *Répertoire de l'École impériale polytechnique.* Paris, 1855.

Marx, Karl. *The Civil War in France.* New York, 1940.

———, and Friedrich Engels. *The Communist Manifesto.* New York, 1955.

Marx, Karl. *Grundrisse: Foundations of the Critique of Political Economy.* Translated by Martin Nicolaus. London, 1993.

Mercier, Louis-Sébastien. *L'An deux mille quatre cent quarante.* London, 1772.

———. *L'An deux mille quatre cent quarante.* Edited by Raymond Trousson. Bordeaux, 1971.

———. *Paris pendant le Révolution (1789–1798), ou le nouveau Paris.* 2 vols. Paris, 1862.

———. *Tableau de Paris.* 12 vols. Amsterdam, 1783–89.

Merruau, Charles. *Souvenirs de l'Hôtel de ville, 1848–1852.* Paris, 1875.

Métral, Antoine. *Description naturelle, morale, et politique du choléra-morbus à Paris.* Paris, 1833.

Meynadier de Flamalens, H[ippolyte]. *Jardin d'hiver: Théorie et pratique, plan, et description pittoresque.* Paris, 1848.

———. *Paris sous le point de vue pittoresque et monumental ou éléments d'un plan général d'ensemble de ses travaux d'art et utilité publique.* Paris, 1843.

Mirbel, and A. Bareau. *Mémoire adressé par une réunion de propriétaires, architectes, et constructeurs de la ville de Paris à messieurs les membres de la commission d'enquête.* . . . Paris, 1829.

Mittié, Stanislas. *Moyens d'exécuter le projet d'embellissements pour Paris.* Paris [1804].

———. *Projet d'embellissemens et de monumens publics pour Paris.* Paris, 1804.

Moléon, Jean-Gabriel-Victor de. *Mémoire sur le quartier neuf de la Villette, sur les avan-*

tages commerciaux, industriels, et agricoles qu'il présente à la ville et au nord de la France et aperçus sur la question de l'entrepôt réel à Paris. Paris, [c. 1827].

———. *Rapports généraux sur la salubrité publique. . . .* Paris, 1841.

———. *Rapports généraux sur les travaux du Conseil de salubrité de la ville de Paris et le département de la Seine. . . .* Paris, 1828.

Monfalcon, J. B., and A.-P.-I. De Polinière. *Traité de la salubrité dans les granes villes suivi de l'hygiène de Lyon.* Paris, 1846.

Mony[Eugène Flachat], Christophe-Stéphane. *Religion saint-simonienne. Le Choléra. Assainissement.* Paris, 1832.

———. *Réligion saint-simonienne. Le Choléra à Paris.* Paris, 1832.

Moreau, M.-F. *Histoire statistique du choléra-morbus dans le quartier du faubourg Saint-Denis (5me arrondissement) pendant les mois d'avril, mai, juin, juillet, août, et septembre.* Paris, 1833.

Normand fils. *Paris moderne, ou choix de maisons construits dans les nouveaux quartiers de la capitale et dans ses environs.* Paris, 1837.

Parent-Duchâtelet, Alexandre. "Des Chantiers d'écarrissage de la ville de Paris." *Annales d'hygiène publique et de médecine légale.* 8, pt. 1 (1832): 5–157.

———. *Essai sur les cloaques ou égouts de la ville de Paris.* Paris, 1824.

———. *Hygiène publique ou mémoires sur les questions les plus importantes de l'hygiène.* 2 vols. Paris, 1836.

———. "Quelques considérations sur le conseil de salubrité de Paris." *Annales d'hygiène publique et de médecine légale* 9, pt. 1 (1833): 243–56.

Paris. *Budget de la ville de Paris. . . .* 46 vols. Paris, 1818–68.

Paris. Conseil Municipal. *Agrandissement et construction des Halles centrales d'approvisionnement.* Paris, 1845.

———. *Embellissements de la Place de la Concorde et des Champs-Elysées.* Paris, Oct. 1834. Report in Bibliothèque historique de la ville de Paris.

Paris. Préfecture de Police. *Arrêté relatif au balayage et à la propreté de la voie publique.* Paris, Oct. 28, 1837.

———. *Ordonnance concernant l'arrosement.* Paris, May 10, 1848.

———. *Ordonnance concernant le balayage des rues de Paris.* Paris, Nov. 14, 1817.

Patte, Pierre. *Mémoires sur les objets les plus importans de l'architecture.* 1769. Reprint, Geneva, 1973.

———. *Monumens érigés en France à la gloire de Louis XV.* Paris, 1765.

Pecqueur, Constantin. *Économie sociale: Des intérêts du commerce, de l'industrie et de l'agriculture, et de la civilisation en générale, sous l'influence des applications de la vapeur. . . .* 2 vols. Paris, 1839.

———. *De la législation et du mode d'exécution des chemins de fer: Lettres adressés à M. le Ministre des Travaux Publics.* Paris, 1840.

Perreymond. "Bilan de la France ou la crise, le misère, et le travail." *La Phalange: Journal de la Science Sociale* 8 (1848): 175–288.

———. *Le Bilan de la France ou la misère et le travail.* Paris, 1849.

———. "Chemins de fer: Système rayonnant; système vertébré." *La Phalange: Journal de la Science Sociale* 5, no. 20 (Feb. 16, 1842): cols. 316–17.

———. "Chemins de fer: Confusion et absence de système." *La Phalange: Journal de la Science Sociale* 5, no. 25 (Feb. 27, 1842): cols. 402–5.

———. "Chemins de fer: Proposition de M. Benoist." *La Phalange: Journal de la Science Sociale* 5, no. 14 (Feb. 2, 1842): cols. 220–22.

———. "Chemins de fer: Le Centre de la France est-il français?" *La Phalange: Journal de la* Science Sociale 5, no. 18 (Feb. 11, 1842): col. 285.

———. "Chemins de fer." *La Phalange: Journal de la Science Sociale* 5, no. 51 (Mar. 15, 1842): cols. 499–500.

———. "Chemins de fer." *La Phalange: Journal de la Science Sociale* 5, no. 58 (Mar. 30, 1842): cols. 615–16.

———. "Comment la France peut prendre le premier rang dans l'exécution des Railsways." *La Phalange: Journal de la Science Sociale* 4, no. 49 (Dec. 22, 1841): cols. 793–96.

———. *Cracovie ou les derniers débris de la monarchie polonaise.* Paris, 1847.

———. "Une Découverte importante pour l'assainissement des villes." *Revue de générale de l'architecture et des travaux publics* 5 (Nov. 1844): cols. 512–15.

———. *L'Espagne démocratique: Compte-rendu des manifestations du 26 mars et du 11 avril 1848.* Paris, 1848.

———. "Etudes sur la ville de Paris." *Revue générale de l'architecture et des travaux publics* 3 (Dec. 1842): cols. 540–54, 570–79; 4 (Jan. 1843): cols. 25–37; 4 (Feb. 1843): cols. 72–79, 79–88; 4 (Sept. 1843): cols. 413–29; 4 (Oct. 1843): cols. 449–58, 458–64, 464–69; 4 (Nov. 1843): cols. 517–28.

———. "De la grande circulation dans Paris, et du livre de M. Hippolyte Meynadier." *Revue générale de l'architecture et des travaux publics* 5, pt. 1 (Apr. 1844): pt. 1, cols. 184–88; 5, pt. 2 (May 1844): cols. 232–35.

———. "Lettre de M. Perreymond à M César Daly." *Revue générale de l'architecture et des travaux publics* 3 (1842): cols. 540–41.

———. "De la Locomotion rapide en France: Grand réseau national, commercial et stratégique." *La Phalange: Journal de la Science Sociale* 4, no. 37 (Nov. 24, 1841): cols. 600–612.

———. "Lutes des ouvriers et des entrepreneurs: Le Travail et les grèves." *Revue générale de l'architecture et des travaux publics* 6, no. 3, pt. 1 (1845–46): cols. 127–38; no. 4, pt. 2, cols. 165–78; pt 3, cols. 301–14.

———. *Navigation aérienne. Système-Petin: Notions élémentaires sur l'aéronautique et sur les sciences accessoires à cet art.* Paris: Librarie Nouvelle, Aug. 1851.

———. *Notions élémentaires sur l'aéronatique.* Paris, 1851.

———. "Nouveau républiques au nouveau monde." *La Phalange: Journal de la Science Sociale* 6, no. 35 (Sept. 18, 1842): cols. 569–74.

———. "Nouveau mode d'emprunt, présénté à M. Humann par M. le Baron Corvajà." *La Phalange: Journal de la Science Sociale* 3, no. 32 (July 14, 1841): cols. 512–13.

———. *Le Pain du prolétaire ou le commerce des peuples: Réponse à M. Thiers.* Paris, 1851.

———. *Paris monarchique et Paris républicain, une page de l'histoire de la misère et du travail.* Paris, 1849.

————. *Physiologie des langues Indo-Européennes: ou introduction à l'étude comparative et raisonnée des mots Sanscrits, Grecs, Latins, Français, Allemands, Anglais, etc.* Paris, 1848.

————. "Physiologie des langues indo-européennes." *La Phalange: Journal de la Science Sociale* 7 (1848): 155–68.

————. *Plantes phanérogames qui croissent aux environs de Fréjus, avec leur habitat et l'époque de leur fleuraison.* Paris, 1833.

————. "Recherches statistiques sur la ville de Paris, publiées d'après les ordres de M. le comte du Rambuteau, préfet de la Seine." *La Démocratie pacifique* 3, no. 119 (Oct. 27, 1844): 2.

————. *De la richesse et des impôts, ou usure et travail.* Paris, 1850.

————. "Salubrité publique." *Revue générale de l'architecture et des travaux publics* 6, no. 1 (1845–46): cols. 25–30.

————. "D'un Système national des chemins de fer en France." *La Phalange: Journal de la Science Sociale* 4, no. 37 (Nov. 24, 1841): cols. 594–600.

———— and Victor Considerant. "D'un Système national de chemins de fer en France." *Revue générale de l'architecture et des travaux publics* 7 (Nov. 1841): cols. 581–88.

Perreymond. "Vicat: les chaux hydrauliques: récompense nationale." *Revue générale de l'architecture et des travaux publics* 6, no. 1 (1845–46): cols. 16–18.

Perreymond, Charles. *Le Portugal devant l'Europe et le monde, ou Les Traités de 1815 et la politique du travail.* Lisbon, 1854.

Picolet, A.V. *Considerations sur la direction des travaux publics de Paris.* Paris, September 1816.

Piganiol de la Force, Jean Aymar. *Descrption historique de la ville de Paris et de ses environs.* 10 vols. Paris, 1765.

Pigeory, Félix. *Les Halles centrales quai de la Mégisserie: Projet adressé à la commission municipale de Paris.* Paris, 1851.

————. *Les Monuments de Paris au dix-neuvième siècle: Histoire architectonique de Paris ancien et moderne.* Paris, 1849.

Polonceau, Antoine Rémy. *Exposé des principaux motifs qui ont déterminé le choix du tracé d'un chemin de fer de Paris à Rouen, au Havre et à Dieppe, par la vallée de la Seine.* Paris, Nov. 7, 1836.

————. *Notice sur l'amélioration des chemins vicinaux.* Paris, 1835.

————. *Observations sur les routes suivies de propositions sur leur amélioration et sur leur entretien.* Paris, 1829.

Poncet de la Grave, [Guillaume]. *Projet des embellissemens de la ville et fauxbourgs de Paris.* 3 vols. Paris, 1756.

Poyet. *Projets de places et édifices à ériger pour la gloire et l'utilité de la République.* Paris, 1799.

Préfecture de Police. *Arrêté relatif au Balayage et à la propreté de la voie publique.* Paris, Oct. 28, 1837.

Préfecture du département de la Seine. *Commission des Halles. Documents à étudier.* [Paris, c. 1842–43].

———. Commission Municipale de Paris. Séance du 11 juin 1851. *Délibération sur les Halles Centrales.* Paris, June 1851.

———. *Rapport de la commission spéciale sur l'étude des chemins de fer et tramways d'intérêt local à établir dans le département de la Seine.* Paris, 1872.

———. *Rapport sur l'emplacement des Halles Centrales de Paris.* Paris, 1851.

———. *Recherches statistiques sur la ville de Paris et le département de la Seine.* 5 vols. Paris, 1821–44.

———. *Recherches statistiques sur la ville de Paris et le département de la Seine.* Vol. 6. Paris, 1860.

———. *Rapport sur les résultats générale du démombrement de sa population.* Paris, 1847.

Quatremère de Quincy, Antoine Chrysotome. *Dictionnaire historique d'architecture.* 2 vols. Paris, 1832.

Rabusson, A. *Affaire du déplacement de la population dans Paris. . . .* Paris, Oct. 15, 1843.

———. *De l'Agrandissement de l'enceinte des fortifications de Paris du coté de l'Est, considéré dans ses rapports avec la défense de la ville. . . .* Paris, 1842.

———. *De la Défense générale du royaume dans ses rapports avec les moyens de défense de Paris.* Paris, 1843.

———. *Du Déplacement de Paris dans ses rapports avec le renouvellement du privilège de la Banque. . . .* Paris, Feb. 12, 1840.

———. *Éclaircisseueurs historiques sur la ville de Paris. . . .* Paris, 1839.

———. *Si le mouvement de déplacement auquel est livrée la population de Paris est contraire aux intérêts de sa défense? Si l'enceinte fortifiée suffira pour l'arrêter?* Paris, 1841

———. *Note sur l'utilité d'attacher à la préfecture de la seine un commissaire du gouvernement pour la question du déplacement de Paris. . . .* [Paris, 1840].

Rambuteau, Claude. *Commission des Halles. Documents à étudier. Projets de la ville.* Paris, 1847.

———. *Memoirs of the Comte de Rambuteau. . . .* Translated by J. C. Brogan. London, 1908.

Roaul, L.V. *Les Nouveau embellissemens de Paris.* Paris, 1812.

Reynaud, Jean. "Villes." In *Encyclopédie nouvelle, ou dictionnaire philosophique, scientifique, littéraire, et industriel . . . ,* edited by Pierre-Henri Leroux and Jean Reynaud, 7:670, col. 2–687, col. 2. 8 vols. Paris, 1841.

———. "Voies de communication." In *Encyclopédie nouvelle, ou dictionnaire philosophique, scientifique, littéraire, et industriel . . . ,* edited by Pierre-Henri Leroux and Jean Reynaud, 7:700, col. 1–712, col. 2. 8 vols. Paris, 1842.

Reynaud, Léonce. *Traité de l'architecture . . .* Paris, 1858, 1863.

Richomme, Fanny. *Paris monumental et historique depuis son origin jusqu'à 1789.* Paris, [1850].

Roch, Eugène. *Paris malade, esquisses du jour.* 2 vols. Paris, 1832.

Ronesse, Jacques Hippolyte. *Vues sur la propreté des rues de Paris.* Paris, 1782.

Rouvières, M. de. *Description du chemin de fer de Paris à Saint-Germain. . . .* Paris, [c. 1836]

Roze, Henry, and A. Roze. *Nouveau projet de Halles Centrales dans la Cité. . . .* Paris, 1853.

Saint-Simon, Henri de and P[rospor] Enfantin. *Oeuvres de Saint-Simon et d'Enfantin.* 47 vols. Paris, 1865–78.

Sauval, Henri. *Histoire et recherches des antiquités de la ville de Paris.* 3 vols. Paris, 1724.

Saussay. *Projet d'ouverture d'une nouvelle voie de communication entre le boulevard St. Martin et Belleville. . . .* Paris, 1845.

Say, Horace. *Études sur l'administration de la ville de Paris et du département de la Seine.* Paris, 1846.

Sedillez. *Discours sur le projet de loi relatif à des embellissemens dans les environs du palais et du jardin des Tuileries.* Paris, 1804.

Senard, J. *Halles Centrales de Paris. . . .* Paris, [c. 1850].

———. *Halles centrales à élever à Paris.* Paris, Dec. 1850.

———. *Halles Centrales d'approvisionnement. . . .* [Paris], Jan. 1851.

Soumet, Alexandre. *Les Embellissements de Paris.* Paris, 1812.

Sucquet, J. P., and L. Krafft. *Hygiène publique. L'Assainissement de la vidange et de la suppression des voieries de la ville de Paris.* Paris, 1840.

Tacheron, C. F. *Statsitique médicale de la mortalité du choléra-morbus dans la XIe arrondissement de Paris. . . .* Paris, 1832.

Teisserenc, Edmond. *Statistiques des voies de communication en France. . . .* Paris, 1845.

[Tell, J.] *Chemins de fer dans l'intérieur de Paris.* [Paris, 1856; rev. 1882].

Tessereau, Dr. *Études hygiéniques sur les Halles Centrales de Paris.* Paris, 1847.

Thiers, Adolphe. "Rapport sur le projet de loi des fortifications de Paris avec différents documents; par M. Thiers (13 janvier 1841)." Document in Série Actualités, Bibliothèque historique de la ville de Paris.

Thiery. *Almanach du voyageur à Paris.* Paris, 1785.

Tisi, R. *Les Édifices modernes de Paris et leur architecture.* Paris, 1860.

Tissot, Amédée de. *Paris et Londres comparés.* Paris, 1830.

Tournon, Antoine. *Moyens de rendre parfaitement propres les rues de Paris.* Paris, 1789.

Vallée, L.-L. *Changements d'organisation proposés pour l'École polytechnique et pour les Ponts et Chaussées.* Paris, 1848.

———. *Exposé générale des études faites pour le tracé des chemins de fer de Paris en Belgique et en Angleterre, et d'Angleterre en Belgique.* Paris, 1837.

———. *Une Loi d'élection.* 3d ed. Paris, Mar. 8, 1848.

Vautier, L.-L. *Chemin de fer circulaire intérieur sur la ligne des anciens boulevards extérieurs et le quai rive droit de la Seine. Avant Projet.* Paris, Mar. 31, 1865.

———. *Chemin de fer circulaire intérieur sur la ligne des anciens boulevards extérieurs et le quai rive droit de la Seine. Mémoire à l'appui du projet.* Paris, 1872.

Vergnaud, [Nicolas]. *Projet d'amélioration et d'embellissemens pour Auteuil, Passy et communes voisines de la capitale. Assaissemens généraux utiles contre le choléra.* Paris, 1832.

Veuillot, Louis. *Les Odeurs de Paris.* 4th ed. Paris, 1867.

Viard. *Projet pour tenir les rues de Paris dans un état constant de propreté.* Paris, 1827.

Villermé, L.-R. "Des Épidémies sous rapports de l'hygiène publique de la statistique médicale et de l'économie politique." *Annales d'hygiène publique et de médecine légale* 9, pt. 1 (1983): 5–58.

————. "De la Mortalité dans les divers quatiers de la ville de Paris. . . . " *Annales d'hygiéne publique et de médecine légale* 3 (1830): 294–341.

————. "Note sur les ravages du choléra-morbus dans les maisons garnies de Paris." *Annales d'hygiène publique et de médecine légale* 11, pt 1 (1834): 385–409.

Vincens, Théodore. *Mémoire sur les moyens d'assainir et d'embellir les quartiers de la rive gauche de la ville de Paris. . . .* Paris, June 15, 1848.

Voltaire [François Marie Arouet de]. "Des Embellissements de Paris" (1749). In *Oeuvres completes de Voltaire,* 29:163–74. Kehl, 1785.

SECONDARY WORKS
Anonymous Works

Les Cahiers de Fontenay: Idées de villes, villes idéals, nos. 69–70 (Mar. 1993).

Hottorff et Visconti. Projets pour la ville de Paris, 1828–1846. Paris, 1989.

La Ville au XVIIIe siècle: Colloque d'Aix-en-Province, 29 avril-1 mai 1973. Aix-en-Province, 1975.

Author(s) Listed

Aguet, Jean-Pierre. *Les Grèves sous la monarchie de Juillet.* Geneva, 1954.

Agulhon, Maurice. *The Republican Experiment, 1845–1852.* Translated by Janet Lloyd. Cambridge, 1973, 1983.

————, ed. *La Ville de l'âge industriel: Le Cycle haussmannien.* Vol. 4 of *Histoire de la France urbaine.* Edited by Georges Duby. Paris, 1983.

Aisenberg, Andrew R. *Contaigion: Disease, Government, and the "Social Question" in Nineteenth-Century France.* Stanford, 1999.

Andia, Béatrice de. "L'Apport des Lumières." In *L'Urbanisme parisien au siècle des Lumières,* edited by Michel Le Moël with Sophie Descat, 10–29. Paris, 1997.

Aron, Jacques. "De Beau à l'utile: une derive irreversible des valeurs urbains?" *Revue de l'Université de Bruxelles* 3–4 (1986): 85–90.

Backouche, Isabelle. "Projets urbains et mémoire du fleuve (1840–1853)." In *La Modernité avant Haussmann: Formes de l'espace urbain à Paris, 1801–1853,* edited by Karen Bowie, 110–22. Paris, 2001.

————. *La Trace du fleuve, la Seine et Paris, 1750–1850.* Paris, 2000.

Ballon, Hilary. *The Paris of Henri IV: Architecture and Urbanism.* New York, 1991.

Barbier, A. A. *Dictionnaire des ouvrages anonymes,* 4 vols. Paris, 1872–79.

Bardet, Gaston. *Naissance et méconnaissance de l'urbanisme.* Paris, 1952.

Barles, Sabine. *La Ville délétère: Médecins et ingénieurs dans l'espace urbain, XVIIIe–XIXe siècles.* Paris, 1999.

Bartier, J., et al. *1848, Les Utopismes sociaux: Utopie et action à la veille des journées de février.* Paris, 1981.

Bauman, Zygmunt. *Postmodern Ethics.* Oxford, 1993.

Becherer, Richard. *Science Plus Sentiment: César Daly's Formula for Modern Architecture.* Ann Arbor, 1984.

Beecher, Jonathan. *Charles Fourier: The Visionary and His World.* Berkeley, 1986.

———. "Fourierism and Christianity." *Nineteenth-Century French Studies,* 22, nos. 3–4 (Spring–Summer 1994): 391–403.

———. *Victor Considerant and the Rise and Fall of French Romantic Socialism.* Berkeley, 2001.

Belhoste, Bruno, Francine Masson, and Antoine Picon. *Paris des Polytecniciens: Des ingénieurs dans la ville, 1794–1994.* Paris, 1994.

Benevolo, Leonardo. *The European City.* Translated by Carl Ipsen. Oxford, 1993.

———. *The Origins of Modern Town Planning.* Translated by Judith Landry. Cambridge, MA, 1967.

Bénichou, Paul. *Le Temps des prophètes: Doctrines de l'âge romantique.* Paris, 1977.

Benjamin, Walter. *The Arcades Project.* Translated by Howard Eiland and Kevin McLaughlin. Cambridge, MA, 1999.

———. *Charles Baudelaire: A Lyric Poet in the Era of High Capitalism.* Translated by Harry Zohn. London, 1983.

Bercé, Françoise. *Les Premiers travaux de la commission des monuments historiques, 1837–1848: Procès verbaux et relevés d'architectes.* Paris, 1979.

Berman, Marshall. *All That Is Solid Melts into Air: The Experience of Modernity.* New York, 1982, 1988.

Bernard, Leon. *The Emerging City: Paris in the Age of Louis XIV.* Durham, NC, 1970.

Bertier de Sauvigny, Guillaume de. *La Restauration, 1815–1830* [Nouvelle histoire de Paris]. Paris, 1977.

Billaz, André, and Ulrick Ricker, eds. *Romantismes et socialismes en Europe (1800–1848).* Paris, 1988.

Blanchard, Marc Eli. *In Search of the City: Engels, Baudelaire, Rimbaud.* Saratoga, CA, 1985.

Blanchot, Christine, and Bernard Landau. "La Direction des Travaux de Paris aux XIXe siècle." In *Paris des Polytecniciens: Des ingénieurs dans la ville, 1794–1994,* edited by Bruno Belhoste, Francine Masson, and Antoine Picon. Paris, 1994.

Bo, Giuseppe Del. *Charles Fourier e la Scuola Societaria (1801–1922).* Milan, 1957.

Boudard, René. "Un Préfet napoléonie en Ligurie: le Comte de Chabrol de Volvic." *Revue de l'Institut Napoléon,* no. 61 (Oct. 1956): 119–30.

Boudon, Françoise, and Françoise Loyer, eds. *Hector Horeau: 1801–1872.* Paris, 1978.

Boudon, Françoise. "Horeau et les Halles centrales." In *Hector Horeau, 1801–1872,* edited by Françoise Boudon and Françoise Loyer, 152–59. Paris, 1978.

———, et al. *Système de l'architure urbaine: Le Quartier des Halles de Paris.* 2 vols. Paris, 1977.

Bourillon, Florence. "A Propos de la Commission des embellissements: La Rénovation du Grand Paris à l'intéieur des fortifications." In *La Modernité avant Haussmann: Formes de l'espace urbain à Paris, 1801–1853,* edited by Karen Bowie, 139–52.

———. "Changer la ville: La Question urbaine au milieu du 19e siècle." *Vingtième Siècle: Revue d'histoire* 64 (Oct.–Dec. 1999): 11–23.

———. *Les Villes en France au XIXe siècle.* Paris, 1992.

Bowie, Karen, ed. *Les Grandes gares parisiennes au XIXe siècle.* Paris, 1987.

————. *La Modernité avant Haussmann: Formes de l'espace urbain à Paris, 1801–1853.* Paris, 2001.

————. "Polaraisation du territoire et développement urbain: Les Gares du Nord et de l'Est et la transformation de Paris au XIXe siècle." 2 vols. Unpublished report. Paris, 1999.

Bowman, Frank Paul. *Le Christ romatique.* Geneva, 1973.

Boyer, Christine M. *The City of Collective Memory: Its Historical Imagery and Architectural Entertainments.* Cambridge, MA, 1994, 1996.

Braham, Allan. T*he Architecture of the French Enlightenment.* Berkeley, 1980, 1989.

Broussel, Patrice, ed. *Victor Baltard: Projets inédits pour les Halles Centrales.* Paris, 1978.

Burton, Richard D. *The Context of Baudelaire's "Le Cygne."* Durham, Eng., 1980.

Cameron, Rondo. *France and the Economic Development of Europe: Conquests of Peace and Seeds of War.* 2nd ed. Chicago, 1965.

Carlisle, Robert B. *The Proffered Crown: Saint-Simonianism and the Doctrine of Hope.* Baltimore, 1987.

Caron, François. *Histoire des chemins de fer en France, 1740–1883.* Paris, 1997.

Casselle, Pierre, ed. *Commission des embellissements de Paris: Rapport à l'empereur Napoléon III rédigé par le comte Henri Siméon (décembre 1853).* Paris, 2000.

Casselle, Pierre. "Les Travaux de la Commission des Embellissements de Paris en 1853: Pouvait-on transformer la capital sans Haussmann?" *Bibliothèque de l'École des Chartres* 155 (July–Dec. 1997): 645–89.

Cassidy, John. "The Prince Prophet." *New Yorker,* Feb. 7, 2000.

Certeau, Michel de. *The Practice of Everyday Life.* Translated by Steven Randall. Berkeley, 1984.

Charléty, Sébastien. *Histoire du Saint-Simonisme (1825–1864): Seize héliogravures.* Paris, 1931.

Chaussinard-Nogaret, Guy. "La Ville jacobin et balzacienne." In *La Ville classique de la Renaissance aux Révolutions,* edited by Emmanuel Le Roy Ladurie, 537–619. Vol. 3 of *Histoire de la France urbaine.* Edited by Georges Duby. Paris, 1981.

Chevalier, Louis, ed. *Le Choléra: La Première épidemie à Paris pendant la première moitié du XIXe siècle.* La Roche-sur-Yon, 1958.

Chevalier, Louis. *Laboring Classes and Dangerous Classes in Paris during the First Half of the Ninteeenth Century.* Translated by Frank Jellinek. New York, 1973.

Choay, Françoise. Introduction to *Mémoires du Baron Haussmann.* Paris, 2000.

————. *The Modern City: Planning in the Nineteenth Century.* Translated by Marguerite Hugo and George R. Collins. New York, 1969.

————. "Pensées sur la ville, arts de la ville." In *La Ville de l'âge industrielle: Le Cycle haussmannien,* edited by Maurice Agulhon, 157–271. Vol. 4 of *Histoire de la France urbaine.* Edited By Georges Duby. Paris, 1983.

————. *L'Urbanisme: Utopies et réalités: Une Anthologie.* Paris, 1965.

————. *The Rule and the Model: On the Theory of Architecture and Urbanism.* Translated by Denise Bratton. Cambridge, MA, 1997.

Chombart de Lauwe, Paul-Henry. *Paris et l'agglomeration parisienne.* 2 vols. Paris, 1952.

Christ, Yvan. *Les Métamorphoses de Paris.* Paris, 1971.

Christaller, Walter. *Central Places in Southern Germany.* Translated by C. W. Baskin. Englewood Cliffs, NJ, 1966.

Cohen, Jean-Louis, and André Lortie. *Des Fortif au perif: Paris, les seuil de la ville.* Paris, 1991.

———, and Bruno Fortier. *Paris, la ville et ses projets: A City in the Making.* Paris, 1988.

Cole, Joshua. *The Power of Large Numbers: Population, Politics, and Gender in Nineteenth-Century France.* Ithaca, NY, 2000.

Coleman, William. *Death Is a Social Disease: Public Health and Political Economy in Early Industrial France.* Madison, WI, 1982.

Corbin, Alain. *The Fowl and the Fragrant: Odor and the French Social Imagination.* Translated by Miriam L. Kochan with Roy Porter and Christopher Prendergast. Cambridge, MA, 1986.

———. "L'Hygiène publique et les 'excreta' de la ville préhaussmannienne." *Éthnologie française* 12, no. 2 (1982): 127–30.

———, Jacqueline Lalouette, and Michèle Riot-Sarcey, eds. *Femmes dans le cité, 1815–1871.* Grâne, 1997.

Cornu, Marcel. *La Conquête de Paris.* Paris, 1972.

Coste, Michel. "Perreymond, un théoricien des quartiers et de la restrucuration." In *Les Annales de la recherche urbaine,* no. 22 (Apr. 1984): 47–56.

Crow, Thomas E. *Painters and Public Life in Eighteenth-Century Paris.* New Haven, CT, 1985.

D'Allemagne, Henry-René. *Les Saint-Simoniens, 1827–1837.* Paris, 1930.

Daumas, Maurice, et al. *Analyse historique de l'évolution des transports en communes dans la région parisienne de 1855 à 1939.* Paris, 1977.

Daumas, Maurice, and Jacques Payen, eds. *Évolution de la géographie industrielle de Paris et sa proche banlieue au XIXe siècle.* 3 vols. Paris, 1976.

Darton, Robert. *The Forbidden Best-Sellers of Pre-Revolutionary France.* New York, 1995.

Davidson, Rondel van. *Did We Think Victory Great? The Life and Ideas of Victor Considerant.* Latham, 1988.

Debofle, Pierre. "La Politique d'urbanisme de la ville de Paris sous la Restauration." 3 vols. Ph.D. diss., University of Paris-Sorbonne, Paris IV, 1986.

———. "Travaux publics à Paris au XIXe siècle: Hommes et programmes (1800–1914)." In *L'Administration de Paris (1789–1977),* edited by Pierre Debofle et al., 42–77. Geneva, 1979.

Delaporte, François. *Disease and Civilization: The Cholera in Paris, 1832.* Translated by Arthur Goldhammer. Cambridge, MA, 1986.

Deleuze, Gilles, and Félix Guattari. *A Thousand Plateaus: Capitalism and Schizophrenia.* Translated by Brian Massumi. Minneapolis, 1987.

Demangeon, Alain, and Bruno Fortier. "The Politics of Urban Space: The City around 1800." *Architectural Design* 48 (1978): 8–13.

Derré, J. R. *Regards sur le Saint-Simonisme et les Saint-Simoniens.* Lyon, 1986.

Des Cars, Jean, and Pierre Pinon. *Paris-Haussmann: "Le Pari d'Haussmann."* Paris, 1991.

Descat, Sophie. "Pierre-Louis Moreau et la Seine." In *L'Urbanisme parisien au siècle des Lumières,* edited by Michel Le Moël with Sophie Descat, 79–92. Paris, 1997.

———. "Pierre Patte: Théoricien de l'urbanisme." In *L'Urbanisme parisien au siècle des Lumières,* edited by Michel Le Moël with Sophie Descat, 58–65. Paris, 1997.

Desroche, Henri. *La Société festive: Du fouriérisme écrit au fouriérismes pratiques.* Paris, 1975.

Desrosières, Alain. *La Politique des grands nombres: Histoire de la raison statistique.* Paris, 1993.

Dion, Jeanne. "Horeau." *Gazette des Beaux-Arts,* Jan. 1914.

Donald, James. *Imagining the Modern City.* Minneapolis, 1999.

Douglas, Mary. *Purity and Danger: An Analysis of the Concepts of Pollution and Taboo.* London, 1984, 1996.

Dufournet, Paul. "Quelques aspects essentiels de l'oeuvre d'Hector Horeau." In *Hector Horeau, 1801–1872,* edited by Françoise Boudon and Françoise Loyer, 145–51. Paris, 1978.

Egbert, Donald Drew. *Social Radicalism and the Arts, Western Europe: A Cultural History from the French Revolution to 1968.* New York, 1970.

Etlin, Richard A. "L'Air dans l'urbanisme des Lumières." *Dix-huitième siècle,* no. 9 (1997), 123–34.

———. *Symbolic Space: French Enlightenment Architecture and Its Legacy.* Chicago, 1994.

Evans, David Owen. *Social Romanticism in France, 1830–1848.* New York, 1969.

Evans Richard J. "Epidemics and Revolutions: Cholera in Nineteenth-Century Europe." *Past and Present,* no. 20 (Aug. 1988): 123–46.

Evenson, Norma. *Le Corbusier: The Machine and the Grand Design.* London, 1970.

———. *Paris: A Century of Change, 1878–1978.* New Haven, CT, 1979.

Farge, Arlette. "L'Espace parisien au XVIIe siècle d'après les ordonnances de police." *Éthnologie française* 12, no. 2 (1982): 119–26.

———. *Vivre dans la rue à Paris au XVIIIe siècle.* Paris, 1979.

Ferguson, Priscilla Parkhurst. *Paris as Revolution: Writing the Nineteenth-Century City.* Berkeley, 1994.

Fernandez-Leveau, Madeleine. "La Dernière enceinte de Paris, 1840–1970." Thèse du troisième cycle, 2 vols., University of Paris VII (Jussieux), 1983.

Filjalkow, Yankel. *La Construction des îlots insalubres: Paris 1850–1945.* Paris, 1998.

Fishman, Robert. *Urban Utopias in the Twentieth Century: Ebenezer Howard, Frank Lloyd Wright, Le Corbusier.* Cambridge, MA, 1989.

Fleury, Michel. "Les Frères Lazare et le Dictionnaire des rues et monuments de Paris." In *Dictionnaire administratif et historique des rues et monuments de Paris,* by Félix and Louis Lazare. 2nd ed., ix–xiv. Paris, 1855, 1994.

———. "Les Projets d'urbanisme de Jaillot (1779). *Cahiers du Centre de recherches et d'études sur Paris et l'Île-de-France,"* no. 50 (Mar. 1995): 141–65.

Fleury, Michel, and Jeanne Pronteau, eds. *Petit atlas pittoresque des quarante-huit quartiers de la ville de Paris (1834) par A.M. Perrot.* Paris, 1835, 1987.

Fleury, Michel. *Souvenirs inédits de M. Le comte Chabrol de Volvic.* Paris, 2002.

————, and François Monnier. "L'Urbanimse éclaré à Paris: Aménagement et législation de Louis XVI à la Révolution." In *Cahiers du Centre de recherches et d'études sur Paris et l'Île-de-France,* no. 12 (1985): 58–68.

Fortier, Bruno, ed. *Métamorphoses parisiennes.* Paris, 1996.

————. *Le Métropole imaginaire: Un Atlas de Paris.* Brussels, 1989.

————. *La Politique de l'espace parisien (à la fin de l'Ancien Régime).* Paris, 1975.

Forty, Adrian. "'Spatial Mechanics:' Metaphores in Architecture." In *The Architecture of Science,* edited by Peter Galison and Emily Thompson, 213–31. Cambridge, MA, 1999.

Foucault, Michel. *Discipline and Punish: The Birth of the Prison.* Translated by Allan Sheridan. New York, 1977.

————. *The Foucault Reader.* Edited by Paul Rabinow. New York, 1984.

————. "The Confessions of the Flesh," in *Power/Knowledge: Selective Interviews and Other Writings, 1972–1977.* New York, 1980.

————. *Madness and Civilization: A History of Insanity in the Age of Reason.* Translated by Richard Howard. New York, 1971.

————. "Space, Knowledge, and Power." In *The Foucault Reader,* edited by Paul Rabinow, 239–56. New York, 1984.

————. "What Is an Author?" In *The Foucault Reader,* edited by Paul Rabinow, 101–20. New York, 1984.

Fourcy, Ambroise. *Histoire de l'École polytechnique.* Paris, 1828. Reprint, 1987.

Francastel, Pierre, ed. *L'Urbanisme de Paris et l'Europe, 1600–1680.* Paris, 1969.

Franklin, Alfred. *Les Anciens plans de Paris. Notices historiques et topographiques.* 2 vols. Paris, 1878–80.

Freedman, Charles E. *Joint-Stock Enterprise in France, 1807–1867: From Privileged Company to Modern Corporation.* Chapel Hill, NC, 1979.

Fritz, Paul, and David Williams, eds. *City and Society in the Eighteenth Century.* Toronto, 1973.

Fuchs, Rachel G. *Poor and Pregnant in Paris: Strategies for Survival in the Nineteenth Century.* New Brunswick, NJ, 1992.

Gaillard, Jeanne. *Paris, la ville, 1852–1870: L'Urbanisme parisien à l'heure d'Haussmann.* . . . Paris, 1977.

Galison, Peter, and Emily Thompson, eds. *The Architecture of Science.* Cambridge, MA, 1999.

Gallice, François. "Les Ingénieurs saint-simoniens: Le Mariage de l'utopie et de la raison." *Recherches contemporaines,* no. 2 (1994): 5–25.

————. "Les Ingénieurs saint-simoniens." Maitrise d'histoire. University of Paris-X (Nanterre), 1993.

Garnot, Benoît. *Les Villes en France aux XVIe, XVIIe et XVIIIe siècles.* Paris, 1989.

Garrioch, David. *The Making of Revolutionary Paris.* Berkeley, 2002.

————. *Neighborhood and Community in Paris, 1740–1790.* Cambridge, 1986.

Gasnault, François, and Henri Zuber, eds., with Shelia Hallsted-Baumert. *Métro-Cité: Le Chemin de fer métropolitain à la conquête de Paris, 1871–1945.* Paris, 1997.

Gaudin, Jean-Pierre. *L'Aménegement de la société: Politiques, savoirs, représentatrions so-ciales, la production de l'espace aux XIXème et XXème siècles*. Paris, 1979.

Geiger, Reed. *Planning the French Canals: Bureaucracy, Politics, and Enterprise under the Restoration*. Newark, NJ, 1994.

Gille, Bertrand. *La Banque en France au XIXe siècle*. Geneva, 1970.

Girard, Louis. *La Deuxième République et le Second Empire, 1848–1870* [Nouvelle histoire de Paris]. Paris, 1981.

Globot, Jean-Jacques. *La Jeune France Libérale: Le Globe et son groupe littéraire, 1824–1830*. Paris, 1995.

Goubert, Jean-Pierre. *The Conquest of Water: The Advent of Health in the Industrial Age.* Translated by Andrew Wilson. Princeton, 1989.

Grad, Bonnie L., and Timothy Riggs. *Visions of the City and Country: Prints and Photographs of Nineteenth-Century France*. Worcester, MA, 1982.

Green, Nicholas. *The Spectacle of Nature: Landscape and Bourgeois Culture in Nineteenth-Century France*. Manchester, Eng., 1990.

Grimsley, Ronald. "Rousseau's Paris." In *City and Society in the Eighteenth Century,* edited by Paul Fritz and David Williams, 3–18. Toronto, 1973.

Guerrini, Maurice. *Napoleon and Paris: Thirty Years of History.* Translated, abridged, and edited by Margery Weiner. London, 1967, 1970.

Haine, W. Scott. *The World of the Paris Café: Sociability among the French Working Class, 1789–1914*. Baltimore, 1996.

Hall, Peter. *Cities in Civilization*. New York, 1998.

Hall, Thomas. *Planning Europe's Capital Cities: Aspects of Nineteenth-Century Urban Development*. London, 1997.

Hammarström, Ingrid, and Thomas Hall, eds. *Growth and Transformation of the Modern City*. Stockholm, 1979.

Harouel, Jean-Louis. *L'Embellissement des villes: L'Urbanisme français au XVIIIe siècle*. Paris, 1993.

———. *Histoire de l'urbanisme*. Paris, 1981.

Harvey, David. *The Condition of Postmodernity: An Enquiry into the Origins of Cultural Change*. Oxford, 1989.

———. *Consciousness and the Urban Experience: Studies in the History and Theory of Capitalist Urbanization*. Baltimore, 1985.

———, David. *Paris, Capital of Modernity*. New York, 2003.

Hayek, F. A. *The Counter-Revolution of Science: Studies on the Abuse of Reason*. Indianapolis, 1952; 1979.

Héron de Villefosse, René. *Les Halles: De Lutèce à Rungis*. Paris, 1973.

Herrmann, Wolfgand. *Laugier and Eighteenth-Century French Theory*. London, 1962.

Horkheimer, Max, and Theodor W. Adorno. *Dialectic of Enlightenment*. Translated by John Cumming. New York, 1994.

Huber, Michel et al. *La Population de la France: Son évolution et ses perspectives*. 3rd ed. Paris, 1951.

Institut National de la Statistique et des Études Économiques. *Pour une histoire de la statistique*. 2 vols. Paris, 1976–86.

Institut pédagogique national. *Paris, croissance d'une capitale.* Paris, 1961.

———. *Paris, fonction d'une capitale.* Paris, 1962.

Jacobs, Jane. *The Death and Life of Great American Cities.* New York, 1961, 1992.

Jacquemet, Gérard. "Les Porteurs d'eau de Paris au XIXe siècle." *Études de la région parisienne,* nos. 29–32 (1971).

Johnson, Christopher H. *Utopian Communism in France: Cabet and the Icarians, 1839–1851.* Ithaca, NY, 1974.

Jordan, David P. *Transforming Paris: The Life and Labors of Baron Haussmann.* Chicago, 1995.

Kaufmann, Émile. *Architecture in the Age of Reason: Baroque and Post-Baroque in England, Italy, and France.* New York, 1955, 1968.

Konvitz, Josef W. *Cartography in France, 1660–1848: Science, Engineering, and Statecraft.* Chicago, 1987.

———. *The Urban Millennium: The City Building Process from the Early Middle Ages to the Present.* Carbondale, IL, 1985.

Kostof, Spiro. *The City Shaped: Urban Patterns and Meanings Through History.* Boston, 1991.

Kudlick, Catherine J. *Cholera in Post-Revolutionary Paris: A Cultural History.* Berkeley, 1996.

———. "The Culture of Statistics and the Crises of Cholera in Paris, 1830–1850." In *Re-Creating Authority in Revolutionary France,* edited by Bryant T. Regan Jr. and Elizabeth A. Williams. New Brunswick, NJ, 1992.

La Berge, Ann F. *Mission and Method: The Early-Nineteenth-Century French Public Health Movement.* Cambridge, 1992.

Lacaze, Jean-Paul. *Paris: Urbanisme d'état et destin d'une ville.* Paris, 1994.

Laisney, François. *Règle et règlement: La Question du règlement dans l'evolution de l'urbanisme parisienne, 1600–1902.* Paris, 1989.

Laporte, Dominique. *History of Shit.* Translated by Nadia Benabid and Rodolphe el-Khoury. Cambridge, MA, 1978, 2000.

Laroulandie, Fabrice. "Les Égouts de Paris au XIXe siècle: L'Enfer vaincu et l'utopie depassée." *Les Cahiers de Fontenay: Idées de villes, villes idéales,* nos. 69–70 (Mar. 1993): 107–40.

Lauriot, Norbert. "L'Adaptation géographique et technique des chemins de fer urbains." Thèse du troisième cycle, University of Paris I (Panthéon-Sorbonne), 1996.

Lavedan, Pierre. *Histoire de l'urbanisme à Paris* [Nouvelle histoire de Paris]. Paris, 1975, 1993.

———. *La Question du déplacement de Paris et du transfert des Halles au Conseil Municipal sous la Monarchie de Juillet.* Paris, 1969.

Le Corbusier. *The City of To-Morrow and Its Planning.* Translated by Frederick Ethehells. New York, 1987.

———. *The Radiant City: Elements of a Doctrine of Urbanism to Be Used as the Basis of Our Machine-Age Civilization.* Translated by Pamela Knight, Eleanor Levieux, and Derek Coleman. New York, 1967.

Lees, Andrew. *Cities Perceived: Urban Society in European and American Thought, 1820–1940.* Manchester, 1985.

Lefebvre, Henri. *The Production of Space.* Translated by Donald Nicolson-Smith. Oxford, 1974, 1991.

Le Hallé, Guy. *Les Fortifications de Paris.* Le Coteau, 1986.

Leith, James A. *Space and Revolution: Projects for Monuments, Squares, and Public Buildings in France, 1789–1799.* Montreal, 1991.

Le Moël, Michel. "Urbanisme et Lumières: Les Idées et les hommes." In *L'Urbanisme parisien au siècle des Lumières,* edited by Michel Le Moël with Sophie Descat, 30–49. Paris, 1997.

Le Moël, Michel, ed., with Sophie Descat. *L'Urbanisme parisien au siècle des Lumières.* Paris, 1997.

Lemoine, Bertrand, and Marc Mimram, eds. *Paris d'ingénieurs.* Paris, 1995.

Lepetit, Bernard. *Chemins de terre et voies d'eau: Réseau de transpoorts et organization de l'espace en France, 1740–1840.* Paris, 1984.

———. "Event and Structure: The Revolution and the French Urban System, 1700–1840." *Journal of Historical Geography* 16, no. 1 (1990).

———. *The Pre-Industrial Urban System: France, 1740–1840.* Translated by Godfrey Rogers. Cambridge, 1994.

Léri, Jean-Marc. "Les Travaux de Paris (1830–1848). Recherches sur la politique de l'urbanisme de la ville de Paris sous la monarchie de Juillet." In *Positions des thèses.* Paris, 1974.

Le Roy Ladurie, Emmanuel, ed. *La Ville classique de la Renaissance aux Révolutions.* Vol. 3 of Histoire de la France urbaine. Edited by Georges Duby. Paris, 1981.

Le Roy Ladurie, Emmanuel, with Bernard Quilliet. "Baroques et Lumières." In *La Ville classique de la Renaissance aux Révolutions,* edited by Emmanuel Le Roy Ladurie, 289–535. Vol. 3 of *Histoire de la France urbaine.* Edited by Georges Duby. Paris, 1981.

Levasseur, Émile. "France." In *Le 25e anniversaire de la Société de statistique de Paris, 1860–1885,* edited by Société de statistique de Paris. Paris, 1886.

Loyer, François, ed. *Autour l'Opéra: Naissance de la ville moderne.* Paris, 1995.

Loyer, François. *Paris: Nineteenth-Century Architecture and Urbanism.* Translated by Charles Lynn Clark. New York, 1988.

Lynch, Katherine A. *Family, Class, and Ideology in Early Industrial France: Social Policy and the Working-Class Family, 1825–1848.* Madison, WI, 1988.

Mairie de Paris. *À la Découverte des Plans de Paris, du XVIe au XVIIIe siècle.* Paris, 1994.

———. *Métropolitain: L'Autre dimension de la ville.* Paris, 1988.

———. *Paris et ses réseaux: Naissance d'un mode de vie urbaine, XIXe–XXe siècles.* Paris, 1990.

Mansel, Philip. *Paris Between Empires, 1814–1852.* London. 2001.

Manuel, Frank E. *The New World of Henri Saint-Simon.* Notre Dame, 1963.

———. *The Prophets of Paris: Turgot, Condorcet, Saint-Simon, Fourier, Comte.* Cambridge, MA, 1962.

Marchand, Bernard. *Paris, histoire d'une ville (XIXe–XXe siècle).* Paris, 1993.

Marrey, Bernard. "Les Réalisations des utopistes dans les travuax publics et de l'architecture, 1840–1848." In *1848, Les Utopisemes sociaux*, edited by J. Bartier et al., 193–215. Paris 1981.

———. "Vie et mort de l'enceinte de Thiers." In *Paris, la ville et ses projets: A City in the Making*, edited by Jean-Louis Cohen and Bruno Fortier, 176–86. Paris, 1988.

Mathieu, Mae. *Pierre Patte, sa vie et son oeuvre*. Paris, 1940.

Mauclair, Placide, and C. Vigoreux. *Nicolas-François de Blondel, ingéneur et architecte du roi (1618–1686)*. Laon, 1938.

McWilliam, Neil. *Dreams of Happiness: Social Art and the French Left, 1830–1850*. Princeton, 1993.

Meier, Richard. *A Communications Theory of Urban Growth*. Cambridge, MA, 1962.

Mercier, Roger. "Voltaire et Paris: Des Rêves d'urbanisme aux pleurs sur Jérusalem." In *La Ville au XVIIIe siècle: Colloque d'Aix-en-Province, 29 April–1 May 1973*. Aix-en-Province, 1975.

Merriman, John M., ed. *French Cities in the Nineteenth Century*. New York, 1981.

Merriman, John M. *The Margins of City Life: Explorations on the French Urban Frontier, 1815–1851*. New York, 1991.

Minoque, Kenneth. "The Escape from Serfdom: Fredrich von Huyek and the Resoration of Liberty." *Times Literary Supplement*, Jan. 14, 2000, 11–13.

Morachiello, Paolo, and Georges Teysot. "State Town: Colonialization of the Territory during the First Empire." *Lotus International* 3 (1979): 24–39.

Moret, Frédéric. *Les Socialistes et la ville: Grande-Bretagne, France, 1820–1850*. Fontenay/Saint-Cloud, 1999.

Morizet, André. *Du Vieux Paris au Paris moderne: Haussmann et ses prédecesseurs*. Paris, 1932.

Mumford, Lewis. *The City in History: Its Origins, Its Transformations, and Its Prospects*. New York, 1961.

Nord, Deborah Epstein. "The Social Explorer as Anthropologist: Victorian Travelers among the Urban Poor." In *Visions of the Modern City: Essays in Literature, Art, and History*, edited by William Sharpe and Leonard Wallock, 122–34. Baltimore, 1987.

O'Brien, Patricia. "*L'Embastillement de Paris:* The Fortifications of Paris during the July Monarchy." *French Historical Studies* 9, no. 1 (Spring, 1975): 63–82.

Olsen, Donald J. *The City as a Work of Art: London, Paris, Vienna*. New Haven, CT, 1986.

Papayanis, Nicholas. *The Coachmen of Nineteenth-Century Paris: Service Workers and Class Consciousness*. Baton Rouge, LA, 1993.

———. "L'Émergence de l'urbanisme moderne à Paris." In *La Modernité avant Haussmann: Formes de l'espace urbain à Paris, 1801–1853*, edited by Karen Bowie, 82–94. Paris, 2001.

———. *Horse-Drawn Cabs and Omnibuses in Paris: The Idea of Circulation and the Business of Public Transit*. Baton Rouge, LA, 1996.

———. "Les Transports à Paris avant le Métropolitain." *In Metro-Cité: Le Chemin de fer métropolitain à la conquête de Paris, 1871–1945*, edited by François Gasnault and Henri Zuber, with Shelia Hallsted-Baumert, 15–30. Paris, 1997.

———. "Urbanisme au Paris souterrain: Premiers projets de chemin de fer urbain et naissance de l'urbanisme des cités modernes." *Histoire, Économie, et Société,* no. 4 (Oct.–Dec. 1998): 745–70.

Paul-Lévy, Françoise. *La Ville en croix: De la révolution de 1848 à la révolution haussmannienne. Éléments pour une problématique générale.* Paris, 1984.

Pellarin, Charles. *Charles Fourier: Sa Vie et sa théorie.* 2nd ed. Paris, 1843.

———. *Une page de l'histoire du Saint-Simonisme et du Fouriérisme: Notice sur Jules Lechevalier et Abel Transon.* Paris, 1877.

Perrot, Jean-Claude, *L'Age d'or de la statistique régionale française (An IV-1804).* Paris, 1977.

Pétonnet, Colette. "L'Espace et les lieux de la ville." *Ethnologie française* 12, no. 2 (1982).

Picon, Antoine. "Les Fortifications de Paris." In *Le Paris des Polytechniciens: Des ingènieurs dans la ville,* edited by Bruno Belhoste, Francine Masson, and Antoine Picon, 213–21. Paris, 1994.

———. *French Architects and Engineers in the Age of the Enlightenment.* Translated by Martin Thom. Cambridge, 1988.

———. *L'Invention de l'ingénieur moderne: L'École des Ponts et Chaussées.* Paris, 1992.

———. "Les Models de la métropole: Les Polytechniciens et l'aménagement de Paris." In *Le Paris des Polytechniciens: Des ingénieurs dans la ville, 1794–1994,* edited by Bruno Belhoste, Francine Masson, and Antoine Picon, 137–53. Paris, 1994.

———. "Le Paris des ingénieurs saint-simoniens." In *Paris d'ingénieurs,* edited by Bertrand Lemoine and Marc Mimram. Paris, 1995.

———. *Les Saint-Simoniens: Raison, imaginaire, et utopie.* Paris, 2002.

Piette, Christine, and Barrie Ratcliffe. "Les Migrants et la ville: Un Nouveau regard sur le Paris de la première moitié du XIXe siècle." *Annales démographique historique* (1993): 263–303.

Pilbeam, Pamela. *French Socialists before Marx: Workers, Women, and the Social Question in France.* Montreal, 2000.

———. *Republicanism in Nineteenth-Century France, 1814–1871.* New York, 1995.

Pinkney, David H. *Decisive Years in France, 1840–1847.* Princeton, 1986.

———. *Napoleon III and the Rebuilding of Paris.* Princeton, 1972, 1985.

Pinon, Pierre. "Les Conceptions urbaines au milieu du XIXe siècle." In *Paris-Haussmann: "Le Pari d'Haussmann,"* edited by Jean Des Cars and Pierre Pinon, 44–50. Paris, 1989.

———. *Paris, biographie d'une capitale.* Paris, 1999.

———. ed. *Les Traversées de Paris: Deux siècles de révolutions dans la ville.* Paris, 1989.

Plessis, Alain. *The Rise and Fall of the Second Empire, 1852–1871.* Translated by Jonathan Mandelbaum. New York, 1987.

Poëte, Marcel. *La Promenade à Paris au XVIIe siècle.* Paris, 1913.

———. *Une Vie de cité: Paris, de sa naissance à nos jours.* 3 vols. Paris, 1924–31.

Pontich, Henri de. *Admistration de la ville de Paris et du département de la Seine.* Paris, 1884.

Popkin, Jeremy D., ed. *Panorama of Paris.* University Park, PA, 1999.

Porter, Roy. *London: A Social History.* Cambridge, MA, 1995.

Poulat, Émile. *Les Cahiers manuscrits de Fourier: Étude historique et inventaire raisonné.* Paris, 1957.

Pouthas, Charles H. *La Population française pendant la première moitié du XIXe siècle.* Paris, 1956.

Prendergast, Christopher. *Paris and the Nineteenth Century.* Cambridge, MA, 1992, 1995.

Procacci, Giovanna. *Gouverner la misère: "La Question sociale en France (1789–1848).* Paris, 1993.

———. "Social Economy and the Government of Poverty." *Ideology and Consciousness* 4 (1979): 52–72.

———. "Sociology and Its Poor." *Politics and Society* 17 (1989): 163–87.

Pronteau, Jeanne. *Edme Verniquet, 1727–1804: Architecte et auteur du 'grand plan de Paris' (1785–1791).* Paris, 1986.

———. "La Commission et le Plan des Artistes." In *L'Urbanisme parisien au siècle des Lunières,* edited by Michel Le Moël with Sophie Descat, 205–17. Paris, 1997.

———. *Les Numérotages des maisons de Paris du XVe siècle à nos jours.* Paris, 1966.

Raban, Jonathan. *Soft City.* London, 1974, 1998.

Rabinow, Paul. *French Modern: Norms and Forms of the Social Environment.* Cambridge, MA, 1989.

Ragon, Michel. *Histoire de l'architecture et de l'urbanisme modernes.* 3 vols. Paris, 1986.

Ratcliffe, Barrie. "Cities and Environmental Decline: Elites and the Sewage Problem in Paris from the Mid-Eighteenth to the Mid-Nineteenth Century." *Planning Perspectives* 5 (1990): 189–222.

———. "The Economic Influence of the Saint-Simonians: Myth or Reality?" In *Proceedings of the Fifth Annual Meeting of the Western Society for French History,* 252–62. Santa Barbara, CA,1978.

———. "Perceptions and Realities of the Urban Margin: The Rag Pickers of Paris in the First Half of the Nineteenth Century." *Canadian Journal of History* 27 (Aug. 1992): 197–233.

———. "Les Périere et le saint-simonisme." *Économies et sociétés* 5, no 7 (1971): 1215–55.

———. "The Saint-Simonians in the French Economy: Towards an Understanding of Ideas, Ideals, and Action." In *Fra Spazio et tempo: Strudi in onore di Luigi DeRosa,* edited by Ilaria Zilli, 2:733–53. 3 vols. Naples, 1995.

———. "Urban Space and the Siting of Parisian Railway Stations, 1830–1847." In *Proceedings of the Annual Meeting of the Western Society for French History* 15 (1988): 224–34.

———. "Visions et (ré)visions des dynamiques de la croissance urbaine dans Paris de la première moitié du XIXe siècle." In *La Modernité avant Haussmann: Formes de l'espace urbain à Paris, 1801–1853,* edited by Karen Bowie, 41–55. Paris, 2001.

Régnier, Philippe. "Les Idées et les opinions littéraires des Saint-Simoniens (1825–1835)." Thèse de doctorat, 3 vols. University of Paris III (la Sorbonne nouvelle), 1982–83.

———, ed. *Le Livre nouveau des Saint-Simoiens. . . .* Tusson, 1992.

Régnier, Philippe. "Les Saint-Simoniens et le mouvement romantique." In *Romatismes et socialismes en Europe (1800–1848),* edited by André Billaz and Ulrich Ricker, 207–23. Paris, 1988.

Reid, Donald. *Paris Sewers and Sewermen: Realities and Representations.* Cambridge, MA, 1991.

Riasanovsky, Nicholas V. *The Teaching of Charles Fourier.* Berkeley, 1969.

Rice, Shelley. *Parisian Views.* Cambridge, MA, 1997.

Riot-Sarcey, Michèle. *Le Réel de l'utopie: Essai sur le politique au XIXe siècle.* Paris, 1998.

Rivière, Émile. *Étude sur le choléra dans les hôpitaux de Paris.* Paris, 1884–85.

Robic, Marie-Claire. "Cents ans avant Christaller . . . Une Théorie des lieux centraux." *L'Espace Géographique*, no. 1 (1982): 5–12.

Roche, Daniel. *A History of Everyday Things: The Birth of Consumption in France, 1600–1800.* Translated by Brian Pearce. Cambridge, 2000.

Roche, Daniel, ed. *La Ville promise: Mobilité et accueil à Paris (fin XVIIe–début XIXe siècle)* Paris, 2000.

———. *France in the Enlightenment.* Translated by Arthus Goldhammer. Cambridge, MA, 1998.

Roncaylo, Marcel. "Le Modèle haussmannien." In *La Ville de l'âge industriel: Le Cycle haussmannien,* edited by Marice Agulhon, 78–117. Vol. 4 of *Histoire de la France urbaine.* Edited by Georges Duby. Paris, 1983.

———. "Preludio all'haussmannizzarione: Capitale e pensiero urbano in Francia intorno al 1848." In *La Città capitale,* edited by Cesare De Seta, 133–47. Rome, 1985.

Rosenau, Helen. *The Ideal City: Its Architectural Evolution in Europe.* New York, 1983.

———. *Social Purpose in Architecture: Paris and London Compared, 1760–1800.* London, 1970.

Ross, Kristin. *The Emergence of Social Space: Rimbaud and the Paris Commune.* Minneapolis, 1988.

Rouleau, Bernard. "Le Plan de Turgot." *Cahiers du Centre de recherches et d'études sur Paris et l'Île-de-France,* no. 5 (Mar. 1995): 131–39.

———. *Paris: Histoire d'un espace.* Paris, 1997.

———. *Le Trace des rues de Paris.* Paris, 1988.

———. *Villages et faubourgs de l'ancien Paris: Histoire d'un espace urbain.* Paris, 1985.

Rykwert, Joseph. *The Seduction of Place: The City in the Twenty-first Century.* New York, 2000.

Saboya, Marc. *Presse et architecture au XIXe siècle: César Daly et la "revue générale de l'architecture et des travaux publics."* Paris, 1991.

Schivelbusch, Wolfgang. *The Railway Journey: The Industrialization of Time and Space in the Nineteenth Century.* Translated by Brayton Harris. Berkeley, 1977.

———. *Disenchanted Night: The Industrialization of Light in the Nineteenth Century.* Translated by Angela Davies. Oxford, 1988.

Scott, James C. *Seeing Like a State: How Certain Schemes to Improve the Human Condition Have Failed.* New Haven, CT, 1998.

Scott, Joan W. *Gender and the Politics of History.* New York 1988.

Sennett, Richard. *The Fall of Public Man.* New York, 1974, 1978.

———. *Flesh and Stone: The Body and the City in Western Civilization.* New York, 1994.

———. *The Uses of Disorder: Personal Identity and City Life.* New York, 1970.

Shapiro, Ann-Louise. *Housing the Poor of Paris, 1850–1902.* Madison, WI, 1985.

Société de Statistique de Paris. *Paris, 1960*. Paris, 1961.

———. *Le 25e anniversaire de la Société statsitique de Paris, 1860–1885*. Paris, 1886.

Stallybrass, Peter, and Allon White. *The Politics and Poetics of Transgression*. Ithaca, NY, 1986.

Sutcliffe, Anthony. "Architecture and Civic Design in Nineteenth-Century Paris." In *Growth and Transformation of the Modern City*, edited by Ingrid Hammarström and Thomas Hall, 89–100. Stockholm, 1979.

———. *The Autumn of Central Paris: The Defeat of Town Planning, 1850–1970*. Montreal, 1971.

———. "Cities, Modernization, and Architecture: Before and after the Paris Building Code of 1901." In *Economy and Society: European Industrialization and Its Social Consequences. Essays Presented to Sidney Pollard*, edited by Colin Holmes and Alan Booth, 175–97. New York, 1991.

———. *Paris: An Architectural History*. New Haven, CT, 1993.

———. *Towards the Planned City: Germany, Britain, the United States, and France, 1780–1914*. New York, 1981.

———. "A Vision of Utopia: Optimistic Foundations of Le Corbusier's *Doctrine d'urbanisme*." In *The Open Hand: Essays on Le Corbusier*, edited by Russell Walden, 216–43. Cambridge, MA , 1977.

Thompson, Victoria E. "Telling 'Spacial Stories': Urban Space and Bourgeois Identity in Early Nineteenth-Century Paris." *Journal of Modern History* 75, no. 3 (2003): 523–56.

———. *The Virtuous Marketplace: Women and Men, Money and Politics in Paris, 1830–1870*. Baltimore, 2000.

Tucker, Richard C. *The Marx-Engels Reader*, 2nd ed. New York, 1978.

Tulard, Jean. *Le Consulat et l'Empire, 1800–1815* [Nouvelle histoire de Paris]. Paris, 1970.

———. *Paris et son administration (1800–1830)*. Paris, 1976.

Van Zanten, Ann Lorenz. "Form and Society: César Daly and the *Revue générale de l'architecture*." *Oppositions*, no. 8 (Spring 1977): 135–45.

Van Zanten, David. *Building Paris: Architectural Institutions and the Transformation of the French Capital, 1830–1870*. New York, 1994.

Vernus, Michel. *Victor Considérant, 1808–1893: Le Coeur et la raison*. Dole, 1993.

Vidler, Anthony. "The Scenes of the Street: Transformations in Ideal and Beauty, 1750–1871." In *On Streets*, edited by Stanford Anderson, 29–111. Cambridge, MA, 1978.

Vigier, Philippe. *Paris pendant la Monarchie de Juillet (1830–1838)* [Nouvelle histoire de Paris]. Paris, 1991.

Virilio, Paul. *Speed and Politics: An Essay on Dromology*. Translated by Marc Polizzotti. New York, 1986.

Von Hoffman, Alexander. "Why They Built Preuitt-Igoe." In *From Tenements to the Taylor Homes: In Search of an Urban Housing Policy in Twentieth-Century America*, edited by John F. Bauman, Roger Biles, and Kristin M. Szlvian, 180–205. University Park, PA, 2000.

Walch, Jean. *Bibliographie de Saint-Simonisme.* Paris, 1967.

———. *Michel Chevalier: Économiste Saint-Simonien, 1806–1874.* Paris, 1975.

———. "Les saint-simoniens et les voies de communications." *Culture technique,* no. 19 (Mar. 1989): 285–94.

Walden, Russell, ed. *The Open Hand: Essays on Le Corbusier.* Cambridge, MA, 1977.

Williams, Alan. *The Police of Paris, 1718–1789.* Baton Rouge, LA, 1979.

Williams, Rosalind. *Notes on the Underground: An Essay on Technology, Society, and the Imagination.* Cambridge, MA, 1990.

Willms, Johannes. *Paris, Capital of Europe: From the Revolution to the Belle Epoque.* Translated by Eveline L. Kanes. New York, 1997.

Index